POLITICS AGAINST MARKETS

POLITICS AGAINST MARKETS

The Social Democratic Road to Power

by Gøsta
Esping-Andersen

Princeton University Press
Princeton, New Jersey

Published by Princeton University Press, 41 William Street,
Princeton, New Jersey 08540
In the United Kingdom: Princeton University Press, Guildford, Surrey

Library of Congress Cataloging in Publication Data will be
found on the last printed page of this book

First Princeton Paperback printing, 1988

Publication of this book has been aided by the Whitney Darrow
Publication Reserve Fund of Princeton University Press

This book has been composed in Linotron Sabon

Clothbound editions of Princeton University Press books
are printed on acid-free paper, and binding materials are
chosen for strength and durability. Paperbacks, while
satisfactory for personal collections, are not usually
suitable for library rebinding.

Printed in the United States of America by Princeton University Press
Princeton, New Jersey

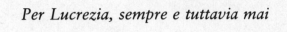

Per Lucrezia, sempre e tuttavia mai

CONTENTS

TABLES

PREFACE

THIS BOOK is the result of a decade-long obsession with social democracy. Both social democracy and I have gone through many changes over the years, and the momentum of change apparently will not subside. In the early 1970s there were probably many obvious signs that a new and more turbulent world order was asserting itself. For an average Danish new-left student, however, capitalism was always capitalism; the academic social scientist is taught to recognize change only after its occurrence. In the early 1970s, too, social democracy entered a new era of political identity crisis; but the average new-left academic was quite unprepared for this and could, with the limited intellectual tools at his disposal, hardly be expected to view social democracy as anything but a milder version of capitalist politics as usual.

But as the 1970s unfolded and research progressed, Leninism had to give way. During a decade of intellectual attention to social democracy my theoretical model has been altered again and again. It is impossible to cling to Leninism when one engages in empirical analysis, juxtaposes different national realities, and searches for the decisive variations. When it is realized that social democracy is not an absolute, when one's sensibilities say that the world would not have been the same without it, a new theory is called for. Therefore, what I wrote then bore only a vague resemblance to what eventually appeared as a doctoral dissertation in 1978. The book I have now written, at first meant to be merely a polished up version of the dissertation, was another five years in the making. For, once again, I came to reject the arguments, theory, and empirical substance of what had gone before—not merely because the realities of socialist parties continued to unfold, but also because the research project itself remained dynamic. To harbor such an elastic theoretical disposition may not be altogether honorable; academics are supposed to launch a paradigm that has staying power.

It is also difficult to avoid falling in love with a subject that has made such a claim on one's attention for so long. As we have learned from George Homans, the more we know of one another the more we will come to like one another. The workings of this principle have undoubtedly helped accelerate my progressive social democratization, both as sociologist and as political man. Then, too, the political milieu has changed around us. When I first began, the phenomenon of social democratic labor movements hardly sparked any interest. For the left in those days, the social democrats were sellouts; for the conservatives, on the other hand, they exemplified the vast and general tendency of end-of-ideology convergence. During the past few years, though, social democracy has once again become a fashionable subject all over Europe and even in the United States. It is difficult to think of a single major work on social democracy written during the 1960s or early 1970s. Since then, however, we have been bombarded with good treatises, and the competition gets fiercer every day.

The reasons for this renewed interest are many. Leftists who rejected the welfare state ten years ago are now rushing to its defense as neoconservatives attack and sometimes even dismantle its accomplishments. A new generation of social democrats have begun to assert themselves, outside the traditional North European strongholds, in such countries as France, Spain, and Greece. And previously Third International parties—notably the Italian Communist party (PCI)—are now looking to the North European social democracies for programmatic and strategic inspiration. The isolated pockets of American socialism have also looked across the seas to learn from Scandinavian social democracy. All these new-generation social democrats are not merely catching up with their older brethren: the rekindled fascination has to do with a fundamental transformation currently under way within the old, established social democratic movements.

It is not that social democratic parties now reject the Keynesian welfare state politics that they once promoted so proudly. In some cases, they may be reluctant partisans of cutbacks and helpless witnesses to rising unemployment, but the transformation of social democracy does not include rejection of the ideology of full social citizenship. What has happened, rather, is that the welfare state project is seen to be in need of programmatic reinvigoration if social democracy is to survive the present and build itself a promising future. The leading social democratic movements, especially in Scandinavia, are perched at a historic crossroads where, for an array of reasons, the leap from a politics of social citizenship to one of economic citizenship must be attempted. This is so because, at the most basic level of causation, the new salaried white-collar strata hold the key to any viable social democratic alliance. Salaried employees, however, will hardly be attracted to traditional welfare policies and will almost certainly abhor excessively emphasized income-equalization programs. Without a broad wage-earner coalition, social democracy will fail to emerge from its present lethargy or even decompose. Accordingly, social democracy is trying to forge for itself a new programmatic profile that can lead to this kind of coalition, and the promotion of economic democracy is becoming the centerpiece of that profile.

A central argument throughout this book is that socialist parties, conceived as strictly working-class movements, are and always have been doomed to fail. Even when optimally mobilized, the numbers of the traditional working classes will be too small to permit socialist majorities, and thus we confront a classic dilemma: should the socialist parties retire into permanent opposition and remain pure, or should they find a class ally? In this I agree generally with the important work of Adam Przworski, but I reject his conclusions: I do not believe that an alliance strategy must doom to failure the social democratic struggle for power.

Behind my greater optimism is a belief that the laws of class structural evolution alone do not dictate the fortunes of socialist parties. Socialist parties are reformist and parliamentarian and, as such, can and must employ what powers they command in order to influence public policy and recast the state. The leading question that runs through this entire study is whether and under what conditions social democratic parties can reform society to their own long-term advantage. My first response to this question is yes, if strong class alliances can be struck. It must be added that these class alliances will have to permit social democracy to implement reforms that at once weaken traditional social divisions and manufacture a pervasive class unity and solidarity. The very institutions and reforms that are implanted must become power resources in their own right. On the other hand, my answer would have to be no if social democratic reforms, and the welfare state more generally, should give rise to new invidious cleavages and equity conflicts—something that is very likely to occur as the state's influence over people's lives steadily mounts.

In brief, the thesis to be argued and demonstrated in this book is that social democratic power depends on a combination of two historical forces: the pattern of class coalitions and the party's conduct of class mobilization through reformist practice. The historical drama of social democracy is defined by the ways in which these forces have coalesced and come apart. I have come to the conclusion that the peasantry was ultimately decisive in the social democratic breakthrough before World War II. Where the peasants were unorganized and politically inarticulate, as in most of Central Europe, they were perhaps susceptible to fascism but were unlikely to enter into political alliances with labor. It was the peculiarly organized and democratic character of the Scandinavian peasantry that enabled social democracy to gain its firmest foothold in the Nordic countries; and it was the absence thereof that stifled socialist parties elsewhere, most notably in Germany. It was on the basis of this popular alliance that Scandinavian social democracy could then proceed to build advanced welfare states and remain faithful to its full-employment promise.

The first historical turning point was therefore the 1930s. The entire postwar social democratic program flowed from it. But the capacity to employ the class alliance in reformist activity varied from country to country, even among the three Nordic countries, and such variation must be included in any explanation of why the social democratic parties' electoral fortunes have diverged. Everything points to the possibility that the present era constitutes a second turning point. Social democracy must supersede its earlier program; in order to launch itself once again on the road to power, it must build a sustainable wage-earner coalition. We might view social democracy, then, as passing through two decisive stages. The popular, peasant-based alliance introduced the stage of social citizenship politics; the new wage-earner alliance is sought as a steppingstone to the stage of economic citizenship politics. If, as I believe, economic democracy must constitute the core program for the second stage, the question then turns on how the transition might be made. It is here that the political spirits of social democracy's reformist past come back to haunt.

By no means unambitious, this book offers a wholly different concept of social democracy from what at present guides both leftist and rightist thought. My arguments, furthermore, are framed in such a way that one might expect a full comparison of all major social democratic movements. Instead, I have chosen methodologically to limit comparisons to the Scandinavian cases. This choice is, I believe, defensible. First, these are archetypal, pure examples of international social democracy. Secondly, the social democrats have held office so long in Scandinavia that the contemporary Nordic state has been heavily influenced by their reformism. Thirdly, though most fail to see this, there is an extraordinary degree of divergence in the accomplishments as well as the political fates of the three Nordic social democracies. Owing to these important variations, it is possible to claim some generality of theoretical application.

Although I have tried not to write more than is necessary, some length is required to provide a meaningful survey of the three social democratic movements and, additionally, of the societies that have given rise to them. Otherwise, this book would hardly make much sense to a reader not exposed to the blessings of a Scandinavian secondary education. Part I presents general historical background but serves primarily to call attention to the social structural causes behind the parties' different evolutionary paths. Part II, reflecting the duality of my theoretical argument, focuses on the political causes that explain the parties' diverse fortunes. In that section, therefore, the variations in Scandinavian welfare state policies, housing policies, and economic management are examined. Chapter 8 details the empirical connections between reforms and electoral support for the social democratic parties. Part III addresses contemporary proposals for economic democracy in light of the parties' struggle for political realignment.

During ten years one cannot avoid accumulating many friends and foes, and I am seriously indebted to both. Rattling off a long list of names in alphabetical order would be infuriating reading for those who feel that they have been specially involved in this project. It might be better to thank each personally and skip the ritual of acknowledgments. Were I to choose this way out, however, it would appear that I had single-handedly accomplished everything. Even though this book bears little resemblance to my dusty dissertation, there are some people whose influence and help then were so overwhelming that they should still be held responsible. This holds for Maurice Zeitlin more than for anyone else, and it applies to Aage Sørensen and Erik Wright. Roger Friedland played a special role because he has always been my favorite collaborator; it is sometimes impossible to say whether my ideas are mine or his. Indeed, our joint project on class coalitions is what first prompted me to consider a revised theory of social democracy.

More recently, the protracted task of preparing this book was made both easier and more complex, more enjoyable and more frustrating, more motivating and more exhausting by the encouragements, criticisms, help, and suggestions I received in the milieus that have surrounded me over the past six years. Barbara Haskell, Walter Korpi, Henrik Madsen, Andrew Martin, Lars Mjøset, John Myles, Orlando Patterson, Alessandro Pizzorno, Adam Przworski, and John Stephens should each be able to discover places where I have exploited his or her wit and thought. Extremely helpful were Peter Katzenstein, who must be one of America's most generous academics; Jon Eivind Kolberg, whom I would like to nominate for the same title in Scandinavia; Walter Korpi, with whom I am now working on a new mastodont project; and Gösta Rehn, who has helped me to avoid becoming a laughingstock in Sweden. If all Nordic social democrats had the attributes of Jon Eivind Kolberg, Walter Korpi, and Gösta Rehn, there could be no such thing as social democratic party decomposition.

The data for this book were not easy to assemble. I am grateful to the Danish Social Science Research Council (Socialvidenskabeligt

Forskningsråd) for the grant that permitted me to conduct the project in its earliest stages. I thank Olof Pettersson and Bo Särlvik for giving me access to the Swedish data; Bernt Årdal, Ola Listhaug, and Henry Valen for making available the Norwegian data; and Hans Jørgen Nielsen for his particularly generous help with the Danish surveys.

From infancy to its present maturity, this book has been a jet-setter. Its (unplanned) conception at Copenhagen University led to delivery at the University of Wisconsin–Madison. Part of the pregnancy was spent at the Institute for Organization in Copenhagen so that the child would not entirely lose its Danish character. Harvard University became its home during the formative years, exposing it to the brutal facts of life. The first cautious steps into the adult world were taken at the University of California at Santa Barbara, and the surfing life helped soothe this painful transition. A year at the Institute for Social Research in Stockholm helped it rediscover its roots. Coming-out parties were held at numerous American universities, at the universities of Copenhagen, Oslo, and Stockholm, at the Wissenschaftszentrum in Berlin, and throughout Italy. The Social Science Research Council even granted it a wonderful week in Hawaii.

I am afraid this book would never have been publishable had it not been for the generosity of so many people and the hospitality of so many places. A final acknowledgment should go to social democracy's intellectual mentor, Karl Kautsky. His classic text, *The Road to Power*, provided me with a ready-made *Prügelknabe*.

Cambridge, Mass.
June 1984

ABBREVIATIONS

AC   Akademikernes Centralorganisation (Danish Academics' Confederation)

ADGB   Allgemeine Deutsche Gewerkschaftsbund (German Trade Union Confederation, before 1934)

AMS   Arbetsmarknadsstyrelsen (Swedish Labor Market Board)

ATP   Arbetsmarknadens Tillägspension (Supplementary Pension Scheme)

CFDT   Confederation Français du Travail (French Trade Union Confederation)

CGIL   Confederazione Generale Italiano di Lavori (Italian Trade Union Confederation)

DAF   Dansk Arbejdsgiverforening (Danish Employers' Federation)

DGB   Deutsche Gewerkschaftsbund (German Trade Union Confederation, after 1945)

DKP   Danmarks Kommunistiske Parti (Danish Communist party)

DNA   Det Norske Arbeiderparti (Norwegian Labor party)

DSF   De Samvirkende Fagforbund (Danish Trade Union Confederation, original name)

EEC   European Economic Community

EFTA   European Free Trade Association

FTF   Faellesorganisationen for Tjaenestemaend og Funktionaerer (Danish Federation of Salaried Employees)

HSB   Hyresgästernas Sparkasse och Byggnadsförening (Swedish Tenants' Savings and Building Association)

ILP   Independent Labour Party (predecessor of the British Labour party)

ITP   Indtaegtsbestemt Tillaegspension (Danish Plan for Supplementary Pensions)

LO   Landsorganisationen (Trade Union Confederation; Denmark, Norway, and Sweden)

NAF   Norges Arbeidsgiverforening (Norwegian Employers' Federation)

NATO   North Atlantic Treaty Organization

NKP   Norges Kommunistiske Parti (Norwegian Communist Party)

OECD   Organization for Economic Cooperation and Development

OMS   Omsaetning og Mervaerdiskat (value-added tax)

ABBREVIATIONS

OPEC	Organization of Petroleum-Exporting Countries
PCF	Parti Communiste Français
PCI	Partito Communista Italiano
PSI	Partito Socialista Italiano
RV	Radikale Venstre (Danish Radical-Liberal party)
SACO	Sveriges Akademikers Centralorganisation (Swedish Federation of Professional Employees)
SAF	Sveriges Arbetsgiverförbund (Swedish Employers' Federation)
SAP	Sveriges Socialdemokratiska Arbetarparti (Swedish Social Democratic party)
SF	Socialistisk Folkeparti (Socialist People's party, Denmark and Norway)
SID	Special og Indisutriarbejderforbundet i Danmark (Danish Unskilled Workers' Federation)
SPD	Sozialdemokratische Partei Deutschlands (German Social Democratic party)
STP	Särskild Tilläggspension (Swedish Occupational Pension Scheme)
SV	Socialistisk Valgallianse (Socialist Election Alliance, Norway); same initials subsequently employed for Norwegian Left-Socialist party (Socialistisk Venstreparti)
TCO	Tjänstemännens Centralorganisation (Confederation of Swedish White-Collar Employees)
TUC	Trades Union Congress (Britain)
VPK	Venstrepartiet Kommunistarna (Swedish Communist party)
VS	Venstresocialisterne (Danish Left-Socialist party)

POLITICS AGAINST MARKETS

ONE

Social Democracy in Theory and Practice

SOCIAL DEMOCRACY is, and has always been, the most successful expression of working-class politics in capitalist democracies. In Northern Europe it has enjoyed virtually a monopoly over workers' votes, and it has been dominant almost everywhere else. Where, as in Italy or France, communism has held sway, the trend is nevertheless toward a "social democratization" of working-class politics. Thus it is puzzling that we have no adequate theory of such a historically powerful force.

Although social democracy may be a pervasive political force, its fate has come to diverge quite sharply from nation to nation. Where once it was unshakable, it is apparently losing ground; where once it was peripheral, it is coming to the fore. It is particularly fascinating to observe that three such historically similar social democracies as the Scandinavian countries are now moving in different directions. Yet, we have no adequate theory to explain the conditions under which social democracy will succeed or fail.

Nearly all theories of social democracy are rooted in the old controversies between Leninists, revisionists, and their "bourgeois" critics. Our task in this chapter is to examine the validity of these contending views, and then to develop a set of testable propositions concerning the conditions that favor, alternatively, social democratic success or decomposition.

The classical debates have consistently been marred by the irritating circumstance that the historical mission is impossible to verify. No social democracy has claimed to have built the Good Society. Since socialism cannot be empirically defined and is nowhere present in the manner prescribed by social democracy itself, our ultimate concern cannot and should not be socialism. However, we can legitimately ask ourselves whether the historical project remains plausible. The notion of a social democratic "road to power" is premised on the assumption that class formation under democratic parliamentary conditions can provide the strength and solidarity needed to transform capitalism. It is also premised on another assumption: that electoral politics and reformist accomplishments will enhance social democracy's progress.

3

Whether Marxist or non-Marxist, most existing theory has concentrated almost entirely on class structural change, in the belief that the logic of labor movements springs from the nature of the social structure. But is this approach adequate for an understanding of how social democracy can mobilize the kinds of power resources required if its promise of a future Good Society is to be made compelling? Reformist socialism has always insisted that its historical task of mobilization and transformation be constructed on the basis of legislative reformism. It is therefore quite odd that there is not one study that systematically attempts to explain trends in social democracy as the outcomes of certain policies. It is on this score, I dare hope, that I have something vital to add.

An Anatomy of Social Democracy

Few writers pause to ask what social democracy is. Party labels alone hardly clarify matters. There exist some self-declared social democratic parties, the Italian version, for example, that few would consider genuine. Eurocommunist parties may, in fact, fulfill many of the criteria normally associated with traditional reformist socialist parties. Some even believe that America's Democratic party is social democratic in nature (Wolfe 1978). Nor is membership in the Socialist International a satisfactory criterion, even if admission is reserved for those parties formally dedicated to parliamentarism and in some way programmatically committed to socialism. It is increasingly difficult to understand why, for example, the PSI is a member while the PCI is excluded. Contemporary catchwords such as Eurocommunism and Eurosocialism bear witness to the growing confusion about who is who in international socialism.

A third, and somewhat more fruitful, method of defining inclusion is to compare party organization. One of the most important historical distinctions between communist and social democratic parties has to do with their principles of party membership, internal authority, and relations between central executive officers and the rank and file. Duverger (1964) counterposes the social democratic party to the loose electoral aggregation typical of the bourgeois party, on one hand, and the centralist and disciplined apparatus of the communist party, on the other. Where the one rarely builds a strong organization with strict membership criteria, the other is typified by exclusiveness of membership, by a "ghetto character" that fosters the creation of an entire world separate from society at large, and by democratic centralism, recurrent purges, and calls for discipline. But, to Duverger's credit, he refuses to make a categorical distinction between communist and social democratic parties; rather, they are viewed as being on a continuum shared by all modern mass parties.

Many social democratic parties were originally "ghetto" parties. Until World War I, all three Scandinavian social democratic parties followed the model of the later communist parties, building a separate socialist world by means of athletic associations, boy scout movements, educational institutions, organized leisure activities and so forth. In respect of centralized authority and strict control over party militants and local cells, a hard-and-fast distinction between communist and social democratic parties is difficult to make. As Michels (1962) has shown, the social democratic party was hardly an open and democratic organization. There is little doubt, too, that the traditional vanguard party model is decaying. Duverger (1964) notes that even the comparatively rigid French Communist party (PCF) could not maintain control of its local cells. By the 1970s, the PCI is only residually a "democratic centralist" vanguard party.[1]

The relationship between party and trade union has had tremendous historical significance. Before World War I, socialist parties usually viewed the trade union movement as a political instrument and hence refused to grant union autonomy. Frequently the parties insisted on collective trade union membership in the party and loyal subordination to party strategy.[2] While the political subjugation of trade unionism was retained in most Third International communist movements, it was abandoned by most social democratic parties. According to Sturmthal (1943), trade union autonomy was crucial in moving social democratic leaders to put aside ideological orthodoxy in order to face the crisis of world depression and further the survival of democracy and the labor movement itself. The emancipation of trade unionism occurred under very different conditions from country to country. In Britain, it was the Trades Union Congress (TUC) that provided the main impetus for the Labour party's formation in 1906 (Pelling 1961). In Sweden and Denmark, the unions were originally under social democratic party control, but divorce came soon after the turn of the century. Even if the Mannheim Resolution of 1906 granted the German unions independent status, the process had not quite been com-

[1] There is one useful organizational criterion for distinguishing social democracy from communism—what we might call the "citizenship rights" of party members. Whereas considerable disagreement is usually tolerated in social democratic parties, a communist party typically purges members who deviate from the official line.

[2] This form of membership still prevails in Sweden and Britain, although individual union members are free to opt out.

pleted before the Nazi seizure of power (Sturmthal 1943; Mommsen et al. 1974a)—at least not to the degree that the ADGB could influence party policy. But postwar communist parties, notably in Italy, have also moved in the direction of granting unions autonomous status.

Organizational characteristics, then, are certainly necessary in any definition of social democracy, but they are not sufficient. They tell us very little about the relation of the party to social structure, to the state, or to historical change. Przworski (1980, 27-28) has provided a definition of social democracy that has the great advantage of being grounded in the parties' strategic choices rather in their professions of ideology. The question is how working-class parties historically have resolved three crucial issues: whether to participate in the political institutions of capitalist society; whether to seek support outside the working classes; and whether to pursue reformist or revolutionary policy. I agree with Przworski on the first two dimensions, but disagree on the third.

The Parliamentary Decision

According to Przworski's definition, social democracy differs from communism in that the former adheres to, rather than opposes, parliamentary democracy. Social democrats, contrary to their Marxist forebears or their Leninist opponents, insist that it is both possible and imperative to struggle for socialism within parliamentary institutions. The decision to commit the proletarian cause to parliamentary procedure did not everywhere evolve with ease. In Britain and Denmark there was hardly ever any contemplation of antiparliamentary strategies. In Germany, the social democrats eventually became the main bastion in defense of "bourgeois democracy," but the party was never quite united on the question. At one extreme were the Lassalleans. For decades, however, the party vacillated between a variety of positions, ranging from acceptance (or cautious distrust) to the almost purely strategic-instrumental view that democracy might be exploited for socialist mobilization. In Norway, the social democrats joined the Comintern during the early 1920s, but even after their departure, the leadership generally opposed the parliamentary strategy.[3]

An important source of ambivalence was concern that the bourgeoisie would not abide by parliamentary rules if the social democrats

[3] Not until the outbreak of World War II did the Norwegian social democrats actually get around to erase formally the last traces of revolutionary commitment remaining in the party program (Dahl 1969).

should finally muster the strength to vote socialism into existence. This was certainly true in the case of the Swedes—at least until the parliamentary crisis of 1918 had been fully resolved (Tingsten 1941)—as well as among the Austrians and Germans (Przworski 1980, 32). If complete and unconditional surrender to the rules of electoral competition and parliamentary majoritarianism is one hallmark of social democracy, the opportunity to surrender varied dramatically before World War II. In Scandinavia, where socialists allied with peasants and farmers in the struggle for political democracy, trust in parliamentarism came relatively easy. Bourgeois resistance there was generally modest, and even under limited suffrage the socialists had managed to gain representation and affect policy at both the local and the national level.

The Question of Interest Representation

The second definitional element concerns the party's strategy for class mobilization. Until 1918, socialist parties typically adhered to the view that the socialist transformation was a strictly proletarian affair. Social democratic parties, until 1918, saw themselves as class parties. To abandon a strict class image, however, does not necessarily mean that a political party becomes class-diffuse.

The issue was partly one of theoretical analysis, partly one of strategic choice. Theoretically, Marxist revisionism—led by Eduard Bernstein ([1899] 1971)—reassessed several fundamental Marxian propositions concerning the evolution of class structure. In opposition to the polarization-cum-immiseration thesis underpinning the justification of the class-oppositional strategy, Bernstein argued that class polarization was countered by the rise of the new middle classes. For a party already committed to parliamentarism, this naturally provoked a reexamination of how the requisite electoral majority would materialize.

Revisionism did not necessarily prescribe broader class alliances, but it did offer a theoretical rationale for their eventuality. The decisive impetus came from strategic choices in the realm of practical politics. The Scandinavian experience of fighting for democracy in unison with liberal farmers opened up new vistas. Liberals learned that the socialists were not necessarily a threat; socialists discovered that significant strides could be made through class collaboration. It seemed logical that additional reforms were possible through ad hoc alliances. Furthermore, while national power still seemed only a remote possibility, socialists occasionally gained influence in local government.

7

Their experience with "sewer socialism" showed that political collaboration with other "progressive elements" on local issues could bear fruit. And, whether or not they had studied Bernstein, socialist leaders themselves began to realize that a strictly proletarian majority was depressingly slow to materialize. Pressed from below to deliver immediate material improvements, socialist leaders were obviously weary of Kautsky's 1904 Amsterdam Socialist International congress resolution prohibiting collaboration with bourgeois parties. As Schumpeter (1970) and Przworski (1980) have put it, the main problem was how to build a majority on the basis of ideological purity alone. If the class party image were abandoned, the party would risk losing its left-wing clientele; by remaining pure, it risked having to wait forever for the socialist opportunity.

Social democracy, then, distinguished itself by the decision to subordinate class purity to the logic of majority politics. The organization moved from "working-class party" to "people's party"; its platform addressed the "national interest" rather than the "proletarian cause." In the words of the late Swedish socialist leader Per Albin Hansson, social democracy strived to erect a "people's home." It is worth noting, however, that the difference between socialist and communist parties does not have to do so much with the actual class composition of the party's constituency as with the conditions under which allied classes are admitted. Whereas the vanguard party admits only recruits who are willing to adhere to its manifesto, the social democratic party is prepared to realign its program in response to current requirements for alliance formation. For communist parties, program dictates parliamentary power; for social democratic parties, parliament dictates program.

Social democratic parties made the choice under a variety of conditions. In some cases, as in Britain and Denmark, there was hardly any debate on the question: pragmatic reformism rarely allowed ideological concerns to interfere. In Scandinavia as a whole, the nineteenth-century experience of collaboration in the struggle for the suffrage made the subsequent working-class–farmer alliance of the 1930s appear more natural. In most countries, unemployment and poverty caused by the wild business cycles of the interwar period forced socialists to reconsider the taboo on collaboration. Above all, the looming specter of fascism and the lesson of Germany spurred the socialists to trade Kautsky for Keynes.[4] Generally speaking, the socialist parties'

[4] This was particularly true in Norway, where farmers were turning toward fascism in the early 1930s. However, the Keynesian economics that resulted from the worker-

ability to appeal to voters beyond the urban, working-class ghettos helped them escape political isolation.

The Reformism Issue

The first two components of Przworski's definition emphasize, respectively, social democracy's relation to the state and to the class structure. The third element focuses on the party's posture concerning social transformation. According to Przworski (1980, 28) social democracy is characterized by a willingness to "seek improvements, reforms, within the confines of capitalism [as opposed to dedicating] all efforts and energies to its complete transformation." Social democracy is without a doubt reformist, but to say this is to miss the point. To differentiate "revolutionary" from "reformist" in this manner assumes that we have a way of knowing when a given policy has long-range revolutionary consequences. In some instances, we probably do. Almost certainly, old age homes will have no revolutionary consequences for the social structure. But in all too many cases, we have no accepted criteria for deciding which actions will merely reflect the status quo and which will accelerate historical transformation. It is all, in the end, contingent upon theory.[5] Two examples will suffice.

The main, if not the only, important demand of the Danish Communist party during the 1950s was "One Krone More per Hour." To someone like Samuel Gompers this would hardly seem revolutionary; but to a communist party wedded to the theory of surplus value, profit squeeze, and capitalist collapse, quantitative change might actually produce qualitative change. To give another example, when social democrats such as Ernst Wigforss proposed industrial democracy and wage-earner funds—reforms that according to Leninist analysis would only prop up the system—they did so on the basis of their theory of "organized capitalism," which suggested that certain kinds of policies have revolutionary consequences in the long run. The Swedish and Austrian Marxists believed that meaningful reforms "within the confines of capitalism" could accelerate socialism, if only a way could be found to nurture the latent socialization of capitalist development.

Thus, depending on the sort of policy and theory espoused, reforms and improvements can either be revolutionary or not. Since we have no generally agreed upon theory, we have no way of knowing. Przwor-

---

peasant coalition was inspired by diligent reading of Stalin's texts on capitalist underconsumption, as well as by exposure to the international Keynesian debate (Dahl 1969).

[5] André Gorz (1967) attempts to distinguish between "reformist" and "revolutionary" reforms. Unfortunately, he points to the problem but does not solve it.

ski's third criterion is therefore of little help. This is not to say, however, that policy is unimportant to a definition of social democracy. I propose to revise the third criterion as follows.

The decisive issue is not whether a movement seeks reforms "within the confines of capitalism," for in reality communists as well as socialists do so. Social ameliorative reforms, such as unemployment insurance or old-age pensions, are promoted by all important labor movements out of simple necessity. Labor movements cannot afford to ignore the fact that economic insecurity, poverty, and unemployment weaken proletarian solidarity and impede class mobilization. Whether the ultimate goal is proletarian dictatorship or a more humane society, the socialists need to eradicate invidious distinctions and mutual hostilities dividing the various sectors of the working class. Both Rosa Luxemburg and Rudolf Hilferding were agreed on the necessity of fighting for the social wage in order to lift up the slum proletariat.

Where social democracy and communism diverge is on the issue of how reforms aid the process of proletarian unity and class formation. With the communist vanguard party, the ghetto model for policy-making prevailed. The movement would take responsibility for the welfare of its constituency. Since the state apparatus was occupied by enemy classes, the strategy naturally called for direct political opposition to state legislation and public schemes. Both Lenin and Bismarck could agree that state welfare schemes might lure workers away from socialism. The essence of the Leninist prescription was that revolutionary class formation and solidarity could be achieved only by creating separate institutions in opposition to the state. Initially, the social democrats shared this view. August Bebel, for example, led the German Social Democratic party (SPD) against Bismarck's social legislation. Social democratic leaders in Scandinavia did likewise when they perceived that bourgeois reformers aspired to divide the working class. But once social democrats had chosen parliament as their battleground, once they had acknowledged the legitimacy of broader class alliances, their strategy for political mobilization and class solidarity had to include efforts to influence government policy. Instead of Przworski's faintly teleological criterion, then, I offer the following: social democracy is a movement that seeks to build class unity and mobilize power via national legislation.

It is easy to see that our three definitional criteria are interdependent. The decision to accept parliamentary democracy compels the party to adopt a majoritarian strategy. Depending on the composition of the class structure, this may entail a stronger or weaker need to aggregate

10

cross-class electoral alliances. The choice of how to implement one's program is cast within the logic of the previous choices. Having opted for parliamentary alliances, social democracy is also forced to seek reforms through parliamentary legislation. It follows that social democracy's ability to develop class solidarity is constrained by its capacity to influence public policy, even if its chances to make policy are in the last instance tied to the development of class structure. Reforms come to mediate between class structure and party power; they affect both. Yet this fact is not typically acknowledged in the classical theoretical positions.

THE THEORETICAL CONTROVERSY

To a fervent social democrat, the theoretical literature must make disheartening reading. Most theories, Marxist or not, project the long-run demise of social democracy. For quite different reasons, Leninists and "pluralist" theory both hold that class structural developments have adverse consequences for democratic socialism.

The Leninist Theory of Social Democracy

The Leninist argument has its roots in the Russian political struggle between Bolsheviks and Mensheviks, on the one hand, and Lenin's long battle against German revisionism, on the other. His attack centered on the question of parliamentarism and class development. Actually, Leninism is little more than a recapitulation of nineteenth-century Marxist orthodoxy. The critique of Kautsky in *The State and Revolution* (Lenin [1919] 1943) reads like an update of Marx's raging attack on the Gotha program of 1875 (Marx [1875] 1978). The Erfurt program of 1891, an attempt to correct many of the faults that Marx found, hardly managed to clarify the precise relation between insurrectionary revolution and parliamentary participation; nor was it clear on the choice between reformism within the system and opposition to the state. Kautsky may have warned explicitly against bourgeois collaboration and social democratic minority governments, but he remained vague about exactly when socialists could adopt a parliamentary strategy.

Lenin, however, was less ambivalent than his mentors. Even *The Communist Manifesto* (Marx and Engels [1848] 1967) allowed for reformism and revolution concomitantly. Its rather anticlimactic conclusion contains a list of first-priority tasks that even the most right-wing laborite could sanction. Similarly, in Marx's analysis of the Brit-

11

ish Factory Acts, one is led to hope that the bourgeois state can be made to serve socialist goals (Marx [1872] 1967, chap. 10). Engels' famous introduction to *Class Struggles in France* (Marx [1895] 1964) can be easily interpreted as an enthusiastic manifesto for parliamentary socialism. Lenin, then, did not merely restate the classical position: he deliberately sought to expunge its revisionist sins.

Lenin's recast Marxian theory is built around three propositions. The first, and most important, concerns the nature of the bourgeois state. In *The State and Revolution* the state apparatus is designed to support bourgeois class power and exploitation. Real power does not reside in parliament, which is merely a "talking shop" and a democratic façade that serves to disguise the fact that power is exercised elsewhere. Consequently, if socialists take parliamentary democracy seriously, they will betray the proletarian cause by helping obscure the nature of class struggle. Even worse, their participation will serve only to perpetuate and strengthen class exploitation, thus delaying the inevitable revolutionary moment. Since parliamentary democracy will never become genuine democracy (workers' councils) and since any state is, by its very nature, a class state, social democracy logically must fail—unless it bends every effort to oppose and destroy the bourgeois state.

Lenin's second proposition flows from his class analysis. In *What Is to Be Done?* (Lenin [1909] 1929, 90) his famous hypothesis on the economism of workers is formulated: "The spontaneous labor movement is able to create by itself only trade unionism, and working class trade union politics are precisely working class bourgeois politics." Left to their own devices, workers are instinctively economistic in their demands and will never discover the level of ideological consciousness required for socialist revolution. Hence, the proletariat will remain unenlightened about its real historical interests, unless narrow economism is replaced by ideological education and unless the trade union movement is brought under vanguard party control. An open mass party would fail to overcome the lethargy of economism.

The third proposition concerns Lenin's view of capitalist development. Without a theory of collapse, he could hardly defend the strategy of opposition to the institutions of capitalism; nor could he plausibly advocate the vanguard party model. The argument, most coherently developed in his tract *Imperialism: The Highest Stage of Capitalism* ([1924] 1939), is premised on the Marxist theory of exploitation, concentration, and monopoly capitalism. Capitalist accumulation, holds Lenin, will culminate with global imperialism, where the reproduction of class exploitation demands an ever more powerful state. But this occurrence will also signal the end of capitalism. While this proposition clearly calls for an international synchronization of proletarian struggles, it also confirms the strategic necessity of nurturing contradictions instead of patching them up by means of reforms and collaboration with the bourgeoisie.

In Leninist theory social democracy is doomed. True, in the short term, given inherent worker economism, it is possible that trade union reformism will hold sway, but long-run developments logically will crush the social democratic promise. First of all, since social democratic parties are prepared to participate in parliamentarism, they clearly mislead workers into believing that participation is power. Since it is not, however, and since the contradictions will become increasingly evident, this betrayal of the workers must at some point become obvious. Moreover, by supporting the bourgeois state, the social democrats will in fact contribute to their own demise, for they will be supporting a system designed to divide, fragment, and exploit their own working-class constituency. When the inevitable moment of revolutionary rupture arrives, the social democrats will be totally unprepared to lead the proletariat. Finally, says Lenin, the demise of social democracy is inevitable because of the activities of the revolutionary communist movement, which according to the conditions for membership in the Comintern, must

> declare a decisive war against the entire bourgeois world and all the yellow, social democratic parties. Every rank-and-file worker must clearly understand the difference between the communist parties and the old official "social democratic" or "socialist" parties which have betrayed the cause of the working class [Miliband 1977, 168].

The Leninist position continues to influence political theory. When he was still a Stalinist, John Strachey believed that social democracy was little more than liberalism in new clothes, a servant of capitalism whose corporatist apparatus helped discipline workers. To these apparent incompatibilities, he adds that in times of economic crisis the party can only retire into opposition or cast itself in the role of "social fascism" (Strachey 1933, 306, 327, 388). Although Leo Panitch is neither polemical nor incoherent, his theory of social democratic participation in neocorporatism shares the same assumption that participation runs directly against the interests of labor, that it is unstable because of rank-and-file revolts, and that it will unleash a militance for which social democracy is quite unprepared (Panitch 1976, 1981).

Adam Przworski et al. (1977a, 1977b, 1980) espouse a more subtle

13

and sophisticated variant of Leninism. Cast in terms of the strategic dilemmas, their version holds that broad electoral appeals will dilute the party's class profile and push ideologically inclined workers to the left. Przworski is willing to entertain the possibility that social democrats may attain the required parliamentary majority for socialist transformation; but, like Lenin, he concludes that it is precisely at this crucial historical moment that parliamentary social democracy is likely to meet defeat (Przworski 1980, 57-58). This is so because the party will be overloaded with popular demands that cannot possibly be satisfied without jeopardizing economic stability and provoking unmanageable crises. The implication is that social democracy will continually vacillate between booms of political mobilization and busts of political defeat. Przworski's argument is both tighter than and empirically superior to most Leninist theories. It rests, however, on two suspect assumptions: first, that the "allied classes" always remain ideologically estranged from socialism; secondly, that social democratic transition politics must begin with "une augmentation substantielle des salaries et traitment" (Przworski 1980, 58).[6] Is it not possible that social democracy can take office and propose socialization in return for an effective promise of wage and consumption restraints?

Sociological Critiques of Marxism

The classical critique of Lenin's theory was developed by Selig Perlman in his *Theory of the Labor Movement* (1926). Perlman agreed with Lenin that economism is inherent in the working class, but disagreed that workers as a class are "objectively" interested in or ideologically prepared for the larger struggle for socialism. Worker consciousness is normally "job consciousness," and revolutionary ideology is mainly a foreign invention, implanted by intellectuals with disregard for the true needs of the proletariat. Perlman's thesis has informed the more

---

[6] Przworski's quantitative analyses assume that the ideological and political preferences of the "allied classes" remain constant over time. This model does not take into account the possibility that, over time, the new middle classes converge with the working class and/or that their political inclinations become increasingly socialist. If that were to happen, the social democratic electoral trade-off dilemma might disappear rather than intensify. Przworski's second assumption appears to rest squarely on the ill-fated experiences of Salvador Allende's Chile and Leon Blum's France. But there is no a priori reason to believe that history always repeats itself. It is possible, even likely, that a social democratic party will enter the transition stage with a package of income-restraint policies in return for some kind of socialization measures. Of course, debate is almost hopelessly impossible because of the difficulty of agreeing on exactly what constitutes an acceptable kind of socialist transition.

general hypothesis that pragmatic American unionism shows Europeans the wave of the future. It is not the absence of socialism in America that requires explanation but, rather, socialism's obstinacy in Europe. Perlman does not reject the importance of class conflict but holds that sharp ideological cleavages are unnatural and will, in the long run, fade.

The Perlman thesis bears a close affinity to the "logic of industrialism" theory (Kerr et al. 1964). If in classical Marxism capitalism leads to class polarization, the industrialism theory predicts convergence and equilibrium. As originally stated in the famous Bull (1922) hypothesis, working-class radicalism is a manifestation of uncertainty and alienation during periods of rapid and explosive industrial change. Where modernization is slow and gradual, the likelihood of radicalism is lessened. Bull's reasoning has frequently been extended to argue that, once the phase of early industrialization has passed, workers will become integrated into industrial society and labor movements will abandon their radicalism (Kerr et al. 1964; Galenson 1949, 1952).[7] Lipset (1960) suggests a social-psychological variant. He claims that both left-wing and right-wing extremism is associated with authoritarianism and worker isolation from the main institutions of modern society.

The theory of industrialism emphasizes, as do latter-day theories of postindustrial society, the importance of class structural change for the decline of socialist radicalism. The proletariat will change as the pathological consequences of early industrialization disappear. But the nature of the upper classes will also change. Schumpeter (1970) argued that the classical entrepreneurial capitalist becomes a historical anachronism as authority and control over production is delegated to modern management. In Galbraith's view (1969), the bourgeoisie surrenders its power to the technostructure. For Galbraith the classical polarity of capital and labor is mediated, especially if economic decisions are based on criteria of social responsibility and technical imperative. Industrialism theory furthermore sensitizes us to the importance of the new middle strata, a phenomenon already noted by Bernstein ([1899] 1971).

The validity of such arguments hinges importantly on the precise nature of the new middle classes and their relation to the traditional working class. Whereas many Marxists will look in vain to the de-

---

[7] Bull's hypothesis, which was formulated with the Scandinavian countries in mind, was empirically substantiated by Lafferty (1971) and Galenson (1949, 1952). One may also view Tingsten's (1941) analysis of the Swedish social democrats as a test of Bull's argument. Lafferty's empirical evidence has been challenged by Klingman (1976).

graded and exploited industrial laborer for the advent of revolutionary consciousness, postindustrial theory recalls an important aspect of Marx's work: the crucial relevance of the growth of productive forces in capitalism. The relative number of industrial laborers is declining, and technically skilled and educated manpower is taking their place. But there is no agreement on the political properties of the new middle strata. They may, as Parkin believes (1972), have a modifying influence on socialist parties. They may, as C. Wright Mills speculated (1951), epitomize the fragmentation, atomization, and privatization of modern mass society, thus implying that class solidarity and collectivism will be shipwrecked. French structural Marxists, like Poulantzas (1975), view these middle strata as the new petite bourgeoisie and, as such, dangerous allies indeed for the proletariat. But if the foregoing consider the new middle strata to be an obstacle to socialist mobilization, writers such as Gorz (1967) and Mallet (1975) find in them a new source of socialist radicalism.

Others find the main agent of change in political democracy. Paradoxically, the argument runs in two directions. Inspired by Max Weber's theory of bureaucracy, Roberto Michels ([1915] 1962) formulated his Iron Law of Oligarchy to account for the decay of German social democracy. According to Michels, the socialist party will contradict its own historical mission of democratic socialism. As it grows into a powerful political movement it will professionalize, bureaucratize, and lose sight of its real purpose as it becomes preoccupied with the demands of day-to-day administration. The party becomes an expression of antidemocratic rule, devoted to the task of its own self-perpetuation. Thus, by the very act of struggling for democracy and equality, the social democratic party generates oligarchy and privilege.

In contrast, "democratization" theories argue that, in the process of state building during the nineteenth and twentieth centuries, the extension of full citizenship rights to the masses diminished social cleavages. For Bendix (1964), Rokkan (1970), and Marshall (1950), a basic source of class cleavages lay in the exclusion of workers from participation and representation in the political system. In this view, most explicitly stated by Marshall (1950) and Lipset (1960), the extension of legal, political, and eventually social rights has secured for the working class effective influence over public policy. Hence, "inequalities no longer constitute class distinctions and therefore do not give rise to class struggles but become socially acceptable [Marshall 1950, 75]." The theories of working-class "embourgeoisement" and "end of ideology" were inspired by postwar prosperity and a new confidence in the strength of democratic institutions—phenomena that eroded old class divisions, both in political attitudes as well as in life styles (Mayer 1955; Zweig 1971; Abramson 1971).

As theorists attempted to explain the British Labour party's declining electoral fortunes, it became fashionable to hold that the socialists had "reformed themselves out of office." Recent backlash theories have much in common with such arguments. According to Wilensky (1975, 68ff., 116-119), welfare state revolts are likely to come from the "middle mass" (a combination of upper-level workers and white-collar employees), owing to tax overload and resentments against welfare bureaucracies. Similarly, Tyrell (1977) and others argue a direct association between social democratic decline and welfare state growth. Generally, the prediction is that as social democracy succeeds in implementing its social reforms, it will alienate its own increasingly affluent electoral base. A related explanation for the decline of socialism in the postwar era holds that democratization and the declining salience of class force socialist parties away from their traditional class image and radical ideology. They become modern catchall parties, designed to capture majorities by appealing to the middle (Lipset 1964; Epstein 1967; Kirschheimer 1968).

All these theories share the assumption that class, as a historical force, is eroding. Hence, social democracy can be expected to decline under two conditions. If it retains its historical mission, affluent and integrated workers in liaison with the new middle strata will reject it. If it should adopt a catchall strategy, it may hold onto voters but will only vaguely manage to distinguish itself from bourgeois parties.

Social Democratic Action Theory

Social democratic theory naturally rejects any view of the party as a passive victim of historical change, whether caused by revolutionary contradictions or the decay of class struggle. Instead, the future of social democracy must flow out of its own actions. Leninism, to be sure, adopts an activist approach, calling upon ideological preparation, organization, and opposition politics to accelerate the fall of capitalism. Social democratic action theory obviously is premised on electoral and legislative accomplishments. The great theoretical problem is how to rescue the promise of the socialist end goal when party activity appears to stabilize the capitalist order (Tingsten 1941; Gay 1970; Lewin 1967).

Modern social democratic theory derives from the controversy between Marxist reformism, exemplified by Kautsky, and the revisionism of Bernstein. Kautsky's position, clearly stated in the 1891 Erfurt

17

program, combines a straightforward Marxian analysis of capitalist development with a program befitting a parliamentary socialist party. The general point is that capitalist development dictates the inevitability of socialism. Accordingly, the main task of the movement is to prepare for the moment when "the time is ripe," a moment that apparently will arise independently of political action.

Kautsky's analysis of class formation is quite deterministic. Because of the concentration of capital and the inevitable proletarianization of most other social strata, capitalism creates its own majority in favor of socialism. The increasingly social form of production ensures that the working class will become a homogeneous and collective agent (Kautsky [1892] 1971, 173). Not much can be done to resolve the basic class contradictions that spell doom for capitalist society. But Kautsky, in contrast to Lenin does not believe that reformism will stop the march toward socialism. On the contrary, parliamentary participation can develop the proletariat's capacity for socialist politics; enlightened reforms can accelerate capitalism's natural progress toward socialism.

It was ideas such as these that brought down the wrath of Lenin in *The State and Revolution*. Clearly Kautsky did take an optimistic view of the bourgeois state. Discussing the advantages of parliamentary participation in *The Road to Power*, he states that "the emancipation of the laboring class is not to be expected from its increasing demoralization, but from its increased strength" (Kautsky [1910] 1943, 38). And in *The Class Struggle*, we read:

> Whenever the proletariat engages in parliamentary activity as a self-conscious class, parliamentarism begins to change its character. It ceases to be a mere tool in the hands of the bourgeoisie. . . . The proletariat has therefore no reason to distrust parliamentary action [Kautsky (1892) 1971, 188].

Yet, Kautsky is never entirely clear on the issue. If these statements suggest that reforms are necessary to uplift the moral fiber of the working class, and that parliamentary action is the instrument, Kautsky takes it all back when he claims that reforms will never help resolve the system's basic contradictions. If capitalism is doomed to collapse on its own accord, then why commit the working class to reforming it? Nor is Kautsky sufficiently clear about exactly when the proletariat should support parliamentarism and when it should oppose it. He insists that, so long as the state is in the hands of the bourgeoisie, the socialists must resist and oppose it. But then, he also holds that parliaments can be trusted when the proletariat forms a "self-conscious class."

This lack of theoretical coherence extends to the question of class alliances. Kautsky admits that socialist comrades can be recruited from other classes, even among the bourgeoisie, but he insists that the party is, and can only be, a proletarian movement. The revolution, which for Kautsky is noninsurrectionary, can be brought about only by the working class (Kautsky [1892] 1971, 159). *The Class Struggle*, however, also calls for middle-class support. For Kautsky these apparent incompatibilities will resolve themselves because, in the long run, capitalism will proletarianize the vast majority. Kautsky and the Erfurt program, then, can offer a convincing theory of socialism only if two key assumptions hold: first, if a proletarian majority actually is imminent; secondly, if the state apparatus can in fact be seized peacefully and made to transform society.

Bernstein's revisionism is characterized by a refusal to accept the first assumption and a disregard for the second. His *Evolutionary Socialism* sets forth an analysis of capitalism that is in direct contradiction with classical Marxism. Instead of showing signs of collapse, capitalism is robust and dynamic, and it is evolving in directions completely at odds with orthodox predictions. Instead of causing misery, capitalism is producing wealth and abundance, even helping to improve the living conditions of workers. Instead of monopolistic concentration, the modern joint-stock company helps distribute wealth and property in a more democratic fashion.

Bernstein's understanding of bourgeois democracy serves to confirm his opinion that capitalism is resistant to cataclysmic collapse. The democratization of the state permits reforms to be undertaken that simultaneously diminish contradictions, allow the productive forces to expand, and benefit the working class. On democracy he was less ambiguous than Kautsky: "Universal suffrage in Germany could serve Bismarck as a temporary tool, but finally it compelled Bismarck to serve it as a tool [Bernstein (1899) 1971, 144]."

If Lenin and Kautsky agreed that class formation was predetermined, Bernstein believed it to be indeterminate. For Bernstein this implied that the party cannot afford to sit and wait for a proletarian majority simply to happen. Majorities have to be created. And since a socialist majority cannot be expected to emerge from unmanageable contradictions, it must be forged in the more mundane world of practical party policy. It therefore comes as no surprise that Bernstein cared less about the future Good Society than about the day-to-day issue of how to build majorities. For Bernstein it was not betrayal to declare

19

that the movement is everything, the end goal nothing. In his view, "the whole practical activity of social democracy is directed towards creating circumstances and conditions which shall render possible and secure a transition of the modern social order into a higher one [Bernstein (1899) 1971, 146]."

Bernstein believed that social democracy must build a broad electoral alliance of all the underprivileged strata and that the movement's success hinges upon its ability to strengthen parliament and legislate the gradual socialization of capitalism. Not only is reformism a salami tactic to bring about socialism, it is the chief source of majority mobilization. If for Kautsky parliaments were a potential tool, for Bernstein they constituted a necessary precondition for social democratic class formation.

Kautsky and Bernstein Synthesized

Austro-Marxism and its Swedish offshoots may be viewed as a synthesis of Kautsky and Bernstein. In Austro-Marxism the theory of capitalist development was recast: first, by explicitly rejecting the breakdown-of-capitalism argument; secondly, by arguing that the organized and planned character of modern capitalism could advance the socialist cause. As Karl Renner would later put it (1953), the case for the coming of socialism can no longer be made in terms of the anarchy of laissez-faire capitalism. Instead, capitalism—owing to state penetration of the economy and the growing dominance of finance capital and cartels—is on its own account becoming an increasingly socialized economic order.

Austro-Marxism shares Bernstein's optimistic view that the state is an autonomous apparatus, increasingly independent of the bourgeoisie. In addition the Austro-Marxists, Max Adler ([1933] 1978) in particular, rejected Kautsky's deterministic class theory. Capitalist development was producing status differentiation instead of mass polarization. Adler, in fact, distinguished five distinct working-class strata. His view of the new middle classes was somewhat ambivalent: large sections were perhaps proletarianizing, but this only added to the problem of status differentiation.[8]

These theoretical propositions led the Austro-Marxists to rethink

[8] Adler emphasizes the classical hostility between labor aristocracies and industrial workers, adding to these the new phenomenon of "bureaucratic" workers. Furthermore, writing during the Great Depression, he gives special weight to the danger of unemployment and its tendency to stimulate antagonisms between workers with and workers without jobs (Adler [1933] 1978).

social democratic strategy. The rise of organized capitalism and the possibility of a rational state suggested a "constructive" rather than a "destructive" attitude toward the capitalist order. Their strategy was to nurture the progressive and suppress the negative tendencies of capitalism. Since the state was not necessarily a machine for class repression, it was natural to advocate a parliament-centered struggle. If capitalism contained the seeds of socialism, one important task for the social democratic party was to bring these seeds to fruition. Bauer's ([1919] 1978) concept of the "slow revolution" implied not only that a parliamentary strategy could succeed, but that it was probably the quickest route.

Party policy had to obstruct the pathological tendencies of capitalism. Since class opposition was more harmful than beneficial to socialism, both Adler and Bauer stressed the necessity of broad alliances between workers, peasants, and the middle classes, advocating reforms that could reconcile internal and external class divisions. A full-employment, welfare state strategy flowed quite naturally from this perspective in that a precondition for social democratic political power was to narrow the gap between unemployed and employed, labor aristocrats and industrial workers, white collar and blue collar. The Austrian socialists thus agreed with Bernstein that social democratic class formation must proceed through practical reformism. But they went further than Bernstein in their wish to connect day-to-day reformist practice to a long-range plan for "slow revolution." In effect, they claimed that short-run measures are steppingstones to the promised socialist end goal.

Early socialist thought in Scandinavia was dogmatically Kautskyan, but after World War I the three social democratic movements parted ways. The Danes essentially abandoned theory; the Norwegians remained loyal to a blend of Kautskyan and Leninist ideas for many years; and the Swedes moved surprisingly close to the Austrian socialists. Hjalmar Branting realized very early that Kautsky's predicted proletarian majority would not arrive in the foreseeable future, and he concluded that a broader electoral strategy was absolutely necessary. As argued by Tingsten (1941), Swedish social democracy was also quick to substitute ideological radicalism for reformism when pressure from below demanded it. By the late 1920s, the party had replaced opposition with participation, socialization with reformism, and class purity with popular alliances. The party leadership was convinced that the mobilization of power required first and foremost the satisfaction of the most pressing popular demands.

As in Austria, Swedish social democracy nurtured a school of creative theoretical talent, among which Nils Karleby (1926) and Ernst Wigforss (1941) stand out especially. They agreed with the theory of "organized capitalism" and believed in parliament's ability to service democratic demands. What distinguishes Swedish socialist thought is its way of situating immediate reforms in the context of a socialist future. Reforms can, in a cumulative way, have revolutionary outcomes. Also, the Swedes were the first to develop a systematic theory in which the sequential order of struggle is reversed. Whereas the orthodox scheme presupposes that welfare and the good life can arise only after the socialization of production, Swedish revisionism holds that political and then social reforms can create the conditions for economic transformation, step by step. "Political citizenship" must precede "social citizenship," and these are in turn indispensable for the third stage, "economic citizenship." Workers must be emancipated from social insecurity before they can partake effectively in economic democracy.

The model, as Korpi (1978, 1981a, 1981b) and Stephens (1979) argue, is premised on a theory of power mobilization. Having chosen the parliamentary strategy, labor's power advantage lies in its numbers; its disadvantage in the scant, and unevenly distributed, resources among wage earners. If political resources rarely come from ideology, political strength must grow out of reforms and full employment, which will endow workers with a greater capacity for participation and solidarity.

In this view, the welfare state is not an end in itself but is a means for altering the balance of class power to social democracy's advantage. Thus, along with the Austrians, the Swedes believe that capitalist crises will only weaken the resources of wage earners. To reform capitalism, moreover, does not automatically imply a betrayal of the socialist promise. Reformism and socialism are compatible because, in the words of Sten Johansson,

> the strength of the Swedish labor movement is due to its ability to reconcile the contradiction between capital and labor, i.e. to adjust successively the conditions of production to the development of the productive forces. The question of "when the time is ripe" becomes . . . the question of the development of the productive forces in relation to production relations [Johansson 1974, 11].

It is difficult to imagine a better dialectical synthesis of Bernstein and

22

Kautsky. Reformism helps accomplish what Kautsky relies on for the day of revolution.

Such analyses may be sophisticated, but they are also ambiguous. They imply that the labor movement can accelerate the arrival of the "ripe time" by adjusting the contradictions. Instead of passively awaiting the day when the balloon will burst or blindly pursuing reforms, social democracy pledges to adjust class relations and social institutions to fit the increasingly socialistic character of the productive forces. The theory is ambiguous in that it cannot specify under what conditions the process of adjustment will have advanced so far that the time is ripe enough. But the ambiguity can be resolved precisely because the theory links reformism with the process of power mobilization. As the balance of class power gradually shifts in favor of wage earners (partly because of structural change, partly because of party policies and organization), the social democrats may pursue salami tactics, slicing away at traditional capitalist prerogatives and replacing them with democratic forms of control.

The Swedish social democrats do not share Schumpeter's (1970) and Crosland's (1967) assumption that effective control has slipped away from the capitalists and into the hands of management. The central task of "functional socialism" is to make capitalists functionally redundant by bringing their traditional powers and prerogatives under collective management. Adler-Karlsson (1967) describes the process as follows:

> Let us avoid the even more dangerous contests which are unavoidable if we enter the road of formal socialization. Let us instead grip and divest our present capitalists of one after another of their ownership functions. Let us even give them a new dress, one similar to that of the famous emperor in H. C. Andersen's tale. After a few decades they will then remain, perhaps formally, as kings but in reality as naked symbols of a passed and inferior stage of development [Scase 1976, 307].

This version, which follows the lead of Karleby (1926), is based on a distinction between the socialization of "flow" and that of "stock." Control over the functions of capitalist ownership, it is implied, is more important than socialization of property per se. It is a twist of irony that Swedish social democratic theory devises a strategy for achieving something that numerous postwar revisionists, most notably C. A. R. Crosland (1967), claim has already come about in Britain.

If the Austro-Swedish model views immediate social reforms as a

23

precondition for economic democratization, a "Keynes plus Beveridge" policy seems to suffice in the view of Crosland. Along with Strachey (1956), Crosland argues that the economic power of the bourgeoisie need no longer be the centerpiece of social democracy's struggles, for the separation of ownership and control is removing that problem. Concomitantly, modern mass production has brought with it a democratization of consumption to the extent that goods produced for "use" have replaced luxury goods. To be sure, Crosland admits that certain irrationalities of the capitalist mode of production persist, but he believes that a mix of Keynesian countercyclical instruments, modern planning, and egalitarian welfare state measures are sufficient to attain the goals of a just society. Crosland is optimistic about the social democrats' ability to mobilize sufficient electoral support for such an endeavor. Once again inspired by Schumpeter, he assumes the eventual emergence of an anticapitalist morality. If today many of Crosland's tenets seem dubious, they nevertheless left a strong imprint on most postwar social democratic movements.[9] The Bad Godesberg program was premised on virtually identical principles, as was the Keynesian welfare state rhetoric of most social democratic parties during the 1950s.

Leninists, Social Democrats, and Pluralists Compared

Lenin held that social democracy could neither contain nor resolve the crystallizing class contradictions of advanced capitalism; participation in bourgeois institutions, moreover, would corrupt working-class politics. In a sense, Lenin relies on a strangely nonmaterialist interpretation. If, on the one hand, the proletarian class is supposed to spring forth according to the laws of capital accumulation, its role as an agent of historical transformation, on the other hand, can be realized only with the support of the vanguard party's ideological consciousness—a seemingly superstructural affair. Similarly, Lenin re-

[9] Ironically, it is where Crosland is most astute that he is overlooked (Bell 1977). He makes the argument that the greatest problem for the socialists is how they will manage to persuade the masses that socialism will prove to be more "fun" and pleasurable than capitalism. Before the war, socialist movements devoted much energy to this question and, with their vast network of social clubs, athletic and boy scout organizations, chess clubs, and so forth, could convey an image of socialism as an enjoyable alternative to the dreariness of industrial life or the vulgarity of purchased leisure. These organizations have decayed, and the typical socialist party has become a predominantly administrative apparatus imbued with rationalist and technocratic notions of efficiency.

lies on a theory of bourgeois parliamentarism to explain why social democratic reforms will help fragment the working class. In the long run Leninism predicts social democratic decomposition, as class struggle under conditions of monopoly capitalism demands the intervention of a revolutionary vanguard committed to the destruction of the very same state that the social democrats have so diligently helped construct.

Paradoxically, non-Marxist theories are often premised on historical-materialist interpretations. Both the "embourgeoisement" and "logic of industrialism" theses hold that socialist class mobilization will flounder because of the technologically determined erosion of class divisions in the economy. In either version, the odds in favor of a social democratic road to power appear desperately poor. Social democratic decomposition is guaranteed under conditions of either class polarization or class harmonization.

The sources of social democracy's own theoretical optimism are variegated. In Kautsky's version, the success of social democracy is virtually predetermined by the inevitable process of proletarianization, although the party is called upon to provide a means of political expression. For Bernstein, class formation is an undetermined process, and socialist advances will flow from the movement's practical achievements. Neither man, however, develops a systematic argument concerning which conditions will promote social democratic success as opposed to decomposition.

On this account, the revisionist theories of Austro-Swedish Marxists appear more sociological. Writing during the tumultuous 1920s and the cataclysmic 1930s, their arguments were naturally more sensitive to the forces that weakened the labor movement and to the necessity of averting economic crises. It is possible to distill the following set of empirically testable hypotheses from these theories. First, social democratic success depends on the party's ability to strengthen parliament's powers. Secondly, that success is contingent on an ability to fight a two-front battle on behalf of and against capitalism. The social fragmentation, atomization, and egoistic competitiveness produced by capitalism must be countered; this means that social democratic power depends on effective control of the business cycle and on the eradication of status differentials among wage earners. Simultaneously, social democratic success will depend on an ability to "realign the conditions of production to fit the productive forces" and steer capitalist development toward its full social potential. Thirdly, as both cause and consequence of the preceding two conditions, the social

25

democratic movement can—if it succeeds in building broad solidarity among its natural constituencies—shift the balance of class power to the advantage of labor.

The Theory of Social Democratic Party Formation and Decomposition

We can now begin to build our theory of social democracy; the simple bivariate theories are inadequate. Social democracy's future cannot be merely a reflection of social structural change, whether that change be embourgeoisement or its opposite.

Although the development of class structure does not determine the politics of socialism, there nonetheless is no doubt that factors such as the relative size of the working class play a fundamental role: they set the limits for social democratic mobilization. Since social democracy aspires to win political office, moreover, and has frequently done so, the long-term success of the movement must be associated with the role of the state. I contend that the process of social democratic class formation depends on the impact of state policies on the class structure. Our theory, then, must specify the relationships between class, state, and power.

The overall argument is that social democracy is historically indeterminate. This is so for the simple reason that none of the social forces that shape it is predetermined. The theory to be presented is built around three key components: class structure, class formation, and class alliance. We will proceed, after first establishing the character of each, to see how they combine to influence social democratic performance.

Class Structure

The case for or against socialism has always been predicated on class structural development.[10] In the Marxist perspective, proletarianization is the necessary (occasionally even the sufficient) condition for socialist success. In pluralist theory, the decline of class cleavages is similarly a necessary (and sometimes sufficient) cause of socialist decomposition. Even a very superficial glance across the globe, however, tells us that class structure alone can hardly explain the wide international variations in socialist party strength. The relative numbers of

[10] The following discussion of class does not pretend to any scientific rigor with respect either to Marxist or non-Marxist class analysis.

the traditional working class (even of wage earners) are quite similar, for example, in the United States, Canada, Britain, Germany, Holland, and Scandinavia, while the fate of socialist parties has certainly varied in those countries. There is hardly any correlation. This does not mean that class structure can be disregarded; rather, it means that we must examine more closely what it is about class structure that conditions politics.

It is useful to distinguish between class structure and class formation. "Class" has to do with the objectively given "empty slots" that exist as a result of the division of labor and that have meaning independent of the attitudes or behavior of the individuals who occupy them (Przworski 1975; Poulantzas 1975; and Wright 1979). "Class formation" has to do with how the individuals who fill the slots engage in collective action; that is, how they constitute a social or political community. The constellation of empty slots may not have a direct bearing on the structure of class formation. Sartre (1968, 96) makes this point rather clearly when he states, "Classes do not naturally exist, but they are made." The fault of the most vulgar Marxism is its tendency to assume that "objective" class location automatically breeds one form of collective action (the socialist kind, naturally).

A rather similar distinction is also made in Weberian and contemporary pluralist sociology. The occupational position of an individual does not dictate status position, nor is it automatically associated with specific political behavior. In the Weberian tradition, status formation is usually described as the rise of interest groups. Both Marxism and pluralism insist that political class (status) formation involves factors that are independent of one's objective position.[11]

The structure of empty slots does play a central role for social democratic ascendance, because it defines the "raw material" upon which communities, alliances, and political mobilization must be based (Przworski 1975). Class structure limits the extent that social democracy can choose to appeal only to workers and prescribes the points at which it must seek class allies. When class allies must be sought, class structure defines the possible allies.

Class structure, conceived of as empty slots, affects the course of social democracy in four respects. First, there is the development of workers. The number of workers relative to numbers in other class

[11] Typically, Marxist and non-Marxist political sociologists alike have studied the process of political class (status) formation according to a simple model that correlates objective class position with voting or other indicators of political behavior. Important examples are Lipset (1960, 1964), Alford (1963), Hamilton (1967, 1972), Abramson (1971), Butler and Stokes (1971), and Rose and Urwin (1971).

categories has an obvious effect on the possibilities for working-class political majorities. Workers, in the sense of traditional manual wage labor, have only rarely constituted a majority in the class structure. Clearly the relative number of workers over time determines the conditions for social democratic power mobilization. Of equal importance is the internal differentiation of worker positions. Even where workers share common status as wage labor, they may be highly differentiated. Class unity is more difficult to achieve under conditions of competition between craft workers, unskilled industrial laborers, and the rural proletariat. A dominance of craft workers over industrial workers tends to make broad solidarity a more difficult task, tending to "corporatize" the labor movement and create jealousies. As has been noted before (Stephens 1979), the relative dominance of industrial workers has historically been decisive for the creation of a cohesive and centralized trade union movement. As Galenson (1952) also shows, skill divisions may cement a dualism in the entire labor movement.

Secondly, variations in the structure of capital undoubtedly play a role, although a dearth of research on the structure and organization of business inhibits precise hypotheses (Schmitter and Streeck 1981). Schumpeter (1970) and Crosland (1967) believed that the decay of entrepreneurial capitalism nurtures a cultural opposition to capitalism; others, especially students of Germany, suggest the opposite, namely that "monopoly capital" has been a leading force behind repression of the labor movement (Abraham 1981; Neumann 1944; Meier 1975). These authors also suggest that export-oriented business was more likely to compromise with labor (see, also, Cameron 1978). The relationship of capital to the state has also been held to play a decisive role, particularly when profits depend on state purchases, as in Germany (Barrington Moore 1967; Gerschenkron 1943). Variations in industrial technology may influence social structure in general and the behavior of labor in particular (Kerr et al. 1964; Blauner 1964). Furthermore, capital concentration and geographical centralization will influence the dispersal or concentration of workers as well as the kinds of tactics to be employed for union organization. Finally, as especially Schmitter and Streeck (1981) suggest, the ways in which business interests are organized play a very important role in how the power of those interests is articulated vis-à-vis the state and organized labor. Kautsky and his Swedish and Austrian disciples premised their entire theory of socialism on the rise of organized capitalism. They believed that the advanced corporate enterprise system is far more amenable to socialist collectivism than traditional entrepreneurial, family capitalism.

28

A third factor, frequently ignored, is the traditional rural and urban petite bourgeoisie. Their importance can hardly be overestimated, for their composition and organization delimit the conditions for class alliance with either labor or capital. As Bernstein observed ([1899] 1971), proletarianization was not occurring at the pace predicted by classical Marxism, and the petite bourgeoisie revealed unexpected staying power. This meant that socialist political majorities were importantly contingent on the political leanings of various petit-bourgeois strata. But as Marx had already emphasized in *Class Struggles in France*, the petite bourgeoisie cannot easily organize itself as a class and is therefore easy prey to demagoguery. The organizational capacity and economic position of the petite bourgeoisie has been historically decisive for socialist movements. Where, as in Scandinavia, family farming induced the formation of cooperatives and associations, their political leanings were likely to favor liberalism, democracy, and social reform rather than fascism or Poujadism, as in Germany or France.

If the position of the petite bourgeoisie has been important, so has the speed of their demise. It is easy to see that this has not simply followed the laws of accumulation. Their survival has frequently been predicated on political intervention, as in case of farm subsidies, laws to protect small shopkeepers against "unfair" competition from large retailers (mandated closing hours, for example), or tax laws favorable to small, independent entrepreneurs. The survival of the petite bourgeoisie has constrained social democratic mobilization in two important ways. First, a strong petit-bourgeois economy generally implies that large sections of the working class are tied to its activities. Such workers are typically both more difficult to organize and intrinsically hostile to economic rationalization and modernization. Secondly, where initial social democratic ascendance and government power was premised on petit-bourgeois alliances, political possibilities were both opened and closed. I shall argue that one of the most important preconditions for social democratic advances in the postwar era is the movement's ability to exchange alliance partners, drop the petite bourgeoisie, and seek a coalition with the new middle strata. Its ability to do so depends on how far the petite bourgeoisie have decayed.

Finally, the rise of new middle-strata categories constitutes one of the most profound changes in the class structure of advanced societies. Rather early on, beginning with Bernstein, socialists recognized that white-collar wage earners would not conform to proletarian status but were evolving into a heterogeneous array of functionaries, salaried employees, and technical and professional cadres, distributed in both public- and private-sector employment. In fact, their lack of a clearly defined class character provoked rather extensive socialist research efforts, such as Adler's (1933) in Austria and Lederer and Marschak's (1926) in Germany. That their location in the class structure is still unsettled is evident as we see Poulantzas (1975) calling them the new petite bourgeoisie, Mallet (1975) describing them as the new working class, and Wright (1979) placing them in contradictory class locations.

It is clear that the middle strata will play a pivotal role once the petite bourgeoisie die out and the traditional working class stagnates. Social democracy cannot avoid the task of building coalitions that unite its old core constituency with the rising white-collar strata. But how? And which strata? Several rough hypotheses present themselves. First, the middle strata are unquestionably a much more heterogeneous entity than either the manual workers or the urban and rural petite bourgeoisie. This suggests that they are less predictably a collective actor and that, to the extent a collective identity can be formed, its roots will probably be variegated. The importance of the state is naturally enhanced where white-collar employment is concentrated in the public sector. The location of the middle strata, in fact, is tightly circumscribed by how the public sector evolves; in some measure, therefore, they are a politically created "class." It can be hypothesized that middle-strata employees centered in collective and public services will have a closer affinity to labor than those in private-sector managerial and supervisory positions, but this could very well depend on the political coloration of the regime that controls public employment.[12] One would expect that the emergence of collective identities among the new middle strata hinge on political factors. "Objective" class location probably plays a lesser role than it does with other classes.

Class Formation

Class formation consists of giving a collective identity to an aggregate of discrete "empty slots"; that is, it is the establishment of a social community whose collective purpose is class representation. For any political movement, however, class formation involves more than the simple activization of empty slots, since people have a host of alternative social identities. For social democracy, class formation therefore implies both a constructive and a destructive strategy. The movement

[12] It would be worth pursuing the hypothesis that in countries like Germany, France, and Italy, public-sector employees will tend to coalesce with bourgeois parties, whereas in places like Scandinavia, they will be more easily allied with the social democrats.

30

must establish class as a legitimate and meaningful political agency and define the boundaries for inclusion. But it must also confront the necessity of displacing alternative community bases—religion, ethnicity, or localism; early "corporative" worker organizations, such as guild and fraternal associations; rival political identities, such as syndicalism or communism; and competitive individualism and market atomization.

Social democratic class formation is a process of power mobilization requiring the establishment of four basic conditions. The maximum penetration within the core of the working class and the development of class unity requires, first, a decommodification of labor and, secondly, the institutionalization of solidarity. Thirdly, social democracy confronts the question of including allied class elements within its political community. The fourth condition is a crucial one: given the nature of class structural development, not to mention the requirement for parliamentary majorities, social democracy will probably not be able to avoid forging political coalitions with other classes.

The market is the first obstacle—and a major one—to the social democratic community. In its pure form, the capitalist market compels workers to behave as discrete commodities; the individual's ability to sell his labor defines his economic and possibly also his social status. Under these conditions, the distribution of working-class resources will spring from the nexus of aggregate demand and personal human capital. As commodities, moreover, workers are atomized, individuated, and fragmented rather than communal. The sovereignty of the market is in general a function of the degree to which workers behave as commodities.

Social democratic class formation, therefore, is first and foremost a struggle to decommodify labor and stem market sovereignty in order to make collective action possible. Only when workers command resources and access to welfare independently of market exchange can they possibly be swayed not to take jobs during strike actions, underbid fellow workers, and so forth. Where the market is hegemonic, the labor movement's future depends on its ability to provide an "exit" for workers that concomitantly ensures collective solidarity.

For the social democratic movement, the decommodification of labor cannot arise from ideology, nor can it await the revolution. Collective social services, unemployment and sickness compensation, employment security, and general income maintenance must be established. Such programs can be established either within the labor movement's own institutions or universally through state legislation. In any case, decommodification policies must be both institutionalized and per-

31

manent to ensure that the market does not reconstitute its natural logic of competition, insecurity, and status differentiation.

In the abstract, solidarity is negatively as well as positively defined. It demands a set of duties and responsibilities toward the community as a whole; that is, a readiness to sacrifice personal gain for the common interest. It also grants the individual a set of rights and expectations from the community. The sort of solidarity required for social democratic formation demands decommodification, but this alone is not sufficient. Alternative bases of communality, identification, and solidarity must be displaced. The fewer the crosscutting pressures on individual workers, the greater the potential for social democratic hegemony.

The creation of solidarity seems always to involve the stick and the carrot. Ostracism, ridicule, peer group pressure, even violence against "deviants" are powerful ways of closing the ranks. But in the long run such methods prove costly, and the carrot is more efficient. Socialist movements have typically pursued two strategies in the quest for solidarity. The classical approach was to construct a workers' world in isolation from the bourgeois environment. This included the establishment of mutual-aid schemes, income-maintenance programs designed exclusively for members and, equally important, cultural and social activities. These served to replace existing, non-class-specific communal and fraternal institutions as well as the market. This so-called ghetto approach was designed to help define workers as the natural universe of solidarity, to cultivate a collective identity, to attract new members, and to tie them to the fate of the labor movement generally.

But the ghetto approach contains some of the same shortcomings that already prevail where workers are differentiated according to guild-type exclusionary communities. Inevitably, it will fail to produce class-universal solidarity. It installs new kinds of divisions between those workers who belong and those who do not. The real danger is that the weakest and most marginal workers are the ones least likely to join, even though they are the ones whose inclusion is most important.

Since the strategy of social democracy is majoritarian, its definition of the solidaristic universe must address the "people," not the "class." Instead of serving those workers who rally readily behind the socialist call, social democracy must actively create its constituency and then attempt to fabricate solidarity. The chief problem is therefore how to transform a differentiated population into a cohesive community, and this involves a combination of movement organization and state policy.

32

In respect of the movement, social democracy depends on the "nationalization" and centralized coordination of trade unionism and on optimal electoral penetration by the party. The first precondition is the victory of vertically organized and nationally centralized trade unionism, which means the subordination and incorporation of craft- and skill-exclusionary unions. The bargaining advantages and disadvantages of each worker must be socialized to the entire working class. Trade union centralization is also necessary for coherence between the union movement and the political party. The second precondition is the ability of the party to claim the political distinctiveness of workers and penetrate deeply into the electorate for optimal voter participation. Party organization and union density are a first-order priority. The tasks of maximum penetration and monopolization of working-class votes include a wide variety of strategies. Many parties have tried to institutionalize a system of collective party affiliation among trade union members; party militants have been asked to escort the blind and the disabled to the voting booth; the party organization has offered bread and circus along with propaganda and education.

The ultimate instrument of social democratic class formation, however, is state policy. The creation of solidarity will depend on reformist accomplishments. But how? In order to legislate such a social democratic community into existence, reforms must institute a universalistic alternative to both individualism and corporatism. Also, resources and living conditions must be distributed in such a way as to cancel out status differentials. A first precondition, we have seen, is to decommodify wage earners and endow all individuals with income and welfare entitlements of such scope that even the marginally weakest (or strongest) worker will refrain from breaking the rules of solidarity. This requires collectivization of those areas of human welfare and need in which the weakest groups are most likely to remain underprivileged under conditions of market provision. It is of paramount importance for solidarity that entitlements and services be universal, generous, and attractive; otherwise, there will be incentives for the better-off to seek private market solutions. As Hirschman (1970) suggests, exit opportunities destroy the basis for broad solidarity. Social democratic class formation depends on the eradication of differentiated entitlements, means-tested and targeted benefits, individualistic insurance schemes, and "self-help" principles. Reforms must avoid situations in which collective services breed discontent between those who pay and those who receive.

The institutionalization of universalistic public and collective programs can be a means of supplanting narrow group identities or individualism with broad social solidarity, for such programs help create a large, if not universal, electoral constituency whose welfare and happiness is wedded to a social democratic state. This should help prevent protest against the "tax state" or the "welfare state." In this sense, universalism means the socialization of duties as well as entitlements. It is hypothesized that social democratic decomposition will result from a failure to institutionalize universalistic solidarity.

One of the greatest dangers to solidarity is the potential for dualism. This will tend to occur where the market is permitted to compete with public provisions, as with occupational pensions or private hospitals and schools. But existing dualisms—traditional civil servant privileges, favorable tax allowances for homeowners, stigmatizing means tests and, above all, cleavages between employed and unemployed—must simultaneously be crushed. Social democracy runs the risk of institutionalizing a dualistic stratification system wherever "welfare state dependents" confront the "self-reliant."

The politics of decommodification and solidarity constitute, thus far in our discussion, a mobilization program that is virtually synonymous with T. H. Marshall's (1950) famous concept of social citizenship.[13] In our perspective, however, social citizenship does not constitute an end goal but is a means by which social democracy can surmount obstacles to its own formation; namely, the problem of resource weakness among workers and the problem of internal differentiation and stratification in its natural political base. Decommodification and solidaristic universalism alone will not suffice for long-term social democratic mobilization. Two problems are involved. One is the inevitable incompatibility of the social citizenship state; the other is the necessity of exercising control over the business cycle.

The welfare state strategy is a natural consequence of social democratic mobilization. It is also the possible source of its demise. Where decommodification and solidarity are promoted through public policy, public expenditures will inevitably escalate: universal services and benefits that address as wide a range of human needs as possible will naturally demand heavy expenditures. If we add to this the criteria that benefits be of equal quantity and quality across the entire population and that they replace market provisions, the state will perforce require extraordinarily heavy tax revenues.

Obviously, less of a political burden is posed when, and if, broad-

---

[13] Marshall's discussion of the concept does not adequately distinguish the "rights" dimension (decommodification) from the "status" dimension. Also, Marshall assumes that the attainment of full citizenship will help resolve traditional class antagonisms.

based financial solidarity exists, the economy is growing rapidly, the incidence of social need has relaxed, and full employment ensures a large and growing income pool to tax. Conversely, when social democracy is concomitantly expected to bring about greater income equality and redistribution, a problem is posed. There is little doubt that universal welfare benefits have a redistributive effect on the expenditure side. As the incidence of taxation grows, however, the tax system automatically loses its potential for progressive redistribution. Under conditions of heavy expenditure, the bulk of taxes must be collected among the largest income brackets, and that happens to be workers and middle-level white-collar employees.

The welfare state is thus in the long run a potentially incompatible strategy for mobilization. If not corrected and supplemented with other policies, it is likely to boomerang and provoke the decomposition of social democracy. This, I shall argue in the following chapters, is precisely the point at which social democratic movements find themselves today. The social citizenship state is at once required and exhausted. A leading hypothesis, therefore, is that unless the social democratic movement manages to relieve the state of its sole responsibility for welfare distribution, decommodification, and solidarity and to reallocate that responsibility in the economy, the movement risks a backlash against the welfare state.

Government control of the economy is the other major precondition for long-range social democratic survival. If the ideological satisfaction of economic socialization pertains only to a peripheral working-class minority, control of the business cycle offers general material satisfaction and reproduction of social democratic unity and power mobilization. As became increasingly clear to the socialists of the interwar era, nothing weakens labor movements so much as economic instability and crisis. In contrast to the rupture strategy followed by Leninism, social democratic class formation ultimately seeks to maintain a full-employment growth economy so that power-resource mobilization can work. The workings of this strategy are complex.

First of all, expansion of the economy is a necessary condition for financing the social citizenship state. Secondly, the guarantee of sustained full employment requires control of the business cycle. Thirdly, the labor movement will be required to help manipulate the form and direction of short- and long-term structural change and, especially, to ensure that other requirements (such as full employment, price stability, and wage equality) are satisfied. Fourthly, control over the process of rationalization and change is important, if not necessary, in order to equalize the working conditions and economic opportunities of workers. Finally, since it is very likely that political interference, resulting from the policies of decommodification and solidarity, will threaten the market's "natural equilibrium," other political instruments are needed to regulate, for instance, the labor market or the credit market.

In general, social democracy must in the long run collectivize and democratize economic power. Where the rate of growth declines, whether because of internal or external forces, the future of social democracy will depend on its capacity to guarantee that adequate levels of investment are maintained, whether or not private capitalists are willing to accept the responsibility. It is doubtful that social democracy will be able to avoid, at one time or another, socializing the investment function.

Class Alliances

Social democracy has almost always been conceived as manual worker politics, and there is no doubt that the movement's main base has been and remains the traditional working class. Yet, to rely on these workers exclusively would prohibit decisive parliamentary majorities. Thus we come to Przworski's class alliance dilemma: additional adherents might be won by diluting the party's programmatic positions; to pursue such a strategy, however, risks alienation of manual workers.

In practice, as Przworski and Sprague's research shows, socialist parties have been able to attract members of other classes without compromising ideology or principles. This can occur spontaneously, from the bottom up, but it can also result from political action. The fabrication of political constituencies is by no means new, nor is it peculiarly socialist. But where the social democrats preside over public-sector expansion, they also help create a vast segment of employees whose personal economic well-being will coincide with the survival of the public sector and with social democratic power. Another possibility is that white-collar employment faces a process of downgrading at the same time that working-class living conditions are being upgraded. Such a process of convergence will ease the dilemma.

In any case, the social democrats have been unable to avoid forging political coalitions with other classes.[14] Moreover, the prospects for, and dangers of, class alliances have varied historically. So long as the traditional petite bourgeoisie are dominant, they constitute the key in

[14] The logic of alternative types of class alliances, and their impact on postwar economic development, has been explored by Esping-Andersen and Friedland (1982). The original inspiration derives, of course, from Barrington Moore (1967).

the electoral competition between bourgeois parties and social democracy. Their structural location and political inclinations are decisive for the rise or fall of social democracy. An alliance with sections of the petite bourgeoisie (the peasantry, say) on the basis of a political quid pro quo is doubly important strategically. It permits the social democrats to "take off" with their reform intentions, and it helps divide and weaken their bourgeois-party opponents. As Castles (1978) has noted, social democratic power is very much a function of bourgeois party disunity. But the relative dominance of the social democrats within the coalition considerably influences the degree to which their reforms must compromise.

Under certain conditions a coalition of the working class and the petite bourgeoisie may be detrimental for social democratic ascendance. There is no doubt that the success of Scandinavian social democracy depended on its twice-demonstrated capacity to coalesce with the farmers—first in the struggle for universal suffrage during the late 1800s and again during the economic depression of the 1930s. The first instance helped avert intransigent upper-class resistance to political democracy and thus helped stimulate the socialists' trust in a parliamentary strategy. The second helped save social democracy from the looming threat of peasant nazification and permitted the party to take office and introduce reforms precisely when labor was being weakened, demoralized, and divided by economic crisis.

A coalition with petit-bourgeois elements will permit the formulation of a specific policy package—typically, welfare reform and full employment in return for agricultural price subsidies—but it will also prohibit the transcendence of that package. A political realignment is therefore necessary when expansion of wage-earner income shares or the need for stronger economic controls becomes incompatible with petit-bourgeois demands. The historically decisive point arrives when the petite bourgeoisie have declined to the point where their numbers have little influence on political majorities (or when their interests directly conflict with those of the workers). At this point, social democracy must be in position to negotiate a new alliance with the rising middle strata. In fact, one of the central conclusions of this book is that the survival of social democratic parties today depends on the potential for such a realignment.

CONCLUSION

We can now restate the general argument. Class structural development cannot be a sufficient cause for either social democratic formation or decomposition. Social democracy must manufacture its own class base, a necessarily continuous process. The "raw material" of the class structure must be transformed into a dynamically expanding social democratic community, and reformism naturally constitutes the vehicle for this. The transformation of the state is therefore the linchpin of social democracy.

We know, however, that the forces of class structural change constrain social democracy's capacity to assume state power unless it is both able and prepared to forge political alliances with other classes. In this respect, the future of democratic socialism has always been decided by classes other than strictly the working classes. The peasants, because they were the largest and perhaps also the most important class during social democracy's infancy, typically held the key to a possible coalition. Indeed, I would go so far as to claim that Scandinavian social democracy would have been aborted had it not been for its ability to ally with the rural classes. Just as the peasantry catalyzed the party's rise to power, they also become a major hindrance to continued social democratic renewal. Such alliances may permit Keynesianism and social citizenship policies, but they are not likely to allow additional encroachments on the economy. Additionally, the peasantry will dwindle as a political force. In this situation, the social democratic road to power will depend almost entirely on the chances of a coalition with the white-collar middle strata.

These theoretical themes guide the study of Scandinavian social democracy that follows. Chapter 2 presents the patterns of social structural development over the past century as these have affected the rise of social democracy. Chapter 3 examines political class formation and the conditions that have obtained for class alliances. In Chapter 4 the trends toward party decomposition are analyzed in relation to the parties' changing social bases. Chapters 5, 6, and 7 mark the analytical shift from the social bases of social democracy to its political bases and present, respectively, the parties' accomplishments in social, housing, and economic policy. By way of assessing the impact of state policies on class politics and party decomposition, Chapter 8 offers quantitative analyses. Finally, Chapter 9 focuses on contemporary plans for economic democracy in order to establish whether a political realignment is in the making.

PART I

The Social Bases of
Social Democracy

TWO

Class Structure and
Social Democracy

THE NATURE of class structural development defines in large part the parameters for social democratic mobilization. Clearly the relative numbers and character of the classes will determine what is politically possible. Even more important perhaps is the classes' organizational characteristics and capacity for self-expression through trade unions, interest associations, and similar representational instruments. The evolution of social democracy will undoubtedly be affected by the degree of trade union centralization and penetration, the degree of capital concentration, the extent of class polarization, and the relative size of the working class.

Social democracy requires the formation of class alliances, and what sets the Scandinavian states apart from virtually all other countries is the role played by the peasantry in the nineteenth century and into the turbulent interwar era. A detailed investigation of the new middle strata in the present era is crucial, for they now hold the key to social democracy's survival. Class structural change, we shall see, may be a "last instance" causal factor, but the formation of class coalitions is the necessary condition.

SOCIAL STRUCTURE AND CLASS DEVELOPMENT

For a mid-nineteenth century observer it would have been difficult indeed to anticipate that the Scandinavian countries would produce such similar and powerful social democratic movements. Sweden and Norway were undeveloped and peripheral nations of peasants; Denmark had always maintained stronger cultural and economic ties to the European continent and could boast a relatively important commercial urban influence. There was little in the nature of these preindustrial Nordic societies that was propitious either for their subsequent convergence or for social democratic hegemony. The eventual outcome must be explained by a combination of late industrialization in a somewhat democratic political setting, an independent peasantry capable of allying with workers, and benevolent historical circumstances.

41

Denmark

In contrast to the experience of many European nations, the modernization of Danish society was facilitated by an early emasculation of the aristocracy. A progressive land reform, passed in the early 1800s, ensured the rise of strong and independent commercial farmers and peasants operating in a tenure system that made family cultivation both feasible and profitable. Several factors contributed to the rise of a liberal and democratically inclined rural population. First, unlike the peasantry of most countries, Danish peasants were blessed with a secular education through Denmark's unique system of universal public education and "folk high schools."[1] Secondly, cooperatively organized family farming was technologically adaptive to changing circumstances. Originally concentrating on grain production, Danish agriculture was quick to rationalize and change when American grain exports began to flood the international markets. With some state aid, Danish farmers moved swiftly into animal husbandry and dairy farming, whose export markets were stronger. This ensured continued prosperity and helped avert proletarianization. It would also dictate the future of Denmark's economic development. Thirdly, the viability of small-scale farmers was importantly influenced by their ability to form cooperative associations ranging from dairies, slaughterhouses, and machine pools to export organizations and marketing outlets. This gave them access to advanced technology and made it possible to dispense with a large work force. Finally, the farmers managed to organize themselves into an articulate political force vis-à-vis the state and the other classes.

Agriculture remained indisputably the backbone of the Danish economy, and farmers continued to be the backbone of the class structure. Farming was export-oriented, tied primarily to the British market. Until the late 1950s, agricultural exports were the most important factor in Denmark's economic development.[2] The unique features of Danish agriculture had a decisive influence on social structural change. First, they enabled a large population of relatively prosperous farmers to persist and eventually to dominate society; even peasants with small holdings managed to survive. Hence, agriculture was not a source of

[1] The purpose of these folk high schools, established under the auspices of N.S.F. Grundtvig, a progressive Lutheran reformer, was to spread enlightenment in the rural areas. Their historical importance cannot be overstated, and to this day they enjoy widespread popularity.

[2] In 1929 agriculture accounted for 70 percent of all Danish exports, and it was not until around 1957 that industrial exports gained dominance (Hansen 1974, 62).

proletarianization. When industry grew, its recruits were either already proletarianized rural workers or domestics for whom urban-industrial life would be a less shocking experience. The extremely slow rate of rural proletarianization in effect hindered the rise of a large, destitute lumpenproletariat. Secondly, the nature of industrialization was affected. Since there was no natural basis for large-scale heavy industry— Denmark commands virtually no raw material resources—industry had to base itself either on the processing of agricultural products (breweries, for example) or on the longstanding urban craft tradition.

The first phase of industrialization, beginning around 1870, was therefore based on small and geographically scattered firms and handicraft shops, which demanded a skilled, apprenticed labor force. Then, as now, there was only a sprinkling of large enterprises. In short, early industrialization did not provoke the severe social and economic dislocations, cultural shock, or massive proletarianization that occurred in other nations. In fact, not until almost a century later did the Danish economy truly come to resemble an advanced industrial nation. Agriculture's share of the gross domestic product continued to exceed industry's at least until the mid-1950s (Hansen 1974, 11ff), and its share of the total labor force remained dominant until the mid-1930s (Andersen 1974). In industry, on the other hand, companies remained very small and craft-based.[3] If agriculture was predominantly export-oriented, manufacturing was directed primarily at domestic consumption. As a result, both agriculture and urban manufacturing developed in a rather petit-bourgeois direction, characterized by a prevalence of independent farmers, artisans, or small-scale entrepreneurs. The nascent working class mirrors this petit-bourgeois structure. Skilled labor and craft workers were dominant; industrial workers were somewhat marginal.

For a long time, then, industrial progress was thwarted by agriculture. Thus, if Denmark was the first of the Nordic countries to begin to industrialize, it also industrialized at the slowest pace. Until the 1930s, the number of farmers actually increased in absolute terms, which suggests very little concentration of landholdings. The rural population first began to decline rapidly during the 1950s and 1960s. Equally resistant to change was the petit-bourgeois character of urban industry and commerce. The chief contributors to wage-labor growth, therefore, continued to be a growing population, greater female labor-

[3] The average number of workers per enterprise in 1914 was thirty-four; twenty years later this average was almost the same (Hansen 1974, 64). Industrial workers accounted for less than 10 percent of the labor force in 1914, and they still comprised 10 percent in 1935 (Hansen 1974, 64).

force participation, and the shift of agricultural and domestic workers into urban wage employment. Accordingly, some of the conditions most frequently cited for the development of radical leftism or syndicalism were totally absent in Denmark.

Compared with the experience of the other Nordic countries, Danish economic development was gradual, slow, and not particularly disruptive. Nor was it very dynamic: a perennial feature has been a relatively slack labor market with recurrent unemployment. In part, this phenomenon may be due to slow economic expansion and the volatile situation of many Danish industries; in part, though, it must be ascribed to the dominant position of agriculture. Since foreign earnings were almost entirely a function of agricultural exports, and since the power of the farming sector prohibited income distribution in favor of the urban classes, the Danish economy's constant problem was a shortage of industrial investment capital. Even if during the Great Depression some rural and industrial concentration did take place, and even if this period also permitted income redistribution, it was really not until the late 1950s and 1960s that class relationships were fundamentally altered.

The preconditions were the liberalization of international trade, falling raw material prices, dynamic international demand and, most important, a weakening of Danish agriculture. During the 1950s and 1960s, as the smaller peasant holdings failed to keep up with the new pace of productivity and the need for large capital investments, major land concentration occurred. Except during the depression, this is the only wave of rural proletarianization to have occurred in modern Danish history. Significantly, the farmers adopted a much more militant stance and managed to wrest substantial income concessions from the state. But their previous economic and political hegemony had been broken.

The "second industrial revolution," from 1957 to the mid-1960s, was very capital-intensive and therefore did not prompt any significant increase in manual workers. Most new employment occurred in the tertiary economy, especially in public services and administration. Thus, in the period between 1950 and 1970 the growth of manual labor was stagnant while the number of employees in white-collar occupations almost doubled. This period was also the first in Danish history to be characterized by sustained full employment, but it is difficult to say whether this would have occurred had it not been for the concomitant expansion of public-sector employment, especially in health and education.

Important changes in the structure of Danish industry certainly took place during the postwar era. Expansion was centered in smaller or medium-size capital-intensive firms directed at foreign rather than domestic markets. Only marginally did this period nurture large industry —shipbuilding being one notable example. But even then, the old craft tradition was very slow to die, and many trades remained incarcerated in anachronistic apprenticeship systems. Hence, the urban economy was very strongly petit-bourgeois not only in retail and commerce, but also in manufacturing and construction.

The old craft industry's resistance to economic rationalization meant that the labor market retained pockets of rigid protectionism. It meant, too, that a large section of the working class was wedded to the preservation of outdated, low-productivity technologies. The overall result was a divided working class. Traditional skilled workers confronted unskilled or semiskilled industrial workers on an array of issues ranging from economic rationalization, technological change, and wage differentials to trade union organization and public economic and social policies.

This dualism has hampered the labor movement's ability to mobilize unity and political coherence and, if anything, conflict tends to prevail over solidarity. The new middle strata of white-collar workers also expanded, as a result of the explosive growth in public employment, and this too nurtured dualism. A large and growing segment is intimately linked to the prosperity and political legitimacy of the public sector.

Norway

The preconditions for industrial modernization in Norway were very different from those in Denmark. Norway was, until the Napoleonic Wars, under Danish rule and, beginning with independence in 1814, remained a protectorate of Sweden until 1905. These historical circumstances have shaped the country's process of modernization. First of all, the aristocracy (being largely Danish) could not play a role in the transition to capitalism. The preindustrial economy was dominated by small and independent peasant holdings that, at best, were precarious. Except in southern Norway, where larger, family-based farming can thrive, the majority of peasants were operating under adverse conditions with respect to climate, soil, and capacity for increased productivity.

Fishing and forestry have always been the backbone of the primary economy, absorbing a large proportion of the labor force and accounting for a very important share of the total economic product.

As Kuhnle (1978) observes, the absence of an aristocracy and the proliferation of small, independent peasants and fishermen combined to make Norway an unusually egalitarian land. It was an equality of poverty, however. Until the late 1800s, fishing was to Norway what agriculture was to Denmark; namely, the cornerstone of the economy and the main source of foreign export earnings. But, unlike Danish farmers, Norway's fishermen were economically weak. In the closing decades of the nineteenth century, Norway's economic structure was importantly changed by the rise of its shipping industry, which soon came to dominate foreign earnings, accounting for 40 percent of the total by the turn of the century (Statistisk Sentralbyrå 1966, 64; Jörberg 1976, 406).[4]

The social structure that sprung up around the triumvirate of weak agriculture, labor-intensive fishing and forestry, and competitive shipping is rather unusual. In both fishing and forestry, a large quasi proletariat developed in the remote regions of the country. This, we shall see, had major consequences for the rise of Norwegian social democracy. In agriculture, a schism existed between the more prosperous commercial farmers in the South and near the cities and the subsistence-based peasantry of the periphery. In shipping, most entrepreneurs were small, and only after the turn of the century—when the steamship overcame sail—did the industry begin to capitalize and concentrate. Finally, Norwegian industrialization came very late, and it was based largely on timber, iron ore, and hydroelectric power.

Preindustrial class conflicts mirror the peculiarities of Norwegian society. In the absence of large landowners, agrarian opposition was directed against the "modern," Swedish-oriented civil service in the cities, a conflict that was partly nationalistic, partly economic—the issue of protective tariffs being salient—and partly cultural, in the sense of a center-periphery conflict on such issues as language, morals, and religion (Rokkan 1966, 1970). If the wealthier southern farmers did not ally with the semiproletarianized peasants and fishermen, neither did they ally with the nascent bourgeoisie. This meant that no power bloc of the right could emerge in opposition to the subsequent claims of labor, but that is getting ahead of our story. Chronically weak, Norwegian agriculture could not fully supply the domestic market and was extremely vulnerable to price fluctuations and adverse

[4] In the latter half of the nineteenth century, the Norwegian merchant fleet was the third largest in the world. Its rise was partly due to the plentiful timber available for vessel construction; later when steel replaced wood, Norway would benefit from its iron ore in the North. In addition Norway was competitive because of its very low wage scale (Dybdahl 1975, 19).

market conditions. To some extent the peasant problem was resolved by heavy emigration to the United States.[5]

Norwegian industrialization really accelerated around the turn of the century—again under unique circumstances. It was based not in the cities but in the periphery, where lumber could be exploited for paper and pulp, and along rivers where hydroelectric power could be produced. The new industries, however, were capital-intensive and thus did not generate a large industrial working class at first. Also, given the lack of domestic capital, these industries were initially formed by foreign capital and, later, by the Norwegian state as well. This meant that an industrial bourgeoisie was slow to emerge, except perhaps in shipping. As in Denmark, moreover, industrialization was slow to develop both in respect of total national product and of labor force participation. Urbanization was very slow, for there was neither an urban industrial proletariat nor an urban bourgeoisie to speak of.[6] As Dybdahl (1975) and Rokkan (1966) note, the Norwegian class structure generated a very special form of social tension and conflict, and center-periphery conflicts often prevailed over direct and naked class opposition.

If industrialization came in a spurt around 1900, it soon leveled off. Industry's share of GNP would remain fairly constant until the 1930s, when a crisis in both agriculture and fishing reduced the number of people employed in the primary economy. Then again, industrial expansion was reversed during World War II when, as a result of the fighting and Nazi occupation, many industries were severely damaged. Norway's entry into the league of modern industrialized nations was, as in Denmark, very much a postwar affair. That event, however, occurred under virtually opposite conditions.

In Denmark it came as a shock wave during the 1960s; in Norway the process was continuous and planned, a state-directed expansion of industry throughout the entire postwar era. The Norwegian state, as we shall examine in some detail in Chapter 7, proceeded to direct finance markets as well as industrial investment—especially in the oil industry—with a strong bias in favor of decentralized regional development. Hence, the social consequences of industrial expansion were almost the opposite of those in Denmark. If small fishermen and, to

[5] Øjen (1968, 35) reports that Norway had the second largest rate of emigration among the European countries during the period 1825-1930, surpassed only by Ireland. More than 1 million people left Norway during this period, and in some years the rate was 15 out of every 1,000 inhabitants. It should be noted, that 25 percent would later return.

[6] As late as 1920, less than 30 percent of the population was urbanized.

some extent, farmers in the South continue to exert a petit-bourgeois influence, the rural petite bourgeoisie are nevertheless weak. In Norway's urban economy, as in Denmark's, manufacturing firms typically remain small; on the other hand, they are less craft-oriented, and the Norwegian working class seems much more homogeneous than the Danish. Also, in contrast to the Danish experience, the new white-collar middle strata of Norway have developed more slowly—in part because the expansion of the public sector there occurred somewhat later and with less explosive force. In Norway, the cleavage between periphery and center has continued to play a dominant role in the articulation of class differences.

Sweden

Sweden is usually considered the most advanced country in Scandinavia, if not in all Europe. At the turn of the century, however, Sweden was certainly one of Europe's most economically backward countries. This gives some indication of the speed and inclusiveness of structural change and economic development

Until the twentieth century, Sweden was an isolated country. In Sweden, too, the power of the aristocracy had been severely curtailed during the eighteenth and nineteenth centuries, both as a result of the nobility's impoverishment and because of the peasantry's ability to assert independence via alliances with the monarchy. What emerged was a powerful absolutist state with a large and very efficient civil service and army. Headed by the king, these managed to accumulate a great deal of autonomous power by balancing the rising peasantry against the declining aristocracy. The army and bureaucracy, in fact, became a safety valve against possible reaction from the aristocracy, absorbing them rather effectively (Tilton 1974). Also, the nobility repeated the experience of their English counterparts by eventually fusing with the rising bourgeoisie, particularly in the developing timber and mining industries.

This centralized, powerful, and relatively independent state bureaucracy came to play a central role throughout modern Swedish history. Anticipating potential popular unrest and economic requirements, it was occasionally instrumental in passing social and economic legislation. The bureaucracy, in fact, came to play a key role in directing and facilitating the transition to modern capitalism.

Sweden, then, embarked on the road to industrialization with an emasculated aristocracy and a somewhat independent peasant population, one that was organized around commercial family farming.

But if land was plentiful, it was not very fertile except in the South. As in Norway, masses of peasants faced impoverishment, and severe peasant unrest was a possibility. Emigration and the character of Sweden's early industrialization, however, diluted this potential.

Emigration was not as great as it was in Norway, but it was nonetheless substantial. In the 1860-1910 period, more than 750,000 Swedes, or approximately 20 percent of the current population, exited the country. Secondly, early industry (centered in mining and lumber) grew extremely rapidly throughout the nation's rural areas, rather than in the cities. This decentralized industrial revolution permitted destitute peasants to take temporary and part-time jobs, thus delaying the process of industrial proletarianization.[7]

Industry was based on iron mining, timber, and electrical power. These industries were export-oriented and—especially during wartime—tended to benefit from high levels of international demand. They were profitable and helped stimulate continued domestic industrial expansion; having sizable capital requirements, they gave rise to rapid and strong capital concentration. The net result was a curious combination of a very concentrated and powerful industrial bourgeoisie and a large mass of wage labor that remained scattered across small milltowns, what the Swedes call *Bruksamhällen*.

But Swedish industrialization proletarianized peasants, not just farm workers, and the influence of old craft industries and artisans was peripheral. The result was a largely industrial wage-labor force whose roots were in the peasantry. In Denmark, family farming and craft industry had helped consolidate a liberalistic, petit-bourgeois state. In Sweden, a timber- and iron-based industrial oligopoly helped perpetuate and strengthen a corporatist central state.

The pace of Swedish industrialization is illustrated by changes in the labor force. In 1870, when 55 percent of the Danish population was in agriculture, the proportion in Sweden was a full 72 percent. By 1901, however, the Swedish rural labor force had declined to 48 percent (Dahlström 1965). In this period, Sweden's industrial labor force grew from 82,000 to 350,000, and by 1914 the value of exports had tripled and the value of manufactured goods had increased twentyfold (Samuelsson 1968). By 1910, the secondary and tertiary labor force had definitely surpassed the agricultural work force (Statistiska Centralbyron 1976, 88-89).

After a few decades of industrialization, Sweden had become the

---

[7] In the late 1800s, more than half of Sweden's industrial workers were employed in rural areas.

epitome of the Marxian polarized class society. The rising bourgeoisie was dominated by the interlocking interests of ten or thirteen leading families, basking under the benevolent gaze of the central bureaucracy and, before World War I, under a conservative regime (Dybdahl 1975). This was not a liberal, laissez-faire bourgeoisie:

> Whatever aspect this nascent industrial enterprise is viewed from, it was as remote from the notion of free, open competition as anything that could be imagined. No entrepreneur ever surrendered to any free play of supply and demand, which was the cherished dream of Adam Smith. Instead, each entrepreneur exercised a relatively complete control over his market [Tilton 1974, 564].

The rise of a domestic bourgeoisie was aided by the Swedish central state. Already in the early 1840s the state had introduced universal primary education for all citizens, and thus the Swedish peasantry was educated. This would prove advantageous later, when educated labor was in demand for nascent industries, and advantageous as well for peasant political mobilization.

Of even greater importance for industrial expansion was public construction of a comprehensive network of canals, railroads, and electric power plants during the middle and late 1800s. A very advanced nationwide infrastructure, then, was ready and waiting. In addition, the Swedish state nurtured capital accumulation through rather heavy-handed protectionist policies (which the Danish farmers had succeeded in opposing), generous lending, and occasional direct investment in large projects.[8] As Tilton (1974, 564) argues, the early concentration and cartelization within Swedish industry was nurtured by public policy. State lending tended to favor the strongest. In some sectors, like mining, the links between the state and private capital became especially intimate. The multiplier effect of iron mining encouraged such intimacy: iron mining and smelting stimulated machine industries, weapons production, and manufacture of sewing machines, bicycles, autos, and aircraft. As in Germany, the state was an important consumer. By the turn of the century, these industries had already become consolidated in huge firms that, to this day, are among Europe's largest: Electrolux, Asea, SKF, and Husquarna, to mention a few.

Confronting this centralized and powerful bourgeoisie was, on one side, a decaying peasantry and a small but healthy farmer class in the

---

[8] High-ranking civil servants were also active participants in the industrial adventure.

South. On the other side, there was the rapidly growing industrial working class, which came from bankrupt peasant landholders (not from the rural proletariat only, as in Denmark). The Swedish working class, moreover, was considerably less craft- and skill-dominated. Compared with either the Danish or the Norwegian rural and urban petite bourgeoisie, those in Sweden had a high mortality rate and a short life expectancy. The pace of industrial concentration accelerated even more between the wars and again in the 1960s.[9]

Class Development Compared

The social structures of the three Nordic nations could hardly have been more different. Denmark remained a "petit-bourgeois" society in both its urban and its rural economy; Sweden seemed to validate the classical prediction of class polarization; and Norway fell somewhere in between. Yet, in all three countries the role of the agrarian and urban petite bourgeoisie declined substantially over time—giving rise not to a mass of manual workers, but instead to the new white-collar strata. Probably to a greater degree than elsewhere, the new middle strata in Scandinavia are concentrated in the public sector. Tables 2.1 through 2.4 show the evolution of occupational structure in our three Nordic countries over the twentieth century.[10]

Unfortunately, the data for Norway prior to 1950 do not allow disaggregation of agricultural and nonagricultural workers. We may assume, however, that in 1900 at least half, probably more, were in the primary economy. Table 2.1 shows a number of trends that are of importance for social democratic power. First of all, note that total manual workers only rarely exceed the magic 50 percent of the entire labor force. It is noteworthy how stable their share is over time, peak-

[9] In 1942, the fifty largest Swedish companies accounted for 16 percent of all employment (compared with only 5 percent in the United States). By 1964, the figure was 21 percent (Stevenson 1974, 44).

[10] Most of the data in these comparative tables are derived from national population censuses and are clearly subject to definitional variations across time and between nations. Methods of classification change. On the other hand, many of the data for Sweden and Denmark are, with some certainty, comparable. For the period 1900-1950, I have used the raw census data compiled by Przworski et al. (1978) with their kind permission. These data have been reclassified in order to facilitate comparability. The major problem of comparability concerns the data for Norway, since that country lacks a systematic series of occupational census data. One particular problem is that Norwegian data sources after 1960 do not distinguish manual and nonmanual categories. I have therefore relied on the electoral survey data for the 1970s. The percentages are calculated on the basis of total labor force, omitting the nonactives but including domestics.

TABLE 2.1. Workers in Scandinavia, 1900-1980
(% of total active labor force)

	1900	1910	1920	1930	1940	1950	1960	1970	1980[a]
AGRICULTURAL WORKERS[b]									
Denmark	19	15	11	10	9	10	7	2	1
Norway	—	—	—	—	—	9	4	2	2
Sweden	15	17	15	13	10	5	3	3	—
NONAGRICULTURAL WORKERS									
Denmark	22	25	27	31	34	39	41	42	41
Norway	—	—	—	—	—	46	48	—	45
Sweden	24	26	33	36	38	46	47	44	44
ALL MANUAL WORKERS									
Denmark	41	40	38	41	43	49	48	44	42
Norway	56	—	49	—	—	55	52	—	47
Sweden	39	43	48	49	48	51	50	47	—

SOURCES: Denmark—for 1900-1940, Przworski et al. (1978); for 1950-1980, Danmarks Statistik (1976, table 2.9; 1981a, 14). Norway—NOS (1978), Statistisk Sentralbyrå (1927, 1933, 1953, 1963, 1971, 1981), Rokkan (1966, 94), Valen (1981, table 6.1). Sweden—for 1900-1940, Przworski et al. (1978); for 1950-1980, Statistiska Centralbyron (1960, 1965, 1981a).
[a] For Denmark, the data pertain to 1975; for Norway, 1977; for Sweden, 1979.
[b] Includes forestry and fishing.

ing around 1950 and declining thereafter. This indicates that a socialist strategy based solely on the traditional manual working class would be denied electoral majorities, even if every marginal worker were to be mobilized. Note, also, the decline in blue-collar workers during the last few decades, a trend that points to the absolute necessity of forging alliances with—or penetrating—other class segments.

Traditionally, rural workers have been more difficult to organize collectively and mobilize politically. Their decline as a proportion of the entire working class should therefore signal greater social democratic potential. We can see (Table 2.1) that in Sweden their share remained very high until the 1930s, after which it declined more rapidly than elsewhere. In Norway, during the first decades of this century, there is reason to believe that agricultural workers, concentrated in fishing and forestry, were fairly prominent, probably even more so than in either Denmark or Sweden. As we shall see, a peculiar characteristic of the earlier period of Norwegian social democracy was its rural profile. The data for Denmark lend quantitative credence to our previous descriptions. Compared with the working classes in the other two countries, the Danish manual working class is perennially smaller; even after World War II, when the country went through a second industrial boom, the ranks of manual workers hardly grew in relative terms. It is therefore to be expected that the dilemmas of class mobilization and alliance have been tougher in Denmark than in Norway or, especially, Sweden.

Table 2.2 shows some of the chief differences in the role of the petite bourgeoisie. Denmark has always had a larger petite bourgeoisie than either of the other Nordic countries. This is partly because Danish industrial establishments are small and plentiful and partly because of the impressive resistance to "proletarianization" within both the rural and the urban petite bourgeoisie. Among Denmark's farmers and peasants there was some decline during the first two decades of the century, but thereafter their share remains constant until the last few decades. The stability of the urban petite bourgeoisie is even more impressive. Not only are they a substantially larger group than their counterparts in either Norway or Sweden, but their role in the class structure is constant until the 1970s.

Norway's petite bourgeoisie have always been fewer. This is, of

TABLE 2.2. Rural and Urban Petite Bourgeoisie in Scandinavia, 1900-1980
(*% of total active labor force*)

	1900	1910	1920	1930	1940	1950	1960	1970	1980[a]
RURAL[b]									
Denmark	28	27	22	19	19	15	11	8	5
Norway	24	—	19	—	—	19	14	10	7
Sweden	31	28	23	21	18	13	9	7	6
URBAN[c]									
Denmark	14	14	14	14	12	14	13	11	9
Norway	10	—	9	—	—	9	10	8	12
Sweden	9	9	6	8	10	8	8	7	7
TOTAL									
Denmark	42	41	36	33	31	29	24	19	14
Norway	34	—	28	—	—	28	24	18	19
Sweden	40	37	29	29	28	21	17	14	13

SOURCES: See Table 2.1.

NOTE. A major source of uncertainty concerning these figures is the problem of how to classify family members who help the head of household.

[a] For Denmark, the data pertain to 1975; for Norway, 1977; for Sweden, 1979.

[b] Includes farmers, peasants, fishermen, and self-employed and employers in forestry.

[c] Includes self-employed and employers in industry, construction, services, commerce, and retail.

course, a corollary of the historically greater importance of rural wage labor and the perennial fragility of Norwegian agriculture. On the other hand, we find that both the urban and the rural petite bourgeoisie—including entrepreneurs—have been slower to diminish in Norway during the postwar era. This may be seen as a manifestation of Norway's predominantly small-scale industry.[11]

Sweden was a considerably more agrarian society than the other two Nordic countries before the turn of the century. The data also reflect the fact that the Swedish peasantry diminished more rapidly in the years just before and after World War II. Another feature of the Swedish class structure is the relatively smaller proportion of urban employers and self-employed. Again, this seems to confirm our picture of a more concentrated urban economy—particularly in industrial manufacture, but also in retail and construction.

Clearly it is impossible to make any sound conclusions regarding internal differentiation within the urban petite bourgeoisie, including the "genuine" bourgeoisie, on the basis of these data. For an appropriate measure of capital concentration and centralization one could compare indices of capital ownership, firm size and sales volume, or the like; or one could compare the distribution of firms by level of employment.[12] Although the former types of indices are perhaps more appropriate, comparable data exist only for the latter.

Table 2.3 shows the distribution of Scandinavian firms by number of employees for the years 1958 and 1979. In both years Sweden has

TABLE 2.3. Distribution of Scandinavian Industrial Establishments by Number of Employees, 1958 and 1979

Employees	Denmark		Norway		Sweden	
	1958	1979	1958	1979	1958	1979
Fewer than 10	52	17	73	60	47	18
10-49	39	60	21	29	39	56
50-199	9	18	5	9	11	19
200 or more	2	5	1	2	3	7

SOURCES: Nordisk Råd (1981, 77); Elvander (1980, tables 5.5-5.7).
NOTE: For the year 1958, Danish and Swedish firms having fewer than five employees have been excluded.

[11] It can also be explained by the Norwegian state's explicit policies in support of the peasantry and other petit-bourgeois sectors in the postwar era.

[12] For a discussion of the validity and appropriateness of alternative measures, see Zeitlin (1974) and Zeitlin and Norich (1979).

a substantially greater proportion of large firms. If we liberally classify firms having fewer than ten employees as petit-bourgeois, we see that Denmark and Norway were more dominated by petit-bourgeois enterprises during the 1950s. Remarkably, Norway has changed little by the late 1970s, whereas Denmark has shifted in the direction of somewhat larger firms, employing between ten and forty-nine workers.

If we turn things around and ask instead how wage earners are distributed among firms of varying size, the differences between Sweden and the other Nordic countries become even clearer. In 1979, 60 percent of all Swedish employees worked in firms having more than two hundred employees; this compares with 39 percent in Norway and 46 percent in Denmark (Nordisk Råd 1981, 77).[13] Naturally these figures also reflect variations among the Nordic countries with respect to the degree of working-class concentration within large enterprises, a phenomenon that is often held to affect working-class radicalism and propensity for collective action. In short, there are sharp differences between the three Scandinavian nations in respect of the role of the petite bourgeoisie and the structure of capital ownership. Sweden is exceptional in its degree of concentration and in the marginalization of its traditional middle classes. Norway is unique in the extent to which the rural petite bourgeoisie especially have persisted during the modern era as well as in the predominance of very small industrial firms. Denmark's rural petite bourgeoisie may have suffered a sharp reduction in the past few decades, but its urban petite bourgeoisie appear very resistant to rationalization and concentration, compared with those of other countries; it is clear, though, that the wave of

[13] Differences in the structure of the retail sectors point up the contrast between Sweden's and Denmark's petit-bourgeois strata. In 1970 there were 85 persons per retail store in Denmark, compared with 160 in Sweden. Of all Danish stores, 82 percent were small independents, while in Sweden the vast majority were chain stores, supermarkets, or cooperatives. In Denmark, 8 percent were chain stores; in Sweden, 40 percent (Handelsministeriet 1973-1974, 3:246-251). The degree of capital concentration in Sweden, in contrast to the other two countries, is very well documented (SOU 1966-1968; Dahlkvist 1975; Åkerman 1973). These studies show that in finance, the three largest firms accounted for 81 percent of total credit issued in 1965 (Dahlkvist 1975, 131). Swedish capital is largely owned and controlled by a small group of families, among which the Wallenberg family is the single most important. These seventeen families exercise de facto control over companies that account for 36 percent of Sweden's total industrial output and that employ roughly 10 percent of the Swedish labor force. One percent of all stockholders own 50 percent of all the shares, and .1 percent own 25 percent of the shares (Åkerman 1973, 36, 40; Dahlkvist 1975, 133). These percentages take on added meaning when one realizes that this .1 percent of stockholders is only six or seven hundred individuals. Sweden's economy may very well be the world's most concentrated, in terms of ownership, and the most interlocked in terms of control.

industrialization experienced during the 1960s produced a decided shift toward medium-size establishments.[14] Such differences should have decisive consequences for the organizability of industry and employers as well as for the potential of corporatist political arrangements between the classes and the state.

From the foregoing data we know that the decline of the petite bourgeoisie was associated with growth among the new white-collar middle strata, by no means a less heterogeneous class than their petit-bourgeois ancestors. If we first consider white-collar employees in the aggregate, we find that prior to World War II there was very little variation among the three Nordic countries. Only after the war did Sweden take the lead in the direction of a modern postindustrial class structure. In Table 2.4 we see that in Denmark and Sweden, less so in Norway, white-collar employees have more than doubled their relative share of the labor force during the past several decades. Sweden took the lead and Denmark followed with a ten-year lag.

The different white-collar strata have not grown at the same rate. Many of the lowest-level routine clerical and, especially, sales jobs have actually diminished or, in any case, stagnated during the era of white-collar expansion. As in many countries, the increase in female participation in the labor force and in part-time work has been concentrated in the lower or middle layers of white-collar work. The bulk of the expansion of the middle strata worldwide has occurred in the

TABLE 2.4. White-Collar Employees in Scandinavia, 1900-1980
(% of total active labor force)

	1900	1910	1920	1930	1940	1950	1960	1970	1980[a]
Denmark	8	10	15	16	18	22	28	37	45
Norway	8	—	14	—	—	20	25	—	34
Sweden	9	11	13	14	18	28	35	40	43

SOURCES: See Table 2.1.
[a] For Denmark, the data pertain to 1975; for Norway, 1977; for Sweden, 1979.

[14] In fact, among the countries surveyed by the Danish government in 1970, only France exceeded Denmark—and then only marginally—in respect of number of stores per capita (Handelsministeriet 1973-1974, 246). Note, however, that, during the 1970s, there was a sharp reduction in small firms and retail stores in Denmark. Incidentally, an industry that has always been especially "petit-bourgeois," construction and building, has shown a slower pace of rationalization. Still, more than 64 percent of Danish construction workers in 1964 were employed in firms having fewer than four workers (Bonke 1976, 74-75).

technical, administrative, and service areas and, in the Scandinavian countries, within the public sector.[15] It is very difficult to assess how the relationship between white-collar and blue-collar workers may impinge on political behavior. Many routine or menial white-collar jobs certainly have a more "objective" similarity to manual industrial work, although such factors as part-time employment may modify the picture. Concomitantly, it is possible that many of the new technical white-collar groups will experience a work situation bearing considerable similarity to that of traditional skilled workers.

Apart from such abstract possibilities, there is little doubt that the structural transformation from petit-bourgeois to white-collar employment decisively changes the parameters for social democratic electoral and political strategy—in all likelihood, in a positive direction. First of all, the bulk of the new white-collar workers are not simply employed in the public sector and services. Rather, they are concentrated in fields such as social welfare or health and education, whereas in the distant past they might have been found in the more repressive organs of the public sector. Secondly, and this will surely vary with degree of unionization, white-collar workers will almost inevitably move in the direction of greater collectivization. Still, there is no doubt that endemic distributional conflicts between blue-collar and white-collar workers will prohibit an easy convergence or cross-class identity.

SOCIAL STRUCTURE AND CLASS ORGANIZATION

In late-industrializing Scandinavia, it is no wonder that trade union growth came late. But if the unions there went through lean times, those same unions eventually became the most powerful in the world. Moreover, labor organizations have counterparts that efficiently articulate the economic interests of other classes. These include not only the employer associations but also federations of industrialists, farmer

[15] For a more extensive analysis and discussion of the middle strata's growth in the Nordic countries, see Goul Andersen (1979) and Therborn (1976). Thus, by 1970, of the 500,000 Danes employed in services, 440,000 were in public-sector jobs; and of the total growth between 1962 and 1972, about 75 percent occurred in public employment (Handelsministeriet 1973-1974, 428ff; Goul Andersen 1979, 112-122). Throughout the 1970s, the increase in public-sector employment was even more phenomenal—mainly due to governmental attempts to counter rising unemployment in the private sector. In Denmark, 300,000 new public-sector jobs were created from 1970 to 1980, while 200,000 jobs disappeared in the private sector. Public-sector employment thus grew from 21.3 percent of the labor force in 1970 to about 32.5 percent in 1980 (Danmarks Statistik 1981b).

and peasant organizations, as well as associations of artisans, retailers and wholesalers, consumers, tenants, and so on.

Among the Nordic countries, Sweden is the most thoroughly organized.[16] Yet all three share a long tradition of association on rather distinct class lines. One remarkable characteristic common to most of these class organizations is their political demarcation. Many such organizations maintain close links with political parties that, in large measure, have come to articulate the politics of their respective interest organizations. This is true as much for the longstanding and unusually intimate relations between the Landsorganisationen (LO) union federations and the social democratic parties as it is for the farmers' associations that found homes in the Danish Liberal (Venstre) party and in the farmers' parties of Norway and Sweden. Employer organizations and the Confederation of Industries and Manufacturers have, as one might expect, cultivated close, if less formalized, ties with the various conservative parties. In short, the linkage of economic organizations and political parties is unusually strong in Scandinavia; the power of a given economic interest group is very closely related to the power of its party.

The early histories of Scandinavian class organization are quite similar. Craftsmen and skilled workers were the first to form unions, and employer organizations appeared at more or less the same time. Danish trade unionism grew rapidly between 1870 and the turn of the century, in close step with industrialization, urbanization, and the dissolution of the guilds. Small, trade-based unions proliferated, and the first test of the embryonic movement came in 1872 when Copenhagen bricklayers, in concert with the socialist party leadership, called a rather disorganized mass strike at Faelleden, a park then situated just outside Copenhagen.[17] The police were quick to break up the strike and imprison its leaders (Bertold 1938). Still, craft unionism continued to flourish as the economy expanded; skilled workers felt little threat of unemployment. The unions were also the main force behind the reconstitution of the Danish Socialist party. The first attempt at central union coordination occurred in 1874, but in this early period it is difficult to distinguish the party organization from the union movement. It seems that most efforts to organize were prompted by fear

[16] Several good overviews of Scandinavian trade unionism exist. See in particular Galenson (1949, 1952, 1968) and Elvander (1974a, 1974b, 1980). Also see Johnston (1962), Elvander (1966), Kassalow (1969), and Kvavik (1976).

[17] Even if the strike ended in disaster, Faelleden has symbolic value for the labor movement and continues to be the final stop of the annual May Day parades.

that wages and jobs would be undercut by competition from migrating rural workers.

In response to labor, the employers did not hesitate to unify. The first step occurred in 1879, when industry and handicrafts formed an association. Yet, it was not until 1896 that a national organization, the Danish Employers' Federation, was formed. The unions followed suit in 1898 with the Coordinated Trade Unions, or DSF (years later renamed the LO, as in Norway and Sweden). On the employer side, industry and handicrafts split into separate organizations after 1910.

The origins of class organization in Sweden and Norway are very similar to those in Denmark, although the process began ten years and twenty years later, respectively. Again, the early unions were concentrated among the skilled workers and craftsmen, although Norway has a history of rural labor organization dating back to the mid-1800s. Such similar historical experiences are not difficult to explain. There was, first of all, relatively little state repression. Norway, in fact, had already attained universal male suffrage and effective parliamentarism by 1884. Furthermore, there was diffusion: the Danish trade unionists and socialists spread the gospel and helped their less advanced brethren to the north erect union organizations. Cross-national synchronization was especially evident with the shift to centrally organized national trade union federations. The decision to move in this direction was made at a Scandinavian labor congress in 1897 (Elvander 1974a). Thus the Swedes constituted their LO in 1898, and the Norwegians followed one year later. Only in Denmark did employer organization precede that of labor.[18]

Although national federations had been constituted, there were no clear rules to regulate the style and content of industrial conflict, which—because of close ties between the social democratic parties and the unions and because of the absence of full democracy in Denmark and Sweden—was easily politicized. It should therefore come as no surprise that the first major confrontation was not long in coming. Denmark again took the lead. In 1899 the DAF countered a small, local strike with a widespread lockout. The union federation, which at that time included only about one-third of all trade union members, was able to hold out for several months. But, threatened with state intervention, the exhausted and nearly bankrupt unions finally agreed to enter into the so-called September Agreement. The unions, in return for recognizing managerial prerogatives relating to the distribution of

[18] The Norwegian Employers' Federation (NAF) was formed in 1900, the Swedish Employers' Federation (SAF) in 1902.

work and the hiring and firing of workers, gained the right to bargain collectively. (This agreement held until 1960, when it was revised.) The employers' association had provoked the confrontation with two goals in mind. First, of course, they wanted to weaken the trade unions and impose the rights of ownership and control. The other motive, also a factor in the subsequent Norwegian and Swedish confrontations, was to force the trade unions to pursue central bargaining instead of following the traditional horizontally based, group-by-group pattern characteristic of craft unionism (Elvander 1974a). In Denmark, the employers succeeded on the first objective but failed on the second. After 1899, trade union growth slowed, but the LO (DSF) failed to shift from horizontal to vertical, industrial organization and collective bargaining.

The Danish LO has continued to resist centralization and industrial organization, and it remains divided between the powerful skilled-labor unions, on one side, and the unskilled-labor unions on the other. The Danish class structure, with its handicraft-centered manufacture, is probably the chief reason for this chronic division. The skilled workers have reigned supreme. In 1913, for example, the LO secretariat included only one unskilled-worker representative, and at that year's congress only 29 out of 386 delegates represented the unskilled industrial workers (Dybdahl 1975, 127).[19] In fact, for a few years during the 1920s, the unskilled workers actually divorced themselves from the LO (DSF). After World War II, the Unskilled Workers' Federation became the largest single element in the labor movement, but thus far it has failed to assert its demand for centralized industrial unionism.[20]

The Norwegian and Swedish LOs also faced tests of strength early on. When the tests came, however, the Swedes and Norwegians were organizationally weaker than the Danes had been in 1899. In Sweden, the first step toward mutual recognition by the LO and the SAF occurred in 1906; in Norway, the year was 1907 (Elvander 1974a, 67). But the situation was not fully resolved until after 1909, when a general strike broke out in both countries. The 1909 strikes were a disaster,

[19] Remarkably, 34 delegates were self-employed, thus attesting to the petit-bourgeois influence over Danish labor in this period.

[20] There have been some moves toward centralization, and an LO congress in 1971 did decide in principle to shift to the industrial pattern of trade unionism. To date, that change is still only a change in principle. For unskilled labor, though large in numbers, is organizationally weak—partly because of their more tenuous market position, but probably also because of an influx of unskilled foreign workers and women into the labor market at exactly the moment when the Danish economy approached full employment in the 1960s.

and the subsequent agreements stipulated harsher conditions than the Danes had acceded to in the September Agreement. Both the Swedes and the Norwegians, moreover, moved toward trade union centralization and vertical, industrial unionism. In Sweden, this was established as a principle in 1912; in Norway, 1923. In neither country, though, was the principle translated into full reality until the 1950s.

A number of peculiar factors account for the drift toward early centralization in Sweden and Norway. First, in contrast to the Danish situation, the unions in this case were confronted with the difficult task of synchronizing and mobilizing industrial action across huge geographical areas in a context of decentralized industry. Concerted action had to put a premium on central coordination and nationwide solidarity. Secondly, in both countries—Sweden especially—the employers were organized in a more centralized fashion, a circumstance that forced labor to reciprocate. Thirdly, the Swedish and Norwegian working classes were not dominated by skilled labor as they were in Denmark. In Norway, the vast majority were rural proletarians; in Sweden, unskilled industrial workers. The unskilled workers were therefore better situated to invoke broad class solidarity over narrower and more exclusionary craft interests. In the Norwegian case, it should be noted, the move toward industrial unionism was countered by a powerful syndicalist movement in the rural West and Southwest, led by Martin Tranmael.[21]

Although membership recruitment stagnated in the Nordic countries following the LO defeats, union growth soon resumed, especially in Norway and Sweden. From 1900 to 1920, membership grew by 270 percent in Denmark, 500 percent in Sweden, and an astounding 2,750 percent in Norway.[22] Unionization in the three countries progressed in a series of historical waves. In Denmark, where labor market conditions were more stable during the interwar period—and where the social democrats were politically stronger—the rate of unionization first crested during the 1920s, with around 40 percent of all wage earners organized. This was followed by a long period of slow growth. It was only in the 1970s that a new wave of unionization occurred, a phenomenon that can be ascribed to the high unemployment in that decade.

[21] Naturally, the 1909 mass strike in Norway helped radicalize the labor movement, but syndicalism was given a further boost by the arrival that year of ousted syndicalists from Sweden. We shall return later to the influence of Tranmael on the Norwegian labor movement.

[22] But note that Norwegian unionization in 1900 was at a very low level (Galenson 1952, App. A).

In Norway, unionization was explosive until stagnation set in during the 1920s. This can be explained by the deep rifts within the Norwegian labor movement following World War I, when the social democratic party split and the majority affiliated with the Comintern. In 1921 the labor movement called a general strike, which failed; this strike had strong overtones of a political mass strike. Unemployment levels were also quite high during this period. A new surge of unionization occurred only after the social democrats had assumed office in the 1930s and the labor market had been stabilized. During the postwar era, trade union membership in Norway has grown at a considerably slower rate than in Sweden. This is probably because Norway is the only Scandinavian country in which the trade unions do not control unemployment funds.

Union membership organization in Sweden was slow for some time following the 1909 defeat and, as in Norway, the 1920s were tumultuous years with respect to labor market conflict.[23] But, following the social democratic ascent to governmental power in 1932, and the renegotiation of relations between the employers and the LO in the famous Saltsjöbaden Agreement of 1938, an organizational surge ensued.[24] Today Sweden is without a doubt the most thoroughly unionized capitalist nation.

The Nordic countries have come to differ in respect of the organizational characteristics of trade unionism: Denmark remains wedded to horizontal, craft-based negotiations; Norway and Sweden are gradually completing the process of centralization and vertical, industrial unionism.[25] The three countries differ as well with respect to white-collar unionism. In Sweden, following the Second World War, white-collar unionization has centered on the TCO (the Confederation of Swedish White-Collar Employees), which, like the LO, has moved in the direction of "industrial" and vertical unionism. Higher-level professional and academic employees formed a separate organization,

[23] Before the 1930s, Sweden and Norway boasted some of the world's highest strike rates (Hibbs 1978; Korpi and Shalev 1980).

[24] The Saltsjöbaden Agreement, combined with the social democratic party's realignment, has been described as the Swedish labor movement's "historical compromise" (Korpi 1981a). Labor finally conceded on rights of ownership and received in return some concessions relating to hiring-and-firing rules as well as a governmental agreement to refrain from intervention. Note, however, that strikes declined dramatically as the SAP formed a majority government in 1935.

[25] In Sweden, the number of separate union federations declined from forty-four in 1960 to twenty-five in 1975. In Norway, the number of such federations declined from forty-three in 1960 to thirty-five in 1973. The number has stayed at around fifty in Denmark (Elvander 1980, 170).

the Swedish Confederation of Professional Employees (SACO), in 1947. Separate white-collar unions have also emerged in Denmark and Norway, but in a less distinct and explosive pattern. In Denmark, white-collar "functionaries" formed an organization (the FTF, or Federation of Salaried Employees) that is similar to the TCO except that it is less coherent and not quite so large. Academic and professional employees also copied the Swedes, forming the Danish Academics' Confederation (AC) in the early 1970s. Danish white-collar unionization was slower to consolidate than in Sweden, but during the 1970s some convergence of organizational penetration seems to have occurred.[26]

In Norway, white-collar employees tried, but failed, to institute a separate trade union federation, again modeled on the Swedish TCO. Instead, the LO has managed to incorporate large numbers of lower- and middle-level white-collar employees. Outside the LO, the situation is chaotic: small and diverse unions, including an organization of academic employees, abound. A number of these separate trade unions even admit the self-employed, thus making exact calculations of wage-earner union membership almost impossible.[27]

The overall result for Scandinavia is a tremendous rise in union membership among blue-collar and, especially after the war, white-collar wage earners. There are, indeed, few nations that can match the level of organizational penetration found in these three countries. If we take Korpi's (1980b, 1981a) cross-national data on unionization, averaged between 1946 and 1976, Sweden scores the highest among eighteen countries, Denmark ranks fourth, and Norway fifth.[28] The long-term rise in trade union membership is shown in Table 2.5.[29]

The Swedish labor movement has enjoyed great organizational success since the 1930s. Norwegian unionization has stagnated since the 1950s, and in Denmark there has been a recent wave of membership

[26] Again, a major factor behind the surge in Danish union membership during the 1970s was the particularly high level of unemployment in Denmark, together with the fact that the trade unions there control the distribution of unemployment benefits.

[27] Elvander (1974b, 76) explains the absence of a central organization of white-collar employees in Norway as the consequence of the early (1930s) emergence of a separate association of public civil servants. This spurred the LO to compete for membership among private-sector white-collar workers. Another factor seems to be the refusal of small, occupationally distinct unions to engage in consolidation.

[28] Austria and Australia rank second and third, respectively.

[29] Note that the percentage figures in Table 2.5 are based on all wage earners, whereas Korpi's data are based on the nonagricultural labor force. Note, also, that the Norwegian data harbor a possible source of error, since unions that include the self-employed have not been counted. The "Other" category for Denmark and Sweden overwhelmingly reflects white-collar unionization.

SOCIAL BASES OF SOCIAL DEMOCRACY

TABLE 2.5. Trade Union Membership in Scandinavia, 1900-1980

	1900	1910	1920	1930	1940	1950	1960	1970	1980
DENMARK									
LO (000s)	77	102	279	259	516	623	818	894	1,250
Other (000s)	—	22	—	52	27	—	196	267	544
% of All									
Wage Earners	18	20	47	37	46	53	62	62	71[a]
NORWAY									
LO and Other (000s)	5	47	143	140	307	488	662	787	967
% of All									
Wage Earners	1	—	18	17	—	50	64	65	62
SWEDEN									
LO (000s)	44	85	280	553	971	1,278	1,486	1,680	2,089
Other (000s)	—	36	21	50	72	290	394	834	1,226
% of All									
Wage Earners	6	12	21	36	50	62	67	81	92

SOURCES: Denmark—Pedersen (1977, app.); Danmarks Statistik 1981a, table 305. Norway—Lorenz (1974, 215); Statistisk Sentralbyrå (1911, 40; 1933, 60; 1934, 239; 1945, 249, 361; 1953, 253; 1963, 62; 1974, 80; 1981, 85). Sweden—Statistiska Centralbyron (1931, 322; 1933, 296; 1942, 315; 1952, 227; 1961, 224; 1971, 243; 1981a, 271).

NOTE: LO = Landsorganisationen.

[a] Since Danish Labor force data are not available for 1980, the percentage figure has been estimated.

growth in blue-collar as well as white-collar unions. A remarkable feature of the 1970s in Denmark is that almost the entire membership increase has occurred among women. It should be obvious that differences in union penetration will affect the long-term strength of the social democratic parties.

TRADE UNIONISM AND THE SOCIAL DEMOCRATIC PARTIES

The beginnings of trade unionism are difficult to distinguish from the beginnings of the social democratic parties. These organizations grew up together and, throughout the history of the Scandinavian labor movement, the two have maintained very close ties. A shared, and historically decisive, feature is the achievement of trade union autonomy from the party at an early date. Yet, from the late 1800s until today, there is little doubt that union power has depended on the success of the party and vice versa.

64

The Danish Social Democratic party was reconstituted and put back on its feet by trade unionists in 1878, following the collapse of its predecessor (Bertold 1938; Bertold, Christiansen, and Hansen 1954-1955). This helped ensure trade union influence over party program, ideology, and policy in a moderately reformist direction. With the reconstitution of the party, the trade unions abolished the earlier practice of automatic collective trade union membership in the party.[30] On the other hand, the trade union organizations continued to mobilize voters on behalf of the social democrats during election campaigns.

Although the trade union and party movements were formally divorced in respect of organization, membership, and program, mutual ties were developed in order to ensure synchrony. With the establishment of a central union confederation and the transformation of the party into a national organization in the 1890s, a system of top-level joint representation was institutionalized. A social democrat is automatically elected to the secretariat of the LO (DSF), and an LO representative is automatically elected to the party secretariat. Also, the LO came to be the primary financial support of various party activities, particularly the party newspaper. The electoral mobilization function of the trade unions, however, diminished once the party developed its own nationwide organizational structure. One of the most important, and most regular, sources of LO influence has been the tradition of recruiting social democratic leaders from the trade union movement.[31] In the long run, though, the nature of Danish trade unionism has also inhibited social democratic party power because the internally divided and fragmented structure of the LO has translated into political incoherence. To a large extent, the party has been placed in a difficult role as political broker between the disadvantaged unskilled sectors and the dominant skilled organizations.

In Denmark, a strong left-oppositional tendency within the trade union movement simply never developed to be transplanted into the political arena. Syndicalism never came to play an important role.

[30] This has meant a much weaker membership base for the Danish social democrats.

[31] At the very beginning, almost all party leaders were trade unionists. The "grandfather" of Danish social democracy, Thorvald Stauning, was—like Gompers—a cigar roller. The present party leader, Anker Jørgensen was previously chief of the Unskilled Workers' Federation. The Danish social democrats, compared with their counterparts in most other countries, have a much weaker tradition of intellectuals in leadership positions. Of all the party's leaders, only two have been academics. This circumstance may help explain the pervasive disregard for theory and ideology in Danish social democracy.

When, after 1918, a communist splinter group broke with the social democratic party, it failed to take many trade unionists away with it. The LO remained solidly social democratic. Throughout its history, in fact, only a few elements of the trade union movement have been captured by left-socialist or communist parties (the seamen's union being one of the few). During World War II, when the communist underground enjoyed substantial support, social democratic hegemony did deteriorate somewhat; and in the post war era internal tensions within the LO have on occasion helped nurture left-wing outbreaks within the union movement. A notable example is that of 1956, when the social democratic government intervened in a general strike and provoked considerable bitterness, especially within the Unskilled Workers' Federation. The rift over membership in the EEC (European Economic Community), around 1970, also stimulated defections within the LO. Both the Danish Communist party (DKP) and the Socialist People's party (SF) managed to penetrate a number of trade unions. But social democratic control was restored after Denmark's entry into the Common Market and especially after the post-1974 economic recession. If the trade union structure has remained largely social democratic, however, formal relations between the LO and the social democrats are occasionally tense, particularly over questions of government-imposed incomes policy.

As might be expected with a labor movement that went from reformism to revolution and back again, relations between the unions and the party in Norway remained uncertain for a long time. Following the Danish pattern, trade unionists played a leading role in the establishment of the Norwegian Labor party (DNA) in 1887. This was prior to the consolidation of a central union federation, and so the party organization simultaneously provided cells for the trade unions. The principle of collective membership in the trade union and the party prevailed. The first structural change occurred with the formation of the LO.[32] Yet, in contrast to the Danish experience, the practice of collective union membership in the Norwegian party continued until the 1925 LO congress.[33] Initially the party was wedded

[32] Until 1957, the LO trade union confederation was actually called the Arbeidernes Faglige Landsorganisation.

[33] During the 1920s, two-thirds of the LO members were collectively affiliated with the party; after the Second World War, however, the system decayed rapidly. By 1966 only about 17 percent of all LO members were collectively affiliated. It should be noted that collective membership, overwhelmingly an urban working-class affair, existed only marginally on the rural periphery, where a large percentage of DNA votes were found (Rokkan 1966).

to a reformist, parliamentary strategy. A series of circumstances, however, prevented the Norwegian labor movement from fully separating trade union activities and organization from those of the party, and during the 1920s the Norwegian labor movement seems to fit more closely the extraparliamentary, class oppositional model.

One important factor was the early centralization of the Norwegian LO. By 1907 it had established a strike fund, and the central leadership exercised considerable power. This provoked dissent on the periphery, especially in Norway's western and southwestern regions where syndicalism was strong. The first major challenge to LO centralism was the 1911 Trondheim Resolution and the ensuing opposition movement. Led by Tranmael—who was inspired by the Industrial Workers of the World (IWW)—the syndicalist movement penetrated both the LO and the party and helped push them toward a strategy of mass action and direct confrontation with the bourgeois state. As a consequence, the trade union movement was politicized and the DNA abandoned its earlier reformist posture.[34]

The decisive break came in 1919, when the DNA chose to affiliate with the Comintern and the LO joined the Amsterdam International. A few years later, the new programmatic and organizational character of the labor movement found expression in an attempt to launch a mass strike whose target was more political than industrial. The movement also tried to establish soviets during the years 1918-1920, although such efforts typically failed. The Norwegian LO and the DNA adopted the same formal system of joint executive representation that was developed in Denmark. But the system collapsed in 1923 when the DNA chose to leave the Comintern: the party split into a minority communist party and a majority DNA.[35] In 1927, when the party was reunified, the institution of joint executive representation was revived.

The Norwegian Communist party (NKP), like that of Denmark, failed to make serious inroads in the trade union movement. After 1927, therefore, the LO remained solidly social democratic. Since the DNA took office in the 1930s, especially since World War II, the principle of joint LO-DNA representation has been greatly extended

[34] It was the rise of Tranmael and syndicalism that helped inspire the "Bull hypothesis," for syndicalism was clearly centered in the more recently uprooted rural population.

[35] When the DNA joined the Third International, a small reformist faction split off and formed the Norwegian Social Democratic party. Incidentally, the syndicalist Tranmael was a prime force behind the DNA's rejection of the "Moscow theses" in 1923, since he refused Moscow's imposition of democratic centralism.

to include LO membership on a multitude of government committees and councils.

It was not until the realignment of the DNA in the 1930s that the LO was fully depoliticized. During the 1920s, the LO was a curious hybrid of conventional trade union and political strike force. This is of course to be expected in a movement dedicated to extraparliamentary action, revolution, and the dictatorship of the proletariat. But an additional reason is that, unlike in Denmark, the state threatened wider repressive action against trade unions, both in its response to mass strikes and in laws designed to weaken the LO.[36]

The 1930s, then, were a turning point for both the LO and the party. But the evolution toward "normality," meaning a firm separation of trade union activities from those of the party, was interrupted during the German occupation of 1940-1945, when the DNA was outlawed and its leaders exiled or sent to concentration camps. After the war, most of the earlier syndicalist and revolutionary characteristics disappeared, although the idea of workers' councils was halfheartedly resurrected after 1945. Postwar relations between the LO and the DNA have been closer and more harmonious than LO-party relations in Denmark. The Norwegian LO has been far more unified, the party has been stronger, and there have been fewer serious disputes between the two—at least until the 1970s.

However, as in Denmark, the issue of Common Market membership threatened to divide the labor movement, and the resultant tensions were worse in Norway. The Unskilled Workers' Federation opposed membership, even if both the LO and the DNA congress favored affiliation in 1972. Strong opposition in a number of separate unions as well as among rank-and-file workers across the country culminated with massive working-class defections from the DNA in the 1973 election. At the 1973 LO congress, the anti-EEC Norwegian Socialist People's party gained substantial support among trade unionists. It is likely that the stronger postwar position of the Norwegian social democrats, compared with the Danish social democrats, is largely attributable to the greater cohesion of the Norwegian LO. On the other hand, it is also likely that continued social democratic electoral progress has been impeded by Norway's slower rate of trade union expansion—especially when compared with that of Sweden—in the postwar era.

Sweden's experience in the early period is hardly distinguishable from that of the other Nordic countries. The first impetus to form a

[36] A 1927 law, for example, prohibited the trade unions from stopping strikebreakers.

party emanated from the trade unions, with some assistance from Danish socialists, in the 1880s. The Swedish Social Democratic party (SAP) was constituted in 1889, two years after the Norwegian party and almost ten years before the unions were confederated in the LO. In this period, the party organization became the central instrument of trade union coordination. When the LO was formed in 1898, however, the principle of collective membership was retained. A few years later, individual trade unionists would have the right to opt out, but the principle has remained a basic feature of the Swedish labor movement to the present day, and a considerable number of LO members are also affiliated with the party.[37] This has given a formidable organizational advantage to the Swedish social democrats, both financially and electorally. It has perhaps also meant a stronger and livelier party organization.

The SAP remained reformist and parliamentarist after 1918, and the left-socialist, pro-Moscow splinter group that surfaced never managed to threaten either the party or the LO, although it did gain considerable local support among workers in the northern mining areas. The LO, on the other hand, recovered from the 1909 disaster and grew rapidly. As noted, its recruits were overwhelmingly industrial workers and so the old crafts influence deteriorated more rapidly than it did in Denmark. Yet, despite a stronger tendency toward industrial unionism, the Swedish LO was slower to centralize than the Norwegian LO—a phenomenon that may have helped avert a strong syndicalist insurgence. Also, the Swedish syndicalists drifted into the communist party (VPK). Thus, for both the party and the LO, the major threats of disunity and fragmentation were averted at an early date.

The central authority of the LO was gradually strengthened throughout the tumultuous interwar period, partly because coordinated action was so important in Sweden's dispersed geography and partly because the labor market was so unstable. The realignment of social democracy in the early 1930s and the subsequent Saltsjöbaden Agreement finally established the parameters of LO-SAP relations. It was a framework that would last until the 1970s.

If we consider the much greater organizational power of the Swedish LO during the past five decades, as well as its unusually homogeneous working-class constituency, it is no wonder that the LO has come to be the dominant partner in the LO-party relationship, particularly in the framing of social and economic legislative proposals. Indeed, the

---

[37] Before 1914 an estimated 80 percent of SAP's membership came from the LO; today the percentage is around 60 percent.

LO commands its own research staff, including academics and well-trained experts. This constellation of factors, not to mention the LO's financial influence, has helped ensure fewer frictions within the labor movement.

In recent years, it is true, some tensions naturally have emerged. For one thing, as Elvander (1980, 178) suggests, the LO's legislative activities have vastly increased. This has posed difficulties for the party, which is compelled to harmonize the demands of workers with those of other classes. Moreover, current problems of growth and full employment, and the LOs proposal for economic democracy, have put new strains on LO-SAP relations. Frictions also resulted from the wave of wildcat strikes that followed the 1969 Kiruna strike, during which workers protested against LO centralism and, indirectly, against the social democratic government.

Occasional difficulties notwithstanding, all three labor movements display unusually strong ties between the trade unions and the party—perhaps most powerfully in Sweden and least so in Denmark. A similar symbiosis has not evolved between the newer white-collar unions and the social democratic parties. Though Norway, where white-collar unionism is so fragmented, is a somewhat special case, the white-collar federations have generally remained neutral with respect to political party. There is no doubt that social democracy's long-term prospects will depend on the political choices and party allegiances of the rapidly growing white-collar employee organizations.

THREE

Class Alliances in the Development of Scandinavian Social Democracy

SOCIAL DEMOCRATIC HISTORY in Scandinavia may conveniently be divided into three periods.[1] In the first period—from about 1870 until World War I and its aftermath—the traditional "class party" model reigned, although socialists and farmers did collaborate in the struggle for democracy. In the second, interwar period, the democratization issue had been resolved, but the political climate remained unstable. Social democratic parties grew remarkably, yet no sound governing coalitions could be formed on either the right or the left. The historical crossroads came with a political realignment that coalesced farmers and working class, transforming "class parties" into "people's parties." This realignment established the parameters of postwar welfare state politics and marks the starting point of the third period. In the postwar period social democracy has generally been dominant, despite occasional bourgeois-party governments and despite the absence of further party growth.

As social democracy entered the 1970s, this third period seemed to be ending. The parties are showing signs of decomposition (or at least stagnation), the political formula of the past has lost its appeal and relevance, and a new set of policies and a new realignment are clearly needed. In response to the new requirements, the parties have embarked on a campaign to redefine themselves as "wage-earner parties." The need to bring the middle-strata employee groups into a social democratic alliance is urgent.

There are, to begin with, a number of shared characteristics that help explain what makes the "Scandinavian model" unique. First, political democratization in the Nordic countries was a comparatively

[1] The following review of Danish, Norwegian, and Swedish social democratic party development and political change draws on these standard works: Westergård Andersen 1974, 1976; Dybdahl 1975; Elvander 1980; Bertold, Christiansen, and Hansen 1954-1955; Bertold 1938; Krag and Andersen 1971; Bille 1972; Bryld 1976; Tingsten 1941; Lindhagen 1972; Hancock 1972; Dahl 1969; Lorenz 1974; Kjeldstadli and Keul 1973; Aasheim 1970, 1971; Valen and Katz 1964; Valen 1981; Rokkan 1966; Paterson and Thomas 1977; Esping-Andersen 1980.

71

smooth and gradual process. Consolidation of parliamentarism and extensions of the suffrage came early in the process of industrialization. Nor were there any drastic reversals of democracy. Secondly, with only minor exceptions, constitutional rules and parliamentary procedures were typically upheld. The political dominance of the aristocracies and the monarchy was weakened at an early date, serious political repression was rare, and there was no Scandinavian parallel to the German *Sozialistengesetz*. A decisive factor was the precocious alliance of peasants, farmers, and workers—with urban liberal support—in the struggle for full democracy. Thirdly, all three countries came to adopt proportional representation, and this without a doubt helped advance social democratic mobilization. Proportional representation tends to place a premium on strong party organization and maximum electoral mobilization, since party competition is fiercer. It may also promote a closer correspondence between social cleavages and political parties. Of course, the conditions for new-party entry will vary according to the percentage of votes needed for representation.[2]

Finally, the unusually strong linkage between class divisions and the party system is related to other peculiarly Scandinavian features. In each country the citizenry is ethnically, linguistically, and culturally homogeneous, a factor that helps reduce the significance of cross-cutting cleavages.[3] In the three Nordic countries, therefore, the profiles of class-organizational political linkage are very similar. Employer organizations have typically found representation in the conservative parties (the Højre in Norway, the Moderate party in Sweden, and the Conservative party in Denmark). Farmers have found a home in the agrarian-liberal parties (in Norway and Sweden, the Center party; in Denmark, the Liberal party), while small landholders have rallied behind the radical-liberal parties. The vast majority of the working class, of course, have mobilized behind the social democratic parties.[4]

For social democracy, the most decisive characteristic of the Scandinavian countries has been the farmers' capacity for self-organization,

[2] The greater proliferation of small parties in Denmark is undoubtedly a function of a very low (2 percent) threshold.

[3] This generalization somewhat obscures the powerful influence of a number of sharp cleavages. In Norway especially there are divisions between "high church" and "low church" Christians as well as between center and periphery. In both Norway and Sweden, other divisive elements, notably the temperance movements, have played a role. For the best discussion of these cleavages, see Rokkan (1966, 1970).

[4] Only rarely have communist parties presented much of a challenge, although recently left-socialist parties have begun to jeopardize social democratic hegemony in Denmark and, to a lesser degree, in Norway.

which set the stage for an internationally unique alliance between liberal farmers and socialist workers. The independent, and politically quite powerful, position of the farmers also meant a more disunited bourgeois bloc, and conflict among the bourgeois parties has been the general rule.[5] In contrast, the social democrats, backed by the powerful trade union movement, have usually had little to fear from the left.

This combination of political system properties is unique and must enter into any explanation of why social democracy has prospered so well in precisely these three countries. Bearing these systemic similarities in mind, we may now turn to the historical factors that are peculiar to each of the Nordic nations.

SOCIAL DEMOCRATIC ASCENDANCE IN DENMARK, 1870-1945

After the 1848 revolutions on the Continent, the Danish aristocracy was compelled to relinquish power to a parliamentary system under the June Constitution of 1849. The strength of the farmers and urban liberals, together with a weakening aristocracy, had helped avert revolutionary upheaval. However, the unusually democratic constitution was amended in 1866 so that the upper house was once again under the control of the landed aristocracy and the king.[6] Full democratic representation was prevented by the power of the upper house to veto majority decisions.

During the late 1800s, therefore, the executive was conservative and parliament was dominated by liberal farmers. The latter were the first to form a political party—the United Left—dedicated to three important goals: representational democracy, reduction of taxes, and liberalization of trade. When the Danish Socialist party came on the scene in the 1870s, it was able to collaborate with the liberals on the question of parliamentarism. It was also in the 1870s that the Danish Conservative party was constituted, in response to the liberal challenge. Conservative control of the government was, until 1901, maintained on the basis of provisional legislation not sanctioned by the lower house, and ministers were directly appointed by the king. The victory for parliamentarism came with the 1901 System Change, when remaining suffrage limitations were eliminated. The liberals immediately formed the first democratically elected government.

The first effort to establish a socialist party failed. In 1871, the

[5] This disunity is, for Castles (1978), the principal factor behind social democratic success in Scandinavia.

[6] The 1866 restrictions on parliamentary representation followed the defeat of Denmark in the war against Prussia and Austria.

initiator, Louis Pio, organized a Danish branch of the First International and devised a somewhat diffuse revolutionary platform. The party crumbled soon afterward when the police broke up a demonstration, imprisoned its leaders, and subsequently bribed them to emigrate to the United States. Some years later, the Danish Social Democratic party was reconstituted by trade unionists and, in 1878, was formally established. During its early years, the party experienced difficulty in mobilizing the working-class electorate, partly because suffrage limitations particularly affected the poorer segments of the working class and partly because the conservatives managed to attract many of the more affluent workers. The social democrats elected two representatives to parliament in 1884, but it was not until after 1901 that the party really began to grow.

The party's first program, the 1876 Gimle program, was a more or less literal translation of the Gotha program. There was remarkable foresight in its slogan "A Century of Social Democracy," for the party commanded hardly any constituency at the time. Its primary objectives concerned electoral mobilization. The demand for universal suffrage and parliamentarism was, until 1901, the leading issue, although welfare reform occupied an important place because of the disenfranchisement of relief recipients and the economic insecurity of unskilled workers.

In the aftermath of the democratic reform, the farmers' Liberal party moved closer to the Conservative party, catalyzing the formation of the Radical-Liberal party (RV) in 1905. This allowed a close parliamentary association between the social democrats and the radicals on issues of domestic social reform as well as military spending. The period gave rise to a pattern of lasting alignments: the conservatives and the liberals were the two dominant bourgeois parties; the social democrats became the largest party on the left; and the radicals occupied a left-of-center position as the natural allies of the social democrats. This left-right axis undeniably reflected the main underlying class cleavages. Farmers and the urban bourgeoisie favored moderation in public spending (except with respect to the military and agricultural subsidies), while workers and small landholders had a common interest in social reform and income redistribution. We can therefore date the Danish worker-peasant alliance, in embryonic form, back to the turn of the century.

The Danish Social Democratic party grew very rapidly, and its strength first became evident in local government. By 1917 the party held a majority in the Copenhagen city council and was strong in several other cities. This allowed the party to pursue many of its social objectives at the local level and may have helped strengthen the party's commitment to a parliamentary, reformist strategy. Unlike the Germans and Austrians, however, the Danish socialists managed to penetrate beyond their urban enclaves.

Nineteen thirteen was a decisive year for social democracy. For the first time, the party's vote surpassed that of the liberals. With almost 30 percent of the vote, the social democrats could no longer remain politically excluded. Cabinet representation was already a fact during the extraordinary circumstances of World War I, when the party decided to permit its leader, Thorvald Stauning, to assume a post in a radical-liberal war government. In fact, only a very small fraction of the party saw anything problematic about participating in the "bourgeois" state.

All four of Denmark's political parties sought electoral power by erecting strong organizational machines around their natural class bases. The term "ghetto party" applies not only to the social democrats but just as well to the conservatives and the liberals. All three tried to get a competitive edge in the race for parliamentary majorities by linking social or cultural organizations to the party. The conservatives, whose base was urban professionals, civil servants, and businessmen, maintained informal ties with employer organizations, various patriotic and cultural associations, as well as youth organizations and athletic clubs. The liberals likewise built an organizational kingdom around agrarian organizations, rural cooperatives, and the folk high schools; considerable energies were devoted to the development of rural social clubs.

But the social democrats clearly outdistanced the rest. This was the period in which the triumvirate of trade unionism, cooperatives, and party organization was consolidated. In the poverty of working-class social and cultural life of the day, the party saw an opportunity to overtake the conservatives. The party press was, for a short period, one of the largest circulating dailies in Denmark. Organization proved a sound investment, yielding large returns in electoral mobilization and party membership.

By the end of World War I, the parties had divided up the population among themselves. Shifts in their relative strength were therefore largely a function of increased political participation and shifts in the class structure, at least until the realignment of the 1930s. The social democrats were the main beneficiaries of this system, especially because there was virtually no leftist opposition. Syndicalism never played a significant role, and the communist splinter group that surfaced after the Russian Revolution failed to attract significant sections of the working class. (The Danish Communist party would enjoy some growth during the high-unemployment years of the 1930s—peaking in 1939 with 2.4 percent of the vote—but the social democrats' crisis strategy in those years effectively limited the drift of the unemployed toward the communist camp.) After 1918 the social democratic ascendance continued. In the 1920 election the party received 33 percent of the vote, and in 1924 the historic moment came when, garnering 36.6 percent of the vote, the party was able to form its first minority government (with Stauning as prime minister). There was surprisingly little hesitation within the leadership to commit the party to government responsibility in the absence of a parliamentary majority. During the next two years in office, the social democrats were eager to demonstrate their capacity to be responsible and competent. Evidently the party saw this as a steppingstone to future electoral success, not as an opportunity for socialist experimentation.[7]

A hallmark of the Danish social democratic movement is its disregard for ideology and theory. It did, however, have an outstanding theoretician in Gustav Bang, who (like the Austro-Marxists) sought to establish an "organic relationship between reformist work and revolutionary goals." But Bang was peripheral among his contemporaries and forgotten by later socialists (Togeby 1968, 107). Neither ideological, strategic, nor tactical questions managed to divide the party. If anything, the arrival of the communists only strengthened the social democrats' solid pragmatism and quest for respectability. The overriding internal cleavage was between the unskilled workers and the dominant, skilled sections of the union movement and the party.

Ousted from office in 1926, the social democrats returned again in 1929 and, until 1940, governed in coalition with the radicals. With the onset of the Great Depression, the Danish social democrats pioneered the Scandinavia-wide political coalition of workers and farmers. In return for promises of agricultural subsidies and trade union wage restraint, both the radical liberals (representing the more leftist

[7] "Historical compromise" was hardly the issue for Danish social democrats, as the following 1919 editorial statement from the party organ, *Socialdemokraten*, reveals: "We have always fought the pseudoradicalism that tries to persuade workers that it is possible to transform the world overnight from hell to paradise. We have . . . distanced ourselves from a certain theoretical radicalism in the German Social Democratic party, and believe that it hesitated too long in trying to attain political influence. . . . [Its problem is] that it has failed to follow the Scandinavian strategy consistently, and at an early date: namely, a firm collaboration between industrial, cooperative, and political action, a healthy harmony of theory and practice, a belief in the ideals of socialism combined with a realistic assessment of what is currently possible, and . . . indefatigable, daily work to increase the power of the people in the state [Bryld 1976, 21-22].

peasants) and the liberals (representing the larger farmers) agreed to sanction an active crisis policy under social democratic political leadership. This alliance would form the basis of a long era of Danish social democratic welfare state politics and would put an end to decades of political instability and shifting minority cabinets.

Although the social democrats' new "people's party" profile was another step toward diluting its working-class ideological image, Przworski's representational dilemma failed to assert itself. Instead of losing working-class support or fueling communist party mobilization, the social democrats in 1935 achieved their greatest election victory ever (46.6 percent of the vote) and their membership surged (Svensson 1974, 132-134). Particularly worthy of note is the fact that youth membership tripled (Dybdahl 1975, 120). Meanwhile, perhaps due to their active crisis policy and attacks on youth unemployment, the social democrats gained at communist expense.

The social democratic decision to realign must also be understood as a response to the looming specter of proto-fascist mobilization and to the fear of a domino effect from Germany. In addition to the party's new coalition strategy and policy formula, there was a redesigned ideology and program. In party rhetoric "democracy" replaced "socialism," and "the people" replaced "working class." Social democracy's 1935 campaign slogan was a patriotic "Denmark for the People," and the new party program elegantly blended appeals to peasants, farmers, small entrepreneurs, workers, and pensioners with promises of antimonopoly legislation, land redistribution, higher rural incomes, unemployment relief, public employment, education, and improved social welfare. Despite its broadened appeal and new cross-class alliance, the party's electoral base remained solidly working class, even if it did make gains among lower-strata white-collar employees and the urban petite bourgeoisie. The bulwark of the party continued to be the skilled worker, who continued to dominate both union organization and party activities.

In World War II, during the German occupation, the Danish social democrats continued to govern, although with the participation of the liberal and conservative parties. Rather than risk open confrontation, the government followed a policy of negotiation. The social democratic prime minister even acquiesced in a German demand to imprison Danish communists. It was not until 1943, when the Danish government refused to impose death sentences on saboteurs, that the break with Germany finally came. Faced with a general strike, the Germans declared a state of emergency, and the government was dismissed. The compromising position of the social democrats, in contrast to the heroic efforts of the communist-organized resistance movement, helped swing the electorate toward the communist party after the war.

SOCIAL DEMOCRATIC ASCENDANCE IN NORWAY, 1870-1945

The push for political democracy in Norway was importantly shaped by the struggle for national independence. Norway's first national constitution had established a quasi-parliamentary system—with only one house—that gave limited and indirect representation to farmers, civil servants, and the propertied classes. The cabinet was appointed and ultimately controlled by the Swedish monarch.

Swedish overlordism and the absence of a landed aristocracy meant that the popular struggle for democracy took on a peculiar form. The chief targets were Swedish rule and the civil service, which represented the Swedish king. Since civil service governance was maintained via Oslo, the struggle for independence exacerbated traditional Norwegian rural-urban divisions. There was a strong cultural dimension, as well: the civil service had its roots in the Danish upper classes (and spoke Danish), while the periphery favored the rural dialects. Of considerable importance, finally, was the homogeneity of the rural population. Since the 1814 constitution had been designed to ensure underrepresentation of the rural areas, a basic revolutionary goal was the elimination of Swedish monarchical control over the cabinet and the institution of a representational parliamentary system. This was achieved in 1884, and Norway became the first Nordic country to introduce a modern parliamentary system. Universal male suffrage followed in 1898, and in 1913 the vote was extended to women.

The conflict over parliamentarism, Swedish sovereignty, and the civil service gave rise to a party system somewhat analogous to the Danish. Farmers and peasants organized behind the liberal Venstre party, while the civil servants and nascent bourgeoisie organized the conservative Højre. The period after 1884 was dominated by the liberals and the conservatives, since the social democratic labor party was formed only in 1887 and did not amount to much until after 1905.

The Venstre had, during the struggle for democracy, united its farmer constituency with urban progressive-liberals. After 1884, the party was increasingly torn from within over questions of urban liberalism versus rural Christian fundamentalism. Although the liberals maintained government control until 1918, they suffered several internal splits in the process.[8] Significantly, these splinter groups leaned toward

---

[8] The first such had occurred in 1888 with the formation of a moderate-liberal party,

the conservative party. This helps explain why the liberals coalesced with the rising social democrats. During the early years, the social democrats supported liberal candidates for parliament, and the liberals embraced social reform. The political strength of the liberal party reached its highest point in 1905, when Norway attained full national independence.

Although the DNA has its roots in the mid-nineteenth-century social movements, one can hardly speak of an urban working class until the turn of the century. Thus, when the party was formally constituted, in 1887, it was very weak. Whereas the Danish party had already gained parliamentary representation by the 1880s, in Norway the party had to wait until 1903. Not until after 1905 did the Norwegian party begin to grow, winning 16 percent of the vote in 1906 and 32 percent in 1915.

Until 1918, the social democrats were a parliamentarist party with a pragmatic, reformist program. By 1919, however, the party had joined the Comintern and was espousing a radical revolutionary program and an extraparliamentary strategy. This sudden transformation may be attributed to a couple of factors. One has to do with the electoral system, which until 1920 was based on single-member constituencies and which heavily overrepresented the largest parties. Thus, despite large electoral gains in both 1906 and in 1915, the social democrats did not achieve commensurate representation in parliament. This did not encourage faith in the parliamentary system and helped win the leadership over to the Leninist view of the bourgeois state. A second factor is the unusually powerful syndicalist influence in the Norwegian labor movement following the 1909 strike. The revolutionary momentum in the movement was given a decisive boost with the 1911 Trondheim Resolution and the subsequent syndicalist opposition movement, led by Martin Tranmael, a journalist who held a powerful position in the West Norwegian party organization. If the syndicalist opposition at first focused its attacks on the centralization of the trade union movement, it soon managed to capture both the unions and the party. With the Russian Revolution of 1917, Tranmael's movement gained de facto control of the party. At the 1918 party congress, a majority—if a somewhat narrow one—voted to transform the party into a revolutionary party of class struggle, dedicated to the task of opposing the bourgeois state and replacing it with

---

which soon thereafter merged with the conservatives. The second took place in 1909, when a libertarian faction broke off, only to disappear in the 1920s. The most decisive split occurred in 1920, when the farmers' organization, in reaction against the leftist drift of the party, formed an agrarian party.

workers' and soldiers' soviets (Elvander 1980, 42). The party affiliated with the Comintern in 1919, and a few years later its reformist wing split off and constituted a separate social democratic party.

For a couple of years, the DNA was committed to extraparliamentary action and managed, for a brief period, to establish an extensive system of workers' councils that included more than 60,000 workers in some two hundred councils (Elvander 1980, 43). Yet the DNA was not a content Comintern member and left it in 1923, when Tranmael and others rejected the principle of democratic centralism. When the DNA departed, a small faction remained and formed a separate communist party. These events, however, did not wholly change the party's attitude toward revolution, even though in practice it increasingly adhered to the rules of the parliamentary game. In 1927, the DNA was reunited with the reformist social democrats and a substantial electoral victory was achieved in that year (37 percent of the vote). This reunification, engineered by the trade union leadership, also helped reestablish a strong working relationship between the party and the LO.

Despite its continued adherence to revolution, the party was oddly enough called upon to form a government shortly after the 1927 elections. The experience was a classic example of the contradiction between revolutionary ambitions and minority parliamentarism. The party proposed a straightforward program for the socialization of the means of production and, as promise became action, the bourgeoisie responded with massive capital flight. With the financial system close to collapse, the government was able to last only two weeks before it was ousted by a concerted bourgeois-party vote of nonconfidence.

As the social democratic party grew and radicalized after 1918, the political system became extremely volatile. The old two-party system of conservatives and liberals had obviously broken down. The 1918 elections gave each party roughly one-third of the vote, but the two bourgeois parties were unable to form a coalition. The problem of mobilizing workable parliamentary majorities was additionally hampered by the introduction, in 1920, of proportional representation. This made it possible for a separate agrarian party to break with the liberals and mobilize its own electorate.

Since the formation of coalition governments was impossible, the 1920s witnessed a long string of weak and unstable minority governments, led either by the conservatives or the liberals, except for the two-week intermezzo of social democratic rule. The left was fragmented as was the right, and this fragmentation mirrored the class organizations. The DNA represented the trade unions, the rising agrarian party represented the farmers' organization, and the conservative party represented employer organizations and civil servants. The once-powerful liberal party decayed as a consequence of its lack of a clear class-organizational base. Its constituency was a hybrid of Christian fundamentalist movements, temperance organizations, and nationalists.

In the 1930 elections, a now-united DNA repeated its mistake of 1927 and campaigned on a revolutionary platform. This provoked fierce and concerted opposition from the three nonsocialist parties and, despite a record electoral turnout, the social democrats lost. The defeat helped strengthen the party's reformist wing, and in the period from 1930 to 1933, the DNA moved rapidly from revolution to reform. The rise of Nazi sympathies among farmers and in the conservative party, combined with the establishment of Quisling's Nazi party, helped to accelerate the DNA's transformation. Following the lead of its Danish counterpart, the DNA began to develop a crisis policy: employment creation, welfare reform, and subsidies to the farmers. In the 1933 elections the party achieved a major victory, getting 40 percent of the vote while the communist share dropped to only 2 percent. Two years later, the party, having succeeded in winning over the agrarians to its crisis policy, formed a government with the first parliamentary majority since 1918. As in Denmark, then, a farmer-working-class alliance gave rise to a social democratic realignment.

The experience of World War II had a peculiar impact on Norwegian politics. Unlike the government of Denmark, the DNA government did not immediately capitulate to the German occupation forces. After the military defeat, king and government went into exile in London. The Germans disbanded all political parties, installed Quisling as prime minister, and initiated an intense drive to Nazify Norwegian society. Several social democratic and, of course, communist leaders were interned in concentration camps. Thus, the Norwegian social democrats could later benefit politically from their more heroic resistance and suffering during the occupation.

While the communist party of Norway did enjoy postwar popularity, the DNA scored an electoral victory that gave it an absolute majority in parliament.[9] A much more important consequence of the war was the DNA's experience in exile. In anticipation of national liberation, the social democrats began in 1944 to prepare a compre-

[9] The NKP received almost 12 percent of the vote in the 1945 elections; the DNA, 41 percent. For the DNA this was actually a slight decline, but because the electoral system tended to favor the largest parties, the DNA managed to gain a majority voice in parliament.

hensive, long-range political program for the postwar period. Including a commitment to both economic planning and welfare state development, the program was cosigned by representatives of all the nonsocialist parties. This implied an end to the prewar state of political polarization and a significant amount of consensus in the formation of postwar policies.

SOCIAL DEMOCRATIC ASCENDANCE IN SWEDEN, 1870-1945

The rise of social democracy in Sweden was perhaps not quite so dramatic as it was in Norway, but neither was it so subdued as in Denmark. Initial mobilization in the Swedish case was constrained by a drawn-out battle for full democracy. As in Denmark and Norway, the power of the nobility had been curtailed at a rather early date, and an independent peasantry had managed to assert itself economically and politically.

Absolutism was formally abolished with the 1866 constitution, which gave Sweden a bicameral parliament much like the Danish one. The constitution granted limited representation on the basis of property qualifications, but with such latitude that well-to-do farmers and urban bourgeoisie could hold a majority in the lower house. The upper house remained under the control of the king and the nobility. The Swedish state was more authoritarian and paternalistic than that of the neighbor countries, but Swedish governments were usually hospitable to expressions of civil liberty and popular demands, and few instances of political repression occurred. As Tilton (1974) has argued, state power could not easily be employed by reactionary groups for repressive purposes.

Yet, the struggle for universal suffrage and representative parliamentary rule was slow to succeed. For one thing, Swedish society did not give rise to a large and liberal-minded class of farmers and urban bourgeoisie. The latter typically favored a paternalistic state, and the former were too weak, economically or politically, to demand constitutional reform on their own. The rising labor movement, therefore, came to play a decisive role in the process of democratization after the turn of the century. The conservatives managed to control parliament until universal suffrage and parliamentarism were finally won in 1918, even if in 1909 political rights were extended to a larger proportion of small landholders and wage earners.

After the turn of the century, the liberals as well as the social democrats grew rapidly, partly because of suffrage extensions and partly because the working class itself was growing at great speed. A loose alliance for political and social reform was formed, and the 1911 elections gave the two parties a majority in the lower house; thus a liberal government was formed, albeit with continued conservative control of the upper house. Only three years later, however, with royal intervention, the government was forced to resign over the question of military mobilization. After World War I, the question of parliamentary reform exploded once again, sparked by general economic crisis and by a political scandal that incriminated the conservatives. Once again refusing to support increased military outlays, the liberals and social democrats demanded that the conservatives step down. Faced by a possibly revolutionary situation and mass demonstrations, the king threatened to intervene on behalf of the conservatives. However, confrontation was averted as leading industrialists and sections of the conservative party, fearing a repetition of the Russian situation, acceded to the demands for full parliamentarism. A liberal government with social democratic participation was reinstalled, and the lingering restrictions on parliamentarism and universal suffrage were eliminated. The foregoing events are a good illustration of the nature of political conflict in Sweden. Confrontations were somewhat sharper than in Denmark, in large measure because of the absence of a powerful liberal influence.

The first political parties emerged with the 1866 constitution. In 1867, the farmers formed the Lantmannapartiet, basically a liberal parliamentary group, and a conservative analogue emerged soon afterward. It was not, however, until the Swedish Social Democratic party was formed, in 1889, that permanent, national party organizations emerged. The liberals formed a party in 1902; the conservatives, in 1904. Aside from the issue of democratization, the main conflict during the nineteenth century had to do with the question of tariffs and protectionism. In comparison with their Danish counterparts, Sweden's liberals were too weak to counter the conservative demand for heavy protectionism.

The social democratic party was established by trade unionists with the aid of Danish socialists. As in Denmark, skilled workers and craftsmen dominated, although under the leadership of Hjalmar Branting, an academic, the Swedish party became more theoretical. Branting was elected to parliament on a liberal ticket in 1897, and in 1898 the party was reorganized into separate political and trade union branches. The SAP did not really grow, however, until a decade into the twentieth century. In 1905, the party managed to send thirteen representatives to parliament, and from then on the pace of electoral mobilization was very rapid. In 1914, the SAP received more than 36 percent of the vote, and by 1917 it was the single largest party in Sweden, with 39 percent of the vote.

The period of liberal political dominance in Sweden, compared with that in Denmark, was short. After 1917, the conservative party began to recuperate, and the liberal party entered a long decline. On one side, the liberals lost ground to the newly founded agrarian party; on the other, it lost to the social democrats. The 1920s were politically unstable, and no party (or party coalition) was able to form a majority government. As in Norway, weak minority governments came and went. Among the three nonsocialist parties, the conservatives remained the strongest; but deep antagonisms prevented them from forming parliamentary alliances, except in cases where they attacked the social democrats, such as in the 1928 election campaign. In 1917, the SAP had suffered a slight setback when a left-socialist splinter group broke with the party, two years later to become the Swedish Communist party. Though the Swedish communists were moderately stronger than their Nordic comrades during the 1920s and 1930s, they never threatened the SAP's dominance.

During the turbulent 1920s, the social democrats failed to clarify fully their programmatic position. Although the union movement had achieved organizational autonomy from the party, and had tried to assert its more "economistic" demands, the party had difficulty choosing between revolution and reform. Granted, it was genuinely committed to parliamentarism, and its main emphasis was on immediate and practical reforms. Yet, the Swedish party was not reconciled to the dilemma of taking office without an absolute majority, and it continued to take programmatic promises of socialization more seriously than the Danish party. The SAP, then, was a party hovering between the Danish and the Norwegian option. Its unusually strong theoretical and ideological tradition may, paradoxically, help explain both its continued radicalism and its eventual resignation to gradual reformism.

Under Branting's leadership, the SAP nurtured a school of younger theoretical talent, such as Ernst Wigforss, Nils Karleby, and Gustav Möller. Later, when the party moved in a more pragmatic direction, the sophisticated and frequently heated theoretical debates within the party lent a vitality that was absent in either Denmark or Norway. This helps explain why the SAP avoided losses to the left as it gradually moved toward pragmatic social reformism. These thinkers, Wigforss especially, were also instrumental in shaping the party's political profile for many decades to come. They managed to eradicate remnants of Marxist orthodoxy, such as the thesis of immiseration and impending

84

capitalist collapse, while simultaneously portraying the party as a movement for socialist transformation (Tingsten 1941).

SAP fortunes wavered during the 1920s. In 1920, and again in 1928, the party went to the electorate with a promise of socializing wealth, a program drafted by Wigforss. Both times it suffered electoral setbacks, as the bourgeois parties mobilized a strong counteroffensive. Concomitantly, Wigforss proposed laws on workers' councils and industrial democracy, but these failed to resonate within the LO (Elvander 1980, 88). Apart from such radical policies, the party was quite confused on matters of immediate relevance, such as the burning question of unemployment. One objective of overriding importance was to reform, on behalf of the trade unions, the state's role in labor market conflicts. As in Norway, the trade unions had suffered a major defeat in the 1909 general conflict, and existing legislation as well as government practice placed restrictions on the trade unions' freedom of action. Thus, even if electorally stronger, the Swedish social democrats were structurally in a weak position, since they had no natural coalition partners.

The five-party system that evolved after 1918 did not lend itself to either bourgeois or social democratic alliances. The right was indeed split, but none of the three bourgeois parties could be counted upon to support social democracy. The liberal party, the most likely candidate in the center, was electorally squeezed between the agrarians and the conservatives, and the agrarians harbored a deep distrust, if not antagonism, toward both the trade union movement and the SAP. As Stjernquist (1966, 121) argues, the social democrats' continued adherence to radical socialization was a source of sharp ideological opposition between the socialists and the bourgeois parties. If, in this period, the social democrats were unable to exert significant political influence, their political exclusion may in the longer run have been an asset. They were saved from having to compromise their politics while still electorally weak. Given the absence of social and economic reforms during the long era of minority governments, the SAP was also in an opportune position when, once in power during the 1930s, it could push through a host of significant legislative changes. Most important, the SAP was not in office when the depression generated massive unemployment.

The Swedish party system became an ideal model in respect of class-organizational penetration. Within the labor movement, the typical Scandinavian pattern of a tripartite union, cooperative, and party organization came to prevail. If initially the Swedish LO was weak, its subsequent growth would make it the strongest in the West. The cooperative movement also became larger and more influential than that in either Denmark or Norway. In addition, the party—because of collective membership and strong local organizations—became an empire in its own right. Thus, the SAP came to command resources for electoral mobilization and organizational dominance that are unparalleled elsewhere.

Among the bourgeois parties, only the liberals lack any powerful link to major interest organizations, and this helps explain the inability of the liberals to mobilize effectively. Like its Norwegian counterpart, the Swedish Liberal party is a hybrid of temperance movements, intellectuals, and white-collar groups. The agrarians count primarily on farmer organizations for support, and the conservatives represent the uniquely well organized and centralized Swedish business interests. There are two important reasons why, in Sweden, the emphasis on building organizational power has been so accentuated. One is Sweden's geographically dispersed population, which makes it necessary to coordinate interests and activities across a huge area. The other is the longstanding tradition of state centralism, which places a premium on well-articulated organizational penetration of and participation in bureaucratic and executive decisionmaking.[10]

After the electoral defeat of 1928, the social democrats began more explicitly to move in the direction of pragmatic reformism. Per Albin Hansson, with his notion of the "people's home," stressed the importance of mobilizing a broader electoral base and, under pressure from the LO and the working-class electorate, perceived the need for an active crisis strategy against rising unemployment. As both Tingsten (1941) and Lewin (1967) argue, the arrival of economic crisis in the 1930s was not interpreted as an opportunity for revolutionary tactics, but as an instance in which the labor movement would be seriously weakened unless it could provide immediate relief. Also, a double fear—of fascism on the right and communism on the left—propelled the social democrats toward political realignment.

Under conditions of mass unemployment, the SAP won a major victory in the 1932 elections, garnering almost 42 percent of the vote, and proceeded to take office (although without a parliamentary majority). Both the liberals and the conservatives suffered heavy losses and a dramatic drop in popular legitimacy. As the population swiftly lost confidence in the principles of budgetary orthodoxy, the liberals

[10] As early as 1913, the still very small SAP managed to have considerable influence on pension legislation because the party leader, Hjalmar Branting, was represented in the government commission that prepared pension legislation. In fact, the 1913 pension reform reflects Branting's idea of universal coverage (Elmer 1960).

and conservatives were held accountable for the worsening economic situation. On top of that, their popularity was strained by their association with a financial crash and with military suppression of a labor strike in Ådalen.

The social democrats proceeded to draft a crisis policy as well as social welfare legislation, notably unemployment insurance. The chief architects were Wigforss and Möller.[11] However, without a majority and refusing to admit the communists, the SAP was compelled to forge a parliamentary alliance with the right. Collaboration with the liberals was out of the question because of their entrenched commitment to austerity policies. The only remaining possibility, the agrarians, appeared at first to be unlikely candidates. As in Norway, the farmers were somewhat attracted to fascism and, at any rate, the agrarian party was violently opposed to trade unionism and social welfare legislation for workers; however, the SAP and the agrarians did have in common a disbelief in liberal orthodoxy. When the social democrats promised to legislate price supports for farmers, therefore, the agrarians agreed to support the SAP's deficit-financed employment programs and welfare legislation. By 1933, Swedish social democracy had entered the era of a farmer-worker political alliance.

Although the real economic impact of the SAP's crisis policies may have been marginal, their political effect was extraordinary. The SAP reaped a great electoral victory in the 1936 elections, while weakening both the communists and the conservatives. With the SAP government and the resolution of labor market relations in the 1938 Saltsjöbaden Agreement came an end to chronic industrial conflict. The labor movement as a whole could now bargain directly—from a position of strength—with the employer organizations and the conservatives to reach mutually acceptable terms for economic and social legislation, economic planning, and the conditions for structural economic change. The labor movement had at last officially recognized the rights of private property ownership in exchange for an assurance that conservative forces would remain loyal to democratic procedure and accept social democratic reforms. In this sense, the 1930s mark a social democratic "historical compromise."

The crisis policies were perhaps not spectacular from a theoretical point of view. Gradually, though, they were amended with ideas of economic planning, developed by members of the famous Stockholm

---

[11] Their analysis and proposals were reprinted in English during the 1930s. See Wigforss (1938, 25-39) and Möller (1938, 47-71).

School of Economics, such as Gunnar Myrdal. These ideas would play a central role in the SAP's postwar program of 1944.

The wartime experience of the Swedish social democrats was quite unlike that of their Scandinavian brethren. Most important, of course, was the circumstance that Sweden managed to remain neutral and avoid German occupation. The SAP admitted the other parties in a joint wartime cabinet, and a major source of tension was whether to concede to German demands and allow a transfer of troops and weapons across Swedish territory (between the Norwegian and the Finnish front). The SAP leadership eventually gave in, meeting with bitter criticism from abroad as well as at home. An additional source of tension was Sweden's continued wartime export of vital resources—such as timber and metals—to Nazi Germany. In 1943, when the German armies were in obvious retreat, the Swedish government finally decided to bring a halt both to German transits and to Swedish exports to Germany.

In the 1944 elections, the social democrats retained, and even increased, their share of the vote from 1936.[12] The communists, however, made important gains, if not so dramatic as those in Denmark. The SAP emerged from the war, then, not so compromised as its Danish counterpart, but also not so heroically as the Norwegian party.

POSTWAR SOCIAL DEMOCRACY

Following quite different paths, the three Nordic social democracies emerged from the 1930s with a convergent politics based on similar alliances with the peasantry that, in turn, permitted Keynesian full-employment policies and social reform. Thus, decades of social democratic hegemony were ensured in a context of political stability. It is this realignment, above all, that has made Scandinavian social democracy internationally unique and given it a degree of power unmatched elsewhere. Few countries can boast such a well-organized and politically articulate peasantry committed to democracy, and those characteristics are certainly essential to the peasantry's ability to forge a mutually favorable policy agreement with labor. In brief, the character of the Nordic peasantry offers the most convincing explanation of why Scandinavian social democracy has succeeded to such an extent, why the Nordic countries pioneered model welfare states and, ultimately, why these three countries came to converge politically.

[12] In the unusual 1940 election, the SAP scored an astounding 53.8 percent of the vote. In 1944, its share was 46.7 percent, compared with 45.9 percent in 1936.

On the basis of the political realignment, the social democrats managed successfully to marginalize their leftist and rightist foes. By shifting the "Downesian center" to social democracy, they also compelled the bourgeois parties to embrace social democratic policies and programs. In this sense, the 1950s and 1960s would appear to confirm Kirschheimer's (1968) theory of a "waning of oppositions." In large part due to the requirements of maintaining a farmer alliance, the 1950s were years of exceptionally bland and uncertain social democratic ideology. As the coalition eventually began to crumble by the 1960s, we witness a new radicalization and ideological renewal.

One should not, however, exaggerate the degree of Nordic convergence. The three social democratic movements have differed importantly in their capacity to consolidate and exercise power. The parties' abilities to reap political dividends from pioneering socioeconomic reforms have been quite divergent and, in fact, are the chief reason why the various parties have experienced such diverse fates in recent years. As Elvander (1980) points out, the Swedes and Norwegians were better positioned than the Danes. In Denmark, important reforms were already in place prior to the war and, besides, the Danish social democrats were less able to push through crucial reforms during the 1940s and 1950s. The balance of political forces constitutes another area of divergence. In Sweden, the bourgeois parties remained particularly weak and divided during the postwar era; in Norway, political consensus helped blunt any possible social democratic distinctions, even if the DNA did remain extraordinarily powerful for decades; and in Denmark, the social democrats were consistently weaker and more subordinate to the political hegemony of liberal farmers.

The fate of postwar social democracy has in all three cases been crucially decided by the party's ability to meet a series of new political challenges. The first such, and perhaps also the foremost, was class structural change. A population decline among farmers and peasants, combined with rapid white-collar growth, has compelled the parties to seek a new political realignment. Just as the social democrats had portrayed themselves as class parties prior to the 1930s and as people's parties thereafter, they were pressed in the 1960s to recast their image as wage-earner parties, in order to align with the new middle strata once the farmer coalition had been doomed. The three social democracies differ importantly in their capacity to forge this new wage-earner alliance, and this constitutes a major reason that the three parties have fared so differently in the 1970s and 1980s. A second challenge began to emerge during the late 1960s as the postwar full-employment, welfare state model became economically strained and politically exhausted. Social democracy's power to recast its policies is intimately linked to its capacity for political realignment. In both instances, the Swedish social democrats have been more successful and, consequently, have avoided serious decomposition. Yet, nowhere in Scandinavia has social democracy been entirely able to stem the tide of political instability and electoral stagnation. The parties' hold on voters has weakened with the rise of new, crosscutting political problems: Danish and Norwegian entry in the EEC, environmental questions, and nuclear power issues. The electorate is not only more volatile but more polarized, and Danish social democracy in particular has found itself squeezed between right and left.

The postwar decades have truly been the "era of social democracy." Electorally, however, the parties have hardly managed to increase their support beyond the levels attained during the 1930s. With only minor fluctuations, their average parliamentary strength has remained rather stable. Hence, the postwar electoral success of social democracy has consisted largely of holding onto prewar gains. All three parties began to experience stagnation and decline during the 1970s, but Denmark is unique in the degree to which social democracy is decomposing. After the following account of social democracy in the context of postwar political development, we shall proceed in Chapter 4 to examine empirical data on the variations in social democratic party decomposition in Scandinavia.

DANISH SOCIAL DEMOCRACY IN THE POSTWAR ERA

The Danish social democrats have never been able to match the level of electoral power they achieved in 1935, but they have held office, in minority or coalition, throughout most of the postwar period. The first test came as soon as Denmark had been liberated from the Germans, in 1945. The communist party was both powerful and popular, owing to its heroic participation in the resistance movement as well as popular admiration for the achievements of the Red Army.

The social democrats pursued a two-pronged tactic to weaken the communist challenge. One was to radicalize their own program; the other was to open discussion on the possibility of merging the two parties. The new 1945 program, *Fremtidens Danmark* [The Future of Denmark], was directly influenced by the Swedish social democrats' postwar program. It strived to co-opt the left without alienating the right. It stressed the party's Marxist ideological heritage and proclaimed the desirability of confiscating large companies, banking and insurance especially. The program called for a commitment to Keynesian countercyclical policies on behalf of the "common good," promising to democratize private enterprise with a mixture of factory- and industrywide councils and central government planning. These promises may have been intended as a radicalization of party program, but their significance was small: most of the program concentrates on short-term administrative issues, such as postwar normalization, rationing, physical controls, and restoration of economic competitiveness.

With respect to the other tactic—to work toward amalgamation of the two parties—negotiations moved quickly, because of the impending parliamentary elections, but broke down almost immediately. The social democrats asked the communists to adopt the socialist postwar program, dismantle the communist press, and merge with the social democratic party organization. In return, the communists were to get a number of "safe" constituencies and cabinet representation. The communists refused and won 12.5 percent of the vote. Consequently, the social democrats were unable to form a government.

Communist party influence dropped significantly in the following election (1947), while that of the social democrats increased. A social democratic minority government was formed, only to be replaced once again, in 1950, with a bourgeois coalition government; after 1953, the social democrats returned as a minority government. Only after 1957 were they able to form a majority government, with the radical liberals, and this coalition lasted until 1964. Thus, though the social democrats may have had some influence over governments throughout the 1950s, their position was weak and their powers were effectively circumscribed by dependence on bourgeois-party legislative support. They were chronically unable to implement major legislative goals, either social or economic, could neither bring down unemployment or shift resources toward industrial expansion, and had to concede to liberal demands for a restrictive fiscal policy and generous agricultural subsidies. Their only notable legislative accomplishment was the much-delayed universal flat-rate pension of 1956. That same year, however, the social democratic government was forced to intervene against striking workers, and this fueled broad attacks from both union leadership and the rank and file; mass demonstrations were held in front of parliament. The farmers, meanwhile, to support their demand for extended agricultural subsidies, refused to market their products. The two "strikes" became intimately linked in the public mind, and as the government conceded to the farmers' demands while legally extending existing union contracts, social democratic legitimacy within its own working-class base was seriously damaged.

These events, combined with the longer-run powerlessness of the social democrats, might have renewed communist party power had it not been for the Soviet invasion of Hungary and the social democrats' general success in blocking communist influence in the trade union movement. Nonetheless, the social democratic party did show early signs of decay. Party membership declined throughout the 1950s, especially among the young, and pensioners began to dominate the party organization.[13] Concomitantly, the party apparatus lost its vitality as meeting attendance dropped and many local branches folded. As local organizations crumbled, the national leadership chose to ignore or bypass party locals altogether, thus heightening a sense of uselessness within the party organization. Candidate nominations, for example, were made less and less by local constituent members and more and more by the national leadership. Michels' iron law was once again given empirical substance.

If the party allowed its traditional organization to crumble and "oligarchize," it also erased whatever remained of its image as a working-class party. The "affluent worker" theme of the 1950s and the visible growth of white-collar employees combined to convince party leaders that the traditional image was antiquated. Yet, while the party drifted toward end-of-ideology, catchall politics, new developments pushed the party in the opposite direction.

The post-1957 coalition with the radical liberals was sufficiently strong to overcome the opposition to active economic-stimulation policies, social reform, and income redistribution. Denmark embarked upon its "second industrial revolution": unemployment was virtually eradicated, wages climbed rapidly, and agriculture's all-powerful hold on Danish policymaking began to weaken. Yet, the social democrats faced a new kind of left-socialist challenge with the formation of the Danish Socialist People's party in 1960, a party programmatically centered on foreign policy issues, particularly membership in the North Atlantic Treaty Organization (NATO). The SF, founded by an expelled leader of the communist party, Axel Larsen, was an immediate success. It gained over 6 percent of the vote in its first election (1960) and, despite most predictions, managed to become a permanent fixture in Danish politics and a steadfast leftist challenger to social democracy. The SF's initial success was largely due to its ability to attract former

[13] According to Thomas's data (1977, 240), the percentage of pensioners among total party membership grew from 5.6 percent in 1950 to 20 percent in 1963. By the early 1970s pensioners constituted 50 percent of the Copenhagen party membership (information provided to me by Ejnar Jørgensen, district representative and member of the party's national executive committee).

communists, but it also attracted dissatisfied social democrats, particularly among the young, who rejected NATO membership and opposed nuclear weapons on Danish soil.[14]

Immediately prior to the 1960 elections, the social democrats had entered into a new agreement with the bourgeois parties on the future of Danish defense and on the continuation of NATO membership, despite pervasive anti-NATO sentiment among the electorate. The SF, apart from its foreign policy position, included in its first congress protocol (1963) the explicit goal of pushing the social democrats to the left and forcing them to return to an agenda of democratic socialism. The intent was to mobilize a left-wing opposition that would force the social democrats to abandon their bourgeois-party alliances and enter a truly socialist coalition.

The social democratic party was not particularly successful in stemming the influence of the SF. The first response of the social democratic leadership was outright hostility. The SF was accused of being a communist party in disguise, attempting demagogically to divide the working-class movement. The social democratic leader, Jens Otto Krag, stated on several occasions during the early 1960s that, under no circumstances whatsoever would he entertain the possibility of collaboration with the SF. Yet, this tactical approach began to boomerang as social democratic policies prompted deep divisions among traditional voters. The SF became a force to be reckoned with.

The first real possibility of collaboration presented itself in the 1964 election, during which the radical liberals decided to leave the government coalition. Yet the social democrats chose to continue as a minority government. After 1964, the most important issues concerned domestic policy, housing reform in particular. The social democrats had initially proposed a reform that stressed egalitarianism but, rather than risk legislation with SF support, they chose instead to forge a broad compromise with the right, thereby seriously eroding the egalitarian thrust of the reform. The SF launched a virulent attack on the social democratic "sellout," arguing that it would not only give disproportionate benefits to homeowners, but would also invite heavy speculation in real estate.[15] The consequences of this political battle were dramatic. In the following municipal elections, the social democrats suffered heavy losses to the SF; in the 1966 national elections,

[14] Logue (1975, 278) reports that 41 percent of SF members surveyed in 1974 stressed the NATO issue as their main reason for joining.
[15] For a detailed account of housing policies, see Chapter 6.

the SF's vote doubled to 10 percent while the social democrats lost ground.

The political situation after the 1966 election was precarious. On one side, the radical liberals transferred their allegiance to the bourgeois parties; on the other, a social democratic majority became contingent on SF support. Krag, noted for his position that "one will insist on a point of view only until one adopts another," was proved right by events. Krag soon came under pressure from within the party as well as from the union movement to enter into negotiations with the SF about possible cabinet collaboration. The Danish social democrats were at a historical crossroads where, for the first time, a pure socialist government was a possibility.

The two parties could easily agree on matters of domestic policy, but the negotiations turned sour when the social democrats refused to reconsider either their allegiance to NATO or the 1960 defense agreement. A formal alliance was therefore ruled out. Yet, it was agreed that the SF would lend ad hoc support to a minority social democratic cabinet. Shortly thereafter, the two parties established an informal joint consultative committee in parliament. The right immediately seized the opportunity, claiming that the arrangement was a covert strategy for creeping socialism and dubbing it the "Red Cabinet." As it turned out, the Red Cabinet lasted only thirteen months and produced little legislation on which the bourgeois parties could not also agree (Damgaard and Rusk 1976, 179ff). It collapsed when a splinter group broke with the SF and formed the Danish Left-Socialist party (VS). Elections were called in 1968, the result of which was a devastating loss to both the SF and the social democratic party. The SF lost almost half its vote from 1966, and the social democrats lost 4 percent.

The saga of the Danish social democrats during the 1960s gives dramatic evidence of the electoral dilemma described by Przworski. The rapid rise of the SF indicated that a large percentage of voters, the young particularly, were disenchanted with bland reformism and compromise with the right. Moreover, the SF was not merely a single-issue party, capable of attracting a marginal element of the young, but was clearly successful among working-class voters. The social democrats were therefore forced to rethink their politics, and from the mid-1960s on they began to address themselves to the threat from the left. If the Red Cabinet experiment was one attempt, a radicalization occurred in other areas, too. In 1969, the social democrats introduced a plan for a fundamental reorganization of the party, placing greater emphasis on participatory democracy and grass-roots activism. That same year, the party presented a program revision, *Det Nye Samfund* [The New Society], that promoted ideas of economic democracy, worker participation in industry, greater public control of savings and investments, active manpower policies, more social housing and, above all, more equality. But, the attempt to move left provoked losses to the right and, even more important, helped unify the traditionally divided bourgeois parties against social democracy. The room for social democratic maneuver therefore remained narrow.

The 1968 election did not mark an unequivocal shift to the right, since SF losses benefited the extreme left as well. It is possible to speak of embryonic polarization and a new volatility among the electorate. The election produced a bourgeois coalition government under a radical-liberal leadership devoted primarily to a program for halting the rapid growth of public expenditure and taxation. This government lasted almost the full four-year term but failed utterly to slow the rate of state expenditure growth. In fact, taxes and spending grew faster than ever. In 1971, when it became clear that the LO would refuse to participate in legislated wage restraint, the government resigned.

Until 1971, the increasing electoral volatility and polarization cannot be ascribed to the advent of fundamentally new political issues. Rather, these were the first manifestations of social democratic demobilization. The party had proved itself incapable of maintaining cohesion on the left when it collaborated with the right. Yet, when it moved to recapture its dissident left, it lost on the right. The underlying problem is that the party presides over an internally divided base, in the trade union movement and in the electorate. A major source of disaggregation after the mid-1960s was party policy itself, especially the 1965-1966 housing agreement. But these issues will be analyzed in subsequent chapters. The point is that, until the 1970s, electoral disaffection was linked primarily to social democracy's performance on traditional left-right issues. After 1971, the trend toward disaggregation, volatility, polarization, and social democratic party decline becomes manifest and explosive with the arrival of new issues.

The 1971 election restored the position of both the SF and the social democratic party, and tacit collaboration between the two was resumed with the formation of a social democratic minority government. It proved to be one of the most tumultuous in modern Danish history. The overriding issue was Danish membership in the Common Market. The social democrats had, chiefly out of economic necessity, backed Danish entry for more than a decade. Denmark's exports were increasingly directed toward EEC nations and, with prospects of British entry, Danish agriculture claimed it could not survive unless Denmark also joined. The issue split the electorate across traditional party lines. The left in general, but especially the SF, formed an unholy alliance with conservative nationalistic forces that opposed entry; the social democrats allied with the major bourgeois parties on a proentry platform. But the social democratic leadership faced violent opposition both from within the party and from important sectors of the trade union movement—especially from unskilled workers. The party was now internally polarized and, to avoid an irreconcilable split, decided to relax internal discipline and allow members to express their independent views in public. As a result, the spectacle of internal party strife became increasingly chaotic as the public referendum approached. In Denmark, unlike Norway, the referendum passed with a majority in favor of entry.[16]

Passage of the referendum was a victory for the party leadership but a disaster for the party. Krag, the social democratic leader, immediately announced his resignation and handed over the prime minister's post to Anker Jørgensen, who in many respects embodied a potential dialectical synthesis. First of all, he was the former president of the Unskilled Workers' Federation but had nonetheless supported EEC membership. Secondly, he was considered to be on the political left and was therefore better positioned to appease left-wing defectors. Finally, his appointment signaled a desire to unify the skilled and unskilled sectors of the LO, centralize the trade union movement, and thereby facilitate labor movement cohesion.

The dialectics failed to work. For one thing, the EEC issue did not disappear, and the old rifts continued to plague Danish political life; the social democratic party had difficulty regaining its legitimacy among the anti-EEC electorate. But other events also conspired to block reunification and reconsolidation. In 1973, urged on by the SF, the social democratic government prepared a new housing bill explicitly designed to redress the inequities of the ill-fated 1965 bill and to recapture the loyalties of renters. The 1965 bill, however, had already created a large working-class clientele wedded to the tax privileges of homeownership. Hence, the new move only exacerbated existing divisions. Led by a right-wing social democratic member of parliament, a splinter group formed its own organization, the Danish Center Democratic party, opposed to higher homeowner taxes specifically and left-wing

[16] The anti-EEC forces called for greater Nordic economic and political unity as an alternative to EEC membership. Negotiations among the Scandinavian countries on the formation of a Nordic Common Market had, however, run aground in 1969-1970.

social democracy generally.[17] This was the first social democratic splinter since the formation of the communist party in 1921, and it was the first right-wing splinter in the party's entire history. The defeat of the housing bill and the breakup of the party forced the social democrats to call for elections in 1973. These came to be known as the Catastrophe Elections.

The remarkable outcome of the 1973 elections can be understood only in the light of political events during the preceding years. After Danish entry into the EEC, farmer incomes improved markedly; as subsidies were eliminated, agricultural prices rose. Although wages also increased, food prices grew even faster and, on top of this, tax rates had climbed very rapidly over the years. The overall result was that working-class households experienced sharply rising taxes and prices while at the same time losing public benefits because of nominal income improvements. The explosion of equity conflicts was additionally dramatized by public revelations that people benefited economically by filing for divorce, going on welfare, or consciously reducing work income in order to restore their eligibility for public benefits while lowering their tax rate.

A controversial tax lawyer, Mogens Glistrup, brilliantly politicized equity resentments by announcing that he paid absolutely no taxes on his million-kroner income and by demonstrating in front of millions of television viewers how everyone could do the same. During the chaotic 1973 election campaign, he formed the new Fremskridts (Progress) party, launching a generalized attack on taxes, welfare programs, bureaucracies, paper-shuffling public employees, and the "conspiratorial politics" of the old anachronistic and professionalized parties. Glistrup's platform presented a petit-bourgeois Poujadism that had tremendous appeal among workers. He managed to exploit popular dissatisfaction over military spending by proposing that Danish defense forces be replaced by a telephone answering service that, in English and Russian, would declare Denmark to have surrendered. He succeeded in pitting workers against public employees by demanding that bureaucrats and teachers be sent out to dig ditches, and he also crystallized latent antagonisms between the employed and the welfare recipients.

These protest parties were the victors of the 1973 election, the Fremskridts party gaining almost 16 percent of the vote overnight and

[17] At LO urging, the social democrats had proposed the plan for collective wage-earner funds in 1973; this undoubtedly added to the right-wing revolt in the party. See Chapter 9 for a more detailed treatment of this issue.

the center democrats almost 8 percent. The social democratic party was decimated, losing about 12 percent. The traditional bourgeois parties (the conservatives, the liberals, and the radicals) also lost heavily. The 1973 election thus signaled the collapse of the old two-bloc pattern of Danish politics and the rise of an entirely new political-cleavage structure that pitted protest politics against the social democratic welfare state model of the previous three decades. For social democracy, this meant heavy losses among its traditional core of voters and the drift of young workers to parties expressing explicitly anti-social-democratic politics.

After 1973 eleven parties were represented in parliament, none of which could form a viable coalition or a plausibly effective minority government. The Fremskridts party was a self-styled parliamentary outcast even if it was the third largest party. Thus, no traditional party was willing, or dared, to collaborate with Glistrup. The end result was a weak, liberal minority government that lasted only until 1975, when the social democrats managed to recapture some of their previous losses with 29.9 percent of the vote. Still, the Fremskridts party retained its position, and the parliamentary situation remained virtually paralyzed. The political climate worsened with the oil crisis and a worldwide recession that hit the Danish economy harder than it hit others. In this context, the social democrats formed another feeble minority government which did not even last two years. Economic crisis and high unemployment helped strengthen the social democrats in the 1977 election, in which they gained 37 percent of the vote. Both the center democrats and the progressives, however, held on to their 1973 position, and a return to "normality" was blocked. At the same time, the left in general, but the communist party especially, experienced a new era of growth.

The social democrats tried, with very little success, to build ad hoc parliamentary coalitions for one economic-crisis package after another. On several occasions, they received LO support for drastic income-policy legislation if, in turn, they could promise legislation on economic democracy. But in every instance the bourgeois parties—and the SF—refused to go along. After the 1977 election, the social democrats tried to build a viable government by admitting the liberal party, but this served only to antagonize the trade union movement. Consequently, this experiment with a "broad unity" coalition also failed, and elections were called again in 1979. The social democrats enjoyed small gains and, for the first time, the progressives began to slip. The social democrats continued to govern, again as a minority and still without any real chance of finding support for an effective crisis policy. In the meantime, the rate of unemployment continued to increase and the economy's imbalance to worsen. In 1981, once again, the social democrats were forced to call elections when no parliamentary agreement could be reached.

The 1981 elections suggest a break with the pattern that prevailed during the 1970s. The social democrats lost rather heavily, and the SF's share of the vote jumped to 11.3 percent. On the right, the progressives lost ground again to the conservatives. The center democrats enjoyed a renaissance. In one sense, the 1981 elections signal a return to the pre-1973 cleavage structure: the Fremskridts party's role diminished, and conventional left-right politics were reestablished. Yet, as with elections elsewhere in Europe, the rise of both the SF and the conservative party signaled electoral polarization. The 1981 elections, then, have replaced fragmentation with polarization, but they have also accelerated social democracy's onward march toward decay. The party did remain in office—with tacit SF support on the left and radical-liberal support on the right—but a workable parliamentary majority, around a broadly acceptable crisis policy, was not forthcoming. The government resigned in September 1982 and was replaced by a right-center coalition led by the conservative party. This, in fact, is the first time in the twentieth century that Denmark has been led by a conservative prime minister.

Since the 1960s, when social democracy's farmer alliance began to break apart, Danish social democracy has been incapable of effective realignment. Although ad hoc attempts to collaborate with the SF were undertaken repeatedly, these have not meant realignment. Again and again the social democrats have been compelled to collaborate with one or more bourgeois parties in order to pass any major legislation. Most decisive have been social democracy's inability to forge a durable alliance of any kind with the new middle strata and its comcomitant paralysis in regard to redirecting its policies. The wave of electoral fragmentation, and now polarization, can be ascribed to this incapacity and paralysis; party decomposition is likewise associated with social democracy's failure to realign.

Norwegian Social Democracy in the Postwar Era

The Norwegian social democrats also displayed symptoms of stagnation and decomposition during the 1970s, although those symptoms were not so severe as the ones experienced by the Danes. Indeed, the Norwegian road to decomposition is a very different one from the Danish. The DNA remained unusually powerful from the 1940s until the early 1960s, when its complete monopoly on government was eventually broken. Enjoying absolute parliamentary majorities for almost twenty years, the party was therefore spared the necessity of constant compromise with the bourgeois bloc. Yet, a remarkable feature of Norwegian postwar politics is the extent to which the bourgeois parties—internally divided as in Denmark—embraced social democratic policies and programs. This pattern of left-right political "consensus" helps explain social democratic stagnation in Norway. More recently, however, the weakness of Norwegian social democracy has primarily been a function of its inability to manage explosive new issue cleavages, notably the EEC issue, as well as its imprisonment within the old coalition of urban workers and the peasantry. A new wage-earner alliance was aborted when it was most needed.

The DNA emerged from the 1930s with a political alliance similar to that seen in Denmark and Sweden, although differing in important respects. For one thing, the bourgeois bloc in general and the farmers' party in particular did not carry the political weight they did in Denmark. The Norwegian tradition of agrarian party opposition to the conservatives ran much deeper and, hence, bourgeois coalitions against the DNA were exceedingly difficult to mount. A second crucial deviation is that the DNA has always mobilized large sections of small peasants, fishermen, and forestry workers within the party, which therefore contains an unusual kind of internal coalition that is largely absent in the other two Nordic countries. This has given the DNA a strong populist flavor and has prevented it from abandoning the old alliance. Thirdly, the Norwegian electoral system worked against parliamentary alliances in government formation by giving overrepresentation to the largest party. Thus, even with less than absolute electoral majorities, the DNA was able to maintain parliamentary majorities until 1961. This implies that governments were strong and effective, and that important legislation could be undertaken without serious compromise or dilution of content. Fourthly, the DNA's wartime experience helped establish its popular legitimacy and strengthened its ability to present social democracy as national-interest politics: labor had stood as the vanguard of democracy and of patriotic defense against the Germans.

Finally, the Keynesian welfare state model that carried social democracy into the postwar era was considerably more radical and aggressive than the Danish version, with its accent on planned economic development, industrial democracy, and collectivism. Since the DNA was capable of implementing such programmatic promises, it was in a position to combine legislative victories with an ability to integrate both moderate and leftist constituencies. Since few reforms had been passed prior to the DNA's rise to power, it was also in a favorable position to portray itself as the vanguard of progressive change and social betterment. Yet, the DNA's ability to profit from this situation was seriously undercut by the bourgeois parties' wartime decision to sanction the DNA program for welfare state development, full employment, and planned industrial expansion. An idyllic left-right consensus was certainly never the case, but the bourgeois parties carefully avoided serious political confrontation. Accordingly, the social democrats were forced to conduct their struggle for supremacy in an environment of consensus. The DNA managed to implant a degree of social democratic hegemony that was probably unmatched elsewhere. The unanticipated consequence of that hegemony is that it hardly served to mobilize loyalty and political passions.

As in Denmark, the 1945 election rewarded the communist party with almost 12 percent of the vote; the DNA lost some ground from its last election, before the war. Yet, the electoral system permitted the DNA to form a majority government. By 1949 the communist party was decimated, and it continued to decline thereafter. The DNA, on the other hand, grew stronger and continued to grow throughout the 1950s. Among the bourgeois parties, the conservatives were strongest; but their inability to coalesce with either the stagnant liberals or the agrarians (after the 1950s, the Norwegian Center party) made them feeble challengers to social democracy.

The DNA was therefore able to consolidate its position on the left as well as the right. Commanding an absolute parliamentary majority and propagating quite radical politics certainly helped the DNA to emasculate its left-wing communist opposition. If some of the more socialistic features of the DNA's program disappeared during the 1950s, the party carried on its policy of state-directed full-employment growth with considerable success. The DNA's economic policy yielded electoral benefits, and there were no instances like those of 1956 in Denmark in which the social democratic government felt compelled to intervene against workers or the unions. Nor was the DNA forced to make the kinds of concessions that would have provoked working-class dissent.

Social democracy's Achilles' heel was its defense policy. As had the Danish social democrats, the DNA agreed to join the NATO alliance despite some internal opposition. As a consequence, the party was plagued by chronic antimilitaristic opposition from within. After a 1960 reaffirmation of Norwegian membership, internal divisions heated up so much that a prominent anti-NATO party member was expelled.

This led to the formation of the Norwegian Socialist People's party. Compared with its Danish counterpart, the SF was a more straightforward single-issue party, programmatically dedicated to the NATO question. That the SF failed to gain substantial support in the following elections is not difficult to explain. Aside from the NATO question, there were not many issues on which a left-socialist critique of social democracy could gain momentum.

The 1961 election, however, did cause problems for the DNA. Though the SF won only 2.4 percent of the vote, and the DNA lost only 1.5 percent, the latter's absolute parliamentary majority disappeared. On the right, a minor realignment occurred, and the conservatives made significant gains at the expense of the liberals and the agrarians. The DNA, then, continued in office, albeit as a minority government and under more difficult conditions. On the one hand, the three bourgeois parties began to put aside old antagonisms and moved in united opposition to social democracy. On the other hand, as the first round of negotiations on EEC membership began, soon after the 1961 election, the DNA's proentry position weakened the party, especially after de Gaulle said *non*. The EEC issue was extraordinarily divisive in Norway, reawakening the old center-periphery cleavage in a way that damaged social democracy. The DNA lost credibility among its traditional rural-periphery constituency, which was fiercely opposed to membership, as well as among leftist urban workers. Since on this issue the DNA was allied with the conservatives, the SF was able to attract voters opposed to EEC membership. In short, the EEC issue provoked new divisions across the political spectrum and harmed the DNA's ability to maintain internal unity. When the issue reappeared, in the early 1970s, these early divisions exploded.

The threat to social democratic hegemony came to the fore in connection with a mining disaster in the state-run King's Bay mines during 1963. A public scandal erupted when it was disclosed that the Ministry of Interior had failed to conduct proper safety inspections. The minister resigned, and the three bourgeois parties—with SF support—toppled the government. A bourgeois coalition government took over until, twenty-eight days later, the SF backed a DNA lack-of-confidence vote. This interlude, if brief, had a tremendous effect on future Norwegian politics. The SF established itself as a left-oppositional force that had to be reckoned with; the bourgeois parties demonstrated their capacity to unite and form an alternative to social democratic government. From 1963 until the election of 1965, the bourgeois parties presented a unified opposition to the DNA and began to prepare a common program.

In the 1965 election, the DNA lost support to the SF, which more than doubled its share of the vote. The bourgeois parties had attained their first parliamentary majority since the early 1930s. Under the leadership of Per Borten, the Norwegian Center party leader, a bourgeois coalition government was formed. As a consequence, Norwegian political cleavages after 1965 seem more like those in Denmark. The bourgeois bloc now presents a coalition of farmers and urban "bourgeoisie" against the DNA, which concomitantly faces competition from the SF. The post-1965 bourgeois coalition resembles its post-1968 Danish counterpart in that it hardly deviated at all from the basic social democratic model.

Despite a somewhat smaller mandate, and a strengthened DNA, the bourgeois coalition stayed in power after the 1969 election. It could do so because the SF had lost its parliamentary seats. The all-encompassing issue after 1969 was, as in Denmark, the renewed issue of EEC affiliation. A parliamentary vote in 1970 showed majority support for entry and, despite its experience in the early 1960s, the DNA leadership stood very strong on its recommendation for membership. The party held two congresses in which a large majority of delegates voted with the party leadership. Still, a substantial minority was militantly against EEC entry, and vehement opposition also came from branches of the trade union movement. As the debate gained momentum, it was evident that the party leadership faced solid opposition from its electorate—especially in the periphery, where popular opposition was almost total.

In Norway, the EEC question inflicted even deeper wounds on the social democratic movement than it had in Denmark. Opponents within the DNA broke with the party and affiliated with the recently created communist and SF umbrella organization, the Socialist Election Alliance (SV), which would spearhead the national campaign against Norwegian entry. Threatened by an unmanageable division, the DNA leadership adopted the Danish strategy and permitted individuals to break ranks with the official party line. Yet, the party was still officially wedded to Norwegian affiliation with the EEC. This naturally accelerated the process of alienation and added to the number of defectors to the SV. The DNA's historical ability to maintain solidarity and unity had collapsed. But the right was equally divided. The strongest EEC supporter was the conservative party, while the center party— and, later, the small Christian people's party—defected and joined the SV's anti-EEC campaign. The liberal party was completely torn on the question and eventually splintered into a pro- and an anti-EEC party. Under such conditions, the bourgeois government clearly could not continue, and the DNA formed a caretaker government until the EEC referendum in 1972.

The EEC issue had created havoc in the political system. The pro-membership bloc comprised conservatives, part of the liberal party, and the right wing of the DNA. The opposition included equally strange political bedfellows: the agrarians, the DNA's left, and the SV. Indeed, the conflict was of such political magnitude that it shattered the traditional left-right axis. With its pro-EEC platform, moreover, the DNA had managed to alienate not only its traditional base in the rural periphery but also the urban, younger generations that fled to SF/SV.

The referendum produced a majority against EEC membership, and this certainly did not help restore legitimacy or confidence in the DNA's leadership. The party immediately resigned from office, and a minority center-Christian government functioned until elections in 1973. At first glance, the 1973 elections appear to be a twin of the Danish Catastrophe Elections. The DNA was decimated, losing more than 11 percent; the big winner was the SV coalition, which gained 11.2 percent. The elections also gave birth to a new, Poujadist-style protest party, Anders Langes party (renamed the Norwegian Progress party). It, too, represented a right-wing populist attack on taxes and welfare state policies, but it was substantially weaker than its Danish counterpart. Except for the surge of left-socialist strength, the 1973 elections would seem to be quite similar to those in Denmark that same year. However, whereas the Danish election was built around massive opposition to social democratic (and bourgeois-party) welfare state politics, the Norwegian election was primarily a consequence of the EEC conflict. Among the bourgeois parties, those that had opposed EEC membership improved substantially. The liberals collapsed. The Norwegian election, then, pretty much replicated the EEC issue cleavages. The only visibly non-EEC-related element in the new political order was the protest party, but its significance was marginal.

Despite heavy losses, the DNA proceeded to form a new minority government. Because of the SV's remarkable gains, and the new divisions among the bourgeois parties, a majority could be formed with SV support. In the 1977 election, the DNA regained most of what it had lost in 1973 and despite the fact that the SV had only attained a level of support equivalent to the SF's pre-1973 average, was able to remain in office. In 1977, the bourgeois parties regrouped into a new alliance of the conservative, center, and Christian parties; the old political order was more or less restored, and the traditional left-right axis once again predominated. The progressives made some gains but could not exert influence commensurate with that of their Danish counterparts.

Norway's oil fortunes in the 1970s spared DNA governments from the necessity of dramatic and divisive crisis policies. Because of North Sea oil, full employment and continued welfare state expansion could be maintained. The social democrats' tried to recapture the dissident left by means of a new emphasis on environmental protection in regard to oil exploration and nuclear power. The Norwegian government had, early on, secured for itself control over all facets of the oil industry, and the DNA now embarked on a cautious policy designed to guarantee that the oil adventure would not jeopardize the natural environment.

Social democratic policies nevertheless helped contribute to party decomposition in the 1970s. After the EEC debacle, the DNA sought to remobilize both the young urban middle strata that had drifted to the left and its traditional constituents in the rural periphery. The party turned to incomes policy and, after a spectacular income settlement in 1973, introduced what was in effect a guaranteed income redistribution for peasants and fishermen. Since this required additional tax financing, in an already steeply progressive tax system, middle-income wage earners were alienated even further. When one couples the DNA's income policies with its strategy of preventing unemployment through massive public subsidies and takeovers of failing industries, not to mention its 1977 decision to impose compulsory wage freezes, it is not difficult to understand why wage and salary earners drifted to the conservative party in large numbers.

Unlike the Danish and the Swedish social democratic parties, the DNA has not undergone a substantial programmatic renewal in recent years. After the war, as mentioned, the party had promoted a more radical ideological profile than its Nordic counterparts. The emphasis on a planned economy was retained much longer in Norway than it was in either Sweden or Denmark and, reflecting its mixed rural-urban social base and its prewar legacy, the DNA made strong pronouncements in favor of localistic, decentralized, and antibureaucratic decisionmaking. From the mid-1950s on, the DNA also moved toward end-of-ideology politics. To an extent, its de-emphasis on planning was the product of bourgeois-party attacks on detailed economic regulation. The party shifted toward a narrower, economic growth ideology but still retained traditionally radical proposals, such as control of finance and workplace democratization. From the 1960s on, the DNA's programmatic statements gave added significance to the importance of decentralized decisionmaking and regional autonomy and development. This was hardly at odds with the bourgeois parties, the Norwegian Center party in particular, but it confirmed rather than questioned the DNA's continued allegiance to the old peasant coalition.

The party's losses in the 1960s did not promote an ideological renaissance. There has been a clear recognition of the need to balance the party's full-employment growth ideology with a greater concern for the human environment. The rising influence of the new women's movement was mirrored in the party's strikingly clumsy promotion of free abortion during the early 1970s, an issue that proved to be unexpectedly divisive and that furthered the rise of antiabortionist movements within the Christian people's party. Entering the 1970s, the party was programmatically hardly any different than before, though greater emphasis was placed on direct participatory democracy and ecological concerns.

Today, the DNA's ideological and programmatic stance lacks the new ideas of economic democracy that characterize both Danish and Swedish social democracy. This may, oddly enough, be explained by the simple fact that the Norwegian social democrats were much more successful throughout the postwar era at actually implementing such policies as greater social control of investments and banking. The DNA's inability to recast its programmatic profile under current conditions of party stagnation, however, may prevent the kind of political realignment necessary for a new era of hegemony.

SWEDISH SOCIAL DEMOCRACY IN THE POSTWAR ERA

Social democracy in postwar Sweden is frequently portrayed as a steady and uninterrupted march toward greater power and political achievement. This impression must be revised. Emerging from the war, the SAP was hardly stronger than the DNA, nor was it at all certain that the social democrats' future would prove especially rosy. By the late 1940s, the SAP was compelled to shelve most of the goals in its 1944 program; strains developed between the LO and the party around 1950; the party's power began to slip during the 1950s; and it slid into a decade of ideological and programmatic uncertainty and lethargy. The break with the Swedish Center party and the 1959 victory on the pension question ensured the SAP a fresh start and greater programmatic creativity, and this in turn helped initiate a new political coalition between white-collar employees and the working class. Yet, by the 1970s, the party had returned to another period of disorientation and electoral decline. It is possible that the SAP's adoption of the economic democracy plan will make possible the kind of realignment that will ensure a new era of mobilization.

As the Swedish social democrats emerged from the 1930s with their version of a farmer alliance and a full-employment welfare state package, they were (compared with the Danes, at least) in a more propitious position. They were electorally stronger and, within the coalition, much more the dominant party. They were also in a uniquely favorable position to benefit electorally from their legislative accomplishments of the 1930s, even if these may now appear rather modest. Their ability to introduce unemployment insurance during the depression, and to bring down the rate of unemployment significantly, helped establish the party as an effective and powerful agent of reform. It should be stressed that the SAP's new legitimacy was not exclusively a working-class affair. Within large sections of the business community, the SAP's ability to revitalize Swedish capitalism helped establish social democracy as the best guarantor of economic prosperity and effective government. As in Denmark and Norway, the postwar popularity of the communists helped radicalize the social democratic program. Communist strength soon declined to its "normal" prewar level as the SAP began to deliver on its promised social welfare programs. For one thing, the Swedish economy was rather buoyant; for another, social reforms could be financed by cutting back on the heavy wartime defense expenditures. Following the Myrdal commission's recommendations, Sweden's social democratic government pursued a powerfully expansionist economic policy that, like Britain's, soon created inflationary pressures and balance-of-payment difficulties which demanded drastic countermeasures.

By 1949, the social democrats were in a politically difficult situation. The bourgeois parties mounted an effective attack on the SAP's mismanaged policy and on its dedication to unpopular economic controls. Placed on the defensive, the SAP suffered losses in the 1948 election and was forced to put aside its planning ideals. The really serious political problem, however, was how to pursue economic stabilization policies that would not antagonize the trade unions. Again following the British pattern, the SAP asked the LO to accept wage ceilings. This provoked considerable tension within the labor movement. The specter of an endless cycle of stop/go policies loomed in the future. The LO's ability to persuade the party to shelve income policies for good and instead implement Gösta Rehn's active labor market policy was, without doubt, a turning point for Swedish social democracy. As Higgins and Apple (1982) convincingly show, the SAP would otherwise in all likelihood have fallen victim to the chronic political paralysis experienced by the British Labour party.

If electorally stronger than the Danish party, the SAP experienced a decade of stagnation during the 1950s. It could not, as the Norwegian party could, count on its 45-46 percent of the vote to produce a parliamentary majority. And so, between 1953 and 1957, the Swedish social democrats refurbished their old alliance with the agrarians (Bondeförbundet). Program and ideology were toned down, and political energies were concentrated on educational reform, a platform on which both parties could agree.

Two simultaneous trends led the SAP to break with the agrarians. One was class structural change; the other was pressure from the LO. Because farmers were disappearing at a rapid rate, the agrarian party was eroding. It was therefore not a promising candidate for membership in future political coalitions. Meanwhile, white-collar employees were increasing. The middle strata had become the new center of party electoral mobilization, both for the social democrats and for the bourgeois parties.

At the same time, the LO was putting pressure on the social democratic government to shift its economic policy in favor of greater state direction of structural change, savings, and investments. The LO also demanded legislation on a supplementary pension scheme that would place workers on an equal footing with the traditionally privileged civil servants. Having initially failed to achieve this through collective bargaining, the LO insisted on legislation and saw the retirement reform (ATP) as a way of meeting two goals at once. It would help accumulate vast savings in collective funds, and it would equalize the pension status of all wage earners.

The ATP question became a historical crossroads for social democracy. If legislated universally, the reform would help cement a broad wage-earner alliance; if, in addition, collective funding were assured, the government would be granted substantial leverage over economic policy. The issue, then, would determine whether the social democrats or, alternatively, the bourgeois parties would lead the rising and increasingly organized white-collar employees. When the SAP proposed the LO plan for a collectively funded ATP, it also invited a break with the agrarians. To compete with the SAP proposal, the bourgeois parties presented various alternative plans, also designed to win over white-collar sentiment.[18]

[18] It was in this context that the agrarian party changed its name from the Bondeförbundet (literally, "association of peasants") to the Swedish Center party—a clear attempt to broaden its electoral appeal to the middle strata.

With the ATP issue, Swedish politics experienced a renewed ideological polarization that ran directly against Tingsten's (1954) prediction only a few years before. The three bourgeois parties attacked the SAP plan as a new, insidious scheme for creeping socialism, but they were incapable of agreeing on any kind of counterproposal. The Swedish Liberal party, in particular, was forced to vacillate because of its dependence on white-collar votes. After prolonged and chaotic conflict, including a referendum and a government resignation, the social democrats managed in 1959 to mobilize a one-vote majority for the reform in the lower house.

These events had lasting consequences for the future of the SAP as well as for Swedish politics more generally. First, the ATP reform helped terminate social democracy's alliance with the farmers. Secondly, divisions among the three bourgeois parties were exacerbated, thus allowing the SAP even greater latitude for Machiavellian tactics. Thirdly, the conflict mobilized the electorate to peak levels, and this mostly benefited the SAP. In the 1960 election, the SAP gained almost 48 percent of the vote; with the communists' 4.5 percent and their implicit parliamentary support, the SAP could now govern with a de facto majority. Fourthly, and this was after all what the conflict was all about, the pension reform vastly improved the social democrats' standing among white-collar voters and their unions. Between 1956 and 1960, SAP support among lower-echelon white-collar voters jumped from 37 to 42 percent, and this was achieved without losing the loyalty of manual workers. A social democratic wage-earner realignment was now in the making.

A final consequence of the ATP struggle was that social democracy proved itself capable of strengthening its position under conditions of ideological mobilization and political confrontation. The bourgeois parties were discredited; the social democrats had been given a new mandate that could be interpreted to mean broad support for a departure from conventional and consensual welfare state policies. During the 1960s, the SAP therefore underwent a radicalization based on LO pressure and a strengthened electoral base. It marched through the decade with a recast program emphasizing extended public regulation and control of the economy, rapid structural modernization of industry, active state direction of investment and housing development and, finally, wage solidarity and income equalization. The SAP was rather successful in legislating reforms in these areas and managed to consolidate further its wage-earner political base. When, in the 1968 election campaign, the social democrats in concert with the LO stressed the need for extended state control of investments, in order to combat unemployment, ideological differences with the bourgeois parties once again came to the fore. This proved to be an advantage for the SAP, which achieved a substantial victory (50.1 percent of the vote).

The SAP's new program, however, was neither strong enough nor free of boomerang effects, and from the late 1960s onward the party's hegemonic position began to slip. If actual unemployment rates increased only marginally, the number of individuals absorbed in the various labor market retraining and employment programs spiraled. The SAP's active labor market policy was being overloaded, and popular fears of unemployment resurged. In addition, indications were that sections of the trade union movement, and of the population at large, were becoming displeased with the centralizing tendencies in policymaking, trade union structure, and industry. The 1969 wildcat strikes in the Kiruna mines enjoyed widespread popular support because they symbolized a sharp criticism of political and trade union centralism and because they accelerated economic rationalization.

A first response was to temper the pace of economic restructuration and manpower mobility; a second was to focus programmatically on workplace democratization reform. To achieve these ends, a series of laws were passed in the early 1970s, although the electoral dividends were less than hoped for. Meanwhile, addressing the regime's lack of adequate investment-direction tools and the call for redistribution of wealth, the LO began to prepare its plan for economic democracy through collective wage-earner funds. The SAP's new emphasis on equality and democratization was evidently inadequate. In the 1970 election the party began its decade-long electoral decline and stagnation, while the Swedish Center party (at first) became the principal beneficiary of the new electoral volatility. This was repeated in 1973 and again in 1976, when the three bourgeois parties performed the historically unprecedented task of uniting in a coalition government led by the centrists.

In Sweden there was no EEC issue to create political havoc, nor did welfare-backlash parties on the right or the left upset the existing balance of party power. Since the bourgeois parties had not yet had a chance to prove themselves in office, it is likely that existing electoral resentment was funneled toward the traditional nonsocialist parties. In other words, while the SAP did lose support, the overall electoral shift was comparatively modest. The bourgeois parties in general, especially the Swedish Center party, could benefit from three basic weaknesses in the SAP's image. First, and most difficult to pin down concretely, was the gradual exhaustion of the postwar social democratic political model which, notwithstanding realignments and radicalization during the 1960s, would appear tired and uninspired in light of the new problems confronting Swedish society in the 1970s. Principally, the SAP did not have a convincing formula for resolving incompatible demands for democratization, decentralization, equality, and ecological preservation, on the one hand, and full employment, growth, international competitiveness, and rising incomes on the other. A two-year economic slump, followed by an unprecedented wage explosion in the latter years of SAP rule, could only help confirm this impression.

A second, and more acute, problem for the SAP concerned the nuclear power controversy, which came to embrace a wider spectrum of environmental and ecological concerns. Nuclear power was an integral component of the LO-SAP full-employment growth strategy, and a large number of reactors were built or planned. The SAP's initial insensitivity and stubbornness on the issues was effectively exploited by the VPK on the left and the Swedish Center party on the right. The SAP thus lost the significant—and growing—"Green movement" and reinforced its image as a centralized machine incapable of harmonizing decentralization and environmental preservation with efficient growth. The SAP's unpopular stance on these issues contributed to its defeat and to the surprisingly strong centrist victory in 1976 (Särlvik 1977).

The third source of the SAP's weakness was, ironically, the LO's behavior on the question of wage-earner funds. Rudolf Meidner's plan for economic democracy had been adopted by the LO congress just prior to the 1976 elections and, in an unusually clumsy move, the LO passed it on to the party for legislative preparation. Embattled on the nuclear power issue and preoccupied with disconcerting pre-election polls, the SAP was taken by surprise. Faced with a media campaign against the unions' newly invented "socialization strategy," the SAP leadership tried to bury the issue by relegating it to an independent commission. But the campaign was well orchestrated and could not be so easily ended. In the 1979 elections, the SAP was again forced to take the defensive while employer organizations and the three bourgeois parties barraged the media with propaganda against economic democracy.

With unanticipated resilience, bourgeois coalition governments remained in power until 1982, although enduring repeated splinters. During its first term, the coalition broke on the nuclear power issue; during the second term, on tax reform. Over this six-year reign, however, the balance of power among the bourgeois parties was importantly altered as the center party—as well as the liberals—decayed, and the conservative party grew. In most respects, these bourgeois governments could not, or dared not, initiate any radical departure from conventional social democratic politics. Full employment remained the overriding priority, and to that end a policy of heavy subsidization of private enterprise was launched. Although budget deficits skyrocketed, there were only feeble attempts at budget cutting. The bourgeois coalition could not survive the 1982 election: the coalition had shown itself to be an inefficient alternative to the SAP, unemployment rates continued to rise, and a last-ditch effort at stabilization policy called for the reintroduction of waiting days for cash benefits—a labor movement taboo.

Armed with a redesigned LO-SAP plan for economic democracy, the social democrats entered the 1982 elections officially committed to that plan's legislation. As before, the new plan was bitterly attacked during the campaign. But the bourgeois parties, given their previous record and their lack of a compelling policy alternative to bring the Swedish economy out of its slump, could not prevent a sizable victory for the SAP. Voters seem to have been less preoccupied with the issue of wage-earner funds than with the immediate threats of unemployment and welfare state cutbacks.

It remains to be seen whether the SAP can forge the new realignment with white-collar groups that is necessary for a strong and stable political future. Clearly the Swedish party has weathered the 1970s better than its Nordic counterparts, partly because it managed to dodge such divisive issues as Common Market entry and partly because it had the good fortune to be forced into opposition just as the economy seriously deteriorated. But the SAP's relative strength cannot be explained by luck alone. In the 1970s, the party may have been stagnant, but it did not suffer sharp setbacks; and, entering the 1980s, the party seemed to be on the verge of a radically new political realignment. One explanation may be found in Castles' argument (1978) that the SAP's power is a direct function of chronic divisions within the bourgeois-party camp. If, in both Denmark and Norway, the bourgeois parties showed a capacity to govern with unity, this was not so in Sweden. The SAP remains skillfully Machiavellian, and the bourgeois split on the tax reform issue in 1981 occurred because the SAP managed to forge a separate deal with the liberal and centrist parties behind the back of the conservatives.

Yet, the real reason behind the bourgeois bloc's structural weakness is social democracy's unshakable power. The general lockout-cum-strike of 1980 demonstrated with utmost clarity that a nonsocialist government is doomed to fail if it should seek to impose unwanted legislation. The employers could not count on political support from the bourgeois government, precisely because it did not dare antagonize the wage-earner organizations, which, after all, represent more than 80 percent of the voters. Similarly, as the waiting-days issue demonstrated in 1982, a bourgeois government cannot afford to tamper with reforms deemed sacrosanct by labor.

Where does this unshakable power come from? In part it lies in the extraordinary unity that springs from a homogeneous and thoroughly organized working class. As we have observed on several occasions, though, the numbers of the working class are in decline and cannot possibly guarantee sustained parliamentary majorities for the SAP in the long run. Accordingly, there is no doubt that the SAP's impressive performance, even during the troublesome 1970s, has been aided by its superior capacity to mobilize the new white-collar groups around political programs designed to appeal to workers and salaried employees alike. This was obviously so in the case of the ATP reform during the 1960s; it is also where the SAP failed to a degree in the 1970s.

In other words, the 1960s were a watershed in SAP history, for it was then that the first links were forged between the traditional manual worker and the new white-collar employee. The alliance, though, was a fragile one, and it remained subject to constant renegotiation. The realignment still has to be concluded and, as the party's current position indicates, some model for economic democracy will have to be factored into the equation. Almost certainly, however, the SAP will also have to relax on its commitments to income equalization.

Still one more feature distinguishes the SAP from its fellow Nordic, if not international, socialist parties. The party's electoral performance is markedly cyclical. But the SAP, in contrast to other parties, seems repeatedly to benefit under conditions of programmatic radicalization and political polarization. The party stood at its strongest in the 1940s, when it promoted state planning and its famous welfare state Keynesianism. During the 1950s, when even the SAP's theoretically inclined leadership embraced the end-of-ideology rhetoric, and when the party seemed to put aside its more ambitious aims in order to accommodate its agrarian allies, voter support subsided. In turn, the SAP enjoyed a new wave of mobilization following the unusually polarized ATP conflict of the late 1950s, and the party was even able to mobilize around promises of strong investment policies in the late 1960s. But when the party retired into programmatic lethargy in the 1970s, it once again suffered losses. Though this connection may prove to be spurious, it should be noted that the SAP's fortunes have improved once again in the highly polarized political climate of the 1980s.

FOUR

The Trend Toward Social Democratic
Party Decomposition

THE CONCEPT of party decomposition is adapted from W. D. Burnham (1970), whose principal intent was to measure aggregate voter fallout and demobilization in the American two-party electoral system. Burnham operationalized the concept as aggregate decline in party votes at elections, combined with trends in voter abstention. Burnham's measures are inadequate or inapplicable in the context of Scandinavian multiparty systems, which are characterized by proportional representation, strong and permanent party organizations, direct links to trade unions and interest organizations, class-distinctive electoral bases, and programmatically distinct political platforms. His concept, however, is still a useful steppingstone for an analysis of social democratic mobilization and decomposition, if altered to accommodate relevant system differences.

First of all, voter fallout is of marginal relevance where proportional representation and relatively low thresholds for parliamentary entry allow new parties a good chance to represent unarticulated interests. Nonvoting would therefore fail to capture electoral alienation from existing parties. Secondly, indicators of party decomposition must be sensitive to the peculiarities of Scandinavian parties and party systems. In contrast to American parties, the Scandinavian social democratic parties are characterized by their reliance on a) strong party organizations and memberships, b) close links with trade unions, c) their traditional anchor in the working classes, and d) penetration into allied class constituencies without running the risk of losing working-class support. Hence, our measures must be sensitive to changes in the incidence of class voting—"the political distinctiveness of class"—and in the class composition of the parties—"the class distinctiveness of the parties" (Alford 1963).

Our overview of social democratic party decomposition in Denmark, Norway, and Sweden will accordingly be based on the following dimensions:

1. Aggregate electoral support; i.e. the social democratic party's percentage share of the electorate in national parliamentary elections.
2. The strength of party splits on the left; i.e. the size of non-social-democratic leftist parties.
3. Trends in social democratic party membership.
4. The political distinctiveness of trade union members; i.e. the percentage of trade union members voting social democratic.
5. The political distinctiveness of social class; i.e. the percentage of working-class and white-collar workers voting social democratic, as opposed to those voting for either a bourgeois party or a non-social-democratic leftist party.
6. The class distinctiveness of the social democratic parties; i.e. the percentages of social democratic party voters according to social class.
7. Generational decomposition.

This last item is of particular importance for a political party. The capacity to mobilize effectively new-generation constituents is an especially sensitive index of possible decomposition, for two reasons. First, we know from electoral research that once developed, early loyalties remain a very important element in the long-term behavior of voters. The social democrats' ability to mobilize every new entering generation is critical for the party's long-range future. Secondly, a party's inability to mobilize new generations probably indicates its failure to realign party program in order to capture salient concerns that develop over the course of time. The social democratic parties were based historically on cleavage structures that attained a degree of permanency and that mirrored the world view of those generations around whom they were constructed. In light of such stability combined with historical change, then, the question is whether the parties manage to incorporate and mobilize new cohorts continuously. Variations in generational support ought therefore to indicate social democracy's ability to re-create electoral loyalties on the basis of dynamic adjustment to new political demands.

TRENDS IN AGGREGATE PARTY STRENGTH

Contrary to what may be commonly believed, the Nordic social democratic parties hardly grew at all after World War II; the great electoral gains were made in the interwar period.[1] The Danes, in fact, never again matched their 1935 performance. The Swedes, on the other hand, broke the magic 50 percent mark on two occasions: during the extraordinary wartime election, they attained 53.8 percent; in 1968, 50.3 percent.

Postwar social democracy has therefore found itself in a prolonged struggle to maintain its position from the 1930s. But the parties' ability to do so has varied substantially. Until the 1960s, the Danish party found its equilibrium at around 40 percent of the vote; thereafter, however, it began to slip. At first the decline was gradual, but in 1973 the party was decimated—dropping from 37.3 to 25.6 percent. Though it managed to recoup some of those losses in subsequent elections, the party seems incapable of regaining anything like its former strength.

The Norwegians and Swedes have performed much better, averaging at around 45-48 percent of the vote. Until the mid-1960s, the DNA remained very stable but then began to drop. As in Denmark, the 1973 election in Norway was a catastrophe for the social democrats, though losses were not quite so severe as in the Danish case. The DNA fluctuated wildly in the 1970s; it returned to normalcy in 1977, but was then defeated in 1981. The Swedish party is, in contrast, a showcase of stability. The SAP hovered at around 48 percent of the vote until the 1970s, and then suffered marginal losses—just enough to force it into opposition between 1976 and 1982. The 1982 election saw the SAP return to its accustomed 1960s strength.

Of great importance for the consolidation of Scandinavian social democracy has been the virtually unbroken marginalization of the communist parties. Their historical extinction was temporarily retarded in the first postwar elections, but since then they have either disappeared—as in Denmark and Norway—or leveled off at a stable 4-5 percent, as in Sweden. After about 1960, however, the situation

[1] The following comparison of decomposition trends is, omitting data on aggregate electoral support and party membership, based on secondary analyses of electoral survey data. The Danish data derive from two separate survey series. In part, I have used Gallup surveys from the Roper Center, covering the 1959-1975 period. These surveys were all conducted at a time close to actual elections. In addition, I was given permission to utilize a series of election surveys (1971-1981) conducted by the Danish political scientists Ole Borre, Hans Jørgen Nielsen, Sten Sauerberg, and Torben Worre. The Norwegian election surveys were kindly supplied by Ola Listhaug, of the Department of Sociology, University of Trondheim, and Berndt Arndt, at Oslo University. The Swedish election survey data have, to an extent, been published in the Swedish Statistical Office's current series, *Allmänna Valen*. However, most of the analyses that follow in this and later chapters were made possible by the kind cooperation of Professors Bo Särlvik and Olof Petersson, who supplied me with their data analyses.

on the left changed importantly. A new noncommunist-left opposition grew steadily in Denmark and has managed to keep a fairly steady 10-12 percent of the vote. Together, the SF and the VS have established themselves as a stable opposition to Danish social democracy. Left socialism also grew in Norway after about 1960, but in a much more erratic way, and can hardly be considered an institutionalized opposition force. Its only important electoral victory occurred in 1973 in the context of the debate over EEC entry.

Social democratic ascendance before the war was primarily associated with the erosion of electoral support for the various nonsocialist parties. It is only in the last decade or so that the bourgeois parties have enjoyed a renaissance, particularly in Denmark. The rise of left socialism in the 1970s was matched by a resurgent right: first, after 1973, in the form of the Danish Progress party and lately with the unexpected rise of the conservative party. A similar, if less extreme, polarization is evident in Norway. Here, too, a Poujadist protest party emerged in 1973, albeit with only modest support. But in more recent years, the conservatives have gained substantially over the DNA as well as the Norwegian Liberal and Center parties. The trend among the Swedish non-socialist parties follows a similar path. In the 1970s it was the Swedish Center party that grew exceptionally; in the early 1980s, the conservatives reign supreme within the bourgeois bloc.

In short, there are both convergent and divergent trends at play in the three Nordic countries. All three are currently polarizing as the conservatives grow at the expense of the centrist parties. It is primarily on the political left that there is important divergence, and the situation is most polarized and fragmented in Denmark. Aside from being the weakest, the Danish social democrats are also the most victimized by splits within the socialist bloc. Their losses have obviously been both to the right and the left, but their primary problem over the past two decades appears to have been the ability of the SF to attract defecting social democratic voters. Leftist party splits have played a lesser role in Norway and Sweden. In Norway, the jump in left socialist power was a temporary phenomenon, spurred on by the EEC debacle. In Sweden, the VPK represents a small, if stable, leftist opposition. Real signs of decomposition are, on this score at least, evident only in Danish social democracy.

PARTY ORGANIZATION AND MEMBERSHIP STRENGTH

The Danish and Norwegian party organizations pale in comparison to the Swedish. Only the latter exhibits no signs of decay. Table 4.1

117

TABLE 4.1. Social Democratic Party Membership in Scandinavia after 1945

	Denmark		Norway		Sweden	
	Number (000s)	% of Party Vote[a]	Number (000s)	% of Party Vote[a]	Number (000s)	% of Party Vote[a]
1945	261	38.8	191	31.5	564	38.7
1950	284	34.9	201	25.0	722	35.5
1955	278	33.2	174	21.0	770	45.0
1960	259	25.3	165	19.2	801	30.4
1964	229	20.3	163	18.5	881	42.6
1970	178	18.2	155	15.4	890	39.5
1974	120	15.4	—	—	1001	42.4

SOURCES: Thomas (1977, 270); Scase (1977, 337-338); Lorenz (1974, 215).
[a] Most recent national election.

shows that both relative and absolute membership rates have declined precipitously in Denmark and Norway since the 1950s. In Sweden, the ratio of members to party votes is stable, and the absolute numbers continue to grow. Although in this respect Denmark and Norway appear similar, the trend actually shows something different. The DNA's party apparatus has always been quite weak but, until the war, the Danish party was almost as powerful and significant as the Swedish. To an extent, this is a self-created problem. In the 1950s milieu of consumption expansion, the Danish social democratic leadership was led to believe that politically organized communal and leisure activities had become anachronistic, and that the party organization had become a political dinosaur.

Yet, organizational decay began to cause alarm as, simultaneously, the party's electoral performance slipped. Steps were taken to reinvigorate party organization in the late 1960s, but to no avail. In Denmark, the party organization is dying, both figuratively and literally. Today, party clubs cater primarily to old-age pensioners (bingo games and coffee), and once the old-generation members die, so will the clubs. This means that party organizations will cease to function as a meaningful tool for electoral mobilization and organizational penetration into the new-generation electorate.

The party organization never played quite as important a role in Norway as it did in the two other countries. Unlike the Danish party, the DNA actually retained the principle of collective membership until the 1950s. In practice, though, the system never functioned, since unions failed to furnish collective membership dues (Elvander 1980,

165). Collective affiliation with the SAP accounts for the bulk of membership, probably 70-75 percent. What is exceptional about the SAP is its ability to attract new individual members, as well. Elvander (1980, 166) reports that the number of individual SAP members more than doubled since the war, and that it continues to grow. If collective affiliation was slowly killed off in Norway, it appears to resist all attacks in Sweden. Opposition to the principle is certainly common, especially among non-social-democratic unionists, but there are no indications that the principle is threatened or will decay.

The Swedish party organization has, like the Danish, undergone substantial reorganization over the years, and the number of separate clubs and affiliates has fallen as the party reconsolidated to conform to the new administrative structure of the Swedish municipalities. It is also possible, even if hard evidence is lacking, that membership activity is on the decline—among young social democrats especially. Still, there is little doubt that the SAP's organization remains extraordinarily vital.[2]

These differences obviously will have an impact on the social democratic parties' performance and fortune. High membership ratios help financially, and they provide an extraordinary network for electoral mobilization and party propaganda. A vibrant party organization also facilitates a closer relationship between grass-roots activities and the parties' parliamentary and organizational elites, thus ensuring the party a better chance to adjust dynamically to social change. As Elvander's excellent treatment of the subject demonstrates, the Swedish social democrats' resources are vastly superior to those of the Danes or the Norwegians. In Sweden, the number of full-time party functionaries is about twenty times as large as in Denmark and five times as large as in Norway. At election time, the SAP has at its disposal 200,000 campaign workers, compared to the DNA's 50,000 and the Danish social democrats' 18,000 (Elvander 1980, 181).[3]

Such quantitative indicators conceal what is perhaps the single most important aspect of party organization; namely, its capacity to implant

[2] Impressionistic evidence gathered by the author during visits to Danish as well as Swedish social democratic clubs points to a vast difference. As indicated, the Danish versions have primarily become coffee clubs for old-age pensioners. The Swedish clubs seem to continue the old tradition of active political and cultural debate and education; study groups are very common, and membership attendance seems surprisingly high.

[3] The three parties' financial resources are a mirror image of their manpower resources. In 1975-1976, the Danish party's budget amounted to about 15 million kroner, the Norwegian budget was 26 million kroner, and the Swedish budget was about 100 million kronor. (Fifteen million of the Swedish party budget were state subsidies [Elvander 1980, 181].)

social democratic "hegemony" in society at large. Naturally, an organizational empire will also permit the party to build informal social networks and sources of influence. Where the party sustains a large army of militants, it can also rely on their ability to penetrate local communities and imbue them with the spirit of social democracy. This task is further aided by the movement's ability to saturate society with sister organizations and institutions, such as cultural centers, educational institutions, cooperatives, and various associations that represent group interests. Again, the SAP is impressively stronger than its Nordic counterparts. Though all three parties boast a huge network of educational centers and consumer cooperatives, the SAP has, in addition, an unusually large organization of pensioners (350,000 members), tenants (624,000 members), and housing cooperative members (340,000). The Norwegian and Danish parties have similar associations, but their membership numbers pale in comparison (Elvander 1980, 186-187).

The importance of party organization for electoral mobilization and party vitality cannot be ignored. It works two ways. On the one hand, it promotes political mobilization. It may also help avert splits, cleavages, and fragmentation. Powerful organization affects broad solidarity, which in turn will be decisive when the party's politics are under strain—as in the EEC debate in Norway and Denmark. Where the party's organizational apparatus has collapsed, issue differences and ideological splits will more readily translate into zero-sum confrontations, precisely because the party will have no framework within which controversies can be debated and differences reconciled. Instead, splits are more likely to produce defections and alienation or, alternatively, a more authoritarian leadership style. In short, the SAP's vastly stronger organizational apparatus is likely both to promote party mobilization and to avert fragmentation and decomposition.

THE POLITICAL DISTINCTIVENESS OF TRADE UNIONISTS

The troubled political and economic climate of the 1970s provoked tensions between the trade unions and the party. In Denmark, such strains had erupted as far back as in 1956, with the general strike, and they resurfaced with the EEC controversy and subsequent government attempts to implement one crisis policy after another. They were manifest, too, in the surge of wildcat strikes, factory occupations, and industrial blockades of the early 1970s, actions that were often leveled against the trade union leadership as well as the government. A number of traditionally loyal social democratic unions began to elect communist shop stewards in these years, although more recently the social democrats seem to have regained control.

Trade union–party tensions in Norway centered on the EEC membership issue and appear to have subsided since that debate ended. The likelihood of intense strains was reduced by the Norwegian oil boom of the 1970s. Whereas Danish workers suffer high unemployment and real-wage decline, the Norwegians face little risk of unemployment and have enjoyed substantial real-wage improvement. In Sweden, also, relations have been less strained. There has not been a single case of direct government intervention in labor market bargaining, and no issue similar to the EEC question has arisen. Although the nuclear power controversy weakened the SAP, the debate probably had little impact on union-party relations, both because the union leadership stood firmly behind the party and because the issue hardly pitted rank-and-file LO members against the leadership. Nor was the SAP in the unfortunate position of having to administer to an ailing economy and defend policies of retrenchment. On the contrary, the bourgeois cabinets' recent attempts to restrict consumption and cut social expenditure clearly mobilized trade unionists against the government. Questions of unemployment and collective wage-earner funds have been a source of tension between trade unions and the party, but these issues are not likely to have provoked trade unionist defections from the SAP.

Table 4.2 shows the percentages of union members who support either the social democratic or the left-socialist parties. The pattern differs in the three countries. Trade unionist support for the Norwegian social democrats actually increased in the late 1970s. Valen (1981) reports that LO workers remained loyal to the DNA even in the cataclysmic 1973 "EEC election."[4] Still, it must be remembered that trade union membership in Norway is considerably lower than in the two other nations.

In Denmark, the split between the social democrats and the left-socialist parties is reflected in the trade union movement. Comparing 1971 and 1977, we notice that leftist gains continue. The percentage of Danish white-collar support for the social democrats is somewhat inflated, however, because it includes only those who are LO members and who are therefore more likely to be social democratic than members of alternative union federations. Still, the trend is similar to that of manual-worker unionists. Since tensions between the Swedish LO and the SAP have been considerably less pronounced than elsewhere,

---

[4] Eighty-one percent of LO members supported the DNA in 1973.

TABLE 4.2. Political Distinctiveness of Scandinavian Trade Union Members
(% supporting parties)

	Denmark				Norway				Sweden			
	Social Democratic		Left Socialist		Social Democratic		Left Socialist		Social Democratic		Left Socialist	
	1971	1977	1971	1977	1965	1977	1965	1977	1970	1979	1970	1979
Manual Workers (LO)	66	63	15	17	67	76	8	3	75	68	6	6
White-Collar Employees (unionized)[a]	46	47	8	13	33	37	5	7	38	37	3	6

SOURCES: Denmark—electoral surveys, 1971 and 1977; Norway—electoral surveys, 1965 and 1977; Sweden—Statistiska Centralbyron 1981b, tables 37-38).

NOTE: Nonvoters have been excluded. LO = Landsorganisationen.

[a] For Denmark, these figures include only white-collar employees affiliated with LO unions; for Norway, LO affiliates as well as independent white-collar unions are included; for Sweden, only members of the Confederation of Swedish White-Collar Employees (TCO).

one would not expect a significant drop in trade unionist support for the SAP. Yet, that is precisely what occurred among manual workers between 1970 and 1979. LO-member defections in Sweden did not go to the communist party, so this means a marked "bourgeoisification" in the 1970s. But, in comparison with the Danish case, the overall level of Swedish LO-worker support for the social democrats remains substantially higher.

On this index of decomposition, the Danish social democrats have gone furthest and, in fact, seem to be experiencing a continuous loss of LO-member loyalty as time goes by. In Norway, LO-worker support for the DNA is actually growing, and left-socialist support is marginal. There are signs of defection in Sweden, but (unlike Denmark) not to the left. Although the data are not yet available, one would expect to find that the Swedish election of 1982 brought LO workers back to the social democratic fold.

THE POLITICAL DISTINCTIVENESS OF SOCIAL CLASS

Over the course of the past century, the social democratic parties have altered their profile to accommodate class structural changes and new conditions for political alignment. The "class party" model gave way to the "people's party" in the period around the 1930s, and when the decay of the petite bourgeoisie no longer warranted a populist profile, the parties saw their future as "wage earner parties," committed to representing a synthesis of working-class and new middle-strata interests. Nevertheless, the parties always remained basically working class.

Even if the social democrats could monopolize the working-class vote, the available numbers would still prohibit a parliamentary majority. In the postwar period, the primary dilemma is whether increased efforts to rally white-collar voters will erode traditional working-class support. In this section we will examine changes in the political distinctiveness of workers and white-collar employees. One way to gauge the capacity of the social democratic party to unite the classes is to trace the extent to which they are politically distinct. Decomposition exists where worker, or white-collar, party support declines and splits.

The Nordic countries typically score very high in comparative studies of class voting (Rose and Urwin 1971).[5] We do not have data on prewar class voting, but we can safely conclude that the rise of the social democratic parties was predicated on the dual process of increasing working-class electoral participation and mobilizing it behind the party. Until the 1950s, the parties also benefited from the relative growth of workers in the class structure. The social democratic parties were overwhelmingly working class, and workers were overwhelmingly social democratic.[6] The question is whether this degree of political distinctiveness might be maintained in the postwar era, when the working class ceased to grow, when traditional working-class com-

[5] In recent years a great number of monographs have appeared on the subject of class, and other social bases of party choice, in the Scandinavian countries, reflecting the accumulation of electoral survey data over the past one or two decades. While most studies are limited to individual countries, there are a number of national comparisons. Among the comparative monographs, see especially Glans (1975), Uusitalo (1975), and Esping-Andersen (1980). The most important single-country electoral studies are Borre et al. (1976, 1979), Särlvik (1966, 1970, 1977), Petersson (1977), Holmberg (1981), Valen and Martinussen (1977), and Valen (1981). The same data have also been presented in Elvander (1980) and Worre (1980).

[6] This is evident from the earliest survey data. Valen (1981) reports that in 1949, 74 percent of manual workers voted DNA. Statistiska Centralbyron (1975b) shows that in 1956, 74 percent of manual workers in Sweden voted for the SAP. And the Gallup survey files for Denmark show that more than 80 percent of workers voted for the social democrats in 1957 (although that survey clearly oversampled social democratic voters). For Norway, Rokkan (1966, 100) has attempted to estimate retrospectively the voting behavior of workers. He suggests that in the period around the 1920s, 76 percent of workers supported the DNA.

TABLE 4.3. Political Distinctiveness of Danish Wage Earners, 1959-1977
(*% supporting parties*)

	1959	1966	1968	1971	1973	1975	1977
MANUAL WORKERS							
Left-Socialist Parties	1	21	14	18	13	13	16
Social Democratic Party	79	64	65	60	38	49	48
Bourgeois Parties	20	15	21	21	48	38	36
N =	(367)	(444)	(382)	(443)	(344)	(314)	(439)
WHITE-COLLAR EMPLOYEES							
Left-Socialist Parties	1	11	7	16	7	11	11
Social Democratic Party	39	31	37	36	28	25	35
Bourgeois Parties	60	58	56	48	65	64	54
N =	(200)	(280)	(301)	(306)	(323)	(330)	(354)

SOURCES: For 1959-1973, Gallup surveys; for 1975 and 1977, Danish electoral surveys.
NOTE: Due to rounding errors, percentages do not always total 100.

munities slowly eroded, and when workers were educated and more affluent.

The data presented in Tables 4.3 through 4.5 do not suggest that this is always the case. In Denmark, the political distinctiveness of manual workers has declined sharply; in Norway and Sweden, moderately. The Danish data for 1959 inflate the level of social democratic support, but even if we deduct a realistic 5-7 percent, or maybe even 10 percent, from the social democratic share of working-class and white-collar voters, there is a straightforward trend over the two decades. Manual workers have become politically fragmented to the absolute detriment of the social democratic party. On one side, a sizable proportion went to the left-socialist parties during the 1960s and remained there. Another, even larger group has defected from the socialist bloc to embrace nonsocialist parties.

The trend can be divided into two periods. During the first, from 1960 to 1973, workers defected to the left. After 1973, there is a new shift, to the right, albeit without much of a left-socialist decline. We should exercise caution, however, before concluding that the Danish working class, belatedly perhaps, is yet another empirical verification of the embourgeoisement thesis. The bulk of post-1973 working-class support for the bourgeois bloc went to the two new protest parties— the center democrats, who were a rightist, homeowner-based splinter from the social democratic party, and the Poujadist progress party.[7]

[7] Of the manual worker, bourgeois-party support in 1973, 16 percent went to the progressives.

TABLE 4.4. Political Distinctiveness of Norwegian Wage Earners, 1957-1981
(*% supporting parties*)

	1957	1965	1969	1973	1977	1981
MANUAL WORKERS						
Left-Socialist Parties	2	8	5	14	6	5
Social Democratic Party	75	69	69	54	64	59
Bourgeois Parties	22	24	26	32	30	36
N =	(592)	(634)	(638)	(484)	(600)	(471)
WHITE-COLLAR EMPLOYEES						
Left-Socialist Parties	1	4	4	9	5	6
Social Democratic Party	39	36	39	32	33	29
Bourgeois Parties	60	60	57	59	62	65
N =	(243)	(404)	(465)	(345)	(469)	(531)

SOURCES: For 1965, 1977, and 1981, Norwegian electoral surveys; for 1957, 1969, and 1973, Valen (1981, table 6.7).

NOTE: Due to rounding errors, percentages do not always total 100.

Danish white-collar employees display similar propensities, if less dramatically. They, too, moved left during the 1960s, but they did not abandon the social democrats. In the 1970s, the social democrats were losing white-collar support to the bourgeois parties. Overall, however, white-collar behavior has been more stable than working-class behavior.

Norwegian class voting has been less volatile. Manual worker, left-socialist support has stabilized below 10 percent—except for the unusual 1973 election. But signs of decomposition appeared in the late 1970s when workers and white-collar employees alike moved to the right. Swedish class voting remained extraordinarily stable throughout the 1960s. The SAP has always enjoyed greater white-collar support, but the party's ability to mobilize these groups was especially impressive in the 1960s. The Swedish social democrats also lost wage-earner appeal in the 1970s, but not so sharply as in Denmark.

In short, the three social democracies diverge in respect of manual worker and white-collar political distinctiveness. In all three cases, the party has lost ground among wage earners, but this has occurred under different conditions and with varying velocity. In Denmark it began much earlier and has been more cataclysmic. The working class there has become politically fragmented, if not polarized. More recently, manual workers have tended to return from the right to social de-

TABLE 4.5. Political Distinctiveness of Swedish Wage Earners, 1956-1979
(% supporting parties)

	1956	1960	1964	1968	1970	1973	1976	1979
MANUAL WORKERS								
Left-Socialist Parties	3	4	6	2	5	6	5	5
Social Democratic Party	74	77	75	77	70	69	68	66
Bourgeois Parties	23	17	19	21	24	25	27	29
N =	(392)	(508)	(974)	(1,055)	(1,380)	(851)	(1,184)	(1,135)
WHITE-COLLAR EMPLOYEES[a]								
Left-Socialist Parties	2	1	1	2	4	3	3	6
Social Democratic Party	49	53	52	54	48	48	43	38
Bourgeois Parties	49	46	45	43	48	49	54	56
N =	(259)	(415)	(841)	(979)	(1,419)	(841)	(592)	(772)

SOURCES: Statistiska Centralbyron (1975b, table 32; 1981b, tables 23-25); Swedish electoral survey, 1976.

NOTE: Due to rounding errors, percentages do not always total 100.

[a] Classification procedures used in the Swedish surveys differ from those used in the Danish and Norwegian surveys. The Swedes included both lower-level and middle-level white-collar employees. It is likely, therefore, that the Swedish surveys encompass a greater variety of occupations.

mocracy. Whether this trend will continue and restore the Danish Social Democratic party to its historical position as the only genuine representative of the workers is impossible to say. So far, we can conclude only that, on this measure, the party has reached an advanced level of decomposition. A distinctive feature of the Danish case is the relation between manual worker and white-collar class voting. If the trade-off hypothesis holds, we would expect an inverse relation in the trend between the two groups. Instead, we find a consistently parallel pattern for both manual workers and white-collar employees: the rise and fall of social democratic support follows an almost identical trend. In other words, a decrease in blue-collar support is not supplanted by an increase in white-collar support.

In Norway social democratic decomposition may be in the making, but not nearly so dramatically as in Denmark. The level of polarization and fragmentation is not especially high, and working-class fallout from the DNA is only moderately strong. What seems to characterize Norwegian class voting is its general drift away from the DNA. As with Denmark, the trade-off hypothesis must be rejected, for declining manual worker loyalties to the DNA are not compensated for by increasing white-collar support. On this variable, Swedish social democracy is hardly decomposing, but the decline in working-class support could, if not corrected, lead in that direction. Similarly, the SAP has lost the hold on white-collar employees that it enjoyed in the 1960s. In Sweden, too, there is no evidence to support a trade-off hypothesis.[8]

THE CLASS DISTINCTIVENESS OF THE SOCIAL DEMOCRATIC PARTY

Class distinctiveness is a central question for social democratic parties. It reflects a party's capacity to appeal to and represent the interests of its core social base. Class distinctiveness is additionally important for the party's ability to formulate a program, an ideology, and a coherent policy agenda. The more homogeneous and unified the base, the greater the likelihood that the party will be able to present a coherent politics, initiate consensus-based reforms, avert internal divisions, and manufacture broad solidarity. There are fewer chances that reformist initiatives will founder on the reef of internal interest conflict. But class purity clearly will not suffice for the attainment of parliamentary socialism, unless the party can attract electoral majorities. To do so, at a time when the traditional working class constitutes a minority, class cohesion must embrace other class segments.

Here we arrive at the crux of the parties' dilemma. Can the social democratic parties include a larger and larger proportion of white-collar constituents without losing manual worker allegiance? As will be recalled, Przworski's answer to this question is premised on class structural development, whereas mine emphasizes the influence of party policy. A comparative test of these two hypotheses will have to await our analysis of party reforms; at present, we will focus on observable trends.

Class distinctiveness—or "class cohesion," as Rose and Urwin (1971) call it—represents a measure of a party's structure. According to Rose and Urwin, who studied European parties between 1960 and 1970, most parties were only moderately class cohesive. The Scandinavian parties, however, scored very high on their index.[9] There is little doubt that the Scandinavian social democratic parties have a long historical

[8] A true test of the Przworski hypothesis, however, must include data on the class distinctiveness of the social democratic party, since the argument is that as the proportion of allied-class members grows within the party, leftist working-class stalwarts will defect. The party is therefore the appropriate level of analysis.

[9] Rose and Urwin's index of class cohesion stipulates that at least 66 percent of a party's votes must originate from the same class. This 66 percent cutoff is quite arbitrary and, as with most similar studies, the class division is a simple manual/nonmanual dichotomy, which implies that white-collar workers of all grades, farmers, and urban self-employed are grouped together.

TABLE 4.6. Class Distinctiveness of Danish Social Democratic Party, 1959-1979
(*% supporting party*)

	1959	1966	1971	1973	1975	1979
Manual Workers	71	72	64	56	61	59
Lower White Collar	12	10	20	31	23	25
Middle and Higher White Collar	7	13	9	10	13	12
Urban and Rural Petite Bourgeoisie	10	5	7	4	3	4
N =	(416)	(401)	(419)	(224)	(519)	(711)
Election Return[a]	42	38	37	26	30	37

SOURCES: For 1959-1975, Gallup surveys; for 1979, Goul Andersen and Glans (1981).
NOTE: Pensioners have been excluded, and housewives have been classified according to the husband's occupation.
[a]Most recent national election.

TABLE 4.7. Class Distinctiveness of Norwegian Social Democratic Party, 1959-1977
(*% supporting party*)

	1957	1965	1969	1973	1977
Manual Workers	70	65	65	64	63
Lower White Collar	8	12	18	13	18
Middle and Higher White Collar	8	9	8	14	7
Urban and Rural Petite Bourgeoisie	14	13	9	9	12
N =	(643)	(682)	(687)	(411)	(652)
Election Return	48	43	47	35	42

SOURCES: For 1957, 1969, and 1973, Valen (1981); for 1965 and 1977, Norwegian electoral surveys.
NOTE: Inactives have been classified according to occupation of the head of household. Due to rounding errors, percentages do not always total 100.

tradition of being class distinctive. The earliest available data show that 76 percent of the SAP's support in 1948 was manual labor (Stephens 1976, 243). In Denmark, in 1954, 83 percent of those voting social democratic were manual workers (Høgh 1956, 16). In 1957, workers accounted for 70 percent of the DNA's voters (Valen 1981, 131).

Let us first look at changes in the class distinctiveness of the three parties over the past twenty years, presented in Tables 4.6 through 4.8. Note that the parties' returns in the nearest national elections have been included in these three tables. Clearly the question of class cohesiveness means something different when the party's electoral share is larger or smaller.

In the Danish Social Democratic party, the share of manual workers has declined, while lower- and middle-level white-collar voters have grown proportionately. The share of urban and rural self-employed has also declined considerably. It is interesting to note that changes in the party's structure seem to reflect its desire to shift from a people's party to a wage-earner party: white-collar employees have increasingly replaced not only the petite bourgeoisie but clearly also the workers. When one compares the trend in class composition against the party's election performance, a pattern emerges: in the 1960s, losses are primarily associated with a fallout of petit-bourgeois supporters; in the

TABLE 4.8. Class Distinctiveness of Swedish Social Democratic Party, 1960-1979
(% supporting party)

	1960	1968	1970	1973	1976	1979
Manual Workers	69	67	65	68	67	65
Lower and Middle White Collar	20	20	25	20	22	24
Higher White Collar	6	9	5	8	8	5
Rural and Urban Petite Bourgeoisie	5	4	5	4	3	4
N =	(663)	(1,458)	(1,801)	(1,047)	(1,040)	(1,147)
Election Return	48	50	45	44	43	43

SOURCES: For 1960-1973 and 1979, Statistiska Centralbyron (1975b, 1981b); for 1976, Swedish electoral survey.

NOTE: Inactives have been classified according to previous occupation or occupation of the head of household. Due to rounding errors, percentages do not always total 100.

1970s, the decline is associated with manual worker fallout and a remarkable increase in the proportion of white-collar supporters. This suggests the following trade-off. During the 1960s, the party was able to unite manual and white-collar workers, and the trade-off was the loss of petit-bourgeois support; in this period the wage-earner party strategy seems to have been crowned with some success. During the 1970s, the trade-off is between manual labor and lower-level white-collar workers—not, as one might have anticipated, between manual labor and middle-level white-collar employees. In brief, as the party's electoral performance has decayed in the 1970s, it has lost ground with the workers.

The Norwegian party has undergone a less pronounced class shift. The proportion of manual workers has declined somewhat, white-collar voters have increased and, surprisingly, there is no real decline in the proportion of petit-bourgeois constituents. Workers have simply given way gradually to white-collar groups. The DNA's somewhat sharp election decline in 1965 was associated with a rise in white-collar members and a fallout of manual workers. The party's second sharp decline, in 1973, produced absolutely no change in the party structure. Finally, the Swedish party shows stability. It should be noted that the petite bourgeoisie have always played a less prominent role in the SAP compared with their role in the other two parties. Unfortunately, the Swedish data on white-collar groups are not entirely comparable with the Danish and Norwegian data because, in the Swedish case, the lower and middle strata are combined. Since variations in the SAP's electoral performance have been small, there is little basis for examining shifts in class distinctiveness as related to shifts in election returns.

Note, also, that Tables 4.6 through 4.8 do not take into account the underlying changes in class structure. A superior measure of a party's class distinctiveness over time would have to control for the "margins"; i.e. include a measure that estimates the degree to which a given class is over- or underrepresented. This we can express in deviation points, which show by how many percentage points a given group in the party deviates from that group's relative size in the total sample. Changes in over- and underrepresentation should more effectively capture relative shifts in the party's ability both to unite its class base and to increase its white-collar share without losing manual workers. (See Table 4.9.)

When controlled for over- and underrepresentation, the data reveal more distinct differences among the three parties. First of all, the Danish manual workers were much more heavily overrepresented until the 1970s, when their position dropped dramatically. The Norwegian and Swedish social democratic parties hold a constant share of the manual working class throughout the period. A remarkable contrast appears between the Danish and Swedish party in the 1973 election. It will be recalled that the 1973 election was a bad one for the SAP and a disaster for the Danish and Norwegian parties. Under similar conditions, the three parties suffered different fates. For the Danish party, the disastrous losses were concentrated among manual workers. In Sweden, the share of manual workers actually increased. In Norway, it was stable. This suggests that in Sweden diminished election returns resulted in a "cleansing" of party structure: the working class essentially remained, while other class elements were the first to leave. In Denmark, the data suggest the opposite: a sharp social democratic party decline is associated primarily with manual worker fallout. This conclusion is strengthened if we recall that working-class overrepresentation increased again in 1977, when the Danish social democrats scored better in the elections. Finally, the DNA's sharp election defeat in 1973 did not affect manual worker loyalties.

Lower-level white-collar support is not always inversely related to manual worker support. In Denmark, the trade-off was clear during the 1970s, even if white-collar increases did not offset manual worker

TABLE 4.9. Class Distinctiveness of the Scandinavian Social Democratic Parties, 1957-1977
(over- or underrepresentation in % points)

	1957-1960	1965-1968	1969-1971	1973	1976-1977
MANUAL WORKERS					
Danish Party	+29	+29	+24	+16	+19
Norwegian Party	+18	+22	+19	+19	+19
Swedish Party	+23	+21	+21	+25	+22
LOWER WHITE COLLAR					
Danish Party	+3	+2	+2	+7	+7
Norwegian Party	-3	-2	-1	-5	-4
Swedish Party	+4	+3	+3	+3	+2

SOURCES: See Tables 4.3, 4.4, and 4.5.
NOTE: The years in which the surveys were conducted in the three countries differ slightly. The years closest to each other have been grouped together so that, for example, 1957-1960 includes the 1959 Danish data, the 1957 Norwegian data, and the 1960 Swedish data. Recall also that the data for white-collar employees are not strictly comparable: the Swedish figures include both lower- and middle-level white-collar employees while the Danish and Norwegian figures include lower-level employees only.

losses. In Norway, there appears to have been no direct correlation: manual worker shares were constant, while white-collar shares declined as the party's election performance deteriorated. This indicates that the DNA is able to maintain manual worker cohesion but is less capable of sustaining white-collar cohesion. In Sweden, the trend is so stable that any possible trade-offs are impossible to detect. This might, of course, indicate that the party is less bedeviled by trade-off dilemmas. To summarize, on our class-distinctiveness measure, only the Danish Social Democratic party appears to harbor serious problems of decomposition, manifested in its inability to unite and hold onto its traditional manual worker base.

POLITICAL GENERATIONS AND SOCIAL DEMOCRATIC PARTY DECOMPOSITION

The study of political generations is a good way to satisfy C. Wright Mills' (1967, 6) insistence that sociology should study the interplay of personal biography and public life. Political generations help connect the immediate experience of individuals with the larger social issues that confront them. Membership in a generation may affect people's consciousness more profoundly than any other form of communal membership, depending on the historical circumstances. Karl Mannheim (1959) was one of the first to give generations a systematic sociological treatment. In his view, each epoch has its own distinct *Zeitgeist*, and generational differences can easily be captured in terms of the rise and fall of each new *Zeitgeist*. As representatives of a unique historical epoch, generations will constitute a social collectivity in their own right—one that cuts across class, religion, and other sources of cleavage. Mannheim also emphasized that once formed, a generational identity will tend to be stable over time. This concept gained popularity among students of the Nazi era in Germany, for it helped them distinguish which segments of society were most or least likely to support Hitler (Heberle 1951; Neumann 1965).

An initial problem is where to draw the line between relevant generations, or cohorts. One might categorize generations by thirty-year intervals, as Mannheim did, or by five-year intervals, as done by Carlsson and Karlsson (1970). It seems more appropriate, though, to define a generation on the basis of theoretical considerations. For our purposes, therefore, a generation will be defined in terms of cohort exposure to a decisive historical event that may be expected to have enduring effects throughout that cohort's later life (Ryder 1965, 850ff; Hyman 1959, 131; Lipset 1960, 279ff; Zeitlin 1966, 493ff). The relevant starting point for a generation, then, should cluster around the time in the cohort members' life cycle when their political identity is decisively formed; that is, during the years of political socialization. Hyman (1959) puts this at around eighteen to twenty-five years of age.[10]

From the foregoing account of social democratic ascendance and decline it should be clear why a study of generation effects might well prove critical. The political realignment of the 1930s was of such magnitude that it must have produced a powerful generational identity. It remobilized the electorate around a political formula that endured into the 1960s. A shift in social democracy's political alignments and programmatic profile began to occur during the 1960s in conjunction with the arrival of unusually large new generations. Their shared generational experience was not lodged in the depression-era politics, but in the welfare state model.

The long-run chances for social democratic power depend on the party's capacity to mobilize new generations whose social identity may differ substantively from that of earlier generations—whose interests and world view might actually conflict with those of the older political generations. Social democracy, in other words, cannot allow generational cleavages to occur; it must be capable of uniting the collective identities of different generations and age groups. Powerful generational cleavages point toward serious problems of social democratic class formation. Significant generational variations in loyalty to social democracy should alert us to the party's inability to recast its politics in order to mobilize new generations without alienating the older ones. A substantial decline in social democratic adherence among young and newly entering generations suggests that a party is heading toward serious decomposition. Ultimately, the party's future depends on the political distinctiveness of new generations.

We should therefore compare the Nordic countries, contrasting generational support for the three social democratic parties over the past two decades. Given the arguments made above, one would naturally predict a much more substantial generational breakdown in Denmark than in the other two social democracies. Table 4.10 suggests that this is indeed the case. Presented are cohort and age support for the social democrats within roughly ten-year intervals. It is therefore possible to

[10] Please note that the following generational analysis will not provide a systematic "cohort analysis," which would attempt to separate age, cohort, and period effects. See Esping-Andersen (1980, chap. 11) for a cohort analysis of the Danish and Swedish data.

133

TABLE 4.10. Generations and Social Democratic Party Support in Scandinavia
(% of electorate)

Age Group	Denmark			Norway			Sweden		
	1959	1966	1975	1957	1965	1977	1960	1970	1979
21-30[a]	50	40	20	45	42	34	60	49	42
31-40	55	39	23	44	49	45	60	51	45
41-50	53	34	30	45	51	51	53	48	43
51-60	50	46	37	44	42	50	45	50	48
61 and older	50	43	43[b]	36	44	44	42	49	47
All Ages	52	40	32	43	46	45	52	49	45

SOURCES: Danish Gallup surveys; Norwegian electoral surveys; Statistiska Centralbyron (1975b, table 35; 1981b, table 31); Valen and Martinussen (1972, tables 9.6, 10.3); Esping-Andersen (1980, tables 11.1-11.12).

NOTE: Nonvoters have been excluded.

[a] In the 1970s, this group comprises voters 18-21 years old.

[b] Because of a coding change in the 1975 Gallup survey, the age groups 51-60 and 61 and older have been "split-pooled." In that year, Gallup coded the older age groups "51-64" and "65 and older," departing from the previous convention. To adjust for this, one-third of the respondents from the age group 51-64 have been pooled with the group 65 and older. The coding change actually made little difference: the age group 65 and older would have scored 44%, rather than the 43% scored by the 61-and-older age group after split-pooling. The same technique has been used, where appropriate, in all subsequent tables; in no case does split-pooling alter the pattern.

examine the "aging effect," the "generational effect," as well as the "period effect."[11]

When we look at Table 4.10, the national differences in age-group voting during the initial year are startling. In Denmark (1959), there is virtually no variance in the voting of young and old, whereas in Norway (1957) and Sweden (1960) the old are significantly less inclined to vote social democratic. At the second time point, the picture has changed: in all three countries, the age groups vote rather similarly. But in the last year, differences are again marked. In Denmark (1975), there is a remarkably strong age-group effect: the old remain loyal to social democracy, the young have virtually abandoned ship. In Norway

[11] "Aging effect" refers to the possibility that party preference changes as people age; "generational effect" refers to the possibility that distinct cohorts systematically behave in different ways; and "period effect" captures the broad historical trend. The first can be deduced from reading vertically down the columns of Table 4.10, the second from reading diagonally from left to right, and the latter from reading horizontally across the rows. It should be emphasized that, at this point, it is not possible to differentiate and isolate the relative impact of aging and cohort effect simultaneously (Glenn 1977).

a similar phenomenon is visible by 1977, although less powerfully so since it seems to be present among only the very young; age differentials are also less extreme. And in Sweden (1979) there are indications, if somewhat weak, of an age variance in which, again, the youngest are less strongly social democratic.

The breakdown in Danish social democratic support among the young cohorts now entering appears especially dramatic in light of the lack of any age variances for 1959. We might also note that the decline among the age groups twenty-one to thirty and thirty-one to forty far exceeds the period decline. The period effect for 1959-1975 is a loss of twenty percentage points; the decline among the age group twenty-one to forty is thirty percentage points. In contrast, the older age groups decline less dramatically than the period effect. In Norway, social democratic loyalties have actually increased among the older age groups, and it is only among voters who are twenty-one to thirty years old that a drop in excess of the period effect occurs.[12] In Sweden, the period effect is a loss of seven percentage points. This was surpassed among the younger age groups by quite a wide margin; yet, the increase among the older age groups tends to offset these losses.

Turning to the question of distinct generational behavior, we might fruitfully contrast the depression-era generation (i.e. those whose early adulthood was formed in the Great Depression of the 1930s and the social democratic ascendance to power) with the welfare-state-era generation (i.e. those who came of political age in the prosperous 1950s and, even more so, in the 1960s). The depression-generation members were about forty-one to fifty years old in the late 1950s; members of the welfare generation enter at about twenty-one to thirty years old in the mid-1960s.[13] In all three countries, the depression generation is politically stable. In Denmark, there is a decline of 10 percent from 1959 to 1975 (i.e. from 53 percent for the age group forty-one to fifty years old in 1959 to 43 percent for the age group sixty-one and older in 1975), but this is only half of the period decline. In Norway, the depression generation remains completely stable, and in Sweden it declines six points, which is a little less than the period effect.

The depression generation contrasts sharply with the welfare generation. The cohort of Danish voters twenty-one to thirty years old that entered in 1966 drops significantly by 1975—more than twice

[12] Note that the Norwegian data for 1957 undersample the DNA's strength.

[13] For Sweden, we have no point of observation during the mid-1960s and therefore have to choose between either 1960 or 1970. Since Sweden's welfare state politics evolved considerably earlier than that of the other two countries, it seems appropriate to chose the year 1960.

the period decline. This group's attachment to the social democrats is therefore very weak. In Norway, on the other hand, the welfare generation shows no such inclination. In Sweden, depending on the measurement choice, there is either a strong decline or no decline in welfare-generation support. I believe it is most appropriate to follow the cohort of voters who were twenty-one to thirty years old in 1960. This group, remember, proved to be extraordinarily strong social democratic supporters in 1960; thus, a decline would reflect a possibly unnatural level of support in 1960. Nevertheless, the welfare generation's decline from 1960 to 1979 is strong—from 60 to 43 percent. Had we taken 1970 as our benchmark for welfare-generation entry, we would not have found a decline stronger than the period effect.

How should we interpret these variegated trends in age-group and generation support for social democracy? Once again, the generally more powerful period decline of Danish social democracy must be noted. The interesting question, then, is how this is distributed by age and cohort. For the Danish Social Democratic party's long-run chances of survival, the situation is ominous. The data suggest that the party has lost its capacity to mobilize young voters and cannot retain the loyalties of welfare-generation voters. It has become a party of old people approaching pensionable age. Unless this trend is reversed, we would have to conclude, the party will decompose as the old die out. We may confidently hypothesize that a fundamental political realignment is a must for Danish social democracy.

For Norway, the data present a different picture. First, they clearly misrepresent the period effect, since the samples do not capture the DNA decline between 1957 and 1977. But the Norwegian party has strengthened its position among older voters, and we can record only one decompositional indicator; namely, the drop in DNA support among voters who were twenty-one to thirty years old in 1977. If this is not reversed, there is a chance that the DNA will follow the downward spiral of the Danish party. On the other hand, the DNA has not lost ground among the welfare-generation voters. This suggests that the roots of the Norwegian party's problems are much more recent than those of the Danish party, and we may suspect the EEC issue to be the principal influence.

Sweden presents a mixed pattern. There are no signs of a strong age-related cleavage, since the difference between young and old voters in 1979 is small. But the SAP leadership should be worried about the decline in loyalty among the "welfare generation." The data on Sweden suggest that the SAP was extremely successful in mobilizing the young in the 1950s and 1960s, but that success seems to have been only a temporary phenomenon. If, in 1960, the party was disproportionately young, today its age composition is even. Though the trend may be to the SAP's disadvantage, there is no sign of decomposition as such.

A critical question has to do with where the younger generations move politically. Three scenarios are possible. Since there is no indication of lower electoral turnout, they must have either moved right or left, or polarized in both directions at once. My interpretation of renewed social democratic mobilization must ultimately rest on which trend prevails.

Table 4.11 reveals a strong left-socialist tendency among the younger cohorts, while the older groups remain quite stable in both their party choice as well as their affiliation with either the left or the right. The left-socialist trend is overwhelming in Denmark, where a full 30 percent of voters who were twenty-one to thirty years old in 1975 supported leftist parties. This cohort had also moved to the right between 1966 and 1975. In other words, this is an extremely fragmented if not polarized cohort.[14] About half of its votes go to parties on the left, or on the extreme right, that explicitly attack social democracy. The pattern is more stable and less extreme among the older cohorts. In Denmark, such "anti-social-democratic" polarization is equally strong among workers. Among welfare-generation workers, 33 percent support left-socialist parties and 8 percent the Danish Progress party; among depression-generation workers the figures are, respectively, 14 percent and 1 percent. In Norway, the degree of polarization is considerably weaker. Younger voters are both more leftist and more rightist than the older cohorts, but the trend is weak and a generational shift against the DNA is not especially evident. Danish and Norwegian youth may have become more bourgeois, but Swedish youth have not. Their support for left parties (notably the VPK) doubled during the 1970s, and their support for the bourgeois parties declined. The remaining age groups are fundamentally stable.

In short, these patterns suggest that the three social democratic parties confront qualitatively different dilemmas of mobilization. The Danish party is obviously decomposing at both ends. Since the younger cohorts' drift to the right is concentrated in the Danish Progress party, that shift would be difficult to interpret as embourgeoisement. Rather, in light of what the progressives stand for, we might view leftist and rightist polarization as two facets of a broad revolt against social

[14] The jump in bourgeois-party support among the youngest cohort is almost completely accounted for by Glistrup's Danish Progress party, which received 14 percent of that group's votes.

TABLE 4.11. Scandinavian Left-Socialist and Bourgeois-Party Support by Age and Generation

Age Group	% Left Socialist						% Bourgeois					
	Denmark		Norway		Sweden		Denmark		Norway		Sweden	
	1966	1975	1965	1977	1970	1979	1966	1975	1965	1977	1970	1979
21-30	21	30	8	11	6	12	39	50	50	56	52	46
31-50	14	11	6	3	2	4	50	62	44	48	54	52
50 and older	7	7	3	3	3	3	48	51	53	52	48	50

NOTE: For sources and explanations, see Table 4.10.

democratic politics in general and the welfare state in particular. In Norway the trend is parallel but not so strong, and in Sweden the decline in younger generational support for the bourgeois parties, in combination with growing support for the VPK, suggests that the SAP's problem is not that it is too leftist for the youthful palate. It is more likely that declining social democratic party support among the younger cohorts mirrors dissatisfaction with the conventional profile of social democratic politics and, possibly, that it reflects a desire to see a more leftist realignment. We will therefore want to pay special attention to generation-based support for social democracy's new policies, economic democracy in particular.

BASES AND OUTCOMES

How is one to explain such disparate political outcomes in such politically and culturally similar nations—especially when one considers that the three social democracies could hardly have been more convergent in the 1930s political realignment and its aftermath? Much of the answer must be sought in social structure generally and class structure specifically. The Scandinavian party systems, and thus the social democratic parties, emerged in a context of distinct class configurations. Industrial capitalism in Denmark was still based on family farming and urban crafts. This ensured a peculiarly liberalistic, petit-bourgeois hegemony that was difficult to challenge since large sections of the working class, and even white-collar employees, remained wedded to its perpetuation.

Denmark's "second industrial revolution," arriving in the 1960s, produced white-collar strata, not manual workers, that structurally and politically inserted themselves between the gradually decaying rural classes and the stagnant (if not declining) and still incohesively organized working class. Moreover, white-collar expansion occurred predominantly in the public sector.

These class structural traits came to define unionism, the longstanding political dominance of liberalistic (but competing) bourgeois parties, and the unrelenting need for the social democrats to compromise and collaborate with parties on the right. Consequently, the social democrats left a great void on the left. As they proved incapable of realigning, that void was filled by new left-socialist parties—parties catering to exactly that blend of manual and nonmanual wage earners which the social democrats could not concoct.

The rural economy of Norway gave birth to a volatile peasantry on the periphery and only a small-farmer stratum in the South. Accord-

139

ingly, the rural classes were in most respects divided. The Norwegian working class emerged as a Russian-style hybrid of quasi-proletarianized peasants and rural workers, with only a marginal urban and craft-influenced segment.

Norway's industrialization—with heavy foreign capital penetration into a rural subsistence periphery—closely resembles that of the typical Third World, dependent-enclave economy. A strong domestic bourgeoisie never emerged. Instead, the civil service remained the bastion of conservatism, and the urban petite bourgeoisie became the bastion of liberalism.[15] If we add to this the deep-rooted and persistent center-periphery cleavage, we can understand why syndicalism came to play such a substantial role in the early labor movement. There was, in addition, no significant independent-farmer class or urban bourgeoisie to build a liberal influence of the magnitude found in Denmark.

The class structure of Sweden developed very much in accordance with orthodox Marxist predictions. Sweden's class structure thus remained more polarized and dualistic, as did the Swedish party system. The urban working class was both larger and more homogeneous than that of the neighboring countries, and this helped establish what is now the world's most powerful trade union movement and social democratic party. While Sweden also had a large semiproletarian rural element, the interests of that sector were able to be incorporated under social democracy in the 1930s crisis policies, even if it did prove to be a difficult element to organize throughout the interwar period. And white-collar trade unionism came to match that of the traditional working class in respect of penetration as well as organization, thus permitting a degree of labor market and political linkage not found elsewhere. In Sweden, finally, there was no rural or urban petite bourgeoisie with sufficient political or economic clout to dictate the terms of class alliances and political outcomes, except perhaps for brief periods. Indeed, this political weakness helps explain the unusually rapid economic demise of the petite bourgeoisie.

Class forces therefore established uniquely different parameters for social democratic mobilization in the three Nordic countries. Those forces came to influence the nature of the state and the content of public policies. Since these, in turn, deeply affect the differential strength and weakness of the social classes, social democratic influence over the state must be considered as both a cause and a consequence of class structuration.

[15] Merchant shipping, however, produced a bourgeoisie whose outlook was predominantly outward-oriented.

It is natural, then, to expect that long-run capacities for social democratic class formation will be increasingly affected by state structure and state policy, if for no other reason than because social democracy has chosen to wage its version of the class struggle through electoral politics and parliamentary reformism. The state becomes the mechanism through which social democracy can best hope to mold the "raw material" of the classes into collective political agents. It is also the mechanism that can present obstacles to the social democratic quest for power, since the growing influence of the state may equally well individualize, fragment, or divide those constituencies upon which social democracy must depend.

Consequently, I propose an alternative theoretical link between class and party, one that places special emphasis on social democratic reforms and their likely impact on social democratic class formation. A specification of how reforms intersect class structure and party mobilization is absolutely necessary if we are to explain why party decomposition in recent years varies so dramatically among the three social democracies. This is so because a strictly class structural explanation will fail. If the three countries have diverged significantly in respect of early class structural development, all indications are that the postwar trend is one of class structural convergence. The Danish class structure, in particular, is beginning to take on the characteristics of the Swedish case as, slowly, the rural petite bourgeoisie are marginalized, the craft character of the working class is weakened, and the new white-collar strata assert themselves as the largest class element. But, aside from class structural convergence, it would be difficult—under any conditions—to identify a direct connection with social democratic party decomposition, precisely because its onset occurs so explosively.

A theory that rests upon the causal influence of state policies can therefore be argued quite plausibly. The question is how to give it empirical specification, and it is to this question that we now turn. Part II of this book will examine variations in the "social citizenship state" erected over the course of the past century. Our attention will subsequently focus on how housing and economic policies differ in their ability to forge unity or nurture fragmentation, how they promote or stifle social democratic class formation.

141

PART II

The Political Bases of
Social Democracy

FIVE

The Social Citizenship State

TODAY, social democracy is virtually synonymous with the welfare state. This is understandable when we consider that social-democratic-dominated countries, particularly in Scandinavia, also boast the most developed social security systems. At the same time it is false to imply a direct causal link. A host of nations, Holland being the most illustrious, display levels of social expenditure that easily match the Scandinavian, yet without experiencing a comparable level of working-class political power.

Generally speaking, it is erroneous simply to equate the two without regard for the content and characteristics of the welfare state. Equal levels of social expenditure may blind us to critical differences in the institutional makeup of welfare systems. High rates of social expenditure do not necessarily imply generosity or commitment to effective social citizenship rights—they may simply mirror a nation's incapacity to deal effectively with such social problems as large-scale unemployment and persistent poverty. No a priori reason exists for assuming that socialists greedily desire heavy social expenditures for their own sake.

There is, as most authorities on the question have pointed out (Briggs 1961; Rimlinger 1971; Flora 1981), nothing especially socialist about the origins of social amelioration and reform. Traditional conservatives, like Disraeli and Bismarck, were eager to promote social legislation as a means of ensuring order and securing working-class loyalties. Liberals were of course more reluctant, but even they gave in when it was politically unavoidable—and when it was eventually understood that social insurance might be beneficial for economic efficiency. In either case, welfare measures frequently evolved without, or actually against, socialist wishes. The politically important issue, then, is not that welfare reforms occurred, but what kinds of reforms the socialists managed to put in place.

SOCIAL CITIZENSHIP AS A SOCIALIST OBJECTIVE

Contrary to what vulgar Marxism sometimes holds, social reformism was not just a social democratic invention to replace abandoned rev-

olutionary politics. Social reform was a vital issue from the very beginnings of working-class organization, whether under reformist or
revolutionary leadership. What has changed over time is the larger
historical role assigned to social policy in the struggle for the Good
Society. The question of social policy has always been a matter of
both pragmatic necessity and theoretical importance.

During socialism's earliest phase, the issue of social reform was
understood primarily in terms of the orthodox view that social amelioration through state action only helped to strengthen capitalism,
divide the workers, and harness the power of the state against revolution. This was the basic point of the 1891 Erfurt program, accepted
by August Bebel in Germany as well as by such Scandinavian socialists
as Gustav Bang (Bryld 1976). Even when the possiibility of social
reform was entertained, it was deemed unrealistic to believe that a
truly emancipatory reform could be wrested from the capitalist system.

But this theory was full of cracks. For one thing, Marx and Engels
concluded *The Communist Manifesto* with a list of undramatic reforms
deemed desirable from a socialist perspective.[1] Rosa Luxemburg and
Karl Kautsky paid tribute to the "social," or "political," wage as a
necessary precondition for uplifting the politically dangerous slum
proletariat (Kautsky [1892] 1971) and for strengthening working-class
unity under conditions of unemployment and poverty. For those loyal
to the classic texts, there were additional justifications for an active
social policy. Thus, socialist demands for pensions and social benefits
were occasionally argued with recourse to the Marxist theory of value;
namely, that the social wage should be granted as a just return on
exploited surplus value (Rasmussen 1933, 144ff).

Theory and ideology aside, the socialists could hardly afford to
ignore social legislation. To the extent that the capitalist market could
not survive without it (Polanyi 1957), and because pressures from
below compelled it, conservatives and liberals were, by the close of
the nineteenth century, deeply engaged in social reform. The socialists
had little choice but to take a stand, if for no other reason than because
bourgeois legislation would "lure the workers away from the correct
path" (Rimlinger 1971, 125). Thus, the SPD bitterly opposed Bismarck's worker insurance schemes; and in Britain the ILP's left, under
Keir Hardie, unsuccessfully opposed Lloyd George's National Insurance Act. In both instances, it was believed, the legislation would
deepen existing cleavages between skilled and unskilled workers. Sim-

[1] Marx's analysis of the British Factory Acts also seems to indicate an optimistic view
of what social reform might accomplish (Marx [1872] 1967, chap. 10).

146

ilarly, the Danish social democrats were adamantly against a conservative proposal for state-subsidized old-age insurance in 1883-1884 because they rejected its self-help character. The enemy lurked within the working class, as well, for privileged skilled workers and craftsmen frequently enjoyed the benefits of—and wished to strengthen—corporatist, guild-type welfare schemes. As can be seen in the writings of Heiman (1929) in Germany, Gramsci (1978) in Italy, and Jungen (1931) in Sweden, socialists were conscious of the need to combat occupational welfare systems because these stood in the way of class solidarity.

In any event, the socialists were forced to struggle for social reform: the workers obviously both needed and demanded it, and it was understood that political mobilization and class unity were difficult to achieve without it. Since existing poor relief typically disenfranchised the recipient, there were electoral gains to be made from its abolition. Equally necessary was the abolition of extreme poverty and economic uncertainty among workers, since these impeded union and party organization and tended to pit workers against each other in the competition for jobs and income. The absence of social protection gave greater power to capitalists and hence perpetuated the labor movement's weakness.

For socialism, welfare policy had to promote three important goals. First, reforms would have to build rather than impede class solidarity. This moved the socialists, very early on, to propose reforms that were universal in their organization and impact, thus diminishing intra-working-class differences and building instead a collective identity. This is why they fought means-tested relief programs as well as state or private insurance schemes: the former would have a powerfully stigmatizing effect, and the latter could only reinforce existing inequalities and privileges, possibly even linking workers to the regime.

The question of how to promote solidaristic policies, and of who was to be included within the embrace of solidarity, was more difficult. Orthodox Marxism prescribed one model; revisionism and parliamentary socialism another. The former, which was typical among most socialist movements until the First World War, was strategically exclusionary in the sense that the struggle was to be conducted on a purely proletarian basis. Accordingly, the "ghetto party" model for working-class unity was designed to immunize workers from bourgeois influence with regard to both ideology and everyday social life. In this context, social amelioration became strictly a working-class affair to be undertaken by the movement—not by the bourgeois state or capitalist employer. The latter model, obviously dependent on parliamentary majorities, would have to define a broader clientele for solidarity since allies were required. Hence, the question of inclusion and the issue of how to design social reforms were resolved with the notion of the party as a "people's home," prescribing policies that benefit the broad masses or even the entire population.

If the first concern was solidarity, the second was to immunize workers from the disciplinary whip of the market. The commodity status of labor in the market was always recognized as an impediment to collectivism. It nurtured competition and uncertainty, and it strengthened the hand of the employer in bargaining as well as in the exercise of authority within the factory. Therefore, for ideological or purely pragmatic reasons, social reform could help free workers to the extent that it decommodified their status; i.e. reduced their dependence on market exchange. Guaranteed adequate benefits in the event of sickness, old age, and unemployment would naturally weaken the power of market exchange and help counter fierce competition when economic conditions were bad. Social entitlements thus became a central reformist objective, and the development of full social citizenship status became a socialist goal, whether or not the party retained revolutionary ambitions. It would be important, however, to influence the exact nature of that social citizenship.

The third, and final, key goal of socialist welfare policy was to further equality. This is partly a residual effect of the first two goals, since solidarity and guaranteed social rights imply equality of treatment and status. Socialists rarely saw social policy as the engine for an egalitarian socialist society.[2] Still, equalization of incomes and wealth was seen as a necessary precondition for attainment of the other two aims. Solidaristic policies necessarily involve a major redistribution both on the finance side and on the benefit side. If greater homogeneity is a precondition for social and political unity, then a reduction of wealth differentials becomes an important task for socialist policy.

It follows that social policy, aside from its humanitarian and altruistic objectives, has a central role to play in socialist power mobilization. One would expect the long-run political fate of social democratic labor movements to be contingent on their ability to implement solidarity, decommodification, and equality through social legislation. Conversely, failure to implement a socialist alternative to liberal or

---

[2] This changed after World War II, when important figures in the British Labour party, such as C. A. R. Crosland (1967), tried to develop a theory of socialism based on Keynesian economics, welfare state policies, and progressive taxation.

conservative social reformism would weaken the capacity for working-class political unity and social democratic power mobilization.

The political risk for a social democratic movement that presides over a divisive welfare state is considerable. If social services are allowed to follow occupational or other social demarcations, broader loyalties are readily sacrificed at the expense of narrower corporate identities. Where private and occupational schemes proliferate, collective identity and loyalty to the public schemes will easily evaporate, especially as the tax rate grows. Socialists therefore risk class fragmentation, divided loyalties, and a greater potential for "welfare backlash" whenever they preside over a welfare state in which liberalistic or conservative principles have been allowed to persist. The advanced process of social democratic party decomposition, especially in Denmark, can be attributed to a pervasively liberalistic welfare state that enhances social stratification and cleavages cutting across class lines.

The Origins of Social Democratic Welfare Policy

Before World War I, and even after, the socialists' position on the "social question" was not especially coherent; occasionally it was self-contradictory. That position consisted of three basic elements: critiques of bourgeois reformism; development of mutual-aid schemes within the "ghetto party" tradition; and attempts to influence whatever reform legislation might happen to be introduced.

When they were small and excluded from political power, social democratic movements could still adhere to the stipulations of the Erfurt program. They viewed workers as their only natural political clientele and were armed with a more-or-less convincing immiseration theory. This meant that socialist leaders elected to parliament exploited what little influence they had to lambaste existing relief institutions as well as bourgeois reform initiatives. In Denmark, the social democrats opposed liberal and conservative party proposals for old-age insurance, maintaining that these would consolidate status differentials and do little to better the lot of the weakest (Rasmussen 1933; Dich 1973).

To ensure order and to compete for worker votes, bourgeois parties were promoting social reforms that, if not somehow countered, might win over working-class allegiance.[3] One socialist response was to de-

---

[3] Thus, Butler and Stokes (1971) have argued that the phenomenon of working-class Toryism, especially among older-generation workers, can be explained by the reformist image of the conservatives dating from the turn of the century.

velop schemes for social protection and collective aid within the movement itself. It was believed that the unions and the party could build a proto-socialist ghetto on the basis of mutual-benefit societies, unemployment funds, institutions for socialist education and culture, housing and building societies, and a myriad of recreational facilities. This would serve the multiple purpose of attracting members, immunizing workers from bourgeois influence and preparing them for collective life in the Good Society, fostering solidarity, and responding to pressing material needs.

The ghetto strategy was, in reality, motivated by several concerns. In part, it was historically determined—to the extent that many members of the "labor aristocracy" already benefited from an array of fraternal mutual-benefit societies. Moreover, in Germany and Denmark (and to a lesser extent in Norway and Sweden), there existed a long and powerful tradition of voluntary health-insurance funds (Kuhnle 1978; Rimlinger 1971; Tennstedt 1976), and these already covered a considerable number of workers. Rather than risk their subordination to a hostile bourgeois state, the socialists perceived a strategic advantage in penetrating them. Since political influence was tied to financial contribution, the socialists logically opposed any legislation that would allocate greater fiscal responsibility to employers. The same issue was even more prominent in the struggle over unemployment insurance.

In Sweden and Denmark, the trade unions had a stake in controlling unemployment funds, which could be used as a weapon during strikes. Employer participation and state influence were both to be avoided. On this matter turned the dilemma of purely union- or state-controlled funds. On the one hand, the labor movement's control over both money and members would be enhanced. But on the other hand, the condition of membership meant that large numbers of unorganized workers would not benefit, thus threatening deeper divisions among workers.[4]

The "ghetto model" remained fairly dominant among Scandinavian social democrats until the turn of the century. But even so, counter-

[4] The fate of unemployment insurance legislation in Germany captures the essence of the conflict. The ADGB wanted to retain union control of the funds as a means to attract members and because it feared that a public scheme would deny benefits to unemployed workers who refused to work during strikes. The SPD, in turn, proposed a public scheme that covered all workers. When finally legislated in 1927, unemployment insurance had become a compromise whereby neither interest was fully served. Coverage was extended to any member of a sickness fund, and the funds were administered by employers and employee representatives together (Preller 1949; Rimlinger 1971). In Denmark and Sweden, the union movement was more successful in retaining control of the funds.

currents took hold. Occasionally, socialist parliamentary representatives would propose ideas or bills that were in direct conflict with prevailing socialist principles. Thus, in Denmark, the social democrats vacillated between autonomous sick-pay funds and demands that the state should cover the entire range of health-care costs (Dich 1973). On the question of old-age pensions, they bounced back and forth between fixed rates and income-related benefits. The Swedish social democrats, more theoretically inclined, were no less undecided on what socialist social legislation ought to look like. Hjalmar Branting was at first enthusiastic about Bismarckian worker insurance. After following the controversies over its introduction in Austria, however, he came out in favor of a nationally inclusive universal scheme that was more like the Danish old-age assistance program, which had been introduced by the conservatives against socialist opposition (Elmer 1960).

Until the 1930s the liberals dominated, and social democratic influence was marginal at best. In Scandinavia, two principles were to prevail. One was voluntary insurance designed to nurture liberal values of self-reliance, thrift, and market participation. The other was a gradual, but incomplete, removal of the stigma associated with poverty relief. The Bismarckian spirit took greater hold among the Norwegian bourgeois parties, and we find a stronger emphasis on compulsory worker insurance. In this period, therefore, a primary social democratic task was to combat "bourgeois" legislation.

But the period was also marked by an energetic search for an appropriately socialist welfare policy. While most Norwegian social democrats remained steadfastly loyal to their antiparliamentary, revolutionary program, the Danes and Swedes engaged in a lively debate on social reform, the most significant contributors being F. Zeuthen and K. K. Steincke in Denmark; Wigforss, Möller, and Jungen in Sweden. By the 1920s, the Danes had more or less abandoned any ideological pretense, and this is mirrored in their approach to the social question. Few had any illusions, and most probably did not care whether or not it could be argued that social policy catalyzed socialism. The party's two most influential spokesmen—Steincke (1920) and the party's leader, Stauning—were moved principally by humanitarian concerns: a vague application of underconsumption theory and the fact of obvious need.[5]

---

[5] There were a few who were inspired by Swedish and Austro-Marxist revisionist theory to claim, as did Frederik Borgbjerg, that social legislation might provide a "transitional link between capitalism and socialism" (Bryld 1976, 105).

Their foremost priority was to abolish the morals- and means-tested relief system, to increase benefits, and to extend coverage to all citizens.

The Danish social democrats were, unlike their Swedish and Norwegian brethren, in the unfortunate position of having to compete with liberal reformism. The Danish liberals and radical liberals had been very actively engaged in social legislation. Hence, a relatively comprehensive network of social services and social insurance (voluntary accident insurance and sick-pay funds) was already in place. This had two detrimental consequences for social democracy. One was that liberalism came to influence social welfare provisions to a great extent. The socialists faced an uphill and tedious struggle to reverse this influence, especially since, once in place, such schemes develop their own devoted constituency. Hence, the principle of voluntary membership remained powerful; the notion of self-help, particularly in health care and sickness compensation, was difficult to reverse. The ideal of private solutions and self-reliance came to prevail to such a degree that jealousies between the haves and have-nots quickly surfaced when the social democrats proposed unitary, universal schemes featuring equal benefits and progressive finance. In short, social democracy was burdened with an already institutionalized liberal hegemony in the domain of social welfare.

The other consequence was that the social democrats were less able to benefit from pioneering social reform (Elvander 1980, 268). Most immediately demanded reforms were already in place; thus, the social democrats had little else to offer than revisions and repairs of existing schemes. As we shall see, this has had profound effects over the long haul. Social legislation could not yield the political-mobilization dividends enjoyed by Sweden's socialists, and continued reliance on the radical liberals—not to mention the liberals—meant that the Danish social democrats were unable to modify social policy in a dramatically socialist direction.

The Swedish social democrats were both more prolific and theoretically more sophisticated in their writings on the social question. The influence of Nils Karleby (1926) was especially important for providing a theoretically coherent link between shortsighted reforms and their future promise for socialism. Like Bauer (1919) and Adler (1933) in Austria, the Swedes were convinced that the socialist struggle had to be based on social welfare legislation—partly because economically insecure and uneducated workers possessed little capacity for socialist participation, partly because the role of the market in distributing social welfare helped divide and fragment workers, and partly because progressive reforms could spur the capitalist system toward greater social rationality.

When the Swedish social democrats eventually assumed government power during the 1930s, they were in a politically fortunate position: the long era of conservative and liberal rule had produced remarkably few social reforms. There was no unemployment insurance, except for financially weak union funds, and insurance coverage for sickness was marginal. Sweden, of course, had been the first nation to legislate a universal old-age pension (in 1913), but benefits were meager at best. In addition, no system of public job creation was in effect when the economic depression led to explosive unemployment. Swedish social democracy was therefore in a very favorable position to reap substantial political dividends from social legislation.

The Norwegians were, until the 1930s, very little concerned about welfare reforms. Their revolutionary, antiparliamentary strategy during the 1920s had clearly ruled out the possibility of participating in bourgeois legislation and, in any case, their chief preoccupation was with the issue of economic socialization. When, in the early 1930s, they finally realigned both program and strategy, existing circumstances were somewhat different from those in the other two nations. First of all, their class-political base was the rural proletariat, on one hand, and urban workers on the other. Secondly, the heritage of social policy was to a great extent influenced by conservative legislation. Voluntary sickness funds were almost wholly absent in Norway and, directly inspired by Bismarck's reforms, Norwegian conservatives had already introduced compulsory sickness insurance by 1909 (Kuhnle 1978). The same thing occurred with respect to accident insurance. As was typical for Bismarckian conservatism, these compulsory state insurance plans were designed exclusively for the working class.

On the other hand, the Norwegian social democrats were also in a position to benefit from the lack of prior welfare legislation. Specifically, there existed no old-age pension system whatsoever, and the old voluntary unemployment insurance program was totally inadequate to cope with depression levels of unemployment, particularly within the rural proletariat.

Despite the wide discrepancies in regard to theoretical understanding, previous reformism, and general political economy, the three social democracies would sponsor virtually identical welfare policies after the political realignments of the 1930s. Whether they were fortunate enough to pioneer reforms or whether their role was limited to the revision of existing schemes, the parties aimed at the same goals: to achieve universal and solidaristic social rights; to equalize the status of workers, farmers, and salaried strata; to secure good benefits and remove various eligibility conditions; and to promote a major income redistribution through flat-rate benefits and progressively financed taxes (Esping-Andersen and Korpi 1984). To the extent that they eventually succeeded in implementing these policies—mostly during the postwar era—the social democratic welfare states were also qualitatively different from either the liberal-dominated welfare systems of the United States, Australia, and even Britain or the conservative variety seen in Germany, Italy, and France.

Hence, universal and equal rights came to prevail over occupationally segregated programs and heavy reliance on private protection. The importance of previous employment and earnings records was gradually abolished, as were means testing and stigma. Most important, the boundary between public and private was constantly pushed back as more and more areas of welfare and distribution were moved from the market to the state.

The congruence of Scandinavian social democratic welfare policy is explained by two critical factors. One was that the parties chose to abandon the ghetto model in favor of parliamentary majoritarianism. They had to cultivate, and fabricate, unity among workers, peasants, and the rising white-collar strata. This naturally led to an insistence on universalism. The other was that the social democrats had come to power on the basis of a similar kind of political class alliance during the 1930s, and they were politically dominant within this alliance. The depression crisis, as in other countries, pointed up the dangers to working-class unity that came with mass unemployment and impoverishment. It also sensitized the social democrats to the possibilities for fascist mobilization among poor farmers and the urban petite bourgeoisie. This suggested a strategy of extending protection and equal benefits to all social classes.

It would be incorrect to claim that the social democrats had a complete blueprint for the postwar welfare state. As they shelved the socialization issue and committed themselves to Keynesian full-employment policy, social reform naturally became a programmatic priority. During the 1930s party energies were concentrated on the immediate problems of crisis management, economic relief and, above all, the unemployment question (Esping-Andersen and Korpi 1984). Not until after the war did a more systematic strategy evolve. Indeed, it was only in Norway that a comprehensive plan was concocted—the *Folketrygd* [People's Security] program. Signed by all parties, this program promised a) to eliminate the need for public relief, b) to guarantee adequate living standards for all, c) to achieve greater equality, and d) to sustain full employment (Lund and Langholm 1967). Though not exactly by careful plan, the social democrats nevertheless did lay the legislative foundations for the postwar welfare state.

In Denmark, it has been noted, the social democrats' achievements were essentially limited to an administrative consolidation of existing schemes. Although the party did triumph in the battle to institution-alize the entitlement principle with respect to social assistance benefits,[6] the 1930s were, generally speaking, not a watershed for Danish social democratic welfare advances. In Sweden and Norway, the social dem-ocrats were in a better position to benefit politically from social reform. In 1934, the Swedish social democrats were able to pass a desperately needed unemployment insurance law, and they also succeeded in con-siderably raising the level of pensions and other benefits. Their ability to legislate a large public-employment program—paying standard wages—was probably just as important from an electoral point of view. The Norwegians, too, were able to pioneer important reforms. In 1936, with support from the bourgeois parties, the social democrats introduced Norway's first old-age pension (which, in fact, followed the existing Swedish plan closely). Disability pensions soon followed, and Scandinavia's only compulsory unemployment insurance was leg-islated in 1938. This last, in fact, is a good illustration of why the universalistic principle was important to social democracy. Given the DNA's large rural political base, and the fact that these groups were difficult to include in a voluntary trade union plan, universal and compulsory coverage was clearly called for.

By World War II, then, the only important difference between the three social democracies was their unequal ability to use social reform as a catalyst for political mobilization. It is with the postwar construc-tion of the welfare state that a politically decisive divergence first emerges. In the remainder of this chapter, we shall examine postwar welfare state development in the three Nordic countries and then compare the factors that arguably could influence social democratic electoral cohesion. These include primarily the degree of institution-alized solidarity, the extent of "decommodification," and the redis-tributive results.

SOCIAL DEMOCRACY AS WELFARE STATISM

If Denmark, under liberal auspices, spearheaded Scandinavian social policy before the war, Sweden was, under social democratic leadership,

---

[6] Although this was a major blow against the relief stigma of the past, the law still contained some residue of the traditionally punitive approach to poverty relief. It can also be argued that the basically administrative nature of the 1933 social reform implied a temporary recognition of the previous liberal system.

the postwar leader. The popular notion of a distinctly Scandinavian welfare state holds some truth. Still, the three countries diverge in respect of their concrete achievements as well as in the political repercussions of their welfare reforms. In any case, there is no doubt that social democracy has been the leading force behind Scandinavian welfare state development, but it has been so under varying conditions. In Denmark, social democratic ambitions have been heavily constrained by liberal, petit-bourgeois interests. Little in the way of direct conflict ever erupted over individual reforms, but this does not necessarily imply consensus. One might say that the Danish social democrats were allowed to expand public social welfare, but not without adhering to liberal notions of how to expand it. As a consequence, the Danish welfare state has become somewhat of an outlier with respect to the celebrated "Scandinavian model."

The Norwegian and Swedish welfare states appear to be very similar in content and structure. To a degree, this can be partly explained by political diffusion; the Norwegians have on occasion simply followed the Swedish lead. But the main explanation is that these two social democracies were a) considerably more hegemonic in the postwar era, b) only marginally pressed to compromise with the bourgeois parties, and c) typically in command of stronger and more permanent parliamentary majorities. Also, as Castles (1978) has emphasized, the chronic divisions between the Norwegian and Swedish bourgeois parties were successfully exploited by the social democratic parties. Nor is the nature of union-party relations insignificant.

Although the Swedish and Norwegian welfare states pretty much converge, the political conditions under which they evolved differ importantly. In Norway, social democratic reforms were pursued with the consent of the bourgeois parties (Kuhnle and Solheim, 1981), dating back to the cooperative postwar program for planned welfare state development (the *Folketrygd* program). The Norwegian reforms, therefore, hardly seem to be a particularly social democratic achievement. In Sweden, several major reforms had to be fought for under conditions of unusually tense left-right conflict. Since the social democrats have emerged victoriously in every instance, they have also been able to profit politically. To some extent this is what happened with the sickness insurance reform of the early 1950s, and it was very much the case with the debacle over retirement pensions in the late 1950s.

The postwar politics of welfare state development can, in all three countries, be divided into two stages.[7] The first runs through the 1950s

[7] This account of postwar welfare state development follows Esping-Andersen and Korpi (1984).

and is characterized by the primary goal of comprehensive social protection with universal and equal flat-rate benefits. The second takes over during the 1960s, when the emphasis shifted in favor of securing more adequate benefit standards, equality, preventive social policy, and stronger entitlements.

The cornerstones of the contemporary welfare state were set during the 1940s and 1950s. All three Nordic countries followed essentially the same principles and plans. The prevailing emphasis was to universalize coverage and equalize benefits within a comprehensive system of protection and to endow all individuals with a citizen right to basic security and welfare. Most legislation was along the lines of Marshall's (1964) social citizenship concept. In this respect, Scandinavian developments as a whole diverged from those elsewhere. Whereas most countries extended social security by including new groups within existing insurance systems (Perrin 1969) Denmark, Sweden, and Norway explicitly broke with the liberal tradition by introducing universal, noncontributory programs. In principle, the Beveridge plan was a guidepost; the Scandinavian reforms, however, went further.[8]

The move toward universalism began with the Swedish social democratic pension reform of 1948. Coverage was universal, benefits were flat-rate, and all contribution- or means-tested eligibility qualifications were removed. The scheme was copied by the Danes in 1956 (although not fully implemented until 1964) and, in 1957, by the Norwegians. It was a victory over both the old relief form of assistance and the insurance system favored by the bourgeois parties. However, it was not a total victory. For one thing, the social democrats could not claim sole responsibility for universal, noncontributory pensions. If, at one time or another, the bourgeois parties had pushed for self-financed insurance, they proved amazingly willing to embrace universal, noncontributory plans whenever popular opinion seemed to favor them. But this is not so surprising when we consider that their political base consisted largely of urban and rural petite bourgeoisie, who were difficult to include in insurance plans.

In the case of Denmark, there was the additional circumstance that most employers were small and could hardly shoulder the social security contribution burdens (Friis 1971).[9] In Denmark, moreover, the social democrats had to concede generous tax incentives for private pension plans (Friis 1971; Vesterø Jensen 1982).

[8] The Beveridge system retained the insurance element, albeit in diluted form, whereas Scandinavian social security largely abolished any connection between financial responsibility and benefit eligibility—except in the case of unemployment insurance.

[9] The Danish social democrats had been aware of this constraint long before the war (Zeuthen 1944).

Another important postwar social democratic demand was for universal and equal child (or family) allowances, a central ideal in the labor movement since the 1930s.[10] In this case, the Norwegian social democrats were the pioneers, in 1946, but the other two countries soon followed. Identical principles would guide subsequent reforms in accident insurance, which once again was universal, compulsory, and state-administered. Once again, too, concessions to liberalism were evident in Denmark, where accident insurance was allowed to continue under private administration.

The first serious political battles came with the issue of medical insurance. The goal of universal, state-financed health care and sick pay dates back to the earliest social democratic program. The German SPD included it in the Erfurt program of 1891; the Danes gave it prominent attention in their somewhat radical 1913 program. But the question was complicated, especially in Denmark, by the fact that the labor movement had simultaneously gained a strategic interest in autonomous sick-pay funds. The issue of health protection, therefore, boiled down to a double issue: a) free and universal public provision of health care and b) state subsidies to health insurance funds in order to reduce the financial burden on workers. In Norway and Sweden, the independent sick-pay funds never played the dominant role they had in Denmark, and there were large gaps in popular protection.

It is thus understandable that Sweden, followed by Norway, led the way in health-care legislation. In Sweden, the issue provoked a political confrontation with the bourgeois parties, for the social democrats wanted universal and compulsory coverage, state financing, and earnings-related cash benefits.[11] The conflict was a protracted one, and it was not until 1955 that the law was passed. The Norwegians more or less copied this scheme one year later. In Denmark, reform had to wait until 1960 and, when it did come, included the usual compromise with liberalism. The state assumed most of the financial burden, but the system remained organizationally within the quasi-autonomous

[10] At first, the chief motive was to counter declining fertility (Myrdal and Myrdal 1934). After the war, however, egalitarian concerns prevailed (Elmer 1978), for it was held that society had a collective responsibility to see that all children, irrespective of family income and size, should be given the same opportunities for growth and advancement. During the 1960s and 1970s, another motive was at work, and the question of sexual equality gained prominence (Baude 1978).

[11] Note that in this instance the social democrats departed from their conventional model of equal, flat-rate benefits. The motive, as with later implementation of graduated benefits, was to ensure adequate income replacement and to place the worker on a par with the privileged civil servant.

health funds.[12] Denmark would have to wait until the reform of 1971 for health insurance to be made completely universal and state-controlled.

The thrust of social legislation in all three countries was to establish what Titmuss (1974) terms the "institutional welfare state." This implies two important commitments. First, society takes over responsibility to provide and guarantee adequate levels of welfare for all members of society; citizen entitlements, rather than family or market contract, constitute the nexus of welfare distribution. Second, socially stigmatizing and degrading forms of public relief are discarded in favor of an inviolable right to a certain level of welfare, to be determined by prevailing societal standards. In both senses, "institutionalization" was a cornerstone of social democratic reform policy. It was, in fact, included in Norway's postwar *Folketrygd* program.

In all three countries, means-tested programs lost their traditional importance during the 1950s. Whatever remnants there were, however, still retained the character of punitive relief. The Swedish social democrats removed such remnants in their 1956 reform; the Norwegians, in 1965. The successive Danish reforms culminated with a complete overhaul in 1974.[13] As a result, means-tested assistance plays a substantially smaller role in the three Scandinavian nations than it does anywhere else.

Notwithstanding occasional opposition to all sorts of reforms, bourgeois-party opposition, especially in Denmark, centered on the institutionalization issue.[14] The debate broke out in the late 1950s and early 1960s, when the Danish economy moved from stagnation to growth and full employment. The bourgeois parties, notably the liberals, claimed that such economic growth eliminated the need for social security expansion. The social democrats, however, supported by their

[12] Nor was the Danish system truly universal, since membership distinctions between high- and low-income families were preserved. The latter had to pay higher contributions, but enjoyed a wider range of free benefits; the former paid only a token contribution, but were not entitled to many benefits.

[13] The Danish reform is fascinating for many reasons. Denmark legislated the basic principle that all citizens should be guaranteed against sudden drops in income and living standards; thus, a guaranteed social income, irrespective of cause of hardship, was institutionalized. This was probably the world's most advanced—and most expensive—social assistance scheme. Unhappily, it came exactly when the Danish economy was sinking into recession and this—coupled with the political uproar over stories of bankrupt millionaires receiving public money to maintain their yachts—caused the program to be revised some years later.

[14] To repeat, in Norway the bourgeois parties had fully committed themselves to welfare institutionalization when they signed the program for *Folketrygden* in 1945.

radical-liberal allies, argued successfully that it was precisely because of economic growth that the long-promised extension of social rights and benefits could be undertaken (Christiansen 1975, 11).

At issue was whether or not a more selective approach should be stressed—whether social expenditures should be targeted only to the needy, assuming that the majority of the population could provide for their own welfare through family, community, and the marketplace. It was the social democrats' ability to win this battle over principles which ensured them sufficient political mandate to institutionalize the welfare state during the 1960s and 1970s. The mandate was tempered in Denmark, where private schemes have been gaining substantial influence.

The social democratic victory on the institutionalization question undoubtedly has much to do with the fact that, by and large, it was already a *fait accompli*. The foundations had been given the task of providing coverage to all citizens, irrespective of market status or employment situation; of separating financial responsibility from benefit eligibility; and of extending collective services to a wider and wider field of social needs. As a consequence, the social democrats had been able to win a large majority of the population over to their model for welfare state growth. The postwar reforms thus turned out to be a sound political investment that would make possible the satisfaction of other ambitions.

But the reforms also had inherent weaknesses. This became apparent when the universal, flat-rate benefits failed to provide adequate levels of income replacement. To compensate for general income growth, governments did introduce indexation and higher benefits, but the problem was threefold. First of all, demographic changes and constant pressure to raise benefits threatened to overload public finances in the longer run. Secondly, a novel kind of poverty was discovered: it became evident that social benefits were inadequate to ensure a decent standard of living among those most dependent on them. Thirdly, the flat-rate principle had inadvertently bred a new social stratification. Higher-income strata would naturally seek to supplement modest public benefits by means of private schemes. Concomitantly, the longstanding tradition of generous social provisions for civil servants seemed increasingly unjust as their ranks swelled. In short, for reasons of justice, equality, and fiscal strain, the social democrats were forced to reconsider the principles of social policy.

Simply to raise the level of flat-rate benefits to adequate standards was obviously out of question, because this would require formidable tax burdens. The only realistic alternative was to implement an earnings-graduated, funded supplementary system that, ideally, would finance itself. That, in fact, is what happened. The Swedish social democrats took the lead, as usual, proposing a universal, supplementary retirement pension in the mid-1950s. To prevent the erosion of collective social solidarity, the so-called ATP pension plan insisted on compulsory membership for all employees in both the public and private sector (with voluntary affiliation for the self-employed); to ensure adequacy, pension benefits were pegged at two-thirds of working income during a person's fifteen best years. Financial responsibility was delegated to employees and employers, the latter assuming most of the burden. The plan, largely designed by the LO, promoted one more goal; namely, that the inevitably huge savings accumulation would be collected in publicly controlled funds.

For the trade unions, the reform would serve to kill two birds with one stone. It would solve the dilemma of old-age pensions without much additional cost to either the state or the workers. Moreover, it would shift responsibility for aggregate savings from the private market to the public realm. Thus, the ATP scheme was not a matter of pensions alone, but was also an effort to complement active labor-market policy with an active credit policy. Naturally, this was unacceptable to Swedish capitalists and the three bourgeois parties, and the plan gave rise to one of the major power struggles in postwar Sweden (Molin 1967).

The employers did not reject the need for retirement pensions, and they were even prepared to foot part of the bill. Their opposition centered around the question of collectively controlled pension funds: these would extend state power over investments, reduce private savings, and violate the principle of free enterprise. Nor were the employers happy about the compulsory element; they preferred a system of private voluntary pensions, which they could preside over themselves. Luckily for social democracy, the bourgeois bloc was its usual divided self, and the issue gave rise to a series of mutually conflicting counterproposals.

The employers' association, the SAF, at first insisted on reaching a settlement via collective bargaining rather than legislation. The conservative party produced its own proposal, pretty much in accordance with the employers' view, and the governing social democrats' alliance partner, the center party (Bondeförbundet), broke ranks by suggesting a third proposal. The basis for a political consensus did not exist; so in 1957 the government had no choice but to relegate the question to a public referendum, which only fueled more conflict. Among the three alternatives, the LO–social democratic scheme received a plurality, but not a majority, of the vote. The bourgeois parties, moreover, insisted that the outcome be interpreted as a majority sentiment against the social democratic proposal.

Faced with political stalemate, fierce ideological confrontations, and a breakdown of the social democratic–centrist alliance, the SAP could neither continue in office nor back down on its commitment. It was forced to call a new election. This did not, however, give it the requisite parliamentary majority to pass the bill, and the stalemate persisted. The issue's eventual resolution gives us in capsule form a good picture of how the ATP conflict helped manufacture the most important post-war social democratic realignment.

A key actor in the drama was the trade union federation for white-collar employees, the TCO. The TCO, unlike the LO, remained in-dependent of any party. Yet, the rising white-collar electorate clearly offered the new margin needed for either social democratic or liberal electoral power. It was therefore decisive when the TCO was swayed to endorse the social democratic proposal during the 1958 election campaign. The liberal party was forced to break ranks with the other two bourgeois parties and move closer to the social democrats. Mean-while, the centrists and the conservatives united behind a private, voluntary pension-insurance plan. The issue was now polarized in such a way that political lines corresponded to class lines: the conservative and the center parties representing employers and the rural and urban petite bourgeoisie; the social democrats moving toward a coalition of blue-collar and white-collar wage earners.

The social democratic minority government, encouraged by broad wage-earner support, presented the ATP bill to parliament. Though the bill passed easily in the social-democratic-dominated first chamber, in the second chamber it was to fall, predictably, on one vote. Even-tually, however, under very dramatic circumstances, a liberal party member was persuaded to abstain and the bill finally passed by a one-vote margin.

If, until this point, Swedish politics appear to have been character-ized by "end of ideology," the ATP battle reinstated with utmost clarity the essential ideological differences between the two political blocs. It is not without significance that the social democrats emerged trium-phant from this their most intense political confrontation with the bourgeois parties. Most observers agree that the social democrats emerged a much stronger party (Molin 1967; Särlvik 1977; Elvander 1980). They had succeeded in deepening divisions among the bourgeois parties and, because the reform proved immensely popular, those par-ties were discredited, as well. The social democrats gained in subsequent elections, especially among the white-collar strata. But, above all, the issue provoked the collapse of social democracy's traditional farmer coalition and helped the movement build a new wage-earner coalition for the future. Herein lies one of the principal sources of Swedish social democracy's continued power advantage.

A few years later, the ATP issue surfaced in Denmark and Norway. But in neither case did it benefit social democracy politically. In Norway, it was again the LO that initiated the debate, and by 1960 an ATP pension agreement had been reached via collective bargaining. Still, the LO insisted on legislation and, after the social democratic government crisis of 1963, the party, pressed by the newly founded Norwegian Socialist People's party, adopted a plan virtually identical to the Swedish version (Rokkan 1966). The Norwegian social democrats, however, were prevented from profiting electorally, for the bourgeois parties, fearing a replication of the disaster that befell their Swedish brethren, also proposed ATP legislation (Elvander 1980, 268). As it turned out, ATP was implemented by the bourgeois government in 1967.

If ATP was beneficial for Swedish social democracy and neutral for the Norwegians, it was a distinct failure for the Danes. In Denmark, the LO urged the social democrats to present a bill similar to the Swedish one. In the context of a legislated incomes-policy package in 1963, the LO was promised an ATP reform. A very modest plan was passed in 1964, and it failed to satisfy most of the demands placed upon it. More limited in scope, the plan called for contributions so low—and coming mostly from the workers themselves—that it could hardly provide a fund for collective investment; benefits were so meager that they scarcely affected retirement incomes.[15] In 1967, during the social democrats' Red Cabinet period, a Swedish-style ATP (in Denmark, ITP) was once again proposed. The bill foundered in its first parliamentary hearing. Inexplicably, the social democrats then laid it to rest and addressed the pension-adequacy issue by adding an income-tested pension supplement (raising the level of the basic benefit) and by passing a law in 1971 on "social pensions," designed to provide for a certain degree of funding in the public sector. In the latter case, however, finances derive only from normal tax revenues.

On the pension issue, then, Danish social democracy proved unable to win over the new middle strata. Ironically, the ITP proposal came

[15] The scheme was not earnings-graduated, and both contributions and benefits are flat-rate. Since it is not cost-of-living indexed, inflation has seriously eroded the value of benefits.

at a political turning point similar to that experienced by the Swedish party in the late 1950s. The traditional coalition with the radical liberals was in disarray, and the latter were drifting to the right as the social democrats initiated contacts with the SF. In Denmark, however, the situation clearly did not permit a realignment. In contrast to what had happened in Sweden, the bourgeois parties of Denmark were unanimous in their opposition and, as a consequence of social democracy's shift to the left, they were uniting rather than fragmenting.

The political repercussions of earlier policy accomplishments must also be taken into account. As part of previous pension-reform agreements, the social democrats had conceded generous tax provisions to encourage private pension plans.[16] But private pensions, whether in the form of company fringe benefits or individual retirement insurance, were chiefly advantageous to higher-income earners who could afford the price as well as benefit from tax advantages. As a consequence, salaried employees were already wedded to private solutions and could not so easily be mobilized in support of a public ATP plan. Previous reforms had encouraged new social divisions that weakened social democracy.

Having led off with the ATP reforms, the Nordic countries—Denmark included—began to inject the principle of earnings-graduated benefits into other programs, such as sick-pay, unemployment insurance, and accident compensation. The goal was to establish a level of earnings replacement so high that individual beneficiaries would suffer no significant net-income loss. Against bourgeois-party and employer insistence that this would encourage worker absenteeism and a breakdown of worker morale, the social democrats managed to legislate replacement rates that almost equaled normal work income. Another achievement, again bitterly opposed by the employers, was the elimination of such eligibility conditions as waiting days for sick pay and unemployment benefits.

One consequence of this new emphasis was that the issue of equality resurfaced. ATP together with the new sickness-benefits reform had eradicated pre-existing differences of status between manual workers and salaried employees. But ATP did not help those too old to be included in the scheme. To correct lingering inequalities among beneficiaries, all three social democratic parties proceeded to introduce an array of income-tested benefit supplements. While this novel em-

---

[16] The most important, and the most problematic, were the so-called index contracts. The public budget would guarantee that private pension-insurance premiums would keep up with inflation. Since inflation rose steadily during the 1960s and 1970s, the burden on the public purse obviously increased.

phasis on selective targeting undoubtedly helped reduce inequality, it was also an important departure from social democracy's traditional commitment to universal entitlements. This, in connection with the necessary growth of tax burdens, has the potential for stimulating an explosive politicization of equity issues. Those who primarily bear the tax burden will naturally also be the ones precluded from eligibility for income-tested supplements. Thus, if the welfare state failed to bring about a powerful solidaristic commitment, the rise of differentiated treatment can more easily provoke tax revolts and welfare state protest.

INCOMPATIBILITIES OF THE WELFARE STATE

The social democratic welfare state tried, with considerable success, to satisfy three fundamental goals. These goals were attained primarily through the state. Hence, latent incompatibilities began to surface as the size of the public sector exploded and full-employment economic growth faded. In all three Scandinavian countries, the social democrats are now facing diminishing political returns from their welfare state program, and a reassessment of the relationship between the welfare state model and the capitalist economy has been forced upon them. The problem is undoubtedly more serious in Denmark, to the extent that the economic crisis there has compelled the social democrats to dismantle a number of achievements.

The problem of incompatibility rests on the realization that a combined commitment to universalism, entitlements, and equality is not feasible within existing state-economy relations.[17] The first problem is what we might call the race between inegalitarian market forces and the attempted corrective measures. The market produces losers and winners, while the welfare state promises status and income equality. The spiraling costs to the public budget as social services and transfers are deployed in the battle against market-produced inequalities testifies to the continued hegemony of the marketplace. The solidarity that is sought through universalization of citizenship entitlements is jeopardized by the market's natural propensity to differentiate and to nurture competition. So long as public policy cannot eliminate this propensity of the market, "government overload" will continue to be a looming possibility.

A second incompatibility is evident where entitlements permit a

[17] I have dealt with this question more extensively elsewhere (Esping-Andersen 1981b and 1982).

degree of worker decommodification that conflicts with market efficiency. The abolition of waiting days and the implementation of generous cash benefits were consciously motivated by a desire to free workers from the inhumane obligation to work when sick or to take undesirable jobs out of necessity. The increase in worker absenteeism and the reduced discipline were anticipated; however, such decommodifying reforms are exploited primarily by workers situated at the bottom of the labor market. So long as bad jobs persist, then, these kinds of entitlements will help diminish worker productivity and stimulate public expenditure at the same time.

The goals themselves are mutually incompatible. By necessity, the expansion of generous and universal social services and benefits requires heavy tax burdens. The more one pursues universalism and entitlements, the greater the need for tax revenues. This means that the public budget loses its potential for substantial redistribution through progressive taxation, since every marginal increase in revenue requirements necessitates a downward extension of the tax scale. Because the bulk of taxable income is concentrated among middle-income households, the inevitable result is that workers and white-collar strata come to bear a disproportionate share of the welfare state burden.

The conflict between these priorities is potentially severe, especially when economic stagnation fuels additional social expenditure in the context of a contracted, or stagnant, revenue base. It is in the resolution of these sets of conflicts that we can find much of the explanation for why the Danish party is decomposing to a much greater extent than either of the other two. A crucial precondition for the resolution of welfare state incompatibilities is to establish effective political control over economic growth. Naturally, full employment reduces the incidence of social problems and maximizes both productive output and taxable capacity. But government ability to control the economy is additionally important to the extent that planned rationalization will help eliminate those industries least capable of providing good working conditions and wages.

As I will show in Chapter 7, there is no doubt that in both Sweden and Norway the social democrats have succeeded in reducing welfare state incompatibilities by such means. The Swedish active labor-market policy is certainly costly, but there is little doubt that it has helped to eliminate low-wage jobs and to shift redundant workers into more dynamic industries. The Swedish and Norwegian labor movements' success with solidaristic incomes policies has helped reduce earnings differentials and hence dampened pressures on the public budget for equalization and redistribution. Similarly, the ATP reforms reduce the public sector's need to provide adequate retirement income, even if they do not have important redistributive effects as such.[18] Unlike the Danish social democrats, the Swedes and Norwegians have managed to transfer some responsibility for aggregate welfare from the public budget to the general economy. This may help explain why welfare state revolt and tax protest were so massive and intense in Denmark, yet so weak in Norway and Sweden.

But if political control of the economy is one precondition, another is the ability to manufacture a level of social solidarity sufficiently strong to immunize the welfare state against equity struggles and tax protest. The welfare state must be organized in such a way that it does not invite conflicts of interest between taxpayers and benefit recipients or nurture jealousies between groups inequitably positioned in respect of welfare benefits and costs. The Danish social democratic welfare state is much more conducive to new social cleavages and electoral protest on these grounds than either the Norwegian or the Swedish state. In the following section, we shall review some measures of welfare state performance in the three Nordic countries. Few important variations seem to be revealed by general aggregate indices, such as level of taxation and expenditure. It is when we turn to structural and distributive indices that more decisive variations appear.

THE CONSEQUENCES OF WELFARE STATE GROWTH

Two inescapable effects of welfare state growth are that the rate of expenditure and the tax rate both escalate. Table 5.1 shows that all three Nordic countries have experienced sustained growth in both areas throughout the 1960s and 1970s. The Norwegian rate of increase has been considerably slower, and the Swedish rate very rapid during the late 1970s. This orthogonality may be ascribed to Norway's extraordinarily strong economic growth rate in contrast to the economic stagnation experienced by both Denmark and Sweden. With respect to explaining national differences in welfare state backlash, aggregate expenditure data seem to provide no clues. In the early 1970s, when protest was at its peak, Denmark and Sweden spent just about the same, and Norway spent considerably less.

In general, if the aggregate levels of either social expenditure or taxation should explain variations in anti-welfare-state sentiment, one

---

[18] In Sweden there is some controversy on this subject. The Secretariat for Economic Planning (SEP 1970, 184) claims that ATP has a major redistributive effect, while Ståhlberg (1981) demonstrates the absence thereof.

TABLE 5.1. Growth of Social Expenditure and Taxation in Scandinavia
(% of GDP)

	Denmark	Norway	Sweden
SOCIAL EXPENDITURE			
1962	10.6	9.7	10.9
1972	19.3	15.8	20.3
1978	26.2	21.9	33.1
TAXES			
1960	26.0	35.6	30.0
1970	40.0	41.2	41.0
1978	42.9	48.7	50.9

SOURCES: OECD (1980a); Nordisk Råd (1980, table 193); NU (1966-1975).

would have anticipated the strongest effects in Sweden—whereas, in fact, no such phenomenon occurred. Heidenheimer et al. (1975) have suggested that the *rate* of tax increase might better explain why the progress party was so successful in Denmark. Table 5.1 does show a phenomenal rate of increase in Danish taxation between 1960 and 1970. Yet, Sweden experienced a similar shock wave in the 1960-1966 period with no apparent protest consequences.

It could be argued that the structure of taxation would play a role in creating broad popular loyalties to the welfare state. Here several aspects must be considered. First of all, to what degree are state finances derived from such various sources as corporate taxation, direct and indirect taxes, and social security contributions? Corporate taxation plays a minor role in all three countries, owing to their policy of encouraging investment through lower taxes on retained corporate earnings. In Denmark such taxes account for approximately 3 percent; in Sweden, about 2 percent; in Norway, if we exclude revenues from the oil industry (OECD 1981), about 3 percent.

With respect to the remaining three forms of taxation, which clearly constitute the overwhelming source of revenue, the question is partly one of progressivity and partly one of visibility, to the extent that Wilensky (1976) is correct in arguing that hidden taxes create greater public tolerance toward high levels of taxation. Table 5.2 presents a functional analysis of the three countries' tax structures. Denmark's tax structure deviates from that of the other two because it relies heavily on direct income taxation, and because social security contributions play a peripheral role. This would seem to confirm Wilensky's

TABLE 5.2. Income Taxes, Indirect Taxes, and Social Security Contributions
in Scandinavia, 1968 and 1978
(% of total tax revenue)

	Denmark	Norway	Sweden
INCOME TAXES			
1968	46.9	36.0	41.7
1978	59.7	34.7	39.7
INDIRECT TAXES			
1968	40.4	36.0	29.7
1978	38.6	34.0	24.4
SOCIAL SECURITY			
1968	4.6	23.2	17.0
1978	1.2	25.2	23.7

SOURCES: OECD (1980a); Danmarks Statistik (1978, table 342); Nordisk Råd (1980, table 186).

argument, since reliance on highly visible income taxes should work to politicize distributional resentment. The only problem with this explanation is that this situation has always obtained in Denmark. If tax visibility is to play a significant role, then it will have to be in combination with other factors, such as rapid, simultaneous tax increases, growing dissatisfaction with the nature of the benefits or with their distribution, or perceived inequality of the tax scale.

This leads us to the question of how financial burdens are distributed, a question that can be approached in several ways. One of these is to depart from the assumption that the larger the share of social security financing imposed on employers or on general government revenues (as opposed to individual contributions), the greater will be the incidence of "financial solidarity," holding the degree of general tax progressivity constant. Conversely, the greater the importance of individual self-financing, the less tolerant the public will be of generous welfare spending for "others." Table 5.3 shows dramatic differences among the three countries in this respect. Financial solidarity is quite high in the sense that general government revenues constitute the major share of social expenditure financing. In Norway, a considerable share is carried by the employees themselves. Both Norway and Sweden have shifted much of the total burden onto the employers. Again, Denmark is an extreme case, and general state revenues cover virtually all social spending.

There is no unambiguous conclusion to be made on the basis of

TABLE 5.3. Social Expenditure Financing in Scandinavia, 1964 and 1975
(% *contribution*)

| | Denmark | | Norway | | Sweden | |
	1964	1975	1964	1975	1964	1975
Government	82	88	53	30	62	65
Employers	3	10	22	47	21	24
Employees	15	2	25	23	17	11

SOURCES: NU (1969, 48; 1978, 50).

these findings. Denmark is consistently the outlier with respect to tax indicators: direct and visible taxes dominate, and general revenues cover virtually all social expenditures. Norway and Sweden are fairly close, although the former gives greater emphasis to indirect taxes and contributions. In part, these differences can be explained simply by Denmark's lack of funded ATP contributions, which surely account for the bulk of social contributions in Norway and Sweden. Moreover, Danish employers have effectively resisted the imposition of contributory levies, whereas the Swedish social democrats especially have managed to shift a larger and larger share of total financing onto the corporations.

On one hand, it can be argued that Denmark's welfare state finances are politically more fragile because they are visible; the absence of direct employee self-financing might add to political fragility if one believes that the perception of a direct connection between one's contributions and one's personal benefits helps create loyalty to the system. But, the opposite could be argued just as well. A strong individualistic flavor could excite egoistic rather than solidaristic commitments to the welfare state. On the one hand, it might give individuals a stronger sense of entitlement (Pinker 1971); but, on the other hand, it could also cause people to reject programs targeted for noncontributors.

THE WELFARE STATE AND EQUALITY

The social democratic promise of the welfare state has always been couched within a broad egalitarian ideology. The precise meaning of equality, however, is rarely specified; it could include equality of opportunity, citizenship status, or income distribution. As many critics began to argue during the 1960s, the social democratic welfare state seems to have failed miserably on the latter dimension.[19]

[19] On Britain, for example, see Titmuss (1962), Wedderburn (1974), and Westergaard

170

The critiques of the social democratic failure to effectuate fundamental income distribution came predominantly from the new left of the late 1960s, and they succeeded in prompting the social democrats to "reinvent" the egalitarian ideal. This was, indeed, the first wave of welfare state revolt in Scandinavia. Social democracy, in concert with the labor unions, responded with both rhetoric and action. All three parties set up commissions to examine the problem, and party programs promised a new era of redistribution. The labor unions, particularly in Sweden, mobilized new efforts to narrow wage differentials between occupations, regions, industries, and the sexes.

There was actually very little room for greater redistribution through tax and expenditure policies. The emphasis on generous universal services and on benefits of equal size and quality for all meant heavy tax burdens, even on modest incomes. Also, though universal benefits may achieve solidarity, their redistributive impact will remain relatively weak. The social democrats generally pursued three policies to further equalization. One was to seek greater progressivity in the tax structure, and to eliminate or reduce tax privileges. Another was to reintroduce income-tested transfer payments, such as housing allowances and pension supplements. A third was to contain and possibly reduce higher-level public-employee incomes; given public employment growth, these had great potential for redistribution, especially to the extent that such incomes were paid out of taxation.[20]

It is notoriously difficult to assess the redistributive impact of the welfare state, especially if we desire cross-historical and cross-national comparisons. The available data seem to confirm my proposition that the expansion of social expenditure imposes limits on the redistributive potential of taxation. Generally, the level of redistribution through the public sector is not much greater today than it was thirty years ago, despite the fact that the size of that sector has tripled in the meantime. For Denmark, a series of studies for the period 1939 to 1971 show that the redistributive impact of taxes and spending has remained rather constant over the entire period—the general effect appears to be that incomes are about 6 to 8 percent more equal owing to welfare state policies. Moreover, it seems that, over time, tax structure contributes less and less to equalization, and that most such is the result of social transfers (Lykketoft 1973).[21] Swedish research also seems to

---

and Reisler (1975). On Scandinavia, see Hansen (1973), Aakerman (1973), and Leion (1970). On social democracy in general, see Parkin (1972).

[20] A fourth avenue of redistribution has to do with concentration of wealth. This problem, which was addressed mainly by the trade unions, gave rise to the proposals for collective wage-earner funds.

[21] These conclusions are based on Olsen and Kampmann (1948), Ussing (1953), Bjerke

indicate that the major wave of equalization occurred during the 1930s and 1940s, but in Sweden—possibly because of greater success in securing full employment—the redistributive effect was greater.

Yet Sweden underwent a second important wave of equalization around the late 1960s and early 1970s. For one thing, the tax schedule was made considerably more progressive in 1971; in addition, the social democrats managed successfully to reduce the income privileges of higher-paid public employees. The net result for Sweden, then, is that incomes, after taxes and spending, are more equally distributed than in Denmark.[22] For Sweden, the difference between pre- and post-tax income distribution is estimated to have been 12.7 percent in 1972 (Sawyer 1976).

In Norway, the major equalization of incomes occurred during the 1940s and 1950s, again in connection with sustained full employment.[23] The Norwegian income tax structure, according to most studies (Sawyer 1976; TCO 1981), is one of the most progressive. This helps account for Norway's very good performance in reducing pre-tax income inequalities. On the basis of incomes statistics from the Norwegian Statistical Bureau (Sawyer 1976), the post-tax distribution is about 13 percent more equal. Note, however, that Norwegian governments have for a long time pursued incomes policy that favors farmers and peasants, a notoriously low income group. Such efforts were stepped up in the 1970s, but it is probably too early to evaluate their impact. Thus, from the rather scant data available, it appears that Norway and Sweden have had similar success at narrowing income differentials, and that Denmark falls far short.[24]

Aggregate indices, such as the Gini coefficient, are not suitable, however, since we are especially concerned with the political effects of welfare state policies. We need to know more about how taxation and social benefits affect the core political base of social democracy— namely, the workers—in relation to other social strata. Table 5.4 shows that the Danish tax structure is considerably less progressive than that of either Sweden or Norway with respect to the position of

(1961), Økonomisk Råd (1967), and Lykketoft (1973). After 1975, when the Danish government changed the income tax schedule in a regressive direction, the redistributive effects of taxation became even weaker.

[22] On Sweden, the principal studies are Bentzel (1952), United Nations (1967), Franzen et al. (1975), Leion (1970), and Spånt (1976).

[23] For Norway, I have relied primarily on Seierstad (1974), Rødseth (1977), Ringen (1979), and Sawyer (1976).

[24] It should also be noted that by most international comparisons Norway and Sweden together lie at the extreme end with respect to income equality (Sawyer 1976; Stark 1977).

TABLE 5.4. Taxes Paid by Typical Scandinavian Industrial Worker Family, Middle-Level Wage-Earner Family, and Top-Level Wage-Earner Family, 1977

Earnings =	Denmark			Norway			Sweden		
	100%	200%	400%	100%	200%	300%	100%	200%	400%
Direct Income Tax and Social Contributions as % of Gross Income	33.0	48.6	59.0	25.4	42.8	57.8	32.6	53.3	68.9
Ratio of Worker to Middle Income		100:147			100:169			100:163	
Ratio of Worker to High Income		100:179			100:228			100:211	
Marginal Tax Rate as % of Gross Income	54.0	64.8	64.8	33.4	60.4	68.4	55.1	80.0	85.0
Ratio of Worker to Middle Income		100:120			100:181			100:145	
Ratio of Worker to High Income		100:120			100:205			100:154	

SOURCES: TCO (1981).

NOTE: Families are assumed to include two children. Worker family incomes are indexed at 100%; middle-level family incomes at 200%; and top-level family incomes at 400%.

an average working-class family compared with that of a middle- or high-income family. As noted, Denmark's relatively poor standing reflects the impact of the 1975 income tax reform, which reduced burdens on middle and upper incomes.[25] But even if the tax systems of Sweden and, especially, Norway are considerably more redistributive from the viewpoint of an average working-class family, it is also these two countries that have been most successful in imposing

[25] It is much more difficult to assess the distributive properties of public social spending because little is known about variations in the public use of services and collective goods. With respect to cash transfers, though, a recent study by the Organization for Economic Cooperation and Development (OECD) shows that the net value of such transfers (as a percentage of gross income) is about the same in all three countries: a typical working-class household receives about twice as much in transfers as a typical middle-income family earning twice the gross income (OECD 1980, table 30).

173

greater income equality through solidaristic wage policies, thus reducing the burden on the public sector.

There are obviously a multitude of ways in which to study earnings inequalities. If we add the problem of change over time, we are faced with the question of how to take into account structural changes in the composition of the labor force. Let us limit our ambitions to three indices of income distribution: between workers and other occupational strata; between the sexes; and between workers, i.e. interindustry wage differentials.

To begin with occupational differentials, the best available comparable data demonstrate remarkably different inequalities in the three Nordic countries. If unskilled worker incomes are indexed at 100, the ratio of unskilled incomes to upper-level white-collar incomes is about 1:3 in Denmark, 1:2.45 in Sweden, and only 1:1.8 in Norway. (See Table 5.5.) For Norway and Sweden, we have comparable data for some years before 1971, and in the latter country it appears that differentials between unskilled workers and top-level white-collar employees have been narrowed substantially.[26]

In respect of wage differentials between the sexes, we face the typical problem that men and women frequently occupy different types of jobs. Nevertheless, differentials clearly have declined over the years, though less so in Norway than in Denmark and Sweden. (See Table 5.6.) Finally, the data on interindustry wage differentials show starkly contrasting trends for the three countries. (See Table 5.7.)

The Nordic countries have taken different paths. Denmark, which

TABLE 5.5. Occupational Earnings Differentials in Scandinavia, 1971
(*unskilled workers = index 100*)

	Denmark	Norway	Sweden
Unskilled Worker	100	100	100
Skilled Worker	140	116	141
Lower White Collar	133	130	134
Upper White Collar	309	181	245

SOURCE: Uusitalo (1975, table 7.11).
NOTE: Data are based on the average income for the gainfully employed in each occupational group.

[26] In 1963, the ratio was 1:310 between unskilled workers and high-level white-collar employees. Interestingly, there do not seem to be any changes between unskilled workers and lower-level white-collar employees (United Nations 1967, table 5.16). For Norway, also in 1963, the ratio was 1:206 (Seierstad 1974, table 14).

TABLE: 5.6. Average Hourly Earnings of Female versus Male Workers
in Scandinavia, 1960-1977
(% of male earnings)

	Denmark	Norway	Sweden
1960	66.5	67.6	69.3
1970	74.4	75.1	81.3
1977	85.5	79.8	87.3

SOURCES: SAF (1978, 1980).

TABLE: 5.7. Interindustry Wage Differentials in Scandinavia, 1960-1977

	Denmark	Norway	Sweden
1960	21.4	25.2	29.6
1970	22.0	25.4	20.0
1977	36.2	25.0	12.6

SOURCES: See Table 5.6.
NOTE: Indices are calculated according to the method developed by Olsson (1980)—industry average (100) minus the average below 100 plus the average above 100. The higher the value, the greater is the wage differential, or wage spread. The data are based on hourly wages, including standard bonuses, piecework rates, and overtime.

initially was the most egalitarian, has experienced a truly dramatic widening of industrial wage differentials during the 1970s; in Norway we find constancy; in Sweden, a remarkable narrowing over the two decades. With respect to Sweden, most of the narrowed differentials can be ascribed to the impact of the LO's solidaristic wage policy (Andersson and Meidner 1973; LO 1980), especially during the 1970s when labor markets were slack. Conversely, the deterioration of wage equality in Denmark during the same decade is probably due to the trade unions' inability to hold onto solidaristic wage negotiations during the severe economic crisis and heavy unemployment, especially among the weaker sections of the industrial labor force.[27] Taken together, the data on inequality suggest interesting differences among the three countries.

First of all, the Danish labor movement has clearly been least capable of bringing about greater equality; the sole exception is in the realm of female-employee earnings compared with those of men. On the whole, Norway has evidently been the most successful on two other

[27] The divided and craft-oriented structure of Danish unionism, however, also played an important role.

fronts: one is the ability to redistribute wealth via taxation; another is the achievement of low earnings differentials between workers and higher-level white-collar employees. Norway seems to have concentrated its efforts on effectuating a redistribution between classes. This is in contrast to Sweden, whose major accomplishments seem to have been concentrated within the working class itself—although the degree to which the earnings gap between workers and high-level employees has narrowed should be noted.

Interpretation of these findings for purposes of political analysis is not easy, since they readily speak to two opposite hypotheses. On the one hand, it could be maintained that efforts to shrink differentials dramatically, within and between the social classes, would provoke serious unrest—particularly among the formerly privileged.[28] On the other hand, one could also expect successful equalization to boost the fortunes of social democracy, especially when one considers that the major challenge from the left during the late 1960s concerned precisely the need for greater equality.

This kind of dual interpretation reflects the reality that contemporary social democracy is exposed to an exceedingly problematic incompatibility once it moves from "people's" to "wage earner" alliances. Income-equalizing platforms were attractive to impoverished peasants and workers alike; such platforms, however, easily estrange the salariat with its time-honored expectation of economic privileges, its anticipation of higher returns for education, and its natural interest in maintaining differentials. If social democracy, in tandem with trade unionism, can shift the process of income equalization over to the labor market, the contradiction may be eased. However, where it is compelled to wage the struggle for equality in public policy—whether through taxation or incomes policies—social democracy is likely to exacerbate the politicization of equity conflicts and impede the chances for a new political realignment. It is this contradiction that the Nordic social democrats must resolve. The Norwegians' exceptionally aggressive drive for equality must enter into any explanation of why the DNA has fared so poorly among white-collar strata in recent years.

THE WELFARE STATE AS AN AGENT OF SOLIDARITY

As already argued, universalism and institutionalism can be viewed as basic organizational principles for the construction of solidarity. The

---

[28] To the extent that social democracy is currently trying to forge an alliance with the new middle strata, moreover, its egalitarian achievements could very well be politically counterproductive.

TABLE 5.8. Private and Public Pension Expenditures in Scandinavia
(*000s*)

	Denmark	Norway	Sweden
Public Pension Expenditure	Kr 17,500,000	Kr 13,351,000	Kr 28,700,000
Private Individual Insurance	Kr 6,260,000	Kr 746,000	Kr 644,000
Private Occupational Plans	Kr 456,000	Kr 188,000	Kr 1,787,000
Private Total as Share of Public Total	38.22%	6.99%	11.70%

SOURCES: Danmarks Statistik (1981a); Statistisk Sentralbyrå (1978, table 7); Swedish National Audit Board (1982).

NOTE: Data for Demark pertain to 1977; for Norway, 1975; for Sweden, 1977. Public pension expenditure excludes civil servant pensions.

former implies that all citizens command an identical status and entitlement to any given benefit; the latter, that collective welfare is distributionally removed from the market, or from charity. A dominance of private market schemes would suggest a situation in which the distribution of welfare among the population closely mirrors market stratification. Table 5.8 presents data on the size of private social security benefits relative to public social security expenditure.

There are problems with the data on private insurance coverage, particularly in the case of Norway.[29] But even if more exact data were available, it would probably not alter the rank ordering among the three countries. Denmark, where private schemes have been allowed to flourish, is an extreme case. As shown above, this is clearly a consequence of the social democrats' necessary compromise with the bourgeois parties, combined with their inability to strengthen collective public pensions through an ATP-style retirement reform. If the private schemes in Denmark were of the general contractual kind (as in Sweden, where occupational plans cover all workers more or less equally), then their fragmentating and divisive effect would likely be smaller. But this is not the case. Private plans in Denmark are chiefly of two kinds: individual contracts and the company occupational funds enjoyed primarily by white-collar employees. There is also evidence that the distribution of individual tax-favored contracts is very uneven

[29] The exact figures on Danish private insurance schemes are higher than those shown in Table 5.8. Official Danish statistics, however, do not include all private plans. This is also true in the case of Norway. The Swedish data are better.

(Vesterø Jensen 1982; Olsen and Hansen 1981). Since the public universal pension is quite modest, the net result is a strong dualism in the entire system. A schism develops between those who are primarily dependent on the public system—unskilled workers and single women—and those who preside over additional private insurance—upper-level skilled workers. Essentially, this schism divides wage earners internally.

In Sweden, where private contractual plans coexist with the public system, their potential effect on solidarity is arguably different. For one thing, private schemes are relatively unimportant in the overall retirement-income package of employees. In addition, the private occupational plans have arisen through collective negotiations and cover all workers, thereby preventing the plans from having much of a stratifying impact. In Norway, the importance of either individual or occupational schemes is so minuscule that they should have no stratifying consequences worth mentioning.

In short, the three Nordic countries' social security schemes differ dramatically with respect to their solidaristic potentialities. The Danish case is exceptional in its divisive properties, and the political consequences are readily identifiable. Broad public support for the universal public pension—which even the former social democratic minister of social affairs, Ritt Bjerregård, is prepared to dismantle in favor of a return to means-tested old-age assistance—has been undermined. Moreover, a vested interest has been generated among the more privileged in the system of generous tax deductions for private insurance. Thus, despite several efforts to do so, the social democrats have been unable to reduce these inequitable forms of tax expenditure.[30] Neither in Sweden nor Norway has the social security system been confronted with similar kinds of attacks.

[30] In August 1982 the social democratic minority government was forced to resign on this issue. To cut social expenditures and raise revenues, the Danish social democrats had proposed to parliament a package bill: they were prepared to make substantial cuts in social security benefits in return for a tightening up of tax deductions among those on the private-pension savings plans.

SIX

The Housing Question

HOUSING POLICY should provide us with a good test of social democratic accomplishments and, as a consequence, of political mobilization or decomposition. For one thing, housing is central to household welfare and historically has ranked especially high among demands from both the working class and the population at large. Secondly, the housing question intersects social and economic policies in a peculiarly complex way. The distribution, standards, and costs of housing are concerns of welfare policy; yet, a frequent motive for government action in housing markets has been to stimulate, or dampen, macroeconomic activity and to promote employment. Housing is easily caught between these two policies when, for example, housing production is consciously reduced for the sake of releasing capital resources to industrial or other investment. In other words, housing policies are a sensitive and possibly contradictory political issue-area. They are a major source of public pressure, and they catch governments—of whatever coloration—in a difficult dilemma between welfare and economic-efficiency objectives.[1]

The housing market constitutes a relatively recent area of advance for the welfare state. Until World War II, government involvement with housing was marginal, typically limited to temporary measures induced by crisis. Local governments would occasionally participate in modest housing schemes for the poor or would, at times, provide rent allowances or introduce rent controls. In the Nordic countries, as elsewhere, housing remained almost exclusively a market commodity (Adams 1975; Donnison 1967; Esping-Andersen and Korpi 1984).

Nevertheless housing has always been an object of political class conflict. As Friedrich Engels held ([1872] 1951), in respect of nineteenth-century England, and as Donnison (1967), Wendt (1962), Hamilton (1967), and Castells (1972) argue concerning contemporary Western Europe, housing policy is frequently motivated by actual or perceived working-class militancy, communist party ascendance, or

---

[1] The dilemma is especially strong in the Scandinavian countries. Because their economies are small and open, the housing market easily affects the balance of payments.

revolutionary upsurge. Such motives have been translated into "Hauss-man tactics" (breaking up neighborhoods) or, perhaps more frequently, "Bismarckian tactics" (co-optation through single-family homeownership plans, residential relocation, and suburbanization). The political dividend projected by conservative or liberal forces was that the working classes would be more loyal to the prevailing social and economic order, less densely packed and angry, and possibly also more divided and individualized.

The realignment of social democracy in the 1930s did not constitute a historical watershed for housing policy as it had for social security and employment policies. In Denmark, Norway, and Sweden, social democratic efforts did step up construction; but these initiatives were employment programs, not really housing policies. Until the Second World War, the social democrats held to a "ghetto model" approach to the housing question, stressing the role of union- or party-sponsored cooperative, nonprofit housing associations for working-class families. The cooperative tradition was especially strong in Denmark and Sweden where, of course, working-class urbanization had proceeded much further than in Norway.

The war imposed a moratorium on new construction, and in Norway it also led to extensive destruction of existing housing—at least in the North. If the war thus inhibited political initiatives, it also helped catalyze postwar reformism to alleviate mounting and acute shortages. In the immediate postwar years, all three social democracies switched to an unusually activist strategy, defining housing policies in welfare terms and moving toward unprecedented public control in the market. Housing policy has been an especially politicized issue in the postwar politics of Scandinavia, fueled by exceptionally severe shortages, poor standards, and distributive concerns. Yet, despite virtually identical policies in the beginning, the nature and consequences of such politicization came to diverge dramatically by the 1960s and 1970s, primarily because the housing policies of the social democratic parties differed.

As we will see, the three strategies could hardly have been more divergent. The Danish social democrats permitted a return to free-market regulation and, via the tax system, encouraged single-family suburban homeownership. The Norwegians decided to retain strong public control over housing finance and distribution, but again with a homeownership bias. Finally, the Swedes favored cooperative apartment development with public control of credit and allocation. Only the Norwegian strategy seems to have been capable of optimizing the multiple goals of alleviating shortages and securing affordability, high standards, and equality without provoking equity conflicts and, thereby, political backlash effects. From a political mobilization perspective, the Danish strategy was easily the most disastrous since it helped fuel sharp equity struggles combined with inflationary real estate speculation. The Swedish strategy was efficient enough for eradicating shortages and creating affordable housing, but its obsession with high-rise apartment dwellings in suburban satellite towns has boomeranged in the 1970s. Given such clearly demarcated differences, housing policy affords us a unique opportunity to test its electoral-impact differentials.

POSTWAR HOUSING POLICIES IN THE NORDIC COUNTRIES

As in most other regions, postwar housing markets in Scandinavia were beset by severe shortages, overcrowding, antiquated dwelling standards, and upward pressures on prices.[2] Very little new construction was permitted during the war, while urban migration simultaneously accelerated. Furthermore, a lack of general upkeep exacerbated the problems.

Still, preconditions varied considerably. The degree of urbanization had remained quite low in both Sweden and Norway, largely because of industrial decentralization, and pressures on urban housing markets were of more recent origin. In both nations there was less of a tradition of working-class slums than in Denmark, a circumstance that naturally affected the nature of housing policies. The Danish housing situation, however, was better than that in the other two countries. Shortages were probably not so intense, and standards were clearly superior on the average (Donnison 1967). Norway faced the additional problem that the German army had destroyed just about everything in the northernmost parts of the country during its retreat.

Given such pressures, the postwar years would obviously see fewer political obstacles to a highly interventionist social democratic housing program. In addition, the social democrats were well positioned to extend state controls in the market, for lingering wartime price-and-material controls were already present. The first housing reforms came, in all three countries, in 1946. Even if they did signal a complete reversal of prewar housing policy with their intention of subjecting the market to extensive government control over finance, pricing, and

---

[2] In this chapter, I shall be treating the housing question in a rather condensed way. Those readers with an appetite for more detail are referred to Esping-Andersen 1980.

distribution, the reforms did not appear to be a dramatic political rupture.

At first, the Nordic nations adopted virtually identical approaches. Existing, quite elaborate controls on materials, dwelling standards, cost ceilings, and the like were continued—although they were gradually relaxed in the late 1940s and early 1950s. But, along with these controls, the state more or less took over the allocation of credit so that almost all new dwellings were built with state loans offering below-market, fixed-interest rates. The primary policy goal in these years was to build as much as possible within the constraints of material shortages, on one hand, and national economic performance on the other. In all three countries it was natural that the social democratic government would give cooperative housing associations preferential treatment in regard to credit supply. Direct public construction was of marginal importance.[3]

In the postwar years, therefore, the combination of public finance and cooperative building was significant. The state furnished the largest portion of total credit, and public-cum-cooperative building accounted for somewhere between one-third and one-half of all construction. In 1958, 73 percent of Danish, 64 percent of Norwegian, and a full 94 percent of Swedish dwellings were financed by state loans. Nonprivate construction accounted for 43 percent in Denmark, 25 percent in Norway, and 57 percent in Sweden in the mid-1950s (United Nations 1966, 25-28, annex 2).[4]

If state intervention was massive in all three cases, its emphasis varied. In Norway, the housing act favored single-family homes. Because of subsidized public mortgages (up to 100 percent), it was assumed that individual ownership would be affordable to all—particularly since such a large share of dwellings were built on a nonprofit basis. In contrast, both Danish and Swedish social democracy favored urban apartment construction during the 1940s and 1950s, most of it in the cooperative and rental sector. As mentioned, the objective was above all to maximize the volume of new construction, since housing shortages were viewed as a more pressing concern than distributional issues or dwelling standards. Since housing policy was general and universal, rather than selective and targeted, it enjoyed widespread political support. Indeed, construction volumes were im-

[3] The exception is Sweden, where joint local-government and cooperative projects are common.

[4] Government housing expenditure was uniformly high: in 1955, 12 percent of total public expenditure in Denmark, 17 percent in Norway, and 11 percent in Sweden (Elvander 1980, 275).

pressive, among the highest internationally (United Nations 1966; Donnison 1967).

Still, the issues of equity, affordability, and distribution remained, compelling the social democratic governments to add such selective programs as rent controls and rent subsidies. In light of continuing shortages, rent controls were retained for the older, prewar housing— particularly in the city of Copenhagen. This, however, tended to fuel increasingly bitter equity conflicts and created severe distortions in the housing market. Elderly inhabitants of prewar dwellings were of course reluctant to move into newer, smaller, and usually more expensive units. Concomitantly, young families with children were forced to choose newer housing, which meant higher rents and less space. The renter population was thus being divided along age lines. In addition, rent-controlled, prewar housing was visibly different. In the old working-class districts of Copenhagen, the vast majority of apartments had no central heating and frequently only communal toilets. Certainly, the housing market had always been harshly segmented by class and income. The practice of selective rent controls, however, provoked new divisions and possibly worsened the perception of inequities. Although similar problems were present in all three countries, they were nowhere more dramatic than in Denmark.

Nevertheless, until the late 1950s the Nordic nations followed a fundamentally similar course in housing policy and, on balance, the social democrats could take pride in their achievements. But the 1950s constitute a historical turning point after which the countries set off in different directions. The basic issue was that new objectives and demands came to the fore, partly because the problem of shortages had been alleviated and partly because of the gradually intensified equity conflicts.[5] In all three countries, the social democrats were forced to reformulate their housing policies.

DENMARK: FROM SOCIAL POLICY TO MARKET COMMODITY

In Denmark the housing question became extraordinarily politicized. The bourgeois parties, backed by powerful interest organizations, held that controls were no longer required now that the shortage problem

---

[5] A Danish Ministry of Housing report (Boligministeriet 1968, 47) showed that rent differentials between pre- and postwar units had become intolerably wide by 1960. In pre-1931 (rent-controlled) units, 60 percent of all households paid less than 10 percent of their income in rent, compared with only 4 percent among those living in units built between 1955 and 1960. More than four times more among the latter group paid over 30 percent of their income in rent.

had been eased. The free market, they argued, should be permitted to regulate prices and credit for new building. Moreover, they could successfully make a case for the market as a superior mechanism, compared with existing alternatives, for supplying housing according to the rich variety of social preferences in the Danish population. The social democratic party, in coalition with the radical-liberal party, was incapable of passing a new bill without collaboration with the right. Moreover, the bourgeois parties' promise of a rapidly growing housing market under laissez-faire conditions—albeit stimulated by generous tax deductions on mortgage payments—would easily resonate within the building trades. As usual, it was difficult for the social democrats to count on unity between the craft-oriented and the industrial branches of the trade union movement.

In 1958, the social democrats entered into a broad compromise agreement with the bourgeois parties and passed a new housing act that departed completely from previous policy. The act stipulated the withdrawal of the state from the credit market, leaving only the private savings-and-loan institutions and conventional banks. Rent controls were to be gradually eliminated and, in return, the social democrats were permitted to strengthen the system of rent allowances for families with children.

The 1958 reform produced new problems, exacerbated by growing inflationary pressures, and equity conflicts grew in scope and intensity. For political reasons a swift termination of the rent-control system was precluded, and the government resorted instead to gradual price adjustments. But prices on new construction grew even faster, and rents in prewar housing therefore remained 40 percent lower than those in new housing (Sørensen 1967). An even more severe problem was the incentive for speculation that arose in the new laissez-faire housing market. As a complement to the 1958 compromise, the social democrats had drafted a bill that would restrict real estate speculation. But they had not anticipated that a united chorus of farmers, landowners, builders, and financial representatives—backed by all the non-socialist parties—would defeat the bill. By the mid-1960s, therefore, the housing situation was once again in crisis.

By then, the political situation had changed quite dramatically. On the one hand, the social democrats had just been severely defeated in 1963 on their land-control bill. On the other hand, they were forced to govern alone after 1964, when the radical liberals left the coalition. At the same time, the new left-oppositional SF had grown unexpectedly strong, and vocalized a bitter attack on the "antisocial" 1958 housing reform. In contrast to what had happened in 1958, the social democrats were now caught in the dilemma of having to choose between a new housing compromise with the left or, as previously, with the right. They opted for the latter, a decision that probably more than any other helped bring about their electoral demise.

The 1966 housing reform essentially reaffirmed the 1958 act. Providing for a gradual elimination of remaining controls over the coming years, it sought to stimulate private homeownership via tax-deduction privileges and encouraged the transfer of existing rental apartments to owner-condominium conversion. The reform further reaffirmed the state's withdrawal from the finance market (although it did provide for a modest loan fund, designed to allocate special credits to co-op builders of lower-income housing). The social democrats also managed to extend the system of income-tested rent allowances.

In two broad sweeps, then, the Danish social democrats had removed housing problems from their social welfare programs, thrusting it back again into the invisible hands of the marketplace. After the passage of the bill, which clearly was the single most important—and most politicized—housing bill ever, political turmoil refused to subside. Massive and vocal opposition came from within the labor movement and especially from the SF. The partners to the compromise praised its soundness, and even the social democratic minister of housing, Kaj Andersen, stated enthusiastically that "we have eliminated one of the largest and most complicated political conflicts" (Wilhjelm 1971, 73).

Yet, opposition from renters remained powerful, and the social democrats lost heavily in the following local elections while their SF opponents leaped ahead. There is no evidence that the reform fueled splits within the social democratic party, but several leaders clearly view it as one of the party's worst political blunders. In the words of the party's finance minister, Henry Grünbaum:

> the agreement on housing was one of the party's major tactical and political blunders. Krag [the prime minister] refused to seek support from the SF, and this forced us to settle for legislation which was less beneficial to the working class, which overwhelmingly benefited homeowners, which did not do much to better the conditions of renters, and which did not result in the establishment of a public housing fund. On this piece of legislation the social democrats would have been wiser to have collaborated with the SF [personal interview, 19 December 1976].

In subsequent years, pressures for a new housing bill continued unabated. Although renter allowances were successively increased,

185

demands came from both the trade unions and the SF to eliminate homeowner tax privileges and increase state control over housing finance. The social democratic party introduced reform bills on several occasions, but these were immediately defeated—one reason being that a larger and larger number of workers had acquired homes and could anticipate tax deductions. In 1973, a social democratic proposal to reduce tax deductions even provoked a rightist splinter that, led by Erhard Jakobsen, proceeded to form the new center democratic party.

The reprivatization of the housing market occurred at a rapid pace. By the mid-1970s only 17 percent of new housing was being built with state loans (compared with 74 percent in 1958), and 82 percent of housing was being built by private undertakings (compared with only 57 percent in 1958). On the supply side, the laissez-faire policy seems to have produced remarkable results. Denmark has the least overcrowding among the Nordic countries and one of the highest standards of housing in the world; the ratio of workers owning their own homes is very high, probably around 60 percent. But the policy has evidently had negative distributive effects: homeowners are favored; renters are disadvantaged.[6] It has also impaired the Danish economy—especially over the past twenty years, during which inflation has helped stimulate heavy speculation in real estate. Finally, laissez faire clearly does not work for social policy goals. Among low-income households, rental costs are almost three times higher in Denmark than they are in Sweden; among middle-income families, they are almost twice as high (Nordic Housing Administration 1981).

NORWAY: INDIVIDUAL HOMEOWNERSHIP AS SOCIAL POLICY

The evolution of housing policy in Norway requires less detailed treatment: few changes have taken place since its inception, and in no case do housing politics seem to have unleashed divisive public controversy. The DNA retained and even strengthened public control over housing finance during the 1950s and the early 1960s, increasing the bias in favor of co-op builders. Gradually, almost all housing was built with state loans. The emphasis on single-family homeownership also continued; but, in contrast to Denmark, this bias is distributionally neutral since tax-deductible mortgage-interest payments play virtually no role at all. Instead, distributive goals have been pursued on the finance side

---

[6] In 1970 the estimated value of homeowner tax deductions was about four times the amount spent on rent allowances and government subsidies to cooperative housing (Wilhjelm 1971, 53).

via government-guaranteed, low-interest loans that provide special discounts to low-income families.

The only major Norwegian reform occurred in 1966, when the bourgeois-party coalition was in government, but existing policies were hardly altered. The state's contribution to mortgage financing was lowered in the case of high-income groups, who would now have to finance a higher percentage themselves. A rental allowance scheme, promoted by the social democrats, was simultaneously introduced with the political objective of guaranteeing that housing costs would not surpass 20 percent of the average worker's income.

Norwegian housing policy, despite its homeowner bias, has been the most consistently and deliberately egalitarian and solidaristic of the three. There is tax equity between renters and owners (many of whom also live in cooperatively built units), and average housing costs are the lowest in Scandinavia. Moreover, average housing cost as a percentage of typical gross family income is virtually the same for renters and owners (Nordic Housing Administration 1981; Elvander 1980; Guldbrandsen and Torgerson 1978).

SWEDEN: FROM SOCIALIZED HOUSING TO REPRIVATIZATION

Swedish governments continued along the lines of the 1946 reform until the late 1960s but, in the early 1970s, began to shift in a "Danish" direction. Sweden had escaped the ravages of the Second World War. Yet, its postwar housing problem was possibly even worse than that of Denmark, partly because of low wartime construction volumes. The big problem was the extremely rapid and sudden migration to the cities during and after the war. Between 1945 and 1955 there was a net migration of 250,000 people (Wendt 1962, 102), and in the course of thirty years—from 1931 to 1960—the urban population grew from 38 percent to 73 percent of the total (Adams 1975). Naturally, then, postwar governments immediately embarked upon a crash building program. An impressive 900,000 new dwellings were built between 1945 and 1960. On a per capita basis, this record was matched only by West Germany (Adams 1975). Indeed, the cities of Sweden were largely built after 1945.

Rent controls imposed during the war were retained to some extent in the older housing, but the equity effects do not seem to have been so disastrous as they were in Denmark. Rent differentials between new and old units were also smaller, in part because public authorities exercised better control over land and building costs. Hence, inflationary effects were checked more effectively.[7]

The approach of the Swedish social democrats was almost exclusively to build apartments—again, with a strong bias in favor of cooperatives. This, of course, helped hold down the costs of such a massive housing program. Moreover, the policy deliberately sought to marginalize free-market forces, an objective that met with considerable success. By 1955, less than 25 percent of new dwellings completed had been initiated by private capital (Wendt 1962, 86-87). If, before the war, housing cooperatives were relatively marginal, the postwar social democratic program established them as pre-eminent on the financial, ownership, and builder fronts. By far the most important cooperative builder in Sweden is HSB (Tenants' Savings and Building Association), but trade union cooperatives also play a large role.

Notwithstanding these ambitious schemes, housing shortages persisted throughout the 1950s, and the queues appeared endless. A new program was therefore launched in the late 1950s with the aim of stepping up construction volumes considerably. The so-called Million program—which was to complete 1 million new units within a ten-year period—actually achieved its goal. This new program was designed to draw its massive financial requirements from the newly established ATP pension funds. As before, priority was to be given to co-op builders and owners. Private financing and single-family housing were further marginalized, while public control of land for housing development was strengthened. To ensure maximum cost efficiency, large apartment complexes in outlying satellite towns were heavily favored. Also, housing developments were planned to cater to a class-and-income mix.

Nevertheless—however efficient or egalitarian, however much authorities tried to emphasize local self-management and community development—the mushrooming satellite developments have been bitterly criticized for their monotonous and bland design, the social and cultural sterility and anonymity that they instill, and the high incidence of alienation and delinquency that they promote (Anton 1975; Adams 1975). These features, combined with long commutes to and from the city, help explain why vacancy rates have often remained quite high and why they may be increasing in some areas. Before the "Million

---

[7] Real estate speculation was kept to a minimum, owing to municipal control of land. To be eligible for state-supplied credit, in fact, housing projects had to be developed on municipally owned land (Swedish Institute 1977; Anton 1975).

program" had even been completed, the social democrats had to address growing popular demand for single-family home ownership.

In its financial design, the Swedish housing policy was a deliberate effort to force out private finance. This was done primarily by artificially setting interest rates below market levels and by providing credit for as much as 100 percent of the total mortgage. Private builders, in contrast, would have to furnish at least 15 percent of the credit themselves. With such broad government control, public authorities effectively controlled the production volume, allocation, design and, to a degree, the pricing of new housing.

The first major reform was undertaken in 1967, when the social democrats deemed the housing-shortage problem to have been more or less resolved. The reform reduced the state's share of total financing by permitting mortgage interest rates to approximate normal market rates more closely. To compensate for the loss of subsidization, however, a new "parity loan" system was introduced—permitting interest payments to be distributed more evenly over the years. While the 1967 reform did reduce government financial regulation, its chief intent was to address egalitarian concerns. Lingering rent controls were finally abolished and replaced by a unique "use value" principle of rent determination, meant to ensure that apartments of equal size and quality cost the same. The base line for cost estimation was to be the co-op associations' apartment units.

But it is the new rental allowance scheme that primarily serves the egalitarian redistributive ideal. Sweden has introduced what is probably the world's largest and most generous rental allowance system. The scope of eligibility is very wide, and the greater part of rent expenditures for pensioners is covered. By 1970, most pensioners and 50 percent of all renters were receiving a subsidy.

The government managed to keep rental allowances more or less equivalent to the amount of tax expenditures handed to homeowners in the form of tax deductions and artificially low imputed rent.[8] However, this state of equitable harmony did not last long. For one thing, the rental allowance scheme was subsequently narrowed. Also, due to the combined effects of a high marginal tax rate, rising inflation, and a widespread desire for homeownership, housing politics during the 1970s—though less extreme—came to parallel those of Denmark. Thus, construction of private, single-family housing grew dramatically in the

[8] Boberg et al. (1974) argue that the total value of tax deductions in 1973 equaled about 2 billion kronor, while the value of rental allowances amounted to approximately 1.75 billion kronor.

1970s, and the issue of homeowner tax deductions has come to the fore in contemporary political debate.[9] Hence, the Swedish social democrats, now back in office, will likely confront an increasingly divisive and politicized housing situation, and electoral fragmentation may very well result.

These national patterns in housing policy differ so widely in their stress on equality, solidarity, and public control that differential electoral impact on social democratic party performance is to be expected. Clearly, Danish social democratic housing policy has been both the most politicized and the most divisive. Clearly, too, the Norwegian policies have been the most equitable and solidaristic while still responding to popular demand for single-family homes. As Elvander (1980) notes, Sweden lies somewhere in between. More to the point, however, it is likely that the SAP will have to bear the electoral consequences of a mounting equity struggle between renters and owners; and it is possible that the growing class differential in this respect will make it more difficult for the party to unite its traditional working-class clientele with the middle-strata homeowners.

[9] It is important to note, though, that the privatization trend in the Swedish housing market differs sharply in respect of class bias. Whereas in Denmark private homeownership became widespread among working-class households, the opposite is happening in Sweden. The proportion of working-class homeowners is actually on the decline, while it is rapidly growing among the middle classes (Frykman 1983).

SEVEN

The Political Business Cycle and
Economic Policymaking

SOCIAL DEMOCRATIC economic policy has been chronically beset by dilemmas. The first, emphasized by Przworski (1980) and Tingsten (1941), has to do with ideology. Socialist parties risk losing left-wing support if they abandon radical demands for socialization; if the parties fail to address the immediate material needs of workers, on the other hand, they will be unable to manufacture parliamentary majorities. Most socialist parties have struggled with this dilemma. For pre-1934 German social democracy the struggle may have been tougher than elsewhere, given the rising communist party opposition (Przworski and Sprague 1977; Nolan and Sabel 1982), but it was nonetheless an issue of considerable importance in Sweden (Tingsten 1941), Norway (Dahl 1969; Elvander 1980), and even in the staunchly pragmatic Danish labor movement (Togeby 1968; Bryld 1976).

Another, related dilemma appears when socialist parties come into actual contact with parliamentary politics. When a party supports policies obviously designed to correct deficiencies in the capitalist system, how can that party simultaneously insist that its policies advance the socialist cause (Lewin 1967)? A variant of this dilemma appears once socialist parties plunge into a long-run commitment to administer the capitalist economy. Social democratic decisions to govern during the Great Depression were motivated by the fear that total economic collapse would only further weaken working-class unity and power. The strategic decision to manage capitalism, however, saddles social democracy with a peculiar problem. As Strachey pointed out in the 1930s, a labor government will easily find itself in the position of having to discipline its own working-class constituency if the conditions for economic growth disappear (Strachey 1933). Hence, management of the political business cycle becomes the linchpin of social democratic political survival.

This set of dilemmas is historically bounded. The first typically found resolution in the social democrats' tacit or explicit decision to put aside the program for state socialization. This choice came relatively easy to the Scandinavian social democrats, once they learned that

191

radical socialization platforms were followed by electoral defeats and massive bourgeois countercampaigns. The second dilemma appeared as the socialists began to participate in public economic policy, particularly during the unstable 1920s. The socialists hardly possessed a workable policy at this stage and, if anything, their economic analyses were confused. The socialization program was of little practical value, and few alternative guidelines for a democratic socialist economic policy were available. The lack of a coherent model is evident just about everywhere. The Danish social democrats found some inspiration in World War I economic controls, and they began to toy with ideas of industrial planning. At the same time, they hovered between a Marxian underconsumptionist analysis and an odd loyalty to orthodox liberal principles of balanced budgets. The Swedes shifted from state socialization to industrial democracy schemes coupled with vague ideas of planning.

Generally, the interwar social democratic model for economic policy evolved into a combination of three basic proposals. One was the idea of workers' councils and industrial codetermination. A second was economic planning. Third was a gradual move toward the Keynesian formula for an active crisis policy. The first two proposals could arguably speak to the long-run promise of socialism as well as to short-term practicality—especially after the Russian Revolution, when workers' councils and planning both became certified socialist policies. They were also theoretically defensible within the social democratic theory of organized capitalism and "functional socialism."

But, as political experience soon demonstrated, bourgeois-dominated parliaments precluded immediate legislation on either meaningful industrial democracy or state planning. The adoption of Keynesian doctrines were considerably more difficult to defend from the point of view of advancing socialism. Where the social democrats faced powerful communist competition for the working-class vote, as in Germany, they could not easily participate in the rescue of capitalism and also claim to be heading straight for the Good Society. The decision to adopt Keynesianism compelled the social democrats to rework the ideological connection between shortsighted economic policy and the future socialist economy. One response was to ignore the ideological issue entirely, as did the Danes (Togeby 1968). Another was to couch it within the analytic framework of functional socialism, as did the Swedes. A third was to articulate an entirely new theory of democratic socialism, as did such postwar British social democrats as Strachey (1956) and Crosland (1967).

The ideological dilemma aside, a basic justification for Keynesianism was, as Michael Kalecki argued, that it could further working-class power. The cycles of heavy unemployment during the 1920s, followed by the chronic unemployment of the 1930s, reinforced the labor movements' age-old understanding that full employment is a necessary precondition for trade union strength and political mobilization. Moreover, depressed economic conditions, particularly in agriculture, might easily propel fascism instead of socialism. The fear of fascism played a key role in the Scandinavian social democrats' decision to collaborate with the farmers' parties on an active crisis policy during the 1930s (Elvander 1980; Dybdahl 1975; Lindhagen 1972).

Once committed to the management of capitalism, the social democrats were faced with the concrete question of how to ensure stable growth and full employment without having to discipline their own working-class base to the degree that political support is lost. The problem is partly one of ensuring full employment, price stability and, in open export economies like those of Scandinavia, international competitiveness. Another part of the problem is that economic growth is the precondition for the social citizenship state upon which the postwar social democrats came to pin their electoral mobilization strategy.

Long-run social democratic strength will depend on the party's capacity to control the business cycle. The question in this chapter is twofold. First, to what extent has social democracy been capable of translating political power into effective control over the economy? Secondly, can variations in economic policy explain differences in social democratic political fortunes? The three Scandinavian social democracies have pursued different kinds of economic policies and differ considerably in the degree to which they have gained control over the capitalist economy.

THE ORIGINS OF SOCIAL DEMOCRATIC KEYNESIANISM

The evolution of Scandinavian social democracy from its infancy to the Keynesianism of the 1930s began with a political convergence, passed through divergence, and ended again in convergence. Until 1914, all three social democratic parties were wedded to the programmatic promise of socializing the means of production as soon as possible. However, none possessed any sort of blueprint for building the new political economy. Since they had no, or very little, access to political power, the issue carried no immediacy. The experience of World War I and the subsequent consolidation of universal suffrage changed this situation substantially.

Denmark

The Danish social democratic leader Thorvald Stauning had partici-
pated in the RV cabinet's wartime regulations and controls. This led
the social democrats to believe that the state could be made to rationalize capitalist production in the common interest (Bryld 1976,
82). The Danish social democrats established a "socialization commission" in 1919, but its report, reflecting the party's growing commitment to parliamentary collaboration with the radicals, rejected
socialization measures and proposed instead a mix of industrial democracy, labor market regulation, and collective bargaining reforms.
The union movement proposed codetermination legislation in accordance with these recommendations; when presented by the minority
social democratic government in 1924, however, the legislation was
immediately voted down.

The period after 1920 produced a break in the economic thinking
of the Danish social democrats. Although the party retained its radical
1913 program, election platforms stressed rather more mundane goals,
such as import regulation, public employment creation, agricultural
subsidies, and greater planning. In the 1920s, the party had embarked
upon the long road to "end of ideology," committing itself only to
policies that were possible given the constellation of parliamentary
majorities and the state of the economy. Yet, such pragmatism was
not free from confusion. On the one hand, the social democratic leadership articulated a primitive sort of Keynesianism, advocating deficit-
financed state support to industry and public works in order to combat
unemployment. On the other, it supported orthodox monetary policies
and refused to vote for devaluation of the krone (Bryld 1976, 91ff).
During its tenure in government from 1924 to 1926, one of the party's
main objectives was to prove its administrative competence and its
adherence to liberal economic policy (Hansen 1974, 40-44).

The Danish social democratic response to the conflict between parliamentary majoritarianism and ideological purity, then, was to stress
political respectability. For example, the social democratic finance
minister, Bramsnaes, tried to calm bourgeois fears by insisting that "it
is important that a social democratic government can keep financial
order in things" (Hansen 1974, 44). The new position was captured
by a 1926 editorial in the party newspaper, *Socialdemokraten*:

> We have penetrated all the institutions of the state, in local as
> well as national government; with the help of information cam-
> paigns and the rise of popular support, we have enforced legis-
> lation that has transformed the old police state into a state in

harmony with society. Thereby, we ourselves have also come into harmony with the state to a much greater extent than it might seem from the outward symbol that the government evolves from our social class. . . . But if the state has indeed been changed into a more valid expression of society, and if the working class has steadily become more unified with society, then we also owe society more and more consideration. . . . The triad of our agitation must now be seriousness, a sense of responsibility, and a sense of the public interest [Bryld 1976, 27-28].

Having refused to support price controls, the social democrats were ousted from office and replaced by a liberal party government until 1929. From then on, however, the social democrats, in coalition with the radicals, held office until the Nazi occupation in 1940. Thus, when the economic crisis arrived, the social democrats had already fully consolidated their political alliance with the small farmers and had already committed themselves to be responsible and rescue capitalism. Very few Danish social democrats viewed the depression as a confirmation of Marx's theory of capitalist collapse. Unlike Hilferding of the German SPD, the Danish party leaders rejected outright state socialization and other, similar measures. By 1929 the party had cemented its image as a people's party acting in the national interest.

The post-1929 coalition led naturally to the promotion of policies benefiting all classes. Coalition programs addressed the common needs of small businessmen, peasants, and workers with promises of anti-monopoly legislation, land redistribution for small holders, unemployment relief and public job creation, education, and welfare reforms. The social democrats' crisis policies emerged step by step rather than according to a general plan. Pragmatic reformism was amply rewarded during the 1932 election, in which the social democrats scored a considerable victory. A genuine economic crisis package had to wait until January 1933, when the social democrats succeeded in forging a compromise with their radical allies and the liberal party. This quid pro quo set the pattern for subsequent crisis agreements in both Norway and Sweden: price supports for agriculture in return for economic relief and public jobs for workers. Yet, the Danish crisis package was also oddly anti-Keynesian. The social democrats made the trade unions accept a temporary wage freeze, a prohibition against strikes, and a devaluation of the krone to help agricultural exports (Olsen 1962; Philip 1939). Wage and price regulations were actually repeated several times during the 1930s, the justification being that a restoration of Danish exports was more important than a Keynesian stimulation of domestic purchasing power (Olsen 1962; Hansen 1974). Surprisingly, this disciplinary action against the trade unions did not provoke significant working-class protest. In the 1935 election, the party scored its biggest victory ever, winning 46.1 percent of the vote.

Probably no other socialist party has made its peace with parliamentary democracy and capitalism so subtly as the Danish party. When the opportunity first arose after World War I, the party hardly hesitated in joining a radical-liberal government. It dodged the ideological dilemma between short-term reformism and the ultimate socialist goal by taking the latter off the agenda. It moved to an all-inclusive "people's party" profile without serious discussion of ideology or strategy. In short, there was never a reason to indulge in an epochal "historical compromise," for labor had made peace with capitalism long before they acquired sufficient power to demand important concessions.

Norway

The voyage from socialist orthodoxy to Keynesianism was considerably more tumultuous in Norway. Indeed, there could hardly be a sharper contrast to the Danish case. The Norwegian Social Democratic party espoused an enthusiastic commitment to socialist revolution after World War I. Joining the Comintern after the Russian Revolution, the DNA accordingly reaffirmed its dedication to a combination of workers' councils and state socialism. In 1923 the DNA broke away, unwilling to embrace the doctrine of democratic centralism. But, even though the DNA bade farewell to Moscow, it remained dedicated to its classic socialist strategy. For five years the party was split into a right-wing reformist group and a revolutionary majority; but their reunification in 1927 was rewarded with electoral success and, to the party's surprise, the king asked the DNA to form the first Norwegian labor government. This saddled the socialists with quite a problem. They had always adhered strictly to the Kautsky doctrine against forming alliances with bourgeois parties or taking office as a minority party. They had upheld the belief that bourgeois democracy was a sham. And they had refused to modify their revolutionary program (Dahl 1969).

The DNA's response was hardly dialectical. Kautsky's prohibition was ignored, but the party stood firm on its revolutionary agenda. The DNA government's program prompted an economic crisis as Norwegian capitalists moved their capital abroad and the financial system threatened to collapse. After only two weeks in government, the DNA was brought down by a vote of nonconfidence from the liberals (El-vander 1980; Dybdahl 1975).

This experience might have inspired the DNA to change political course, as the Swedish social democrats had when they were defeated on a socialization program. But the opposite happened. The strategic dilemma came to the fore in the ensuing party debate (Rokkan 1966). On one side, the revolutionary wing held that the defeat only gave additional proof that bourgeois democracy could not be trusted. The other wing argued that the party needed to moderate its policies in order to mobilize stronger parliamentary majorities. The debate was carried by the revolutionary wing, and the DNA went to elections in 1930 with a radically socialist platform. The bourgeois parties—and the press—launched a massive counterattack and, profiting from a record-high electoral turnout, succeeded in mobilizing votes against the DNA. The socialists had failed to gain new votes with their revolutionary program.

This signaled a turning point, and the DNA proceeded to alter its political course. A number of factors contributed in the process of realignment. First, the shifting bourgeois governments of the unstable 1920s had typically adhered to procyclical economic dogma, generally of the restrictive, deflationary kind. Investments had been slack, and rural indebtedness reached crisis proportions. Yet, for those workers who kept their jobs, the 1920s had produced real wage growth. The agrarian party was naturally in confrontation both with the bourgeois parties and with the labor movement; in this polarized political environment, Norwegian farmers began to drift toward Nazism. Secondly, the quasi-proletarianized peasants and fishermen on the periphery, it was discovered, were rallying behind the DNA with urgent demands for economic relief, not ideological satisfaction. At the local level, social democratic politicians were deeply engaged in the implementation of relief policies. Thus, the party leadership's commitment to ideological purity obviously clashed with grass-roots desires. Thirdly, it is also possible that the economic crisis hit Norway harder than it did the other Scandinavian countries. The rate of urban unemployment was higher, and the poverty suffered by the peasants was certainly worse. This may also help explain the much heavier influx of rural populations into the DNA (Dahl 1971).[1]

In the period from 1930 to 1934, the DNA's reformist wing began to assume leadership, and the party worked its way toward a practical

---

[1] Dahl reports (1971, 91) that at least 10 percent of the DNA's membership came from workers in forestry and agriculture.

crisis program. Within the party, Ole Colbjørnson was an important influence. His thinking was largely formed by exposure to Soviet economic planning and Stalin's interpretation of underconsumption theory, and his first proposal was for state socialization of investment. In collaboration with Ragnar Frisch, however, the Soviet influence was weakened, and by 1934 the party could present a crisis program advocating productive public-employment creation, deficit-financed industrial stimulation (including subsidies to firms), and economic relief (Nordvik 1977; Elvander 1980).[2]

As the party had now demonstrated its commitment to both parliamentarism and practical reformism, its electoral fortunes improved.[3] The DNA gained 40.1 percent of the vote in 1933. But the leap toward political realignment did not take place until 1935, when the DNA entered into the basic quid-pro-quo agreement with the agrarians, promising agricultural price supports and income distribution in return for their parliamentary support of unemployment relief and the active crisis policy.

Since government imposition of incomes policies had already been undertaken by the bourgeois government in 1934, the DNA was spared the difficult task of imposing wage restraint on its working-class constituents (Dybdahl 1975). The DNA's crisis program of 1934, fiscally more "Keynesian" than the Swedish version, called for a 37.5 percent increase in public expenditure, 60 percent of which was to be borrowed (Nordvik 1977, 290). Yet, in practice, the 1930s crisis policies were more cautiously expansive and, in adherence to the requirements of alliance with the agrarians, mention of socialization was dropped (Mjøset 1981). As in Denmark, the party's leap from revolution to reformism and its embarkation on an active crisis policy weakened the communist party.

Although the final outcomes were strikingly similar, the Danish and Norwegian social democracies passed from socialist orthodoxy to Keynesian economics in virtually opposite ways. The choice to align with the peasantry finally ensured social democratic convergence. This, we shall see, was also the overriding factor in Sweden. Still, the formation of peasant–working-class alliances is probably not a sufficient explanation for the rise of the Scandinavian model. Of considerable importance was the evolution of ties between trade unions and the

[2] This program also called for active state involvement in industrial development and direct state planning, thus testifying to the party's continued adherence to its past.
[3] The DNA did not formally recognize parliamentary rule until 1939.

party. As Sturmthal (1943) argues, trade union political autonomy meant that ideological dogma was countered with union pragmatism.

In Denmark, both conditions had presented themselves at a very early date. On one side, the social democrats were forced to acknowledge the economic and political supremacy of agricultural interests. The decision to collaborate was importantly influenced by the strong liberal-reformist inclinations of the rural petite bourgeoisie and, of course, by their historical partnership in the struggle for universal suffrage. On the other side, Danish trade unionism had asserted its independence from the party even before World War I; thus, bread-and-butter unionism easily came to prevail over the lukewarm and muddled ideological principles of party leadership (Galenson 1952).

In Norway, the two forces of compromise could not make their imprint on social democratic politics until very late. First, the configuration of the social classes was qualitatively different. For one thing, there was a stronger and more permanent antagonism between the old conservative forces and the liberal farmers. For another, the rural classes were themselves deeply split. The rural propertied classes aligned themselves behind the liberal and, later, the agrarian party while, unlike anywhere else, the large mass of quasi-proletarian small landholders, forestry workers, and fishermen found a political home in the social democratic party (Rokkan 1966). Paradoxically, this internal peasant-worker combination may explain both the DNA's longstanding revolutionary profile and its eventual reformism. With an eye to the Russian experience, it was easy to conclude that a rural-urban proletarian constituency was the stuff of revolutionary stragegies. But, during the economic crisis, this same class constituency helped persuade the party leadership to abandon revolution for relief policies. Secondly, the situation within the trade union movement was very unsettled until the 1930s. The Norwegian LO was formed late, but it grew explosively in the first decades of the century. It had already centralized and adopted the principle of industrial unionism by 1912. Yet, a powerful syndicalist movement prevented the LO from pushing the party toward economistic reformism (Elvander 1980, 38-43; Galenson 1949).

Sweden

At first glance, Swedish social democracy might seem to lie midway between the Danish and Norwegian versions. As in Norway, the social democrats had no ready-made political allies, and they sustained an ideological radicalism longer than the Danes. But the Swedes were quick to put aside socialist orthodoxy and were more accommodating to both parliamentarism and capitalism than the Norwegians. The Swedish road to a "historical compromise" in the 1930s is not just a "middle way." In Sweden, the party followed its own unique course.

The Swedish rural classes were quite different from those of either Denmark or Norway. In Sweden, unlike Norway, there were no lingering masses of rural quasiproletarians, easily attracted to socialist policies. But neither was there an overwhelmingly large and powerful class of independent farmers wedded to liberalism. As in Denmark, the social democrats had fought for democracy side by side with the agrarians; after its attainment, however, there was little else that could unite the two parties politically. In Sweden there was no liberal-reformist political force of sufficient strength to compel the social democrats into early acquiescence. Nor was the Swedish party capable of bringing the rural, or urban, petite bourgeoisie closer to social democracy. With no room for political compromise, with a virtual stand-off between statist conservatism, weak liberalism, and social democracy, the 1920s were a period of chronic instability and ineffective minority cabinets.

The balance of political forces was unsettled, and there was very little to indicate that the Swedish social democrats, together with the LO, would become the world's strongest labor movement only a few decades later. Pressured from all directions, the party attempted in the 1920s to walk the political tightrope between ideological rigor and pragmatic reformism. As in Germany, a combination of both was seen as the only possible way to avoid heavy electoral losses to either the left or the right. It is therefore not surprising that SAP programs and policies express a certain political schizophrenia.

Under Branting's leadership, the party constantly attempted to meet the promise of socialism by means of mundane reformism. In 1911, the SAP agrarian policy seemed to want to antagonize everyone and yet no one: "Agricultural lands should, according to circumstances, be divided into large-scale operations . . . or small plots under conditions that strengthen the rights of the user and the viability of the land [Severin 1969, 30]." The 1920 program sounded the call for immediate socialization of natural resources, banks, and large companies. Unlike the Danish party, the SAP was still prepared to antagonize large farmers with a demand for collectivization of farmland (Lindhagen 1972).

The Swedish social democrats were actually asked to form a government in 1920 and, though in the minority, they accepted. The LO was ambivalent, if not hostile, but the party leadership began to pre-

pare legislation along the lines of the 1920 party program. This served
only to unite the otherwise conflicting bourgeois parties behind a
strong antisocialist campaign, and the bill was defeated. After less than
one year in office, the party had been ousted. Suddenly required to
translate vague ideology into legislative reality, the party constituted
a "socialization commission" to recommend an appropriate strategy.
But the commission, chaired by Rikard Sandler and influenced theoretically by Wigforss and Karleby, never produced a final report after
its sixteen-year term.[4]

For the SAP, the 1920s were a period of fundamental programmatic
revision. The Swedes, unlike the Danes, did not shelve the socialization
question; nor did they stick to the dogma of state nationalization, as
the Norwegians had. The Austro-Marxist-inspired strategy for "functional socialism" crept into programmatic revisions during this period,
and the socialization of *flow* rather than *stock* came to be advocated.
The party (Wigforss in particular) began to stress planning and industrial democracy.

The remodeled formula for socialization was evident in the party
platform for the 1928 election. Ernst Wigforss proposed a plan for
inheritance taxation that would have sharply reduced the transfer of
wealth and capital between generations. To offset the consequent drop
in savings, he proposed that the wealth taxes be allocated to a public
investment fund—an idea that, in weaker form, would find its way
into social democratic legislation during the late 1960s.[5] The new
program for economic socialization invited a repeat of the bourgeois
antisocialist campaign, and the SAP suffered a major setback in the
1928 election (Tingsten 1941). Still, the party's programmatic delib-
erations occurred against the backdrop of a genuinely pragmatic approach to immediate policy matters. The party was reinstated in office
from 1921 to 1923 and, with the economy in a deep slump, attempted
to carry out a program of welfare reform and relief legislation. The
bourgeois parties, however, refused to vote for unemployment relief
to workers engaged in industrial disputes, and the Branting cabinet
was forced to resign. The social democrats experienced a third term
in government, from 1924 to 1926, but were again brought down
when the liberals refused to extend unemployment benefits and cash
relief. With the economy once again in recession, the social democrats
were unable to bend the liberal commitment to budgetary austerity.

[4] Sandler did write two unofficial reports during the 1930s, but their practical significance was nil since, by then, socialization was out of the question.

[5] There are also obvious similarities with the recent Meidner plan for economic
democracy. On this theme, see Wigforss (1981).

As noted, Swedish social democracy during the 1920s bears more than passing resemblance to that of Germany. Both socialist parties attempted to tread the narrow path between pragmatic reformism and socialist ideology; in both cases, moreover, any attempt to choose one or the other was effectively blocked. The bourgeois parties readily reconciled their differences whenever the social democrats proposed even modest welfare reforms, and so the social democrats were prevented from choosing the straight reformist strategy. But the radical option was equally impossible, for bourgeois forces had no difficulty in mobilizing electoral anxieties against the socialist specter. Unlike the German party, however, the Swedish social democrats did not decompose under the pressure of growing communist opposition, on one side, and growing reactionary forces on the other. The Swedes had not compromised their position with the workers by partaking in controversial legislation, whether support for military appropriations or state repression of worker uprisings; nor were they forced to devote most of their energies to the defense of democracy. In both 1923 and 1926, they chose to resign from office rather than collaborate in unacceptable legislation. Then too, Swedish farmers, unlike those of Germany, were organized and politically articulate.

After three bitter experiences of cabinet participation without power, the SAP leadership began to re-examine its conditions for holding office. A parliamentary majority became the precondition for participation (Elvander 1980; Landauer 1959). But it was evident that the class structure would not evolve into a strictly working-class majority within the foreseeable future. The question of political alliances thus returned with added significance. However, the constellation of Swedish politics held no promise of a natural class ally. The SAP leadership had traditionally viewed the liberals as their most natural coalition partner; as the liberals' doctrinaire commitment to laissez-faire economics only strengthened with the economic crisis, however, this possibility was ruled out. Even more remote was the outlook for an alliance with the peasants' party, the Bondeförbundet. The social democrats had always opposed price protection for farmers; the Bondeförbundet was generally against welfare protection for the working class—rural workers in particular—and harbored a great hostility toward trade unionism (Lindhagen 1972, 236-242).

Worsening economic crisis broke the stalemate. The social democrats had the great fortune of being out of office when the crisis arrived, and the liberals in power refused to deviate from their balanced budget ideas. As conditions grew worse for workers as well as peasants, popular belief in the economic wisdom of liberalism eroded. The overall result of the 1932 elections was a blow both to the conservatives and the liberals—and marked gains for the social democrats, who received almost 42 percent of the vote and 104 seats in parliament. Still without a majority, the social democrats were persuaded to form a government alone, and they began to prepare legislation to counter the economic crisis.

The crisis package, developed by the new finance minister, Ernst Wigforss, contained no socialization measures. It proposed to stimulate employment and aggregate consumption; to legislate public works projects, welfare reforms, and public relief. The program called for a budget deficit rather than increased taxation to cover additional public spending. It also stipulated that public employment projects pay according to prevailing wage rates (Wigforss 1938; Möller 1938). It was in effect the first consciously designed Keynesian program to be adopted anywhere in the world (Tingsten 1941).

Still, the social democrats had no parliamentary majority to carry out an active crisis policy. The liberals continued to insist on balanced budgets, and the Bondeförbundet appeared as unlikely an ally as ever, having launched a bitter antisocialist campaign during the 1932 election and blaming the unions for the economic crisis of agriculture (Söderpalm 1976). On the other hand, with the collapse of agricultural prices and confidence in the liberals, farmer opinion shifted in favor of social democracy, especially when the SAP leadership expressed a willingness to grant subsidies to agriculture. With the famous 1933 agreement, the SAP and the Bondeförbundet formed a coalition, whereby the latter supported Wigforss's deficit-financed stimulation package in return for agricultural price supports.

Under the leadership of Per Albin Hansson, the social democrats consolidated their new ideological position. Remnants of their old class profile were eliminated, and the appeal was broadened to include all the economically weak, a reorientation expressed in Hansson's famous "People's Home" slogan (Berkling 1982). The combined effect of active crisis management and a broadened ideological message appeared to reward the SAP when, in the 1936 elections, it scored a huge victory with almost 46 percent of the vote.

The economic crisis measures seemed to be strikingly effective. By 1939, the rate of unemployment had fallen below 10 percent (Lindbeck 1975, 23). In reality, though, the Keynesian stimulation package probably had a stronger symbolic significance than it had direct economic influence. Indeed, the increase in government expenditures barely surpassed 1 percent of GNP between 1933 and 1934. In large measure, Sweden's rapid economic recovery was the result of generous amounts of good luck. In 1931 the Swedes had already abandoned the gold standard—under the liberals—and the krona happened to be undervalued against foreign currencies. This obviously helped Swedish exports when foreign demand began to pick up in the mid-1930s (Lundberg 1968; Lindbeck 1975; Jörberg 1976). The tragic irony of the SAPs success was that the jump in demand for Swedish iron and lumber products coincided with the Nazi rearmament drive.

Thus, as Lindbeck suggests (1975, 33-34), the significance of the government's expansionist economic policy lay in its principles rather than in its tangible results. Politically, it proved to be a boon. The SAP could convincingly assert that its reformism profited not only workers but the entire nation. It helped convince anxious capitalists that active state intervention under social democratic administration was preferable to the class struggle that reigned under bourgeois-party cabinets. The social democrats, then, emerged in the 1930s with an acceptable positive-sum formula for capital and labor. This was especially so after the 1938 Saltsjöbaden Agreement, which finally concluded the Swedish "historical compromise." With this realignment, the Swedish labor movement had made its peace (or, rather, its truce) with capitalism.

THE POSTWAR MANAGEMENT OF BUSINESS CYCLES

The road to social democratic power (or, at any rate, to office) was based on a combination of active crisis policy and coalitions with the rural classes. This alliance became the foundation of the long, and largely uninterrupted, reign of social democracy. In addition, the nature of the alliance continued to define the scope and limits of postwar economic policy. It sanctioned active stimulation policies with a commitment to sustained full employment—but only so long as social democracy could agree to put aside its more daring program for socialization and state planning.

The economic policy model that emerged would naturally begin to encounter its own incompatibilities as its long-range effects came to fruition. The dilemmas of postwar social democracy are very much entwined in its capacity to overcome these incompatibilities. The first problem would be how to reconcile full employment with price stability and an orderly balance-of-payments situation. The second was that the thrust of active industrial promotion would inevitably clash with the interests of social democracy's rural allies. This—combined with the income-distribution problems that arise when farmers, on one side, and rising middle strata on the other lay claims to favorable income shares—compels social democracy to seek an escape from its self-imposed limitations in regard to state direction of the economy.

The structure of the political coalitions, and social democracy's power within them, came to differ considerably in the three Nordic countries. Such circumstances, we shall now see, have caused significant variation in the ability of the three parties to manage the business cycle successfully.

Liberal Hegemony in Denmark

The Danish social democrats may have been the first to forge the coalition for active political management of the business cycle, but they have stalled in every attempt to extend state control beyond conventional aggregate monetary and fiscal policies.[6] Throughout the postwar era, the Danish party has failed to achieve public dominion over labor and capital markets and has only marginally exerted political influence over the nature of economic structural change. The social democrats have thus been unable to prevent either pervasive speculation or unproductive use of the country's resources. On several occasions, social democratic governments have been forced to discipline the trade unions, by means of incomes policies and economic crisis packages, in order to re-establish international competitiveness and economic stability. Except for the decade of the 1960s, and the early 1970s, the party has been unable to guarantee full employment together with price stability and a healthy balance of payments. All in all, then, social democracy has been captive to virtually uncontrolled business cycles.

Social democratic economic failure cannot be attributed to an unwillingness to assert greater political control. There has been continuous pressure from the union movement, particularly from the powerful Metalworkers' Federation and the Unskilled Workers' Federation (SID), for greater state control over investment and for managed structural change. On several occasions, the social democrats have presented bills, or plans, designed to accommodate such demands.

The reasons for Denmark's weak economic performance under social democracy are many. One obvious factor is the divided and craft-dominated trade union movement, which weds much of the working class to archaic forms of enterprise; internal consensus has been dif-

---

[6] The following account of Danish postwar economic policy makes extensive use of the following standard sources: Hansen (1974), Schmidt (1971), and Handelsministeriet (1973-1974).

ficult to achieve. Another crucial factor has been the precarious international position of the Danish economy. The country has no natural resources except for its fertile soil. Thus, export performance comes to hinge upon a fragile balance between the price of imported capital goods and raw materials, on the one hand, and international demand for Danish manufactured goods on the other. Agricultural exports were for a long time the crucial element in the Danish economy, and they have continued to constitute a "bottom line" with respect to the balance-of-payments situation and foreign exchange revenues. Policy options have been tightly circumscribed by the necessity of giving due consideration to farmers' interests and demands. The character of Danish industry has clearly also been an impediment. Except for a sprinkling of large firms—mostly in shipbuilding—Danish industry is typically a combination of traditional artisan production—furniture and design—and small-scale manufacture, most of which is quite vulnerable to small changes in costs and demand.

These structural impediments find expression in the continued lack of a parliamentary constellation that might make possible a more aggressive social democratic economic policy. The bourgeois parties, representing both rural and industrial capital, have held an automatic veto against greater state control. Farmers and small industries alike, via unusually powerful lobby groups, have secured their own economic survival by means of state protection and subsidization. But the social democrats' subservience to "bourgeois" economic policy has also provoked a substantial left-socialist opposition, calling for much more radical policies.

The postwar social democratic program presented a radical approach to economic policy with its emphasis on extensive macroeconomic planning, industrial stimulation, and public regulation of production and finance. Following the debates within Swedish social democracy, the Danes advocated the continuation of wartime regulation and physical controls, combined with planning and an active fiscal policy, to prevent a relapse into recession (Bille 1972). This abnormal radicalism must be understood in light of the strong challenge of the Danish Communist party immediately after the war.

As the bourgeois parties successfully exploited popular resentment against controls, and as inflationary pressures forced upon government a restrictive fiscal policy at the expense of full employment, this burst of social democratic action soon calmed down. Throughout most of the 1950s there was effective opposition to policies for full employment and industrial growth. The period was marked by austerity policies, tight credit, balanced budgets, and sluggish growth with very high unemployment rates.[7] Almost complete dependency on agricultural exports prevailed, and farmer organizations effectively blocked any active Keynesian plan for full employment. Public-sector expenditure growth was not permitted to exceed GNP growth, and balanced budgets were held up as the condition for any social democratic reform initiative. Thus, during the entire 1945-1957 period, the major instrument against unemployment and slack economic activity was the stimulation of construction by lowering the discount rate. Since this quickly fueled inflation and threatened to jeopardize the balance of payments, however, governments vacillated in an endless series of stop/go measures (Hansen 1974).

High unemployment rates helped keep down industrial wages and, when a massive strike and lockout broke out in 1956, the social democratic government was forced to intervene by legislating a settlement previously vetoed by the workers. After the mid-1950s, the position of agriculture deteriorated so much that its prior hold over economic policy was weakened. This allowed a shift to more aggressive stimulation of industry. Behind the weakened position of the farmers was a serious decline in agricultural prices on the international market, combined with a saturation of Danish agricultural export capacity (Hansen 1974, Westergård Andersen 1974). Because farmer incomes fell so dramatically, there was demand for additional government compensation and export aid. At the same time, however, world demand for Danish industrial products showed signs of improvement, in large part owing to the formation of EFTA (European Free Trade Association) and the general liberalization of trade. For the first time in history, Danish industrial exports exceeded agricultural exports.

The shift had a profound effect on the possibilities for economic policy. Dependence on agriculture had weakened, and continued reliance on agriculture to generate foreign exchange for industrial growth was impossible. Another critical factor in the realignment of economic policy was the outcome of the 1957 election, in which the social democrats together with the radicals finally obtained a parliamentary majority. The new government launched an industrial-stimulation policy, based on capital borrowing abroad combined with a reduction in corporate taxes, state credit to key industries (especially steel), and a less restrictive fiscal policy. These policies fueled a strong industrial expansion, and economic growth after 1957 was twice the previous

[7] In the 1946-1960 period, Danish unemployment hovered at around 10 percent. Real GNP growth per annum (1950-1957) was the lowest among the OECD countries: 2.7 percent, compared with 3.5 percent in Norway and 3.3 percent in Sweden (Hansen 1974, 148).

rate; fixed-asset formation in manufacturing grew by 20 percent annually.

To a degree, the burst of industrial investment was helped along by relatively low wages. All in all, the year 1957 signals a change in the balance of power between the social classes. Not until the farmers' "monopoly" on economic policy was broken, therefore, could a social democratic coalition government shift economic resources to industrial employment and investment. But the farmers did not resign themselves to the new political economy. The shift provoked one of the most dramatic class confrontations in modern Danish history.

The decline in farmer incomes led the agrarian interest organizations to demand state compensation and protection. In 1958, the social democrats granted farmers a price compensation for domestic production. This was extended again in 1959, but in 1961 the farmers demanded compensation amounting to 550 million kroner (about 1.5 percent of 1960 GNP). Because of the inflationary impact of such subsidies, and their distributive impact on income shares, the trade unions were fiercely opposed. A government counteroffer, amounting to 300 million kroner, was refused by the farmers organizations and the liberal party. The conflict exploded when the farmers went on a production strike. Mass demonstrations and serious confrontations took place, and the social democratic prime minister, Viggo Kampmann, was compelled to reach a settlement with the liberals, conceding a 425 million kroner subsidy to the farmers over a two-year period. The political victory of the farmers meant that rural incomes became additionally politicized.

The outcome of the conflict just described illustrates the continued power of Danish farmers to assert their interests over both labor and industrial capital. In effect, the 1961 agreement was a circumscription of the "1957 breakthrough," since the farmers had managed to reverse a marked redistribution from agriculture to wage earners and industry. Instead of braking the social democrats' dependence on famers, the conflict had forced a renegotiation of the political settlement of the 1930s. The capacity of the farmers to reassert their position politically is a major factor behind the Danish social democrats' stalled move toward greater political control of the economy.

The political settlement of 1961 dampened industrial progress as public moneys were dedicated to rural subsidies. Moreover, these subsidies slowed the progressive rationalization of agriculture, making it possible for less productive and less competitive farms to survive. Basically, farmers could not be forced to finance wage growth in industry. As a consequence, the Danish economy has been subject to

208

intense inflationary pressures, for class conflict over distribution easily becomes a stalemated, zero-sum affair between wage earners, industrial profits, and farm incomes. The repeated recourse to incomes legislation throughout the 1960s and 1970s can be understood only in this light.

To reduce the immediate inflationary pressures of the agreement, the government placed a temporary stop on new construction and tried to create budget surpluses. The rapid decline in unemployment, however, combined with a longstanding wage lag, permitted the unions to negotiate a 23 percent increase in nominal wages between 1960 and 1962. Concomitantly, public expenditure jumped dramatically because of the recent pension reform and other social welfare measures. The result was a 10 percent rate of inflation during 1961-1962. This period, in fact, is frequently referred to as the "income binge": farmers got subsidies, workers got wage increases, and the population got a marked increase in the social wage. The negative impact on the balance of payments forced the social democratic government to negotiate an incomes-policy solution, the 1963 "package deal" (Ibsen and Vangskjaer 1976; Hansen 1974; Schmidt 1971).

The so-called package deal was motivated partly by the destabilizing effects of the preceding income explosion and partly by the failure of a recently legislated value-added tax (OMS) to reverse the wage-price spiral and dampen consumption.[8] The policy comprised an array of legislative elements that the government refused to implement unless passed by parliament in their totality. The act included a freeze on collective agreements for two more years, price stabilization, removal of taxes from the wage indexation system, and subsidies to agriculture. Incomes of public employees and pensioners became tied to wage developments among LO workers; sickness cash benefits were increased; and special compensation was paid to low-wage workers, in part to offset the regressive effects of the OMS law. The government also promised the LO that it would prepare legislation on supplementary labor market pensions (ATP).

This incomes settlement contained all the classic ingredients of corporatist incomes policies. Wage-earner incomes were frozen in return

[8] At first, the OMS surtax was meant to be levied at the retail level, but political pressure from the Association of Retail Merchants led the social democratic government to implement it at the wholesale level instead. The OMS bill was introduced despite the vocal opposition of the Unskilled Workers' Federation. Although the OMS issue is a minor one, it testifies to the balance of power in Danish politics. The labor movement bent to the demands of petit-bourgeois organizations, even when this meant going against the interests of its own core constituency.

for improved social benefits and the prospect of continued full employment with price stability. The price controls were ineffective, so the total effect was a redistribution away from wage earners—although the lowest-paid sections of the working class clearly did improve their relative position (Munk et al. 1980, 56-57; Hansen 1974).

The package deal probably helped restore economic stability, but it also contributed to political instability. For the struggle over income shares was additionally politicized, and recourse to incomes policy in the first place exposed the greater need for public control of the economy. During parliamentary negotiations, the bill had been opposed from both right and left. The Danish Socialist People's party opposed the bill partly because it meant governmental interference with trade union autonomy in collective bargaining, but also because the SF wanted to focus attention on the need for greater state direction of investment. The package deal did little to solve the basic problem of how to promote a more rational and efficient use of the nation's resources.

In this period, the social democrats' main effort to combat speculative use of resources was their 1962 land reform bill. In the context of rapid urbanization, the social democrats had for years prepared legislation to permit greater public control of land use combined with reduced incentives for speculation. When the bill was presented in parliament, it was effectively blocked by a bourgeois majority. The social democrats then presented it for a popular referendum in 1963. The campaign became unusually bitter as the liberals and conservatives proclaimed it a covert attempt to socialize land. In turn, the social democrats defensively tried to convince the electorate that it was primarily a technical matter of stricter zoning. Finally, the bill was defeated, and this helped perpetuate the chronic problem of inflationary land speculation with its associated unproductive absorption of capital.

If the period until 1957 was marked by farmer domination of economic policy, the ensuing period has been characterized by a strangely dynamic stalemate. The 1960s in Denmark, as elsewhere, produced very high growth volumes with sustained high industrial investment rates. There was, in fact, a "second Danish industrial revolution" (Hansen 1974). This expansion, however, was very unsettled. The eradication of unemployment meant that the trade unions could push up real wages.[9] Yet, working-class strength produced destabilizing consequences. For one thing, the continued power of farmers meant

[9] During the 1960s, unemployment averaged only 2 to 3 percent.

that income gains in the urban economy necessitated agricultural compensation. Another factor was the uneven capacity among industries to offset wage pressures with improved productivity. This was particularly so in the case of firms producing for domestic consumption, such as those in the building sector. Working-class strength fueled wage-price spirals. Since the organizational strength of employers as well as workers in unproductive sectors blocked economic rationalization, their survival posed additional pressures for new incomes-policies agreements.

Although industry overtook agriculture in respect of exports, labor force participation, and share of national income, the great expansion during the 1960s—especially after 1965—occurred in services generally and public-sector activity especially. Public expenditure grew faster than GNP, and noneducational welfare spending grew at an annual rate of 5.1 percent between 1960 and 1968.[10] Agricultural employment declined, industrial employment was stagnant, and public-sector employment began its phenomenal growth.

The change in economic activity was not accompanied by a realignment of political power. Hence, wage pressure among blue-collar workers, the rising white-collar strata, and public-sector employees was stronger than productivity growth and not offset by relative income losses by other classes. This distributive stalemate nurtured creeping inflation and balance-of-payments difficulties, although some of the pressure was released by public and private borrowing from abroad. This permitted high investment rates and full employment to continue, even if productivity increases repeatedly failed to match wage growth.

The trade union movement and the rising left-socialist opposition mounted a concerted campaign for enhanced public control of credit and structural change in the economy. Yet, except for a few marginal reforms and a series of failed legislative attempts, the social democrats were unable to respond. Therefore, incomes policy remained the only viable instrument for economic stabilization.

The first important effort to exercise control over the economy occurred in 1967, when the social democrats—heavily pressured by the LO—proposed the ITP plan, along the lines of the previous Swedish ATP reform. It was specifically designed to augment the extremely weak 1964 reform and to funnel savings into collective pension funds. The bill never got beyond a first parliamentary hearing, and when the Red Cabinet collapsed shortly afterward, the idea died.

[10] After 1968, welfare expenditures exploded, increasing about 18 percent annually on the average.

Economic policy thus continued to be of the last-minute, crisis-management variety. In 1967, when the British devalued the pound, Danish agriculture was again threatened. The social democrats could respond only by devaluating the krone and imposing a new sales tax, this time levied at the retail level. This maneuver led directly to the downfall of the social democratic government, since the SF refused to sanction a policy that would reduce wage-earner purchasing power. The radicals, who had traditionally allied themselves with the social democrats, now coalesced with the other two bourgeois parties and formed Denmark's first unified nonsocialist government.

The period around 1966-1967 was ripe for a fundamental political realignment. The social democrats were in a position to cement a new wage-earner alliance with the SF around the ITP issue, just as the Swedish party had done during the late 1950s. But in this case the social democrats hesitated to break with the center. Tactical indecision aside, however, the objective circumstances had already asserted themselves when the various proposals for a more radical economic policy were aborted. One must also consider the ramifications of the social democrats' compromise housing agreement, in 1965-1966, and the social democrats' commitment to NATO as well as Danish entry into the EEC, both fiercely opposed by the SF.

Although the new bourgeois government sponsored a tight credit policy to dampen inflation and reduce balance-of-payments deficits, the opposite happened. By 1970, inflation was back to 6 or 7 percent per annum and, amazingly, taxes as a percentage of GNP rose from 33 percent in 1969 to 44 percent in 1971 (Munk et al. 1980, 58). This was in part a consequence of reforms already legislated during the social democratic tenure. But the failure to dampen either public-sector growth or inflation led the bourgeois government to propose a new round of incomes policies in 1970-1971, and the unions were asked to accept a continuation of existing contracts. In confirmation of Warren's thesis (1972), the LO refused to abide with incomes policies under a nonsocialist government, and the bill was aborted.

The social democrats were returned to office in 1971, as a minority government with implicit backing from the SF. The new government continued the previous restrictive fiscal and monetary policies and proposed a 10 percent import tariff. The question of Danish entry into the EEC overwhelmed all other issues. EEC membership was supported by the bourgeois parties and the social democrats; it was vehemently opposed by the SF and the other leftist parties. The issue was an extremely delicate one for the social democrats because large sections of the LO, particularly the metalworkers and the SID, were opposed.

The social democratic party itself was deeply split. In 1972, a public referendum produced a majority in favor of entry, but the issue clearly hurt the social democrats in the following elections.

Growing economic instability forced the government to dampen public-sector expansion and to renew its struggle to gain public control over economic change. In 1973, the social democrats proposed the joint LO–social democratic plan for economic democracy through collective wage-earner funds. The plan, designed to overcome the stalled condition of Danish economic policy, was meant to trade off wage-earner income restraint with an accumulation of investment capital in collective funds.[11] However, the bill was blocked by the right and was even opposed by the SF. When it proposed a gradual reduction of homeowner tax privileges, in December 1973, the government fell.

In concert with labor movements abroad, the Danish entered the 1970s with a burst of ideological radicalization. The party's 1969 program, *Det Nye Samfund* [The New Society] commits the party to do battle against inequality and launches the struggle for a democratization of economic life. The party leader Anker Jørgensen sought to underline the party's new leftist image by positioning it "to the left of the center." At the September 1977 congress, this new ideological profile was filled out with the adoption of a new program, *Solidaritet, Lighed, og Trivsel* [Solidarity, Equality, and Well-Being], in which the party confirmed its intent to eradicate unacceptable inequality and concentrated economic power by means of redistributive policies and economic democracy reforms (Socialdemokratiet 1977). But this recast ideology has had little effect on practical party policy in the economic crisis of the 1970s.

This attempt to launch economic democracy as the new vanguard of party policy was an immediate failure. The new program did not help weaken the left-socialist opposition, which, in fact, labeled it class betrayal; nor did it command much enthusiasm among workers. At any rate, the social democrats were forced onto the defensive following the disastrous December 1973 elections and the post-1974 economic recession. During the 1970s, within the context of rising unemployment, the social democrats had no choice but to sanction a combination of repeated incomes-policy settlements and restrictive fiscal policies.

The economic recession after 1974 clearly hit Denmark harder than it did most other countries. Unemployment averaged 11.2 percent of the insured labor force between 1975 and 1979, and there was a steady

[11] The issue of economic democracy is described in Chapter 9.

decline in investments from 1973 to 1978.[12] Deficits on the balance of payments increased fivefold (in current terms) between 1975 and 1980 and, equally troubling, public-sector debt burdens skyrocketed.

Governments have had but two remedies against chronic unemployment: one was to increase public-sector employment (from about 500,000 in 1970 to about 800,000 in 1980); the other was a system of generous, and very expensive, unemployment benefits. Despite increases in public employment and recent employment creation programs (directed particularly at the young), the overall level of unemployment has shown no tendency to drop. With no active labor-market policy apparatus, such as that enjoyed by the Swedes, overt unemployment could not be easily absorbed by such activities as retraining or sheltered employment.

Danish social democratic economic policy turned in the 1970s to step-by-step crisis management. The main instrument has been voluntary or compulsory incomes policy: in 1975, with legislated compulsory arbitration; in 1976-1977, with a demand for voluntary wage restraint; in 1979, with a legislated two-year extension of existing contracts (although this time with compensation to low-wage workers). In each case, the social democrats attempted—and failed—to complement wage discipline with economic democracy legislation. But wage restraint without the desired economic democracy reform seriously strained relations between the LO and the social democrats during the 1970s—almost to the breaking point during the 1978-1979 social democratic–liberal government.

Public debt burdens are reaching crisis proportions owing to the combined effect of declining tax revenues (because of economic stagnation) and rising unproductive expenditures (because of unemployment). This has forced social democratic governments to participate actively in public expenditure cutbacks. Thus, the social democrats are again caught in a dilemma, for such cutbacks exacerbate unemployment[13] while casting social democracy in the role of dismantling previous legislative achievements. During the late 1970s, the social democrats tried to erect an apparatus for active employment policy, though without noticeable success. There has been some ex-

---

[12] This unemployment rate translates to about 6 percent, when calculated on the basis of total labor force (Nordisk Råd 1980, table 46). The period is marked by a disinvestment rate of −2.2, for 1973-1976, and −0.6, for 1976-1978 (Munk et al. 1980, 50).

[13] The 1975 budget called for a savings of 185 million kroner by laying off more than 3,000 teachers. It was discovered that the "savings" from these layoffs disappeared because of the need to pay additional unemployment benefits.

pansion in temporary job creation programs and in wage subsidies to employers who agree to hire the long-term unemployed. But a more institutionalized approach to labor market policy remains blocked by the nonsocialist parties. Of the 9 billion kroner spent on labor market policies in 1979, a full 84 percent consisted of unproductive cash assistance to the unemployed (NU 1980a, 1:102).[14]

In conclusion, Danish social democratic economic policy has been imprisoned in the liberal mold. In the 1970s the capacity for political direction of the economy was hardly greater than it was before World War II. The social democratic crisis maneuvers of the 1970s only reaffirmed the capitalist economy's continued authority over social democracy.

Toward a Planned Economy in Norway

The structural parameters for postwar economic management in Norway are unique.[15] First, Norway's capital stock was severely damaged during the war and, thus, the process of industrialization was somewhat retarded. With its overwhelming attachment to natural resources such as hydroelectric power, forestry products, and metals, the Norwegian economy has had something of an enclave quality. Secondly, agriculture has remained weak and relatively unprofitable, while fishing has constituted a dominant export sector. Thirdly, the industrial sector appears to be dualistic. The large companies, built on metals and forestry products, have thrived on strong international demand and have secured a degree of economic freedom for Norway through export earnings. The state has come to play a key role in terms of both ownership and control within this sector. On the other hand, consumer-goods manufacturing has been underdeveloped and dominated by small companies. The upshot of these circumstances is that the Norwegian economy is an unusually open one,[16] but less vulnerable than others because its major export commodities have enjoyed sustained international demand. Moreover, the overall economic struc-

[14] This compares with only 10 percent in Sweden and 43 percent in Norway, where credit controls have been the chief instrument against unemployment.

[15] The major works on postwar economic policy that have been used in this chapter are Statistisk Sentralbyrå (1965), Haarr (1982), Mjøset (1981), Eriksen and Lundestad (1972), and Bergh (1977). On the topic of incomes policy, see Leiserson (1959), Schwerin (1980, 1981a, 1981b), and Cappelen (1981a, 1981b). On industrial policy, consult Grønlie (1977), Cappelen (1981a, 1981b), and Sejersted (1978).

[16] As a share of GNP (1950), exports constituted 38 percent in Norway, 28 percent in Denmark, and 22 percent in Sweden. By 1970, the figures were, respectively, 42 percent, 28 percent, and 24 percent (OECD 1980a).

ture, like that of Denmark, has been dominated by the primary sector; yet, Norwegian agriculture, unlike that of Denmark, has been weak.[17]

Conditions in Norway were therefore more opportune for the social democrats to promote industrial expansion and to insert the state as a key agent in this process. Given the pervasive sense of national solidarity stemming from the war, the DNA's ability to mobilize a consensus around its postwar "Work for Everyone" economic program (like the *Folketrygd* program, signed by all the parties) and, finally, the DNA's absolute parliamentary majority, the social democrats were in a very favorable position. They gained conservative support for their active industrialization program, which embraced government subsidies, credit controls, planning, and direct state engagement in such industries as iron and metals (Mjøset 1981). They gained trade union support for their long commitment to wage and consumption restraint, partly because this promised growth and full employment and partly because savings were funneled into collective public institutions. Moreover, the social democrats achieved continued support from the peasantry and rural periphery because the DNA's commitment to agricultural and fishery rationalization was coupled with a commitment to raise their relative income shares and protect prices. Very few forces in Norwegian society would have preferred Danish-style government passivity in regulating postwar economic growth.

Postwar economic policymaking can be divided into four distinct periods. The first, from 1945 to 1952, is marked by unusually deliberate and ambitious planning and regulation. The second, from about 1952 to the early 1960s, parallels the international trend toward liberalization and reaffirmation of market forces—although a broad political consensus for continued active state involvement in credit allocation and investment persisted. The third, from the early 1960s to the early 1970s, inaugurates a resumption of *dirigisme*, uninterrupted even under bourgeois-party rule after 1965. Finally, after 1973, the combination of international economic crisis and the advent of Norwegian oil production causes a sharp break with the past. DNA governments increase the state's direct role in investments and ownership, pursue extraordinarily strong countercyclical policies, and turn to a very active use of incomes policy. An overriding problem for the DNA throughout this sequence has been how to reconcile its aggressive

[17] In 1946, primary-sector employment (agriculture, fishing, and forestry) accounted for 30 percent of Norway's total labor force, compared with 28 percent for Denmark in 1940 and 25 percent for Sweden in 1940 (Elvander 1980, 59).

industrial promotion program with the pressures for protection, subsidization, and economic preservation that were brought to bear by the rural, periphery-based classes.

As elsewhere, postwar reconstruction in Norway involved extensive state regulation, rationing, and controls. In Norway, however, the combination of detailed microeconomic and general macroeconomic planning was both more powerful and more permanent. Also, the reconstruction program, drafted in London in 1944 and signed by all the parties, could be implemented in relative freedom from compromise because the DNA controlled a parliamentary majority. In addition, since the economy was severely damaged[18] and since a string of industries (especially in the hydroelectric and metal industries) had been seized by the Nazis, there was, as in Austria, a ready-made case for state nationalization or guidance within vital industries. And, besides, Norwegian industry was very weak.

But it was probably the design of the program that most of all ensured consensus. The DNA, unlike the Danish party was able to promote state-controlled industrial accumulation because rival political resistance was nullified.[19] The plan was a beautiful example of positive-sum politics. Although industrial accumulation called for planned, long-term wage restraint and consumption sacrifices, it was acceptable to the LO—and the rank and file—because it promised full employment. Also, with guaranteed price and profit controls, and government direction of investments, wage moderation would not produce unacceptable profits. Even with price and profit controls, the plan was welcomed by industrial capitalists because it promised an abundant supply of cheap credit and wage restraint under conditions of full employment. It also promised mobility of manpower from the primary to the secondary sector through planned agricultural rationalization. Finally, and perhaps most important, the peasantry, small fishermen, and the forestry sector could embrace the model—despite its clear intent to rationalize the primary economy—because it also promised considerable income compensation and price subsidies. Aside from the intent to rationalize the primary sector, government activist planning and investment policy was, and remained, overwhelmingly biased in favor of capital-goods-producing industries as well as those

[18] Fifty percent of Norway's merchant and fishing fleet had been sunk, or was inoperable, and 18.5 percent of the nation's capital stock had been destroyed (Leiserson 1959, 22). The volume of industrial output was, in 1945, only 57 percent of the 1938 level (Statistisk Sentralbyrå 1965, 365).

[19] Bourgeois resistance to planning rarely addressed the goal itself, and political conflicts generally centered around technical-administrative questions (Elvander 1980).

industries linked to Norway's natural resources. Small consumer-goods manufacturing was generally left to market entrepreneurialism (Sejersted 1978).

The social democrats erected a formidable apparatus for planned and controlled industrial expansion. Loyal to their prewar radical tradition, they immediately introduced a system of *Bransjeråd* (planning councils) and *Produktionsutvalg* (production committees) designed to promote democratic participation in matters of investment, planning, and industrial organization. The councils, however, were soon diluted into organs for joint consultation and lost their role as decisionmaking centers. Considerably more important was the establishment of state credit and finance, designed to exercise control over the allocation of investment capital. The system included state investment banks for industry (*Tiltaksfondet* and *Den Norske Industribanken*), for housing (*Husbanken*), and for agriculture and fishing (*Landbruksbanken* and *Fiskarbanken*). The latter were given the task of rapid capitalization and rationalization within the primary economy to ensure its economic viability, and equally important, to promote mobility of manpower from rural to industrial employment.[20] Planning was further aided by state ownership of important industries, particularly in energy.

Finally, the whole package of controls and planning was based on a system of quasi-voluntary incomes policies. Beginning with the 1944 London agreements, the state came to play a central role in setting the pattern for wage and incomes developments. Instead of imposing compulsory wage legislation, the Norwegian social democrats have relied on the willingness of the LO and the NAF to abide by the Public Wage Board's guidelines. When negotiations between capital and labor fail to result in agreement, the system of compulsory arbitration is set in motion. In Norway, in contrast to Denmark, wage conflicts could generally be reconciled without recourse to direct legislative intervention (Elvander 1974a; Schwerin 1981a).[21]

[20] It is interesting to note a marked difference between the Norwegian and the Swedish approach to state-directed economic transformation. Whereas the Swedish social democrats primarily used the active labor market policy to effectuate controlled change, the Norwegians have generally relied on their active credit policy to accomplish the same thing.

[21] On only two occasions has there been any overt, state-imposed incomes policy: in 1947 (for nine months) and in 1979. However, compulsory arbitration has occurred many times since the war, and there has also been voluntary LO abidance with the Public Wage Board's guidelines (Cappelen 1981a, 112). The system of directed wage settlement seems to have spurred very little rank-and-file protest (Schwerin 1981a, 1981b), thus going against most current theories of neocorporatism.

The planning model for this first period worked extraordinarily well: unemployment remained very low, inflationary pressures were effectively controlled, and both investments and real wage incomes rose constantly (Leiserson 1959; Statistisk Sentralbyrå 1965). Much of the success of DNA planning may lie in its technical proficiency, but some must also be ascribed to the organizational environment. As Galenson (1949) noted, the NAF is both highly centralized and unusually "solidaristic" internally.

Since similar organizational characteristics hold for agriculture, fishing, forestry, and merchant shipping, the environment for corporatist negotiations is peculiarly hospitable. But clearly the model would have broken down were it not for the DNA's capacity to rely on trade union acquiescence. The LO has accepted continuous wage planning, partly because it is preferable to compulsion and partly because the system includes built-in safety valves. Thus, it allows for a certain degree of local wage drift, and centralized LO wage settlements (with or without compulsory arbitration) are, on occasion, replaced with decentralized bargaining.[22]

The harmony of class relations was disrupted in the early 1950s over the question of continued price and profit controls. The social democrats wanted them to be continued, but a bourgeois countercampaign succeeded in moving the DNA toward liberalization. The liberalization of economic policy that began after 1952 was nevertheless not so far-reaching as that which occurred elsewhere in Scandinavia.

The planning apparatus was to some extent dismantled. Price, dividend, and profit controls were abandoned in 1953-1954, and the planning councils were allowed to die. Also, government allowed greater trade union autonomy in wage bargaining—although the practice of setting guidelines for acceptable wage increases was retained. On the other hand, the social democrats continued their selective direction of investment credit within the context of a low-interest lending policy. Except for financial and investment direction, however, economic policy was predicated on a far greater reliance on market forces in the allocation of both incomes and manpower. Within the system of negotiated guidelines, the LO allowed subordinate federations greater autonomy in contractual negotiations. To a degree, the solidaristic

[22] The LO had already turned to centralized, nationwide negotiations in the 1930s, and the central LO executive exercises considerable control over its member federations. Also, like the Swedish LO, the Norwegian LO has since 1938 committed itself to solidaristic wage bargaining in favor of low-income workers. It is more than likely that the Norwegian social democrats' greater success with planning-cum-incomes policy is attributable to the organizational cohesion of the LO.

wage-setting goal was sacrificed in favor of a restoration of wage differentials.[23]

Fortunately for the social democrats, economic liberalization proved equally successful in respect of sustained economic growth with full employment, price stability, and balance-of-payments stability. Some threatening signals appeared during the mid-1950s when a combination of relaxed price controls and rapid growth produced inflationary pressures and substantial balance-of-payments deficits. The social democrats were potentially losing their grip on the business cycle.

The DNA responded with a mix of restrictive fiscal policies, requests for voluntary union-wage restraint, and controls on the level of financial credit to be made available (Statistisk Sentralbyrå 1965). However, the decision to lower the subsidy on food prices, combined with imposed wage restraints, fueled sporadic strikes. The government responded by reinstating subsidies. Thus, despite some signs of disequilibrium in the late 1950s, social democratic policy continued to live up to its guarantee of full employment, real wage growth, and price stability.[24] The policy of state-directed industrial expansion was also successful with respect to its secondary objectives. The volume of investments remained high at the expense of current consumption; and it succeeded in shifting manpower and capital into manufactures and industry, especially into the export-oriented and dynamic sectors, while rationalizing the primary sector.[25] In addition, the social democrats kept their promise to the farmers concerning income equalization.[26] Finally, the social democrats further increased state control of the capital markets. By 1958-1961, public savings as a percentage of total savings exceeded 50 percent (Seierstad 1974, 78), and public direct investment constituted perhaps one-fifth of the total (Furre 1971, 307; Seierstad 1974, 79; Statistisk Sentralbyrå 1965, 131), although this was targeted primarily for traditional capital-goods-producing industries.

[23] Decentralized negotiations took place in 1952 and 1956. Apparently, the LO's decision to temporarily relax its solidaristic wages policy was motivated by the discovery that unskilled workers were beginning to outpace the skilled workers (Leiserson 1959, 127).

[24] Unemployment averaged 2 percent; from 1946 to 1957, real wages grew by 44 percent. The rate of GNP growth per capita from 1946 to 1957 was an average 2.9 percent, the highest in Scandinavia (Leiserson 1959, 94; Nordisk Råd 1980, table 172).

[25] Net investment as a percentage of net domestic product averaged 20.1 percent from 1951 to 1960 (Seierstad 1974, 86), and agricultural employment fell by 50 percent while industrial employment grew by 40 percent (Leiserson 1959, 130; Sejersted 1978).

[26] Agricultural incomes increased by 80 percent and forestry-fishing incomes by 118 percent in the 1946-1955 period (Leiserson 1959, 130).

In the 1960s a number of circumstances prompted the social democrats to bolster political control of economic activity. But this third period also heralded a reorientation of policy objectives. For one thing, there was a drastic shift toward decentralized, regional development policy; for another, the growth of public expenditures—especially on the social policy front—generated a move toward all-inclusive, corporatist incomes-policy bargaining in which the social wage began to figure prominently in income settlements.

The move to favor decentralized regional development had its political origins in the growing unrest among the DNA's traditional allies in the rural and provicial constituencies, particularly when rapid industrialization and rationalization began to take its toll on local communities. The promotion of decentralized local development began in earnest with the establishment of the *Distriktenes Utbygningsfond* (Regional Development Fund), which actually was a major extension of the already existing Northern Norway Plan of 1951. The new fund, however, was designed to promote investment throughout Norway by a means of direct state investment as well as generous subsidies for local industrial development and reorganization. At the same time, the social democrats strengthened other state finance institutions, such as the Housing Bank and the Export Credit Bank.

But the early 1960s produced political problems for Norwegian social democracy, particularly with respect to its ability to command political consent. Suddenly the DNA faced leftist opposition with the formation of the SF splinter party. In the 1961 elections, the DNA lost its parliamentary majority, and the SF gained. On the right, the nonsocialist parties began to form a common opposition program after decades of disunity (Rokkan 1966). Although neither the SF nor the bourgeois parties presented a radical challenge to the social democratic model for economic policy, the DNA's hegemony was slipping. Its problems were ultimately linked to shifts in the class structure. The decline within the traditional rural constituency was matched with the growth among middle-strata, white-collar groups. While the DNA's new regional development program and bolstered agricultural subsidies were designed to recapture waning loyalties among the former, the party had greater difficulty attracting the latter (Rokkan 1966). These were unmistakable signs that Norwegian social democracy was due for a political realignment.

The DNA's new policies may be viewed in light of these structural trends. As mentioned, the new attention to local and regional modernization was a response to crumbling support among the DNA's traditional rural base. A first attempt to accommodate the rising white-collar strata consisted in lowering the tax rate, for middle-income, white-collar wage earners were particularly hard hit by high marginal tax rates (Rokkan 1966). A watershed for modern Norwegian social democracy came in 1963, when a disaster in one of the state-owned mines fueled a public scandal and the social democratic minister of the interior was forced to resign. The DNA government was brought down and replaced with a tripartite bourgeois-party government (which, however, lasted only twenty-eight days). When the social democrats resumed office, it was with conditional SF support. This had the effect of pushing the DNA to the left.[27]

The social democrats' strategy for realignment was built on a) a more aggressive approach to state direction and control of the economy, b) industrial democracy, and c) the promotion of an ATP-funded, earnings-related retirement pension, very similar in form and content to the Swedish version. The ATP policy clearly spoke to the desire for a political alignment of workers, white-collar strata, and the rural population. With its promise of higher pensions, funded capital accumulation for additional regional development, and greater government control of the economy, the proposal seemed to benefit everybody. The tactic apparently helped the DNA win greater electoral support from the new white-collar strata, but it did not prevent the party from losing the 1965 elections to a coalition of bourgeois parties.

The bourgeois alliance, under center-party leadership, was to last until 1971. However, nonsocialist government policies were hardly at odds with social democracy's. The Christian people's party in the coalition insisted on an active social policy profile; the center party, on continued favorable treatment of its rural base. During its tenure, the bourgeois government legislated the final elements of the *Folketrygd* program for full social protection as well as the DNA-sponsored ATP pension plan.[28]

The bourgeois government actually strengthened the tradition of

[27] The Norwegian SF's opposition to the social democrats, unlike that of its Danish counterpart, seems to have been confined to the question of NATO membership and, later, to the issue of EEC affiliation. Nor has the Norwegian SF presented a major threat on economic policy issues (Westergård Andersen 1976), although it did push the DNA to give greater attention to economic democratization in the 1960s (Mjøset 1981).

[28] On this score it may be more appropriate to speak of an imposed consensus. The bourgeois parties could hardly avoid implementing the longstanding promise of the *Folketrygd* program. With respect to the ATP reform, it would have been politically dangerous to oppose ATP, especially in light of its overwhelming popularity when introduced in Sweden. The bourgeois parties there had suffered bitter defeats because of their opposition to the reform, and it is clear that the Norwegian bourgeois parties wished to avoid a similar fate (Elvander 1980).

strong public control over the credit market, especially in regard to the new regionalism. Public credit institutions for planned industrial rationalization and research development were established, and in 1969 the regional development fund was expanded considerably. Agrarian subsidies and the longstanding tradition of government participation in wage settlements were also continued. The 1968 collective agreements were, in fact, a classic example of corporatist incomes policy in which the LO abided by wage restraint in return for government-supplied price guarantees, improved social benefits, and a shorter work week (Cappelen 1981b). The bourgeois coalition's downfall was precipitated by the EEC issue.

Norway, like Denmark, had for many years negotiated for membership in the EEC and, again, the issue had provoked deep divisions both within parties (especially the DNA) and between parties. Fortunately for the social democrats, the bourgeois parties were in office when negotiations began. Since the center party was against membership, while the liberals and conservatives were in favor, the coalition fell apart in 1971. The subsequent social democratic cabinet was equally beleaguered, and the DNA continued official negotiations on membership despite powerful opposition from both within the party and from the left socialists. In Norway, however, in contrast to Denmark, the EEC referendum of 1972 produced a majority against membership. This did not resolve the instability that had suddenly beset Norwegian politics. The social democrats stepped down that year and were followed by a brief interlude of bourgeois government. In the 1973 elections, the DNA suffered heavy losses while the anti-EEC socialist left scored a fantastic victory. A minority DNA government with left-socialist support ensued.

The explosiveness of the EEC question in Norway can be understood only by recognizing that this issue crystallized the long-run tensions created by postwar policy with respect to the pattern of class coalitions. Unlike Danish farmers, who enthusiastically advocated EEC membership, the rural populations of Norway saw EEC membership as a colossal threat to their survival and as a direct contradiction to the powerful localism and regionalism espoused on the periphery. The DNA's official stance in favor of entry, therefore, prompted its erstwhile allies to forge a temporary alliance with the leftist, urban, white-collar-based SF in bitter opposition. With the EEC conflict, then, the DNA had simultaneously estranged its old rural allies and its potential white-collar allies. The party's struggle to resurrect itself and recapture political support must enter into any explanation of the DNA's altered policy course during the 1970s. If, on one hand, this struggle had to be waged in the context of a severe international economic contraction, the discovery of vast oil resources, on the other hand, gave the faltering DNA government the requisite room to maneuver.

In response to the worldwide recession that occurred after 1974, the DNA embarked upon what may very well be the world's greatest Keynesian, deficit-financed stimulation policy. If the years 1970-1973 had produced wage stagnation, the government-designed income agreement of 1974 increased government spending by 1 billion kroner in the form of reduced employee contributions to social security, tax reductions for middle-income wage earners, subsidies, and greater social spending (Cappelen 1981a, 192). The promotion of real income growth was additionally strengthened in subsequent years through a series of packaged income agreements. Besides real-income expansion for urban wage earners, an astounding redistribution of wealth in favor of the rural populations was undertaken.[29] The final round of the income agreements, in 1977, cost government an additional 2 billion kroner (Cappelen 1981a, 194). Not only were income redistribution and expansion employed as a means of addressing the collapse of the DNA alliance, but the party also embarked upon a wave of economic democratization reforms in the 1970s, including improvement of working conditions, enhanced worker participation in company decisionmaking, and democratization of banking.

These expansionary incomes policies went hand in hand with a concerted countercyclical effort: to prevent unemployment and to shelter Norwegian industry against the general drop in international demand and, particularly, against the nation's vastly reduced international competitiveness. Norwegian per-unit labor costs jumped to 25 percent above the OECD average (OECD 1978) and perhaps even higher (Sejersted 1978; Haarr 1982). Drawing on anticipated oil revenues, the government launched between 1975 and 1978 a deficit-financed program for selective industrial subsidization, including an expansion of investment credits, loans, and direct state investment in industry. These stimulation measures, moreover, were coupled with a low-interest policy and a substantial growth of active labor market programs, such as employment training and job creation (NU 1980b).

The DNA government received strong criticism, especially from the conservatives, for its decision to subsidize troubled, if not bankrupt, firms; this, it was held, would block the necessary structural adaptation

---

[29] The idea was to bring rural incomes on a par with average worker earnings in a series of transfers to begin in 1976, and the effects were almost immediately visible. The income share of agriculture, fishing, and forestry combined rose from 20.2 percent in 1970 to 29.5 percent in 1978 (Cappelen 1981a, 160).

of Norwegian industry to more competitive markets (Sejersted 1978; Haarr 1982).[30] Besides its expansionary fiscal and monetary policies, the DNA government initiated a marked shift toward direct state engagement in investment allocation. In 1973, the *Industrifond* was established as a superstructural credit institution that would consolidate the existing network of public credit supply. More important, though, government began a major wave of direct investment in the form of stock purchase. Excluding the oil industry, in which government holds majority ownership, state-held stock as a percentage of the total increased from 18 percent in 1970 to a full 30 percent in 1978 (Olsen 1980). If Statoil were included, the figure would jump to roughly 50 percent.

Up to and including the 1977 election, the DNA maintained its commitment to countercyclical expansionary policies; after being restored to office, however, the party made a volte-face and initiated a series of restrictive measures. Norwegian industry remained vastly uncompetitive, huge deficits had accumulated on the balance of payments and, borrowing on future oil income, the public deficit skyrocketed from 1 billion kroner in 1975 to more than 8 billion kroner in 1978 (Mjøset 1981).[31] With smaller than anticipated oil revenues, the restoration of stability would clearly necessitate a contraction of fiscal and monetary policy.

Beginning in 1978, the DNA government abandoned its low-interest policy, undertook a devaluation of the currency, sharply curtailed selective subsidies to industry, and imposed a price freeze. This was followed, in 1979, by a legislated wage freeze, which was supplemented in 1980 by an imposed ceiling on permissible wage drift (Schwerin 1980; Cappelen 1981a; Haarr 1982). In place of the liberal industrial subsidies, a relatively modest program to promote industrial rationalization and new product development was inaugurated in the context of a general plan for industrial rejuvenation. Until 1978, the government had successfully managed to prevent unemployment and, although the cost was high, the DNA could hold firm to its fundamental principles. After 1978, unemployment has shown a modest tendency to climb.

The Norwegian social democrats have, in recent decades, set in place an unusually elaborate apparatus for government management and

[30] Haar's excellent analysis of the subject, however, casts some doubt on whether in fact this subsidization program merely rescued lame-duck companies. He suggests instead that it may have helped maintain Norway's productive capacity under very unfavorable circumstances.

[31] Total public debt in 1978 was 40 percent of GNP (Nordisk Råd 1981, 179, 186).

control of economic development and business cycles. Indeed, apart from the troubled 1970s, it would seem that the party's economic policies have been crowned with success. Unemployment has almost never exceeded 2 percent, the rate of savings and investment has been both high and stable, industrialization has proceeded very quickly, and general economic growth has been healthy and sustained. It is, of course, impossible to determine whether the same results would have been forthcoming under laissez-faire conditions (the Danish experience), but it can be argued that much of Norway's economic success has depended on its "free ride" in the expansionary international markets of the 1950s and 1960s. Still, one must admit that the DNA has been able to deliver the promised—and politically necessary— stable full-employment growth.

The 1970s mark a decisive turning point. Had it not been for the happy coincidence of huge oil revenues, the DNA would likely have been forced, like the Danes, into defensive crisis management. Yet, even with the benefits of the oil cushion, the pressures on DNA policy that evolved with the EEC controversy seem to have pushed the party into a series of political and economic rescue operations that eventually boomeranged. Redistributive income policies were intended to appease the party's rebellious allies, but they fueled politicization and equity conflicts over income shares—especially as the post-1978 situation demanded a freeze on wage-earner incomes. Subsidization policies were intended to preserve employment, but they exposed the party to heavy and probably effective criticism from the right.

Above all, the apparent problem with the DNA's economic policies in the 1970s was that they failed to help move the party toward a modern and promising wage-earner alliance with the new middle strata. The extension of huge income transfers to the rural classes bears witness to the party's continued imprisonment in its traditional alliance; and those transfers may well have contributed to the alienation of the white-collar strata, which traditionally have opposed the DNA's sharply redistributive tax policies. A further problem for political realignment is that the DNA's existing policy formula has exhausted itself, as evidenced by the party's 1979 decision to shift to incomes-policy legislation and to permit unemployment to rise. Moreover, unlike the Swedes—or even the Danes—the DNA has no political formula, such as collective wage-earner funds, with which to transform a negative-sum conflict between profits and wages into a positive-sum model for recapitalization. However, one must remember that the construction of a policy model for a broad wage-earner alliance is especially difficult for the Norwegian social democrats, for white-collar employees have no central, coordinated trade union organization to protect their interests. At any rate, with no new political program to offer under current conditions, and having pushed large numbers of white-collar employees into the arms of the conservative party, the necessary social democratic realignment appears far off.

The Swedish Model

Sweden was in a particularly favorable position when the war ended.[32] Neutrality had spared the country from devastation and economic plunder, and Sweden's capital equipment was intact. Moreover, Sweden had enjoyed a comparative advantage during the war as exporter of critical war-related goods, such as iron and lumber. This comparative advantage extended beyond the conclusion of the war because Sweden was one of the few European economies capable of running at full capacity.

The political situation was a mixed blessing for social democracy. The SAP had dominated the wartime coalition government, especially after the extraordinary 1940 elections gave it 53.8 percent of the vote. Although the party lost votes in the 1944 election (when the communists suddenly doubled their share), the postwar position of both the LO and the SAP was extremely strong. Unlike the Norwegians, though, the Swedish social democrats could not rely on a heroic image to manufacture a broad national consensus for a social democratic future.

All in all, the success of the labor movement's economic policies is primarily due to its advantage in the balance of political power. If the movement could not force the bourgeois parties into consensus, it could rely on a combination of its own strength and the perennial disunity among the three nonsocialist parties. Also, in contrast to the saga of Danish social democracy, the Swedish movement was not chronically forced to bend to liberal doctrine. The structural constraints on Swedish economic policy were generally quite different from those in Denmark. Export revenues and balance-of-payments stability never hinged on one dominant yet fragile product, such as agricultural commodities. Instead, even more than in Norway, high-

---

[32] The story of Swedish economic policy in the postwar period has been told many times, and there exist several excellent overviews in English, among them Lindbeck (1972) and Martin (1973, 1975, 1979, 1981). With respect to the standard Swedish sources, I have relied particularly on Södersten (1974), Andersson and Meidner (1973), and Edgren et al. (1970). The following account closely follows Esping-Andersen 1980 and Esping-Andersen and Friedland 1982.

quality iron ore deposits and ample supplies of timber and electric energy provided a cushion against the world economy. Nor did Swedish social democratic policy have to contend with a proliferation of anachronistic, craft-based industries in which employers and workers alike were wedded to protective survival measures. Rather, the industrial structure was dominated by large, heavily capitalized and concentrated companies in which control was effectively centered in a few hands. Swedish capitalists were rather easily persuaded to accept state participation in economic rationalization.

Given these conditions, major advances toward social control of capitalism had to wait longer than in Norway but much less than in Denmark. One important constraint on postwar economic growth was that it could not possibly proceed on the basis of low wages and idle labor reserves. The Saltsjöbaden Agreement, furthermore, had ruled out the option of direct state intervention in wage negotiations. This meant that, from the very start, the SAP's great policy dilemma was how to ensure constant full employment without inflation.

Social democratic stabilization policies follow a clear chronology. In the immediate postwar period, economic policy was couched within orthodox demand-management prescriptions. During the 1950s, the LO and the SAP moved in tandem toward the celebrated policy of structural change and rationalization via active labor market policies. By the late 1960s this was clearly not enough, and the SAP sought to complement active labor market policies with investment direction. By the mid-1970s, the postwar political formula was exhausted as Sweden became caught in the grip of the new international economic disorder, and economic conflict turned into a zero-sum battle between wages and profits.

The social democrats' famous postwar political program, *Arbetarrörelsens Efterkrigsprogram*, called for a concerted strategy of economic planning and democratic control of private capital. The program put aside nationalization goals and advocated a deregulation of wartime physical controls. Instead, the emphasis was on a mix of active fiscal policy, to stimulate demand, and macroeconomic planning of aggregate resource allocation. On both counts, however, the program boomeranged. The bourgeois parties, exploiting popular resentment over controls, were able to force the social democrats away from their planning program when, in the 1948 elections, the SAP lost votes to the right. In the case of active stimulation policies, the social democrats had exaggerated the threat of a postwar recession. The result was inflation and balance-of-payments problems, as full employment engendered large wage increases and squeezed profits. In

228

short, the social democrats faced a situation very similar to that in Britain, and their solution, like that of the Labour government, was to impose upon a reluctant LO a two-year freeze on wages.

Although the incomes policy had helped restore equilibrium to the economy, it also endangered the equilibrium of Swedish politics. The LO made it clear that further resort to incomes policies would be entirely unacceptable. Such policies violated the LO's prized ability to bargain freely in the labor market, and they permitted employers to accumulate profits at the expense of wages. But, aside from such standard objections, the LO was also concerned that wage discipline jeopardized solidarity, for the strongest workers could more easily take advantage of wage drift. In contrast to their British counterparts, however, the Swedish trade unionists managed to present a constructive political alternative to an endless series of stop/go measures: the famous Rehn model. According to the LO economist Gösta Rehn, incomes policy was objectionable not only in respect of wage solidarity goals, but also because controls would later unleash a wage explosion. Controls allowed dynamic companies to reap unacceptably high profits and, at the same time, protected inefficient and unprofitable companies.

The Rehn model was adopted by the LO in 1951 and, eventually, by the social democrats as well.[33] It was a brilliant application of neoclassical economic theory to the needs of the labor movement. The idea was to resolve the full-employment–inflation problem by a combination of aggressive wage-solidarity bargaining, active manpower policy, and restrictive fiscal policies to effectuate structural change in the economy. The system of solidaristic wage bargaining was to equalize wages across industries and regions; across-the-board wage pressure was to be applied in such a way as to reward firms that could increase productivity and to punish firms that could not. Thus, collective bargaining would help drive out weak firms, which—in Rehn's analysis—are the ones particularly open to inflationary price compensation against wage pressure. The Rehn model thus eliminates traditional trade union defensiveness against manpower layoffs in declining industries, substituting an aggressive rationalization policy, in which layoffs are tolerated and even encouraged. The problem of manpower redundancies, in turn, is resolved by the institutionalization of an "active manpower policy," which guarantees that laid-off workers be

---

[33] Gösta Rehn, who collaborated closely with Rudolf Meidner, first published his theory of full-employment stabilization policy in 1948, in a *Tiden* article entitled "Ekonomisk Politik vid Full Sysselsättning." The LO version (1951) was published as *Fackföreningsrörelsen och den Fulla Sysselsättningen*.

spared the individual risk and cost of rationalization. To ensure the smooth transition of labor from declining to growing industries, Rehn's active manpower policy relies on central coordination of worker retraining and education, employment exchanges, sheltered employment, and local job creation for workers who are unwilling, or unable, to move.

By socializing the risk of technological unemployment, the Rehn policy naturally removes a major impediment to rapid rationalization and structural change. By helping shift manpower to more efficient and profitable firms, the policy enhances the economy's competitive potential under full employment and high wages, while at the same time removing the need to subsidize weak firms in the interest of maintaining jobs.

At first hesitant, the social democrats decided in 1956 to promote the active labor market policy. In subsequent years, the Swedish Labor Market Board (AMS), set up in 1939, was given the resources to promote labor mobility, training, and employment creation. A parastatal institution with rather autonomous status and with strong corporatist overtones, the board is composed of three representatives from the LO, two from the TCO, one from the SACO, and three from the SAF.[34] Institution of the active labor market policy meant an advance for social democratic management of the economy. Government, in liaison with the trade union movement, thereby acquired political leverage over structural change (although indirectly more than directly, since it relies on labor mobility to stimulate the desired capital mobility). The policy may be viewed as a Swedish analogue to the Norwegian use of credit controls to direct economic change.

The AMS rapidly became an extraordinarily important and powerful device for regulating the economy. Its budget, initially rather modest, increased considerably as its authority was expanded and as the speed of rationalization picked up during the 1960s.[35] The expansion of the AMS's sphere of operation is attributable partly to unforeseen consequences of rapid structural change and partly to deliberate policy. First of all, economic rationalization gave rise to a lopsided pattern of development, featuring a growing concentration

[34] This composition ensures that a unified LO-TCO vote will command a majority.
[35] In 1956, AMS expenditures were only about 125 million kronor. By 1971, they had increased to more than 3 billion kronor (about 2 percent of GNP). From 1976 to 1981 expenditures hovered at 2 or 3 percent of GNP, per annum. Generally, about 60 percent of AMS expenditures are earmarked for employment creation and 40 percent for mobility-stimulating activities, such as training and improved matching of jobs and employees (Johannesson 1982, 52-53).

in large cities and, especially in the North, stagnation. By the mid-1960s, popular resistance to mobility was growing, and the AMS was saddled with the task of providing a greater amount of sheltered employment than had been envisaged (Berglind and Lindquist 1972). In 1965 the regional development policy, giving preferential treatment to industries locating in declining areas, was considerably reinforced. It was logical that regional development and industrial location policy were managed by the AMS. Another field in which AMS authority was expanded was housing policy, since reliance on rapid labor mobility assumed the existence of a ready supply of housing. After the introduction of a crash program for housing construction in the 1960s, huge amounts of pension-fund capital were funneled through the AMS for housing development. In addition, the AMS holds authority over the social democrats' previously legislated "investment reserve system."

The investment reserve system was established before the war but was vastly expanded in 1956, primarily in order to facilitate management of the business cycle. The scheme invites corporations to place as much as 40 percent of their annual pretax profits into a closed public account, to be frozen until the government approves its release. The advantage to business is a substantial tax savings on corporate profits; the advantage to government lies in the potential for adjusting to business cycles by allowing the release of capital during slumps and withholding capital as the economy overheats. The scheme originally assumed full managerial control over how released funds were to be invested, but the AMS has increasingly tried to bring its influence to bear on the geographical distribution of such capital.

The active labor market policy was undoubtedly successful with respect to stabilization and full-employment growth. But it also caused individual hardship for workers forced to move, undergo retraining, or "volunteer" for early retirement (Berglind and Lindquist 1972; Berglind and Rundblad 1978), although such hardship would undoubtedly have been worse under conditions of laissez faire. Unquestionably the policy has enhanced the power of the labor movement, helped to avert unemployment, and permitted the unions to bargain for wage increases with less risk of wage-price spirals. It has obviously also given the social democratic government greater power to conduct economic policy for structural change. In addition, it has helped the trade unions pursue income equalization through solidaristic wage bargaining (Meidner 1974). There is some evidence, too, of a salutary effect on economic performance, although the magnitude of that effect is difficult to assess (Lindbeck 1975). It has probably helped dampen

231

the inflationary pressures of a full-employment economy, and it has aided the rate of investment and productivity growth within expansionary sectors (Andersson and Meidner 1973). Finally, the export sector's share of total production increased to 40 percent by 1970, thus strengthening Sweden's balance of payments.

But the policy was not free from problematic side effects. As noted, the dedication to economic efficiency took a human toll that, despite the protective umbrella of the AMS, has been considerable. Secondly, it fueled an astounding rate of capital concentration and exacerbated the problem of unequal distribution of wealth (SOU 1968; Dahlkvist 1975; Spånt 1975). This posed a particularly difficult dilemma for the labor movement. According to the LO, growing inequalities of wealth are a byproduct of solidaristic wages policy, since workers in highly profitable industries are forced to underutilize their bargaining power.[36] A third shortcoming of the active labor market policy is its inability to ensure adequate rates of new investment. In the late 1960s, there were signs that wage pressure was squeezing profit levels so much that capitalists were unwilling, or unable, to compensate with productivity improvements (Edgren et al. 1970; Bergström 1971). While the rate of investment declined, market wages as well as government social expenditures grew very fast. Aside from this resurgence of the unemployment-inflation dilemma, the active labor market policy itself began to produce bottlenecks. The rate of manpower redundancies surpassed the AMS's capacity to transfer labor to expanding industries in a smooth fashion. When labor-market mobility alone proved insufficient for long-range stable growth, the LO began to pressure for state direction of investment.

The investment reserve system had perhaps been successful with respect to the allocation of investments throughout the business cycle. But it was an inadequate means of controlling the distribution of investment across industries.[37] The issue for social democracy, therefore, was how to supplement the active manpower policy with an active investment policy.

[36] It was primarily the problem of excess profits through solidaristic wage policy that inspired the LO to request adoption of Rudolf Meidner's proposal for employee capital funds.

[37] By 1970, the investment reserve funds contained over 4 billion kronor, representing more than half the rate of industrial investment in that year. The influence on aggregate investment can be seen from the fact that a major release of funds in 1968 accounted for 11 percent of total private investment (Lindbeck 1975, 150). Also, since the system mainly favors companies having large assets and a capacity for long-range corporate planning, it naturally strengthened the process of concentration.

The issue of investments immediately centered on the enormous amount of capital accumulated in the ATP pension funds. The SAF urged that capital be released in the private credit market; the LO demanded that it be channeled into a public investment fund. Rising unemployment in the mid-1960s helped convince the social democrats of the need for a concerted investment policy, and in 1967 they agreed to the LO's demands, legislating a state investment bank financed by the "fourth ATP fund." The reform was a major campaign theme for the social democrats during the 1968 elections; the party's ability to convince voters that such a reform would attack the unemployment problem helps explain the SAP's unusual electoral success in that year.

Initially, the bank's lending was targeted for housing construction, and only a third was allocated to industrial investment. But after 1974, when the housing program had ended and the unemployment problem resurfaced, the social democrats began to dedicate a greater share to industrial development and stock purchase in private companies. Thus, government became a major shareholder in the development of a new steel mill in the North and bought stock in such companies as Volvo.[38]

The government record with respect to economic policy was, until the 1970s, quite favorable from the labor movement's point of view. Industrial reorganization and rationalization were rapid, and the policies did force companies to streamline production, cut unnecessary costs, and invest in advanced technology. Despite Sweden's high labor costs, export competitiveness was maintained. Even with constant full employment, the average rate of inflation during the 1960s was no higher than in most West European nations. Remarkably, this was achieved with one of the world's lowest unemployment rates—rarely exceeding 2 percent. Simultaneously, public-sector spending grew twice as fast as GNP as the social democrats consolidated their welfare state apparatus.

By the early 1970s, however, the social democratic model came under severe strain. The two principal problems were, first, continued full employment and, second, the problem of income-and-wealth distribution. To begin with the latter, the late 1960s had produced a trade-off between wage growth and profitability; as the public sector grew, the room for real-wage improvements narrowed rapidly. But the question also extended into the broader issue of greater social

[38] The steel mill project turned out to be a minor disaster for the social democrats, partly because of enormous cost overruns and partly because of uncommonly bad timing. The mill's establishment, for one thing, happened to coincide with a worldwide crisis in the industry. When the bourgeois parties assumed power in 1976, they decided to bring the project to a temporary halt.

equality. To some extent, tax reforms and social expenditures had managed to redistribute incomes; the solidaristic wage-bargaining process had also helped narrow differentials. Yet, overall, the emphasis on efficient structural change during the 1960s had ignored the goal of greater equality. In short, income redistribution became important both because of egalitarian promises and for reasons of price stability when union wage pressure and public expenditure growth exerted themselves on the economy. The overriding question had to do with whose wallet would be lightened in order to redistribute incomes.

On this question the social democrats had the luck of stumbling upon a ready-made target when, in 1971, the association of professionals and civil servants, SACO, made use of its newly won right to strike for higher salaries. The strike was unpopular, especially among LO and TCO workers, who claimed that earnings differentials were already too high and who would also be paying for those higher salaries through higher taxes. The social democratic government was therefore in an opportune position to respond with a general lockout. After a protracted struggle, the SACO finally gave in and, as a consequence, the social democrats reaped a major distributive victory.[39] From the LO's perspective, however, the real issue of equalization has to do with the distribution of wealth. We shall later see how the original Meidner plan and subsequent proposals for collective wage-earner funds became a major strategy for social equality.

The issue of continued full-employment growth came to the fore as Sweden entered the 1970s, particularly as a result of restrained fiscal and monetary policy. In addition, the negative byproducts of economic rationalization had begun to be felt. One indicator was the AMS's growing burden with respect to absorbing redundant manpower, together with the rising cost of avoiding open unemployment. As mentioned, AMS expenditure had grown to 2 percent of GDP by 1971. The number of workers absorbed in various AMS activities, moreover, had grown to 2 percent of the labor force in 1971. Simultaneously, the rate of worker absenteeism rose, and worker militancy erupted with a series of wildcat strikes in 1969-1970. Not only that, but the economy was showing definite signs of long-term stagnation and structural imbalance. Despite concerted efforts to supply capital to growth sectors, the necessary recapitalization of Swedish industry was hindered by high interest rates and entrepreneurial reluctance to invest (Meidner 1978). Gross investment as a percentage of GNP declined

[39] The defeat of the SACO led to a substantial real-income decline among professionals in the public sector.

from an average of 25 percent in the 1960s to 20 percent in the 1970s (LO and SAP 1978). Since productivity improvements could no longer offset the rise in direct and indirect labor costs, the conflict between wages and profits became inflationary, and Swedish exports lost their competitive edge.[40]

After the 1971-1973 recession, the government asked the LO and the TCO to hold back wage increases voluntarily in return for a legislated refinancing of social security contributions. But, as a consequence of wage lag and the high rate of marginal taxation under inflationary conditions, restraint was followed by a wage explosion. This, of course, exacerbated the problem of high wage costs and export decline.

When the social democrats lost in 1976, indications were that their model for economic policy no longer worked. Labor market negotiations began to depart from the traditional pattern of harmony. In the 1977 wage rounds, the employers refused to bargain on the basis of the LO proposal, hoping that their militant stand would be backed by a sympathetic bourgeois cabinet. Negotiations lasted a record seven months. Moreover, wage negotiations could no longer escape politicization. On one side, the unions began to demand a reduction of the high marginal tax rate. On the other, the SAF demanded that employer payroll taxes be slashed and that absenteeism be combatted with longer waiting periods for sick pay. The state, however, is ill-equipped to absorb heightened distributive conflicts, and the public deficit more than tripled—from 3.5 percent of GNP to 12 percent of GNP—between 1976 and 1981 (Tholin 1982, 4).

Clearly the public fiscal crisis was exacerbated by the nonsocialist government's crisis policies. After 1976, it vastly expanded the social democrats' scheme of subsidizing company inventories to counter a decline in activity and, thus, in employment. Yet, government projections of a resurgence in exports proved too optimistic. By 1977, the value of accumulated inventory equaled 2 percent of GNP (Geiger 1978). In addition, the fear of rising unemployment under a nonsocialist government led to heavy subsidization of threatened industries, such as shipbuilding, and to subsidies for company-sponsored training programs. Meanwhile, the rate of open unemployment has slowly increased and the rate of "disguised" unemployment (i.e. manpower redundancies absorbed in the AMS) has mushroomed, accounting for an additional 5 percent of the labor force.

[40] The inflation rate during the first half of the 1970s was double the rate in the 1960s.

In Sweden, government has clearly lost its grip on the economy as a long string of successful stabilization policies for structural change has been replaced with British-style, lame-duck subsidization and serious structural imbalance. It is debatable to what degree the collapse of the Swedish model for economic policy was caused by the shift to nonsocialist government after 1976. Naturally, the social democrats insist that they would have done everything differently, and there is some truth to the claim that they would have been better positioned to restrain union demands. Yet, a major cause of Sweden's jeopardy was the post-1973 OPEC price explosion, coupled with bad timing. The wage explosion of 1975-1976 (under a social democratic government) meant that Swedish exports priced themselves out of the market exactly when the international economy began to rebound (Martin 1981; Tholin 1982). Furthermore, such crisis measures as inventory subsidization had begun under the SAP government prior to 1976. Indications are that the real problem is the inability of existing policies to cope with the combined effects of the new international economic order and the domestic economic structure of the 1970s and 1980s.

As the economic situation has worsened, political conflict over economic policy has sharpened. All political parties are agreed that the core problem is how to finance a new growth machine. The conservative party has had considerable electoral success with its neoliberal vision of reprivatization and much greater reliance on market forces. The social democrats, after their 1981 congress, finally committed themselves to economic democracy as the centerpiece of recapitalization. Ultimately, victory for either side depends on an ability to win support from the new middle-class electorate. The present struggle over a new model for Swedish economic policy is therefore a question of political alignment. The only chance for social democracy lies in its capacity to forge a new white-collar–blue-collar alliance behind economic democracy.

A COMPARATIVE ASSESSMENT OF BUSINESS-CYCLE CONTROL

The three Nordic countries have developed very different mechanisms for political control of the business cycle. The Norwegian social democrats have primarily emphasized planning with credit control and, lately, government purchase of industrial stock. The Swedes have relied primarily on labor market regulation, but after the mid-1960s they also began to promote a more active government role in investment. Finally, the Danish social democrats have failed to institute public direction and control of finance, labor market, or investment behavior. In all three countries—but especially in Norway and Denmark—government intervention in income determination assumed major proportions during the 1970s.

To estimate the degree of public economic controls, one can take two paths. One is to compare policy instruments believed to have a strong influence on the economy. The other is to compare data on economic performance and assume that cross-national variations may be ascribed to differences in the countries' control apparatus. Government potential for exercising control can be captured by such variables as government share of total credit supply, government share of new fixed-capital formation, and levels of expenditure on labor market regulation.

If we begin with the assumption that large labor market expenditures reflect government capacity to manipulate the behavior of the labor market, we see that the Swedish commitment exceeds by far that of the other two countries. In Sweden, such labor market activities (excluding the cost of unemployment compensation) accounted for 2.24 percent of GDP in 1979. This is more than four times the volume in Denmark (.53 percent), despite Denmark's more serious unemployment problem. The very low Norwegian figure (.28 percent) can be explained by the lack of a tradition for active labor market policy and, of course, by the virtual absence of any unemployment problem during the 1970s (NU 1980b, 1:102; Nordisk Råd 1980, table 171).

A high rate of labor market expenditure may not directly reflect control over the market, for it may simply express efforts to absorb persons who would otherwise be openly unemployed. On the other hand, manpower training or job creation must be substantially better than open unemployment from the labor movement's point of view. The cost to the public budget is probably no greater than that of unemployment assistance; and the expenditure is undoubtedly more productive, since the recipients at least produce some kind of socially valued product. Furthermore, few would doubt that employment or retraining has a less demoralizing effect on individuals and families than long-term open unemployment. It should also strengthen labor movement cohesion and solidarity as well as trade union power vis-à-vis employers.

Our second indicator is the degree of public control over the finance and credit markets. There are three important ways in which government can affect credit and investment: through its influence on total lending, through its share of the bond market, and through its impact on capital formation. Table 7.1 compares the three Nordic countries

TABLE 7.1. Public-Sector Share of Credit Market in Scandinavia,
FY 1978/79

	Denmark	Norway	Sweden
% of Total Lending	1.44	52.40	24.68
% of Total Bond Holdings	11.80	32.48	44.48
% of Total Gross Fixed-Capital Formation	12.98[a]	37.70	18.39

SOURCES: Danmarks Statistik (1978, tables 322, 371); Statistisk Sentralbyrå (1980, table 91); Statistiska Centralbyron (1980, tables 439, 483); Nordisk Råd (1980, table 166).

NOTE: The public sector includes local and central government, public banks, credit institutions, and investment funds, postal banks, social pension funds, and related state institutions.

[a] Data are for 1974-1975.

in terms of public-sector share of total lending, bond holdings, and capital formation. Norway clearly occupies a vanguard position, while in Denmark public credit is largely subordinate to the free market. Again, the indices of public credit supply may not reflect *actual control*. It is, for example, clear that a large share of total government lending is concentrated within the housing sector (especially in Sweden).[41] Still, one would expect that the larger the public share of total credit, the greater the government's capacity to decide on allocation. Hence, broader social priorities would influence the credit market.

Public control of capitalism should also be enhanced where government share of direct investment is high and where the government owns a considerable part of industry. On these counts, too, one would expect Norway to score especially high, given the extent of government direct investment and stock purchase during the 1970s. If we take publicly owned companies as a percentage of all firms (in respect of sales volume), Norway scores highest with 10 percent and Sweden yields 7 percent. In Denmark, publicly owned companies occupy such a peripheral position that their share of total sales volume is close to zero (Elvander 1980, 266).[42] The government share of gross fixed-capital formation is again considerably higher in Norway and lowest in Denmark.

Combining all these factors is not easy. Yet, it seems obvious that

[41] Of all public lending in Sweden, the housing sector absorbs approximately 22 percent (Statistisk Sentralbyrå 1980, 200).

[42] As mentioned, the Norwegian government holds 30 percent of all non-oil-related stock and 50 percent if oil is included.

Denmark is extraordinarily liberalistic, in the sense that government has very little leverage over either the labor market or the capital market. In contrast, Sweden stands out with respect to labor market regulation, while the Norwegian state emphasizes involvement in the credit market and direct investment. Hence, one would expect the economic performance of Norway and Sweden to be far superior to that of Denmark—assuming that there is a direct relation between capacity for control and actual performance in the areas of full employment, price stability, and stable growth. We should keep in mind, however, that one cannot control adequately for the decisive factor of "objective economic vulnerability."[43]

At first glance, the evidence seems to bear out our expectations. On balance, both Norway and Sweden have performed much better in terms of maintaining full employment at a given level of inflation. But in Sweden economic growth has been slower. (See Tables 7.2, 7.3, and 7.4.)

During the 1950s, Denmark maintained price stability, albeit at the cost of slow growth and high unemployment. The period between 1960 and 1973-74 was quite different: growth and inflation were high; unemployment was low. The real test, of course, is the period of "stagflation" from 1974 to 1980. Here, the Danish performance is dismal on all three counts: growth was once again slow, unemployment was very high, and the rate of inflation was the worst in Scandinavia.

Norway's record is almost always the best of the three. GDP growth was consistently high throughout the 1950-1979 period, and the rate of unemployment must be the lowest in the world over so many years. Moreover, this was achieved with generally lower inflation rates than

TABLE 7.2. Average Annual Rate of Real GDP Growth Per Capita in Scandinavia, 1950-1979

(%)

	Denmark	Norway	Sweden
1950-1960	2.5	2.9	2.7
1960-1970	4.0	3.9	3.8
1970-1979	2.3	4.0	1.7

SOURCE: Nordisk Råd (1980, table 172).

[43] For open economies, such as those of Scandinavia, the importance of exports can be used to gauge "vulnerability." Norway, then, appears to be far more vulnerable than the other two countries, for its exports account for 42 percent of GNP, compared with 28 percent for Denmark and 29 percent for Sweden (OECD 1980a).

TABLE 7.3. Average Rate of Unemployment in Scandinavia, 1955-1979
(%)

	Denmark	Norway	Sweden
1955-1959	9.3	1.7	2.0
1960-1969	3.3	1.2	1.5
1970-1974	3.6	.8	1.8
1975-1979	11.2	1.3	1.4

SOURCE: Esping-Andersen and Korpi (1984, table 6).

NOTE: Cross-national comparisons of unemployment rates are problematic. The figures for Denmark exaggerate unemployment because Danish statistics are based on membership in unemployment insurance funds. If, instead, Danish labor-force survey figures are used—and these are probably comparable to those for Norway and Sweden, at least for the 1970s—the rate of unemployment in Denmark becomes 1.3% for 1970-1974 and 6.1% for 1975-1979.

TABLE 7.4. Average Annual Rate of Inflation in Scandinavia, 1951-1980
(*consumer price index*)

	Denmark	Norway	Sweden
1951-1960	3.4	4.5	4.6
1960-1973	8.2	7.0	6.6
1974-1980	10.7	9.2	10.4

SOURCES: Nordisk Råd (1980, table 160); OECD (1970, 1980a).

in either Denmark or Sweden. Norway's performance in the late 1970s, of course, despite high inflation, would likely have been much less impressive were it not for the oil boom.

Until the social democratic engine ran out of steam in the 1970s, Sweden's performance more closely resembled that of Norway (although Sweden's GDP growth was slower during the 1950s and 1960s than either of the other two Nordic nations). Inflation was lower than in Denmark until the 1970s, but higher than in Norway. What is remarkable is the low rate of unemployment during the stagflationary 1970s. This is certainly attributable to the social democrats' achievements in labor market policy.[44] But in terms of growth and price stability, the "Swedish model" has performed poorly in the 1970s.

Until the 1970s, the indices of economic performance seem to confirm our expectations; that is, the greater the capacity for public direction, the better should be the potential for maintaining full em-

[44] These policies continued under the bourgeois governments from 1976 to 1982.

ployment without inflationary damage. A trade-off between full employment and inflation certainly exists, as is clear when we register the steadily growing inflation rate at constant levels of unemployment. Norway and Sweden seem to fit Hibbs's (1977) finding that strong labor parties hold onto full employment, even at the expense of inflation. Denmark's record of high inflation and high unemployment in the 1970s provides evidence against the argument.

The maintenance of full employment under bad as well as good economic conditions is a social democratic achievement in its own right. If attained at the expense of real incomes, however, the political benefits of full-employment policies might easily be undercut by worker frustration over long-run, or at least periodic, income restraint. The development of real incomes in light of the indicators discussed above would therefore constitute an important additional index of government economic performance. Obviously, an index of real-wage growth tells only an incomplete story, since distributional issues are concealed and since such an index does not take into account compensatory social wage improvements. Table 7.5 shows the evolution of hourly real earnings in manufacturing for the three Nordic countries.

Sweden experienced the strongest real-wage growth in Scandinavia during the 1950s. That position was taken up by Denmark during the lively 1960s, and by the 1970s, real wages were growing much more slowly in Sweden than in the other two nations. Danish growth during the 1970s is quite remarkable, given Denmark's economic difficulties and high unemployment.[45] In summary, Sweden has been characterized by sustained full employment in a context of moderate-to-high inflation, relatively sluggish growth, and slow real-wage increase. Nor-

TABLE 7.5. Development of Real Wages in Scandinavian Manufacturing, 1953-1979
(% *increase*)

	Denmark	Norway	Sweden
1953-1959	19	25	30
1960-1970	98	62	77
1970-1979	72	74	48

SOURCES: ILO (1960, 1970, 1979); Statistiska Centralbyron (1980, table 285).
NOTE: The data are based on hourly, pretax wages, deflated by the consumer price index, and pertain to adult males only.

[45] If we take only the latter 1970s, real wages stagnated in Denmark between 1976 and 1979 and in Sweden between 1976 and 1978. No stagnation or decline occurred in Norway until after 1979.

way has, over the long haul, performed best with respect to full employment, economic growth, price stability (until the 1970s), and wage growth. Denmark has performed badly both in terms of full employment, especially during the 1970s, and in terms of inflation; however, in growth rates and wage development Denmark has surpassed Sweden during the past two decades.

Public-sector budgets have come to play a central role in the determination of the business cycle and employment picture, as we have seen for all three countries—in the 1970s especially. There is no doubt that a major weapon in the battle against unemployment has been the expansion of public-sector employment. Indeed, had it not been for a tremendous rise in public employment in Denmark, the rate of unemployment there would certainly have been twice as high.[46] A similar trend is evident in the other Nordic countries. Also, the rate of early retirement has grown dramatically. Public deficits and debt have been relied on to dampen the repercussions of economic stagnation. The debt burden has grown dramatically in all three countries; but the best indicator of serious imbalance and crisis is the trend in *interest paid* on public debt, partly because this acts to constrain alternative government-program expenditures and partly because of the distributive properties of such payments.

In Denmark, total public debt as a percentage of GNP increased sixfold between 1973 and 1980. Both Norway and Sweden held a rather high public debt throughout the 1970s, with a rising trend. In terms of interest on public debt, however, there is little doubt that Danish finances are especially troubled. In Norway, the interest payments remained high throughout the period of DNA expansionary policy, but began to stabilize after 1979. In Sweden, interest on public debt began to grow rapidly after 1977.[47]

Owing to oil revenues (which showed a welcome rise after 1979), Norway is the only one of the three countries that has been able to administer such immense debt burdens without recourse to extraordinarily tight economic policies. Yet, all three nations have embarked upon cutback policies—in Denmark, especially after the conservative-

[46] Public-sector employment grew from 21.3 percent of the labor force in 1970 to 31.7 percent in 1979 (Danmarks Statistik 1981b).

[47] In 1973, total public debt as a percentage of GNP was 5 percent in Denmark, 26 percent in Norway, and 24 percent in Sweden. By 1980, the figures were, respectively, 33 percent, 38 percent, and 37 percent. Interest on public debt as a percentage of 1980 GNP was 6.4 percent in Denmark, 4 percent in Norway, and 3.5 percent in Sweden (IMF 1973, 1976; Danmarks Statistik 1981a, 1981b; Nordisk Råd 1981, 179, 186; Swedish Ministry of Economic Affairs 1976/77–1982/83).

led government took office in 1982; in Norway, both under the DNA government, after 1979, and under the present conservative coalition government; and, in Sweden, under the SAP's current administration. That such programs are proceeding under bourgeois sponsorship in Denmark and Norway may well mean a reversal of social democracy's dwindling fortunes. (Even this is questionable, however, given the broad popularity of the bourgeois government's "final attempt to clean up the Danish economy.") The SAP, without doubt, faces a major test of its legitimacy, although the party can exploit the widely perceived incompetence of previous bourgeois governments.

The twin issues of unemployment and income distribution will likely have the greatest impact on social democracy's ability to forge a political realignment that can recapture long-term party dominance. Some version of economic democracy through collective employee funds (or citizens' funds) is conceivably the only realistic way out for social democracy: the parties would be able to persuade the trade unions to moderate wages in coming years in return for a share in the resulting profits and, accordingly, for control over a growing proportion of investment resources. The adoption of such a scheme is not a realistic prospect for the near future in Denmark; the Norwegian DNA has no such plan at all. Only in Sweden, therefore, does the realignment have some prospect for fruition. This theme will be addressed in detail in Chapter 9. For now, let us turn to the question of whether, empirically, variations in social democratic policies can account for the different electoral fates of the three parties.

EIGHT

The Political Causes of Social Democratic Party Decomposition

WE ARE NOW in a position to return to the initial question. To what extent are variations in party decomposition associated with postwar policies and reforms? Although social structural change must enter into any analysis of the rise and fall of the social democratic parties, it fails to explain why Danish social democracy has proceeded so much further along the road to decomposition and decay than the other two varieties. Why have Danish workers and white-collar employees, in contrast to those of Norway and Sweden, moved both left and right in vocal opposition to social democracy?

Standard theoretical models have little to say in this regard because they typically fail to acknowledge that the social democratic process of class formation is decided politically; that the class unity and mobilization requisite for social democratic power must ultimately rely on the party's capacity to influence government policy. When social democracy is parliamentarian, its power depends on parliamentary action.

The pessimism that Leninist theory accords to the parliamentary strategy flows from doctrinaire assumptions that are not entirely convincing, especially since we have no single historical example in which the class-oppositional strategy has produced the desired political results. The point is that we must recast our analysis and attempt to identify the *conditions* under which the proposition may, or may not, hold. It is very possible that social democratic decomposition reflects socialist parliamentary failures; but since not all social democracies are decomposing, one must be able to explain why some are and others are not. This is where an analysis of the relationship between party policies and electoral shifts becomes decisive.

The welfare state, it is often held, signifies social democracy's departure from the "real" socialist struggle. Leninism argues that social democratic policies amount to little else than socialization of the costs of reproducing labor power, legitimation of an exploitative economic order, or acceptance of the "negative byproducts of capitalist growth." This view, I have argued, is entirely false, for without a strategy of

244

social citizenship policies, social democratic class formation must certainly fail.

Depending on its organization, scope, and content, the welfare state's political effects will vary dramatically. It may introduce new divisions in the class structure; it may fragment or individuate workers; and it may unleash unmanageable and destructive equity or status conflicts. On the other hand, the welfare state may help manufacture broad class (even cross-class) solidarity and social democratic consensus. In short, the social citizenship state is a variable, not a thing. The essential precondition for solidaristic results is that the welfare state be constructed along the following parameters. First of all, its primary social as well as political function is to strengthen the weakest section of the working class. It must therefore decommodify workers so that they will possess sufficient resources to engage in broad solidaristic activity. However, defense of the weakest segment requires that the strongest participate—that internal differentials be eradicated. Hence, solidarity must be built into all programs as a universal phenomenon. The social citizenship state, then, is compelled to pursue two goals if it is to aid social democratic class formation: it must both establish universal solidarity and marginalize the market as the principal agent of distribution and the chief determinant of peoples' life chances. Basically, the entire population must become wedded to the fate of the social citizenship state and must have an incentive to promote its cause actively.

The dangerous alternative to social democracy is residual welfare-statism, in which the state becomes the champion of the destitute or of weak minorities while permitting the majority of the population to acquire welfare and resources in the marketplace. This inhibits the formation of solidarity, for privileged workers will give their political support to private welfare programs and will be more inclined to oppose the tax burdens associated with delivery of social citizenship rights to the weak. Failing to get universal consent for welfare state politics, social democracy will permit the market to further the interests of the stronger segments of the population. Under such conditions, social democracy is likely to lose the long-run struggle between politics and market and, as it seeks to expand the role of the welfare state, is likely to engender divisions between its welfare state clientele, on one hand, and the main body of wage earners on the other. Needless to say, this will allow the bourgeois opposition forces greater opportunity to gather worker support behind their challenge to social democratic welfarism. In contrast, where social democracy manages to establish universal solidarity behind the social citizenship state, liberal advocates

245

of the market will be delegitimized and social democracy itself will be ensured greater hegemony. Under such conditions, we are also more likely to find bourgeois-party consent to the social democratic program, thus diminishing their ability to offer a plausible political alternative to social democratic rule.

In respect of social policies, therefore, I postulate that social democracy will decompose to the extent that the social citizenship state nurtures divisions between sections of the working class specifically and the population more generally. The foregoing overview of welfare state politics in the three Nordic countries points to the distinct possibility that this is so. The Danish welfare state is undoubtedly the one most likely to divide, fragment, and pit groups against one another. Neither the Norwegian nor the Swedish welfare state exhibits similar propensities. Hence, a broad-based welfare state revolt would naturally be more likely to occur in Denmark. We shall subsequently see whether the Danish welfare state revolt is uniquely stronger and whether it correlates with the social democratic party's decomposition. If my hypothesis is correct, then one would also expect that the welfare state revolt will be weaker in the other two nations and that social democratic decline will not correlate with welfare state issues.

The second area in which social democratic policies will have an important influence on class formation is housing policy. Again, as in the case of social welfare policies, the weakening of social democracy would seem to be associated with its inability to manufacture a solidaristic housing policy. Housing policy constitutes a very good test case. For one thing, it has been a highly politicized issue in all three countries during the postwar era. Secondly, the social democratic parties have given this issue an extraordinary amount of attention. Thirdly, there are few policy areas in which the conflict between market and political allocation has become so intense and problematic. Finally, housing is obviously a central component in peoples' overall view of their living standards. Like conventional social policy, housing policy must counter equity conflicts as well as divisions between sections of the population. The likelihood of such problems occurring is greater here than perhaps in any other area—precisely because it is so difficult to design a policy that, at once, guarantees affordable dwellings of high quality, eradication of housing shortages, and equity between homeowners and renters.

As shown in Chapter 6, housing policy has become an Achilles' heel especially for Danish social democracy, although the Swedish party's strategy also has a built-in backlash mechanism. Danish housing policy has stimulated divisions between renters and homeowners, and it is likely that this helped produce social democratic decomposition. In Sweden, a renter-owner split is likely to develop, and broad dissatisfaction with the drab, satellite model of cooperative apartment should also be present. Even if Norwegian housing policy did stress individual homeownership very heavily, it was constructed on solidaristic principles and with such an immense public subordination of market forces that a significant political backlash is not to be expected.

Then there is the problem of economic policies. Electorally, there are three important dimensions of economic policy that must be taken into account. First, a promise to socialize the capitalist economy may enjoy ideological support from others besides students and intellectuals, although ideological desires for socialization may not be restricted to conventional state confiscation or directly worker-owned means of production. Ideological desires alone, however, would probably be limited to a marginal segment of the social democratic electoral base were they not fueled by additional, more pressing concerns.

Two such factors are likely to operate. One, leaving ideology aside, is that the power and legitimacy of social democracy will be seriously imperiled if it cannot secure sustained full employment and growth. The strength of wage earners and their collectivities depends directly on full employment and, as socialists learned during the 1920s and 1930s, nothing weakens solidarity so much as economic crisis. Maintenance of full employment, however, may incur a heavy cost if it must rest on repeated political regulation of wages and incomes. Obviously, social democratic governments operating within small and open economies (like those of Scandinavia) will not be able to control against the international economic order; restrictive economic policies cannot be avoided under conditions of international economic recession. Yet, it is precisely under such conditions that it becomes decisive whether social democracy can or cannot find a resolution to the zero-sum trade-off between wages and jobs—i.e. whether an acceptable form of wage restraint can be found. This leads us to examine social democracy's capacity for control over such factors as prices and investments.

The other factor that will eventually compel social democracy to stress political control of economic growth is the dilemma of welfare state financing. Discontinued economic growth and high unemployment will endanger the welfare state edifice from two sides at once, for these increase the demand for social expenditures and decrease the basis for revenues. It is more than likely that electoral attitudes toward the welfare state will correlate with attitudes toward economic policy, especially under conditions of welfare state expansion and slow eco-

247

nomic growth. In general, there is every reason to expect that social democratic party decomposition will be positively related to weak performance in controlling the business cycle.

There is one final reason why political control of the economy will come to play a central role in social democratic party power, and that is the long-run impossibility of promoting social citizenship without beginning to address the issue of economic citizenship rights. This issue, however, will be treated separately in Chapter 9.

A METHODOLOGICAL PREFACE

As those who have attempted cross-national statistical comparisons know, validity problems pose serious obstacles for comparative analysis. This is certainly the case in the following analyses, based on election-survey data files. The data sets used comprise repeated electoral surveys and, for Denmark, Gallup survey files as well. Cross-fertilization has to a degree occurred, although the wording of questions often differs. A problem of comparison from the start, therefore, is that questions addressing identical phenomena (especially welfare state attitudes) do not permit strict comparisons. A second quite serious problem is that it is difficult to determine whether a respondent's answer reflects his/her evaluation of the existing order of things or whether it expresses his/her desired order.[1] A third serious problem with this kind of cross-national comparison is that similar answers to similar questions can mean something different from country to country, depending on the unique context prevailing in each country. We must try to keep in mind our knowledge of system differences, in order to catch such possible contextual effects.

Unless noted otherwise, the data reported below derive from the electoral survey files. For Sweden, where access to data tapes is extraordinarily difficult, I have benefited from the generous assistance of Professors Olof Petersson and Bo Särlvik in supplying me with the requested runs.[2]

---

[1] For example, an expressed negative assessment of welfare state programs can indicate that the respondent rejects the kind of welfare state that has come to exist, but that he/she may be happy wiith another type; or it can indicate that the respondent rejects any kind of public commitment for social welfare.

[2] With respect to the Danish data, I am especially grateful for the assistance of Professor Hans Jørgen Nielsen. Professors Henry Valen, Berndt Årdal, and Ola Listhaug are equally deserving of thanks for their assistance to me in gaining access to the Norwegian data.

SOCIAL CITIZENSHIP AND PARTY DECOMPOSITION

Welfare state revolts mushroomed in the 1970s. The dramatic rise of Mogens Glistrup's Progress party helped place Denmark at the forefront of this international phenomenon. Norway gave birth to a parallel political movement, although the Anders Langes party did not gain the stature and electoral backing that the Danes enjoyed. In both instances, the progressives launched a direct attack on the entire welfare state edifice, ranging from questions of taxation and bureaucracy to the irrationalities of supporting welfare state parasites. In Sweden no such political party emerged, and there is little sign of any significant welfare state backlash. Researchers in Sweden have identified the presence of antitax sentiments (Särlvik 1977), but these have prevailed over many years—even in 1968 when the SAP scored one of its greatest electoral victories. One can also note that electoral unwillingness to accept cutbacks in welfare state programs came to the fore in the 1982 election, when Swedish voters vocally rejected the bourgeois government's proposal to cut spending in order to reduce taxes and alleviate budget deficits.

There are several theoretical explanations for the backlash movements of the 1970s. From one perspective, the problem has to do with overloaded government and the decay of traditional citizen restraint as entitlements and interest groups managed to place greater pressure on government than it was equipped to manage (Huntington 1975; King 1975). Another argument centers on the tax rate. Rose and Peters (1978), for example, hold that tax revolts occur when take-home pay falls as a consequence of either slow GNP growth or accelerating public expenditures. This view disregards the possibility that voters may wish to pay higher taxes and reduce disposable earnings in return for improved services and public transfers. A third perspective, exemplified in the work of Wilensky (1976), suggests that the degree of tax and welfare backlash can be explained by the visibility of taxes, the level of corporatism, and the age of the party system. The tax bite alone has no direct effect on backlash proclivities.[3]

None of these perspectives offers a plausible explanation of why the three Scandinavian countries differ so sharply in respect of overt welfare state backlash. In the early 1970s, social expenditures as a percentage of GNP were very similar in Denmark and Sweden, lower

---

[3] Wilensky's conceptualization and measurement of backlash is somewhat questionable since it includes antispending, antitaxation, and antibureaucratic sentiment as well as racial, ethnic, or minority factors (e.g. the George Wallace vote in the United States and resentment against guestworkers in Switzerland).

in Norway. The same holds for per capita taxation. All three countries have experienced periods in which the spending volume and tax rate grew with tremendous speed. In Sweden, that period was the 1960s; in Denmark, the late 1960s; and in Norway, the 1970s. Real-wage growth has increased more quickly in Denmark and Norway than in Sweden; yet, Denmark and Norway both experienced a stronger anti-welfare-state movement. When the Danish welfare revolt exploded in the early 1970s, there was hardly any difference in the ratio of visible to invisible taxes in Denmark and Sweden. Moreover, the age of the party system was the same for all three nations and, obviously, social democratic dominance had been both stronger and more permanent in Sweden than in either Norway or Denmark. Sweden is known to be one of the Western world's most centralized and corporatist systems, but so is Norway.

In short, the evidence does not clearly support any of the conventional theories of welfare state backlash. There is another, very important issue with which we must deal: the outbreak of electoral protest against social democracy has not been limited to the new Poujadist "flash parties." Any theory of the relation between welfare state revolt and social democratic decline must be able to explain the growth of the left-socialist opposition.

Correlates of Welfare State Program Attitudes

Except in Norway, there is a general trend toward greater and greater dissatisfaction with the welfare state and, concomitantly, a decline in the degree to which the electorate desires welfarism to be extended. As Table 8.1 shows, negative attitudes were extraordinarily high in Denmark during the early 1970s but, in the late 1970s, subsided to "Swedish levels." Note that this coincides with mounting economic crisis and the beginnings of cutbacks in Denmark; in Sweden, cutbacks were not even contemplated until 1981.[4] If solidarity has eroded in these two countries, albeit regaining some strength in Denmark, it remains overpowering in Norway. The pattern of attitudes in Norway, by the way, has been cyclical, modest leaps in anti-welfare-state sentiment occurring during the protest year of 1973 and in 1981, when defections from the DNA were high.

[4] Before 1981, the Danish case had differed radically from the other two, but in that year the Danish and Norwegian cases became identical. The marked drop in Danish anti-welfare-state attitudes by 1981 might be caused by different wording of survey questions, although the steady decrease over the 1970s, suggests that favorable opinion had been growing.

TABLE 8.1. Trends in Electoral Support for the Welfare State in Scandinavia
(% response to survey questions)

	Denmark[a]				Norway[c]				Sweden[d]		
	1973	1975	1977	1981[b]	1965	1973	1977	1981	1968	1976	1979
Anti–Welfare State	83	74	66	52	10	24	10	18	41	61	67
Neutral, Accept Status Quo	4	12	14	12	42	56	48	58			
Support Extension of Welfare State	13	14	20	36	48	20	42	24	51	32	27
N =	(433)	(1,318)	(1,074)	(868)	(1,366)	(1,070)	(1,345)	(1,414)	(2,419)	(2,536)	(2,673)

SOURCES: Danish electoral surveys, 1973–1981; Norwegian electoral surveys, 1965–1981; Holmberg (1981, 250).

NOTE: "Don't Know" responses have been excluded.

[a] From 1973 to 1977, the Danish question was worded as follows: "Too many receive social benefits who do not really need them (Agree/Neutral/Disagree)."

[b] In 1981, the Danish question is identical to the Swedish question, except that Danish respondents could choose from among "Agree," "Neutral," or "Disagree," whereas Swedish respondents were restricted to either "Agree" or "Disagree."

[c] The Norwegian question is worded in such a way that respondents were required to indicate a preference for less social welfare, the status quo, or further extension of the welfare state.

[d] The Swedish question was worded as follows: "Social reforms have gone so far that the state should reduce rather than increase its efforts (Agree/Disagree)."

Even with different wording, the Danish data for the early 1970s would confirm the expectation that voting in the 1973 Catastrophe Elections was influenced by powerful backlash sentiment throughout the population.[5] No such extreme opinions have been voiced in either Sweden or Norway. Since Swedish respondents are forced to choose an either/or answer, the Nordic data are not comparable. We must assume that some would otherwise have opted for the status quo and that attitudes both for and against are therefore likely to be inflated. Still, the data suggest that the SAP's welfare state lost much of its legitimacy in the 1970s. The rekindled support for the Danish welfare state in the late 1970s and especially in 1981, when the responses are comparable, could be the consequence of cutback policies in the midst of the deep economic crisis.

But the question is also too generally formulated to get a sense of voters' beliefs about the social democratic welfare state. Alas, more pointed survey questions are scarce except for Norway. Danish voters were asked in 1975 whether they favored a rollback of child welfare allowances, and only 37 percent said yes. In 1981, as the government prepared to reintroduce waiting days for daily cash benefits, 40 percent agreed with the cutback. A special Norwegian study in 1980 demonstrated consistent and broad backing for virtually all individual welfare programs. The highest level of willingness to see cutbacks occurred with respect to unemployment compensation, yet even this was only 20 percent of respondents.[6] In Sweden, only 19 percent in 1979 rejected further extensions of day care for children (Holmberg 1981, 228).

On balance, one would conclude that electoral solidarity behind the welfare state is vastly more powerful in Norway, gradually eroding in Sweden during the 1970s, and weakest in Denmark (although in the process of resurrection). At this level of analysis, however, it is difficult to connect welfare state opinions with the fate of social democracy. To test my theoretical arguments, it is necessary to establish the degree to which the welfare state causes divisions, fragmentation, and erosion within social democracy's traditional and potential social bases.

Table 8.2 presents summary indices of voters' balance of opinion

[5] A 1974 Gallup survey, asking a more comparable question—whether respondents agreed that the welfare state had "gone too far"—shows similarly high anti-welfare-state attitudes, although these were less extreme among socialist voters (Nielsen 1975, 133).

[6] Here I rely on data kindly supplied to me by Professor Jon Eivind Kolberg. See, also, Kolberg and Pettersen (1981).

TABLE 8.2. Attitudinal Balance on Scandinavian Welfare State by Social Class and Party Preference

	Denmark (1977)[a]				Norway (1977)				Sweden (1976)[b]			
	All	Left	SD	Bourgeois	All	Left	SD	Bourgeois	All	Left	SD	Bourgeois
Workers	−47	−19	−44	−56	+39	+52	+39	+24	−10	+20	+2	−66
Lower White Collar	−41	−25	−7	−90 }	+39	+81	+43	+30 }	−36	+34	+7	−72
Medium/Upper White Collar	−33	−16	−11	−65	+24				+24	+83	+11	−53
Entire Sample	−44	+9	−38	−64	+32	+65	+39	+26	−29	+40	+5	−61

SOURCES: Danish electoral survey, 1977; Norwegian electoral survey, 1977; Swedish electoral survey, 1976.

NOTE: Attitudinal balance scores are derived by subtracting the percentage of anti-welfare-state responses from the percentage of pro-welfare-state responses. See Table 8.1 for details on the survey questions. "Don't know" and "Neutral" responses have been excluded. SD = social democrats.

[a] It is important to keep in mind that the wording of the Danish question in 1977 was quite different from that of the Norwegian and Swedish questions. Comparability cannot be assumed. Admittedly, the wording of the 1981 Danish survey question would have made it more directly comparable; however, the scores in that year were not typical of scores during the 1970s. Because the 1977 data fall in the middle with respect to the degree of anti-welfare-state feeling, it is hoped that they constitute an "average" Danish response for the 1970s.

[b] Remember that Swedish respondents were restricted to an "Agree/Disagree" answer; therefore, the Swedish scores probably over-dramatize voter attitudes.

on the welfare state by class and party preference. These indices measure the percentage of pro-welfare-state attitudes less the percentage of anti-welfare-state attitudes and should tell us the relative strength of these attitudes. Again, there is no doubt that protest attitudes in Denmark are much higher, regardless of social class or party preference. Sweden occupies a middle position, and in Norway the positive consensus prevails among all classes and parties. For Denmark, there is less variance between social classes than might have been expected, and negative attitudes prevail among leftists, social democrats, and rightists alike. There is, however, a clear tendency for white-collar strata to exhibit stronger attitudinal polarization, depending on party sympathy. This, as one might expect, correlates with the private-sector/public-sector division in white-collar employment.[7] For one thing, private-sector employees are far more likely to support the Poujadist progressives (Nielsen 1979, 66; Goul Andersen and Glans 1981, 28). For another, public-sector middle strata are more than twice as likely to support the SF, which in later years has been the most vocal defender of the welfare state against both social democratic and, now, bourgeois-party cutbacks. Another special feature of Denmark is the especially low support for the welfare state among workers—even leftist and social democratic workers.[8] In terms of age and generational membership, the most significant finding is that young workers and low-level white-collar employees are likely to be anti-welfare-state, while this is not true for the rest of the population.[9]

In Norway, the welfare state enjoys broad support, irrespective of class or party preference. There is a slight tendency among public-sector white-collar employees to be more approving than their private-sector counterparts; there is absolutely no age or generational effect.

[7] During the 1970s, there is a noticeable shift in party affiliations among white-collar strata, depending on whether the employee works in the public or private sector. In 1971, differences were virtually nonexistent: 13 percent in both private and public employment supported left socialism; 26 percent in the private sector and 28 percent in the public sector supported the social democrats. By 1979, 8 percent in the private sector and 20 percent in the public sector supported left-socialist parties; 33 percent versus 39 percent, respectively, supported the social democrats (Goul Andersen and Glans 1981, 28). Such trends toward political polarization do not appear to be present in Norway or Sweden (Holmberg 1981, 304).

[8] Note, however, that the distribution of attitudes is very different when (in the 1981 survey) the question has to do with a cutback in daily cash benefits. Then workers and low-level white-collar employees share strong, pro-welfare-state attitudes, whereas higher-level white-collar employees and other social classes hold negative attitudes.

[9] Among young workers the opinion balance in 1977 was -64; among the old, -48. For low-level white-collar employees, respectively, the balance was -66 and -42.

It is true that negative opinions increased in 1981, and here we are able to detect the first signs of discord. The sharpest drop in support occurs among white-collar groups, especially among upper-level white-collar employees. (For all white-collar employees, the opinion balance falls from +39 in 1977 to +1 in 1981.)

The Swedish picture differs importantly from that of the other Nordic countries. In the aggregate, anti-welfare-state attitudes run quite high, but the divisions are radically different. In Sweden there is a wider gap between workers and the middle strata than there is elsewhere. Sweden's working class is the more loyal to the welfare state, whereas in Denmark workers are less loyal than upper-level white-collar employees. Moreover, the issue seems primarily to turn on traditional left-right cleavages: both leftists and social democrats have positive opinion balances, while those of bourgeois-party voters are strongly negative. It is particularly significant that age-group differences contrast sharply from those in Denmark. The young (eighteen to twenty-four years old) are far more supportive of the welfare state than voters in the age group thirty-five to sixty-four or even the older-than-sixty-four population.[10] This is clearly very important for social democracy's longer-run chances of sustaining broad solidarity behind the welfare state. It also suggests that welfare state issues do not necessarily pit the younger, working population against elderly welfare recipients.

All in all, the Danish welfare state has engendered dramatically more negative politicization than either of the other two social democracies; in Sweden, however, popular loyalties were evidently on the wane during the 1970s. If welfare state consensus is virtually universal in Norway, protest appears almost universal in Denmark. Yet, within this broad attack one finds symptoms of divisions between young and old as well as between public- and private-sector employees; backlash sentiments are unusually strong among working-class voters. These symptoms confirm one's impressions of the precarious position faced by the Danish party's welfare state politics. On the other hand, it should not be forgotten that popular support is on the rise now that the social effects of the economic crisis have taken hold and the welfare state is being subjected to major cutbacks.

The Swedish welfare state is more embattled than might have been anticipated. The social democrats seem to be losing the white-collar support that was gained with the ATP reform in 1960. But, most of all, the socialist parties are being pitted against the bourgeois block.

[10] In 1976 the opinion balance for these three age categories was, respectively, −2, −32, and −22.

TABLE 8.3. Strength of Support for Danish Political Parties by Social Class, Trade Union Membership, Class Identification, and Attitude toward Welfare Expenditure, 1977

| | Dependent Variables | | | | | | | |
| | Left Socialist | | Social Democratic | | Bourgeois | | Progress | |
	B	Beta	B	Beta	B	Beta	B	Beta
INDEPENDENT VARIABLES								
Class	−3.407*	−.204*	−.693*	−.151*	1.800*	.167*	.573	.074
Union Membership	3.895*	.245*	.840*	.192*	−2.191*	−.214*	−.771	−.104
Class Identification	−.213	−.064	.429*	.467*	.219	.102	−.512*	−.329*
Attitude	−1.479*	−.271*	−.219*	−.146*	.492*	.140*	.743*	.293*
$R^2 =$	.249	.249	.376	.376	.140	.140	.259	.259

SOURCE: Danish electoral survey, 1977.

NOTE: $N = 374$; Beta = standardized coefficients; B = unstandardized coefficients. An asterisk indicates $P = .001$. The dependent variables (party "thermometers") are scales from −100 to +100 according to the degree of disapproval or support. The independent variables were scored as follows: Class—1 = working class, including low-level white collar; 2 = higher-level white collar, urban and rural employers, and the self-employed. Union Membership—1 = nonmember; 2 = member. Class Identification—scaled 1 to 5, where 1 = low identification with working class and 5 = high identification. Attitude—answer to the question "Too many receive social benefits who do not really need them" scaled 1 to 5, where 1 = strong disagreement and 5 = strong agreement.

The issue, therefore, seems to center on classic political conflict instead of new, sharply defined social cleavages.

In order to understand better how the Danish welfare state revolt has influenced social democratic party decomposition, we can estimate how attitudes, compared with traditional social-position variables, affect the strength and direction of party choice. Table 8.3 presents a multivariate regression analysis for Denmark, showing strength of voter support for party alternatives given the level of anti-welfare-state sentiment and controlling for social class, trade union membership, and working-class identification.

A few preliminary clarifications of the model are perhaps necessary. It tries to explain strength of party support by structural variables and by attitudinal variables related to public policy.[11] The model presented is considerably reduced. Previous analyses, not shown here, found that income level had absolutely no influence on party sympathies and was also uncorrelated with the level of welfare state resentment, mainly because income correlates strongly with class. The results of Table 8.3 are quite interesting. For one thing, they show that the determinants of party support differ dramatically from one party to another. In all cases other than the bourgeois parties, moreover, the model has rather strong predictive value.

First of all, being a worker is significantly related to support for both the left socialists and the social democrats, and *not* being a worker is significantly related to bourgeois-party sympathies. Class position plays no role in support for the Danish Progress party—the coefficients are not significant. Secondly, trade union membership helps explain support for both the left socialists and the social democrats, and bourgeois-party supporters are likely to be nonunionized. Again, trade unionism plays no role with respect to progress party support. Thirdly, strength of working-class identification has no bearing on support for left socialists, but it is extremely important for social democratic party support. (Class identification alone explains 22.9 percent of the variance, while class and trade unionism together explain only 8.5 percent.) One should note that the *absence* of class identification is importantly related to progress party support (explaining 12.2 percent

---

[11] The dependent variables are constructed in the form of "thermometers." Respondents were asked to grade the party from −100 to +100; a strongly negative score was to indicate dislike and vice versa. The scaling of party sympathy in this way permits us to analyze the relative importance of various independent variables in a multivariate statistical test, while at the same time avoiding the problem of how to scale parties on a left-right continuum. It also allows us to study the determinants of support for each party, or party groups one by one.

of the total variance). For all four parties, finally, attitudes on welfare spending play a significant role. Pro-welfare-state attitudes explain left-socialist support quite powerfully, and anti-welfare-state beliefs are very strongly related to progress party support. In the case of the social democrats and the bourgeois parties, welfare state attitudes play a role, but not a particularly strong one.

Overall, these results suggest that the welfare state issue has had a significant polarizing effect on the Danish electorate. Note that the strongest defenders of welfare spending are to be found on the extreme left and that the strongest opponents, the progressives, are on the extreme right. Table 8.3 also suggests that the left socialists have lured working-class trade unionists away from the social democrats, and that the progress party's supporters are to be found primarily among those least affiliated with social democracy's traditional working-class core. In addition, since structural factors (such as class position, trade union membership, and class identification) explain much of the social democrats' support, while welfare state attitudes play only a small role, we may speculate as follows. As the Danish Social Democratic party lost supporters during the 1970s, its core base still comprised those that have always been most social democratic, while those with a weaker connection to the traditional working class defected as major issues, such as the welfare state issue, exploded. If this interpretation is correct, then social democratic party decomposition in Denmark reflects the party's inability to form a strong allegiance outside its working-class core, combined with a repulsion of supporters when party policies become objectionable.

The Taxation Issue

Taxation can easily be an Achilles' heel for the social democratic welfare state. The issue is partly one of solidarity. Are people prepared to follow the principle "From each according to his ability, to each according to his need"? Overall levels of tax resentment should convey the social democrats' achievements in this regard. For the analytical purposes of this book, it is even more important to detect whether the issue of taxation threatens to alienate rather than unite the traditional working class and the new middle strata on income-distributional grounds. Fortunately, the surveys of all three Nordic countries asked identical questions with regard to taxation.[12]

[12] Respondents could choose from among three answers in regard to the level of taxation on higher incomes: a) it should be reduced; b) it should remain as is; or c) it should be raised.

When one considers that the Danish Progress party's spectacular rise in 1973 was expressed primarily in terms of a tax revolt and when one considers, moreover, the generally more politicized nature of the Danish welfare state, one would anticipate a weak level of tax solidarity. In terms of issue saliency, taxes—not surprisingly—ranked first in 1973. In later years, voters began to show less concern about taxes as unemployment and the economy overtook all other problems in the public mind. At the same time, though, tax solidarity has steadily declined. Steeper progressivity (and, therefore, higher taxes on higher incomes) was favored by 69 percent in 1973, 57 percent in 1977, and only 50 percent in 1981. Conversely, less progressivity was favored by 21 percent in 1973, 27 percent in 1977 and 40 percent in 1981.

Still, tax progression is clearly an issue that divides workers and the new middle strata. In 1981, when tax solidarity was especially low, workers presented an opinion balance of +30 in favor of more progression; low-level white-collar employees scored +7, while middle- and higher-level white-collar employees scored −37. That the social democratic program for income equalization pits workers against the middle strata is even more apparent on another survey question. When respondents were asked whether they favored more or less equality of incomes, the opinion balance was +1 among workers, −26 among lower-level white-collar employees, and −60 among middle- and higher-level white-collar employees. The most striking finding here is that proequalization opinions prevail among social democracy' traditional alliance of workers and small farmers (including pensioners), standing in sharp opposition to white-collar strata.

Given reduced salience, however, one would expect that electoral tax attitudes explain less of the variance in party preference. This can be seen in Table 8.4, which displays a model identical to the one shown in Table 8.3, except that welfare spending attitudes have been replaced by tax progression attitudes. The total explained variance has declined for the left socialists, the social democrats, and the progressives. Favorable attitudes toward greater tax progression are significantly related to left-socialist support (explaining 3 percent of the variance). They are not significantly related to social democratic support and, most surprisingly, they are not powerfully related to progress party support—although, as one would anticipate, there is a negative effect. In short, by the late 1970s tax issues are less significant in determining voter allegiance, and they do not fuel a polarized attack on social democracy as welfare-spending attitudes do. Moreover, it appears that the Danish electorate is more solidaristic with respect to taxes than it is with respect to welfare programs. Still, this does not

TABLE 8.4. Strength of Support for Danish Political Parties by Social Class, Trade Union Membership, Class Identification, and Attitude toward Tax Progressivity, 1977

	Dependent Variables					
	Left Socialist		Social Democratic		Progress	
	B	Beta	B	Beta	B	Beta
INDEPENDENT VARIABLES						
Class	−2.344*	−.140*	−.550*	−.120*	.342	.044
Union Membership	5.129*	.320*	1.046*	.238*	−1.250*	−.168*
Class Identification	−.199	−.059	.431*	.468*	−.532*	−.342*
Attitude	.929*	.182*	.103	.074	−.213*	−.090*
R^2	.216	.216	.361	.361	.183	.183

SOURCE: Danish electoral survey, 1977.

NOTE: $N = 374$; Beta = standardized coefficients; B = unstandardized coefficients. An asterisk indicates $P \geqq .01$. Attitude is scaled 1 to 5, where 1 = strongly in favor of less progressivity and 5 = strongly in favor of more progressivity. For an explanation of the other variables, see Table 8.3.

mean that tax resentment played a secondary role in the formative stages of the welfare state tax revolt. First of all, the high salience of the issue in 1973 suggests that taxes played a central role in shifting voter loyalties. Secondly, 80.5 percent of the 1973 sample demanded that the rate of income taxation be lowered.[13]

Norwegians may be enthusiastic about welfare programs, but they are also more dissatisfied with taxes than the Danes. Several studies confirm that the tax issue has been very salient for many years (Valen 1981; Valen and Martinussen 1972). Thus, it comes as no surprise that virtually all respondents (90 percent) favor tax reductions for *lower-income* earners. But there is also a stronger propensity among Norwegians to favor lower taxes on *higher incomes*.

In the 1965 Norwegian survey, 35 percent agreed that there should be tax reductions on higher incomes; this hardly changed in 1969 and 1977 (34 percent and 37 percent, respectively). These values are markedly higher than in Denmark during the 1970s and stand in sharp contrast to the overwhelming popularity of welfare programs. Note, however, that the degree of tax resentment is stable over time, suggesting that there is no direct correlation with the ups and down of

[13] Among Danish Progress party voters the figure was 83 percent.

DNA support generally. Secondly, there is considerable variance in tax attitudes by class and party support. In 1965, and again in 1977, attitudes concerning tax progression were polarized between left socialists and DNA voters, on one side, and bourgeois-party supporters on the other. Similarly, workers were strongly opposed to tax reductions for higher-income wage earners, while white-collar employees and the self-employed were in favor. (See Table 8.5.)

The issue of taxation in Norway is therefore one that is generally more politicized and, even if it does follow the conventional left-right political cleavage, it also pits workers and white-collar employees against one another to a greater degree than seems to be the case in Denmark. Fewer Norwegians than Danes are neutral. The combination of class and party polarization on this question suggests that the tax issue may have been a major source of the DNA's electoral problems in the 1970s. Finally, the Norwegian data reveal the same kind of farmer-worker coalition, favoring egalitarianism, against the middle strata, who prefer to sustain differentials.

Taxes have also been a persistently salient political issue for a decade or more in Sweden (Särlvik 1977; Holmberg 1981), though never as salient as general economic and labor market conditions. But it is doubtful that popular irritation with high tax levels has had a detrimental influence on SAP support in past elections. Särlvik (1977, 99) notes that the level of disapproval, as it has remained constant since the 1960s, cannot explain the SAP's decline during the 1970s.

Overall tax resentment is less extreme than in Norway or Denmark. In 1976, 24 percent advocated lower tax progressivity (27 percent in 1979), while 61 percent advocated more progressivity (60 percent in 1979). For Sweden we can benefit from a detailed 1969 survey on tax opinions (Vogel 1974). Although 63 percent believed that the tax burden should be "reduced at any cost," the 1969 survey nonetheless indicates that tax resentment declines when the level of taxation is considered against the kinds of benefits one receives from the state. More than half the respondents agreed that, if one considered the benefits, taxes were reasonable. Tax evasion, moreover, was opposed by almost everyone. Finally, the data showed very few differences in opinion according to social class or party preference.

A very similar profile emerges from the survey data for 1976, when respondents were asked whether they favored lower or higher taxation on high incomes. (See Table 8.6.) First, in comparison with Norway, there seems to be much greater consensus across social class on the desirability of progressive taxation. Even higher-level white-collar employees show an opinion balance favoring progressive redistribution,

261

TABLE 8.5. Attitudes toward Tax Progressivity in Norway by Social Class and Party Reference, 1965 and 1977
(% favoring)

	1965				1977			
	Less Progressivity	Status Quo	More Progressivity	Opinion Balance	Less Progressivity	Status Quo	More Progressivity	Opinion Balance
CLASS POSITION								
Workers	20	30	50	(−30)	27	9	50	(−32)
Low White Collar	30	26	44	(−14) }	46	11	39	(+7)
High White Collar	60	14	26	(+34) }	36	17	43	(−7)
Farmers	28	24	48	(−20)				
PARTY PREFERENCE								
Left Socialists	22	25	52	(−30)	9	9	82	(−73)
Social Democrats	20	20	60	(−40)	26	10	64	(−38)
Bourgeois-Party Supporters	55	16	29	(+26)	54	13	33	(+21)

SOURCES: Norwegian electoral surveys, 1965 and 1977.

TABLE 8.6. Attitudes toward Tax Progressivity in Sweden by Social Class
and Party Preference, 1976
(*% favoring*)

	Less Progressivity	Status Quo	More Progressivity	Opinion Balance
CLASS POSITION				
Workers	19	9	70	(−51)
Lower and Middle				
White Collr	27	11	62	(−35)
High White Collar	38	14	48	(−10)
Farmers	26	13	54	(−28)
PARTY PREFERENCE				
Left Socialists	9	9	83	(−73)
Social Democrats	17	7	74	(−57)
Bourgeois-Party				
Supporters	33	13	49	(−16)

SOURCE: Swedish electoral survey, 1976.

a phenomenon that was not found in Denmark or Norway. Similarly, even the bourgeois parties favor equalization—again, a unique result for Scandinavia. If, therefore, taxation has been a source of popular resentment for many years, it is evidently not an issue that has polarized or fragmented the electorate, and there is very little to suggest that it alienates key constituencies from social democracy. Holmberg (1981, 257) reports similar findings for 1979.

The Political Effects of Welfare Policies

With respect to taxes and spending, the three Nordic nations display very different voter-reaction contours. Denmark is the only one in which a genuine welfare state backlash has occurred, the advent of a protest party in Norway notwithstanding. This backlash is most sharply expressed in terms of welfare expenditure, but note that tax fatigue was strong in 1973 when the protests climaxed. Anti-spending and anti-taxation sentiments abated during the 1970s, but this does not necessarily portend social democracy's rescue. In the early 1970s, it is true, the backlash movement decimated the social democrats and drove voters, including large sections of the working class, toward the right. But there is evidence to suggest that social democracy's engagement in cutbacks from the late 1970s on has pushed voter groups toward the SF—which has assumed the role of welfare state defender.

In Norway, despite fluctuations, welfare state programs enjoy sacrosant status among all layers of society, and protest seems obsessed instead with the DNA's egalitarian tax policies. Tax resentments seem chronic, moreover, and the issue polarizes left and right, as well as workers (with farmers) and the middle strata. This curious mix of welfare state consensus and tax irritation may help explain both why the Glistrup-style backlash party emerged and why it never really succeeded. Given such broad backing for the welfare state, the backlash party could not launch a frontal attack as it had been able to do in Denmark. On the other hand, there is reason to believe that the taxation issue accounts for the DNA's electoral problems in the 1970s, for the party's vocal egalitarian platform evidently prevented it from mobilizing loyalties in the middle strata. This may very well constitute the nexus of the DNA's class realignment problems.

The Swedish electorate behaves quite differently from the Norwegian electorate. Heavy taxes may cause irritation, but there is no doubt that they rest on a broadly shared solidarity and consensus. The SAP's egalitarianism commands the kind of hegemonic consent that welfare programs do in Norway. On the other hand, the visible trend toward falling support for welfare state reforms should cause alarm in the Swedish Social Democratic party. These general trends, moreover, conceal the fact that the population is becoming more divided and polarized on the welfare state question. Among its core constituencies, and on the left generally, consensus behind the welfare state is intact; it has slipped badly among the white-collar strata and within the bourgeois bloc. Still, as we know, six years of bourgeois-party rule did virtually nothing to dismantle the welfare state, or even reduce it. When, in 1982, the attempt was finally made, the labor movement had no problem rallying the electorate against it.

This experience, incidentally, contrasts with that of Denmark, where both social democratic and now a bourgeois government have cut deeply into welfare state programs. Even though popular protests against cutbacks are proliferating, there is no momentum to block the cutbacks. In short, the level of popular consensus remains much more fragile in Denmark, and welfare state issues continue to disrupt electoral politics. But it does not contrast with Norway. Even if the DNA was seriously defeated in 1981, that cannot have been because of welfare state reforms; the conservatives mobilized on economic policy and taxation issues, not on welfare state backlash.

HOUSING POLICIES AND PARTY DECOMPOSITION

The social democratic response to the housing question differed dramatically in the three Nordic countries. In Denmark, the social democrats permitted remarketization of housing supply and distribution, combined with generous tax incentives for single-family homeowners. Sharp inequities between renters and owners were practically built into the reform, and the housing issue became one of the single most politicized questions in postwar Danish policymaking. The social democrats—pressed from the left—promised repeatedly, yet failed, to eliminate some of the more extreme inequities, and the issue never disappeared (partly because large numbers of voters had become dependent on favorable tax deductions).

The Norwegian and Swedish social democracies took exactly opposite paths in the struggle to solve the housing problems of the postwar era. In both cases, though, housing policy favored a considerable extension of public-sector intervention, primarily through state financing and preferential treatment for cooperatives. The net result was that housing shortages were eradicated along quite solidaristic lines.

These housing policies differed in one important respect, however. In Norway, individual family homeownership reigned supreme, but in such a way as to suppress any possible inequities between renters and owners in regard to taxation and net housing cost. The Swedish social democratic solution was perhaps equally solidaristic, but the decision to stress apartment construction in satellite towns was not altogether a fortunate one. As inflationary pressures mounted and the marginal tax rate increased, the entire model began to crumble in the 1970s. New inequities emerge as tax-privileged private homeownership mushrooms. Yet, in Sweden, in contrast to Denmark, an extraordinarily generous rent-allowance system has helped correct the problem of tax inequities. In short, one would not expect to find an electoral backlash effect in the Norwegian case, and in Sweden the politicization of housing policy is so recent that expected effects may still be weak. Only in Denmark would one predict a massive impact of housing policy on the electorate's party choices.

In Denmark, one would expect the first dramatic electoral effects to appear after 1965. Table 8.7 shows that the 1965 reform helped push renters over to the SF, which made the housing bill its major campaign issue in the 1966 elections. We might note that the bulk of renter defections to the SF came from the social democratic party, and that the social democrats' position among homeowners was actually

TABLE 8.7. Party Preference in Denmark by Housing Status and Social Class,
1960-1975
(*% supporting parties*)

| | Workers | | Nonworkers | |
	Owners	Renters	Owners	Renters
1960				
Left Socialist	—	2	—	1
Social Democratic	78	79	14	24
Bourgeois	22	19	86	75
1966				
Left Socialist	9	27	5	13
Social Democratic	73	55	16	26
Bourgeois	18	18	79	61
1975				
Left Socialist	6	29	2	22
Social Democratic	46	39	5	26
Bourgeois	39	26	79	37
Progress	9	6	14	15

SOURCES: Gallup surveys, 1960-1975.

strengthened at the same time. The new housing-based schism is especially strong among workers. A second turning point in the saga of Danish housing policy came in 1973, when the social democrats introduced a bill to reduce the tax privileges of owners and improve the position of renters by means of additional subsidization for builders of co-op apartments. This move, however, proved to be even more detrimental to social democracy in electoral terms. Many workers had been able to purchase a house by the 1970s, and the new legislative initiative threatened their interests, jeopardizing their capacity to finance a house frequently mortgaged to the chimney top. Because of the right-wing Danish Center party splinter, based on the defense of homeowner interests, the bill was never actually passed. Certainly the huge electoral shift to the right in 1973 was not simply a question of housing policy; as Table 8.7 shows, however, the social democrats did suffer exceptionally heavy losses among homeowners in 1975.

In other words, the repeated consequence of housing policy was to increase the political significance of housing inequities among the electorate. Moreover, the social democrats eventually created a clientele wedded to tax-privileged homeownership. Survey data reflect this political effect. In 1971, there was a popular majority in favor of abolishing homeowner tax advantages (an opinion balance of +4). By 1981, all voters except for pensioners were opposed (an opinion balance of −33). Workers, then, are as radically opposed to abolishing such tax advantages as the middle classes.

We can estimate, in the case of Denmark, the relative importance of housing in party choice over the entire period, by regressing party preference on social class and dwelling category, and then compare the results for the years 1960, 1966, 1968, 1973, and 1975.[14] One would expect the regression coefficient for the dwelling variable to vary in strength according to the degree of politicization surrounding the issue at the time. The coefficient should jump substantially in 1966 and again in 1973 and 1975.

Table 8.8 suggests that housing status became crucial for party choice on both occasions. Comparing the unstandardized coefficients, we find that the housing variable jumps from .136 to .326 ($t = 2.235$) between 1960 and 1966. Still, social class remains dominant. By 1968, the situation has stabilized, but a second wave of politicization occurs, as expected, in 1973 and 1975. The housing coefficient jumps from .277 to .800 ($t = 2.933$). In this second period, however, class voting has declined sharply, so that in 1975 the housing variable is actually stronger than the class variable.

A comparison with the data for Norway and Sweden presents some empirical difficulties. After 1965 the question of housing status was not included again in the Norwegian surveys until 1981, and we have no information on housing status for Sweden in the 1960s survey. This obviously impedes any effort to generalize. Yet, as can be seen from Tables 8.9 and 8.10, the distribution of owners and renters, by social class, is surprisingly similar in the two countries. In Norway, if we hold social class constant, there was no polarization between homeowners and renters in 1965—and this is especially important with respect to the DNA's crucial working-class base. There are slight differences among white-collar and petit-bourgeois groups, but these do not amount to any kind of cleavage. As expected, there are no indications that housing policy in Norway produced new political cleavages during the 1970s. The data for 1981 indicate that the DNA has

[14] The three variables entered into the equation were scored as follows: *Social Class* (working class = 1, non–working class [excluding pensioners] = 2 ; *Dwelling Type* (renter = 0, owner = 1); and *Party Choice* (left-socialist parties = 0, SF = 1, social democratic party = 2, centrist parties = 3, bourgeois parties of the right = 4). The analyses are based on Gallup-survey data files. Since these do not contain the "thermometer scales," I was forced to score the dependent variables in this less satisfactory manner.

TABLE 8.8. Party Preference in Denmark by Housing Status and Social Class,
1960-1975
(*regressions*)

	B	Beta	R^2	N
INDEPENDENT VARIABLES				
1960				
Social Class	1.122	.588 ⎫	.376	800
Housing Status	.136	.072 ⎭		
1966				
Social Class	1.059	.482 ⎫	.288	822
Housing Status	.326	.151 ⎭		
1968				
Social Class	1.085	.508 ⎫	.320	753
Housing Status	.277	.130 ⎭		
1973				
Social Class	.793	.351 ⎫	.192	714
Housing Status	.425	.198 ⎭		
1975				
Social Class	.762	.284 ⎫	.246	790
Housing Status	.800	.296 ⎭		

SOURCES: Gallup surveys, 1960-1975.
NOTE: *Beta* = standardized coefficients; B = unstandardized coefficients. For all coefficients $P \geqq .001$.

lost voters overall, but the defections have been very evenly distributed between renters and owners. We may conclude, then, that the highly equitable character of Norwegian housing policy has helped prevent housing-related political cleavages.

Swedish housing policies have also placed considerable emphasis on equity, although in recent years private ownership has come to occupy a very privileged position in regard to taxation—the unanticipated result of high marginal taxation and inflationary pressures. In addition, it is generally agreed that the uninspired and drab apartment complexes that were erected under the "Million program" induced those who could to choose the more pleasurable alternative of private home-ownership. It is evident (see Table 8.10) that the housing situation of voters (again, if we hold social class constant) matters very little in terms of party choice. Since differences between renters and owners are negligible, one must conclude that housing does not induce new electoral cleavages. Note, however, that the real momentum of home-

TABLE 8.9. Party Preference in Norway by Housing Status and Social Class, 1965 and 1981
% supporting parties)

	Left Socialist		Social Democrats		Bourgeois Parties	
	1965	1981	1965	1981	1965	1981
WORKERS						
Renters	4	10	71	49	25	41
Owners	7	7	71	52	22	41
WHITE COLLAR						
Renters	7	7	34	26	58	67
Owners	2	9	32	29	66	63
PETITE BOURGEOISIE						
Renters	4	—	24	—	72	—
Owners	1	—	19	—	80	—
All Renters	5	12	51	34	43	54
All Owners	4	4	46	38	50	58

SOURCES: Norwegian electoral surveys, 1965 and 1981.
NOTE: "Don't Know" and "Neutral" responses have been excluded.

ownership increase and rising tax-benefit inequities began in the early and middle 1970s. Yet, as shown in Table 8.11, such events do not seem to have affected voters' party choices very much. The only noticeable change is a slight increase in renter support for the left socialists, combined with a decline in renter support for the social democrats. It is possible that greater polarization will emerge if present trends are allowed to continue and if the SAP, which returned to government in 1982, fails to reverse the creeping dualism inherent in the structure of the Swedish housing market.

In summary, Danish social democratic housing policies have helped shatter the unity of the party's natural social base. Once the social democrats took the initiative to attempt a reform of housing policies, renters were pushed heavily to the left, while homeowners were pushed to the right. Housing has become a fundamental axis of electoral polarization and a core component in social democratic party decomposition. The data for Norway are too limited for a genuine comparison, but there is little reason to suspect that the situation is even close to the Danish one. Sweden seems to occupy a middle position. Overall, it does not appear that housing policy has helped create new electoral cleavages. But it is possible that the Swedish social democrats may end up facing a scenario analogous to the Danish one if they do not

269

TABLE 8.10. Party Preference in Sweden by Housing Status
and Social Class, 1976
(% *supporting parties*)

	Left Socialists	Social Democrats	Bourgeois Parties	N =
WORKERS				
Renters	6	69	25	(498)
Owners	4	62	34	(584)
WHITE COLLAR				
Renters	7	39	54	(321)
Owners	2	31	67	(521)
PETITE BOURGEOISIE				
Renters	3	21	76	(67)
Owners	1	15	84	(215)
All Renters	6	55	39	(886)
All Owners	3	42	55	(1,320)

SOURCE: Swedish electoral survey, 1976.
NOTE: "Don't Know" and "Neutral" responses have been excluded.

TABLE 8.11. Party Preference in Sweden by Housing Status, 1979
(% *supporting parties*)

	Left Socialists	Social Democrats	Bourgeois Parties	N =
Renters	9	49	40	(1,007)
Owners	3	42	54	(1,556)

SOURCE: Statistiska Centralbyron (1981b, table 43).

manage to correct currently developing inequities. The SAP should be
alarmed that renters are beginning to harbor left-socialist sympathies.[15]

THE POLITICAL BUSINESS CYCLE AND PARTY DECOMPOSITION

One important factor that permitted a social democratic realignment
in the 1930s was the party's decision to shelve the socialization ques-

[15] That a dwelling-based political division is possible can be surmised from the results
of the 1979 electoral survey reported in Holmberg (1981, table 12.1). Forty-four percent
of the respondents agreed that tax privileges for homeowners must be reduced; this is
almost the exact same figure as the percentage of renters.

tion. This move imposed upon the social democrats new dilemmas of electoral judgment concerning their economic performance. The entire welfare state program has been both objectively and subjectively contingent on the social democrats' capacity to guarantee both stable growth and full employment—objectively, because without it the foundations for welfare state expansion will be absent; subjectively, because trade union and broad working-class acquiescence and belief in the postwar social contract has been contingent on full employment. Beyond the objective of full employment with growth, it is easy to see why large segments of the labor movement would make more ambitious demands for planned and controlled economic development. This would be the case especially when full-employment wage pressures conflict with the requirements for price stability, the balance of payments, and international competitiveness. In addition, one cannot ignore the salience of more ideologically inspired demands among workers and intellectuals for visible progress toward the promised democratic socialist economy.

Several questions, therefore, remain to be addressed with respect to social democratic economic policies. First, to what extent is it a political liability for social democracy to abandon the classic socialization strategy? Secondly, to what extent are variations in social democratic electoral performance related to the movement's capacity to implement public control of the economy? And, finally, what is the relationship between voter dissatisfaction with the welfare state, on one side, and economic performance on the other?

Classic Policy Options

A core element of the Leninist critique is that social democracy betrays the working class when it abandons the commitment to socializing the means of production. If this were historically correct, a powerful latent demand for state socialization would have to be present and would constitute a basis for rejecting social democracy. But the social democrats' actual strategy of seeking control over the business cycle could possibly backfire if the traditional conservative insistence on the sanctity of laissez faire should indeed manage to convince the electorate.

These two alternative scenarios can be tested with electoral survey data. On balance, these data (see Table 8.12) suggest that the decision to shelve the socialization issue was politically safe for social democracy. Popular enthusiasm for such measures remains modest at best. In Denmark, where the question was worded more strongly they are

271

TABLE 8.12. Electoral Support in Scandinavia for Laissez Faire and for State
Socialization of Means of Production
(*attitudinal balance scores*)

| | Denmark (1981) | | Norway (1977) | | Sweden (1976) | |
	Laissez Faire	Socialization	Laissez Faire	Socialization	Laissez Faire	Socialization
CLASS POSITION						
Workers	− 6	− 37	0	− 5	+ 18	− 16
White Collar	− 10	− 52	+ 11	− 39	+ 30	− 30
PARTY PREFERENCE						
Left Socialists	− 41	+ 14	− 59	+ 64	− 49	+ 71
Social Democrats	− 23	− 39	− 12	+ 13	− 10	+ 1
Bourgeois-Party Supporters	+ 22	− 80	+ 31	− 79	+ 65	− 75
Entire Sample	+ 2	− 55	+ 7	− 25	+ 27	− 38

SOURCES: Danish electoral survey, 1981; Norwegian electoral survey, 1977; Swedish electoral survey, 1976.

NOTE: With respect to laissez faire, respondents were asked whether or not they favored abolition of state intervention in the private economy. Swedish respondents were restricted to an "Agree/ Disagree" answer; therefore, the scores on this variable are likely to be inflated for Sweden. With respect to socialization, the question referred only to "large corporations" in the cases of Norway and Sweden, but to the entire economy in the Danish case; therefore, negative opinion in Denmark is probably inflated. The attitudinal balance scores are derived by subtracting the percentage of those against from the percentage of those in favor. "Don't Know" responses have been excluded.

unambiguously rejected by all except (marginally) the left socialists.[16] In Scandinavia only the Norwegians actually have historical experience with socialization policies (immediately after the war and again in the 1970s, especially in the oil sector). This may help explain why opinions are more favorable among workers generally as well as among leftists and social democrats. In Norway, too, the issue has provoked stronger left-right polarization than in either of the other two Nordic nations.[17] Sweden falls somewhere in between but, like Norway, is polarized on

[16] However, one should note that voter support for socialization of the means of production went up in Denmark during the 1970s. Thus, in 1971 the opinion balance (for the total sample) was − 71, versus − 55 in 1981.

[17] The long-term trend in Norway, however, seems to be against socialization. In 1965 the level of support for such measures was considerably greater—a total-sample balance of − 15, compared with − 25 in 1977.

the left-right axis. Social democrats in both Sweden and Norway still seem to have some affection for the classic doctrines.

The socialization issue has not weakened social democracy's legitimacy in a serious way in any of the Nordic countries, but it is difficult to determine whether it has had no effect whatsoever. On the one hand, there is strong wage-earner opposition, particularly in Denmark. On the other hand, the left socialists in Norway and Sweden may rob social democracy of its leftist constituencies on this score—a phenomenon that would validate Przworski's thesis. If that is the case, however, the effect would have to be quite marginal: remember, the Swedish VPK has remained stagnant for more than three decades, with roughly 5 percent of the vote, and the Norwegian left socialists follow a cyclical, boom-and-bust pattern linked primarily to the EEC conflict. Moreover, in Norway the distance between the left and the DNA is not especially great.

The laissez-faire option is, in contrast, more attractive to Scandinavian voters. We may note that these surveys fall at a peculiar historical conjuncture in all three countries. Traditional social democratic policies for managing the full-employment economy have, if not collapsed, at least demonstrated their shortcomings vis-à-vis the new economic order. Meanwhile, the conservative parties—following the international trend—have resurrected their old ideology of free-enterprise capitalism and have, with no little success, persuaded voters to shift allegiance. For each of the three countries, the survey data reflect the situation just prior to bourgeois-government takeovers (albeit with a three-year lag in Norway). It is therefore possible to interpret positive responses concerning laissez faire as voter rejection of social democracy's record in respect of government economic regulation—or, to put it a different way, as a measure of the extent to which conservative free-enterprise ideology can assert itself against social democracy.[18]

In all the Nordic countries, laissez faire is rejected by leftists and

[18] It is important to note, however, that voters may refer to a great variety of things when they express a desire for less (or more) government regulation. They could, with bureaucratic excesses in mind, be rejecting the maze of detailed regulations that enter into any market transaction; or they could be objecting to government intervention in wage negotiations. The latter interpretation may have some validity at least for Denmark, where, as Goul Andersen shows (1979, 246-247), both manual worker and white-collar wage earners vehemently oppose government intervention in collective bargaining (and where intervention has been frequent). In short, the answers to the laissez-faire issue are difficult to interpret. But it is probably safe to use them as a gauge of basic dissatisfaction with the kind of regulated economy that social democracy has pursued since the 1970s, as well as an index of the ease with which the conservative option has undermined social democracy's legitimacy on this score.

social democrats alike; but in Norway, and especially in Sweden, the situation is very much polarized between the political blocs. Bourgeois-party adherents in Sweden are exceptionally pro-free-enterprise.[19] The data in Table 8.12 also suggest that broad dissatisfaction with the regulated economy even characterizes large sections of the working class and the new middle strata. In this respect, though, Denmark is the exception—perhaps because the Danish party's record with government economic regulation has been strikingly weak, and perhaps also because bourgeois governments have played a much larger role in postwar policymaking. If the laissez-faire question is a little difficult to interpret one-dimensionally, the opinion profile in the three countries nevertheless does suggest rather marked disillusionment with social democracy as well as a surprising readiness to embrace the conservative alternative (at least under present circumstances).

Social Democratic Business-Cycle Control

A sound assessment of the electoral consequences of social democratic economic policy must examine voter reactions on questions that actually reflect the policies that have been enacted or at least pursued. The electoral surveys contain a series of questions designed to capture voter preferences concerning the publicly controlled economy. When the specified objective of more state control has to do with investment allocation, full employment, or even the reduction of "capitalist power," aggregate electoral opinion is favorable (although there are differences, depending on party affiliation and class).

In Denmark (in 1971), there was a net majority in favor of publicly controlled lending for both housing and industry. Among left-socialist and social democratic voters, the net majority was very strong (Borre et al. 1976, 140). In Norway and Sweden, the surveys asked respondents about the need for greater state economic control to ensure full employment. The results (see Table 8.13) are surprising. Support was virtually identical in the two countries during the late 1960s but, by the middle and late 1970s, they parted ways. In Norway, the data

[19] To a degree, one would expect that the more extreme scores in Sweden result from the absence of a "status quo," neutral-response alternative. Yet, it is also tempting to interpret these polarized scores as reflecting the debate over collective wage-earner funds, an issue that figured very prominently in the 1976 election campaign. The bourgeois parties were very successful in persuading Swedish voters that wage-earner funds were a socialization policy in disguise. A comparison with the data for 1968 supports this interpretation: in that year, the opinion balance was −6 among workers and +13 among white-collar employees.

TABLE 8.13. Attitudinal Balance in Norway and Sweden on Need for Greater State Control of the Economy to Ensure Full Employment

	Norway		Sweden	
	1969	1977	1968	1976
All Voters	+9	−21	+8	−4
CLASS POSITION				
Manual Workers	+38	0	+36	+42
White Collar Employees			−8	−9
Private Sector	−30	−66	—	—
Public Sector	+12	−22	—	—
PARTY PREFERENCE				
Left Socialists	+56	+77	+79	+69
Social Democrats	+43	+23	+43	+42
Center Party	−32	−59	−22	−41
Liberals	−16	−62	−31	−46
Conservatives	−50	−82	−63	−73

SOURCES: Norwegian electoral surveys, 1969 and 1977; Swedish electoral surveys, 1968 and 1976.

NOTE: The attitudinal balance scores are derived by subtracting the percentage of those against from the percentage of those in favor. Danish electoral surveys did not include a question on this matter.

reveal a trend among all but left socialists toward less support for, even opposition to, state controls to maintain full employment. In Sweden, there is a trend in the same direction, albeit much weaker. What is more important, Swedish voters have become significantly more polarized on the issue. Manual workers have moved even more in favor and white-collar employees have remained about the same, implying a marked shift to the "right" among the self-employed, farmers, and upper-level white-collar groups.

The new polarization is especially pronounced with respect to party support: left socialists and SAP voters remain overwhelmingly in favor; bourgeois-party voters express strong opposition. This is also the case in Norway, but social democrats are concomitantly less in favor and left socialists markedly more in favor. In other words, Norwegian voter opinion in general, and the DNA's natural political base in particular, increasingly seem to be rejecting one of the centerpieces of postwar DNA policy. In Sweden, on the other hand, the SAP is given a stronger mandate by the workers to pursue such policies, even if under more polarized political conditions.

The heightened politicization of the full-employment issue may strengthen the SAP. Average voter evaluations of the SAP's position on employment issues improve considerably between 1973 and 1976; a clear majority believes that the SAP is superior to the bourgeois parties on the question of handling employment problems (Petersson 1977, 377, 397).[20] For Norway, one would have to come to the opposite conclusion. The DNA's new controls and subsidies to sustain jobs appear to have been unfavorably received, even among workers. These reactions, furthermore, may have helped strengthen the bourgeois parties. In other words, it is possible that the DNA's decline during the 1970s is associated with its full-employment economic policies, and that the bourgeois parties' vocal criticism of the DNA's lame-duck subsidizations were effective. The Norwegian data do suggest that, at least under certain conditions, social democratic policies to control the economy may demobilize the wage-earner electorate.

How may one explain this divergence between Norway and Sweden? First, one would have to note how important, comparatively, the issue of full employment is. It is quite evident that fear of unemployment would be minimal in Norway and increasingly acute in Sweden. Secondly, the political guarantee of full employment has never been as intimately connected with the DNA in Norway as it is with the SAP in Sweden. Ideologically and programmatically, the Norwegian "political consensus" embraced full employment, and this would have been borne out during the reign of the bourgeois coalition in the buoyant 1960s. In contrast, the SAP has always stood as the exemplification of the full-employment guarantee, and the symbiosis of trade union and party is stronger on this question than on any other. The SAP's image as the last bastion against unemployment could only be strengthened when levels of unemployment increased during the post-1976 bourgeois coalition governments. Thirdly, the implicit meaning of the statement that greater state control of the economy is required for full employment will naturally be received differently by the Norwegian and Swedish working classes.

The distribution of public opinion changes when the question of state control is rephrased in more explicit class-conflict terms. When the statement reads, "If the state cannot control the private economy,

[20] According to Holmberg's 1979 data (1981, 99ff), voter evaluations of the SAP on the issue of employment improved even more between 1976 and 1979. In contrast, Norwegian voters appear less convinced about which party will best protect full employment. The vast majority believe it makes no difference, and the remainder are surprisingly split between the DNA and the bourgeois parties—although the DNA does have a slight edge (Valen 1981, 321).

TABLE 8.14. Attitudinal Balance in Norway and Sweden on Need for Greater State
Control of the Economy to Prevent Leaders of Banks and Industry
from Wielding Too Much Power

| | Norway | | Sweden | |
	1969	1977	1968	1976
All Voters	+35	+8	+46	+34
CLASS POSITION				
Workers	+72	+40	+68	+56
White-Collar Employees			+30	+24
Private Sector	+30	−26	—	—
Public Sector	+58	+12	—	—
PARTY PREFERENCE				
Left Socialists	+68	+85	+72	+89
Social Democrats	+56	+42	+71	+63
Center Party	+5	−10	+19	+10
Liberals	+26	−6	+8	−2
Conservatives	−1	−48	−35	−40

NOTE: For sources and explanation, see Table 8.13.

the leaders of banks and industry will gain too much power," then
the level of agreement increases markedly. (See Table 8.14.) Yet, some
of the tendencies observed earlier are still present. In Norway, we
again see fading enthusiasm for a state-controlled economy during the
1970s. Among workers—even though they remain strongly in favor—
the drop is significant. This is also true for white-collar employees,
especially private-sector employees. The distribution of support by
party affiliation shows polarization between left socialists and social
democrats, on the one hand, and bourgeois-party voters on the other.
In Sweden, the decline of support is much smaller. The comparison
with 1968 data may be unfortunate, for in that year voter support for
greater control over banks and industry was at an all-time high.[21] The
1976 attitude balance is quite similar to that in most previous years,
and since the level of agreement jumps again in 1979, we would be
wrong to interpret the trend as deradicalizing. With respect to Norway,

[21] According to Holmberg (1981, table 12.6), those who agreed that the state should
increase its control of the economy in order to reduce the power of leaders in banking
and industry comprised 55 percent in 1964, 64 percent in 1968; 57 percent in 1970,
59 percent in 1973, 56 percent in 1976, and 62 percent in 1979. Unfortunately, we
have no way of knowing whether a similar problem of comparison obtains for Norway,
since data are available only for 1969 and 1977.

several differences may be noted. If we concentrate solely on 1976 (a typical year) for Sweden, the data suggest that the SAP enjoys very strong backing, among manual labor and white-collar groups combined, for radical economic policies. But the issue pits socialists against the bourgeois bloc, although some support can be found in the center.

In Norway, the issue was pretty much consensual in 1969 but, since then, it has become even more polarized than in Sweden. This new polarization seems to benefit the bourgeois parties at the expense of the DNA. One may also note a greater differentiation between the DNA and the left socialists. In short, in conformity with our previous findings, the DNA seems to be losing consistently on radical economic policy issues, while it is doubtful that this is so with the Swedish party. One way to put it is that the Norwegian electorate may be withdrawing its support for DNA policies to control the economy, as these found articulation during the 1970s, while Swedish voters seem to be sanctioning further social democratic advances in the direction of a more controlled economy. The difference between manual worker and white-collar attitudes is perhaps the most crucial one. The gap between manual labor and white-collar employees has widened dramatically in Norway, and this could reflect the DNA's inability to unite the two within a broad wage-earner coalition.[22] The SAP's capacity to unite manual labor and white-collar employees around economic issues, on the other hand, does not appear to have been impaired. Indeed, one outstanding feature of the Swedish data is the smaller attitudinal gap that exists between the two wage-earner categories.

The Danish surveys did not include questions about state economic controls as related either to full employment or to the power of bankers and industrialists. Instead, respondents were asked whether they favored greater government control over investment. If a comparison with the Norwegian and Swedish cases is to be made, the first thing to note is the stronger and more persistent demand among Danish voters for state-controlled investment. The opinion balance among all voters was +30 in 1971, +40 in 1973, and +42 in 1977. Similarly, manual workers are much more favorably disposed than their Norwegian and Swedish comrades, while Danish white-collar employees score rather similarly to their Swedish counterparts. By party affiliation (in 1977) there is overwhelming agreement among left socialists (+79), social democrats (+70), and even progressives (+36). To understand

---

[22] The same gap was evident with respect to the issue of state control for full employment as well as on the taxation issue—though not on the question of social welfare reform.

TABLE 8.15. Strength of Support for Danish Political Parties by Social Class, Trade Union Membership, Class Identification and Attitude toward State Control of Investments, 1977

| | Dependent Variable | | | | | | | |
| | Left Socialist | | Social Democratic | | Bourgeois | | Progress | |
	B	Beta	B	Beta	B	Beta	B	Beta
INDEPENDENT VARIABLES								
Class	−2.698*	−.161*	−.551*	−.120*	1.198	.111	.383	.049
Union Membership	4.159*	.262*	.854*	.195*	−2.017*	−.197*	−1.027*	−.139*
Class Identification	−.152	−.046	.438*	.476*	.203	.094	−.544*	−.350*
Attitude	1.105*	.188*	.216*	.133*	−.908*	−.239*	−.301	−.110
$R^2 =$	.210	.210	.371	.371	.170	.170	.189	.189

SOURCE: Danish electoral survey, 1977.

NOTE: $N = 374$; Beta = standardized coefficients; B = unstandardized coefficients. An asterisk indicates $P \geq .01$. Attitude is scaled 1 to 5, where 1 = strongly opposed to investment controls and 5 = strongly in favor of investment controls. For an explanation of the other variables, see Table 8.3.

these trends, one must remember that the current economic crisis is especially severe in Denmark, and that the Danish social democrats have been far less successful at advancing programs to control the economy, especially with respect to investments.

One remarkable thing about these high levels of electoral agreement is that they are virtually identical to the levels of electoral disagreement with "welfare-statism." A large number of Danish voters seem both to be dissatisfied with the welfare state and to want greater political control of the economy.[23] It is therefore possible that the defections from social democracy among the electorate, particularly from among the workers, is a double-barreled dissatisfaction with both welfare state spending and the lack of active investment policies. Thus, welfare state protesters tend to drift to the right; investment-control protesters move left. The data in Table 8.15 suggest that this may in fact be the case.

[23] While Danish *workers* who support the progress party tend to harbor extreme anti-welfare-spending attitudes, those same workers favor investment controls. (The attitude balance for 1977 was +62.)

Pro-investment-control attitudes are strongly related to left-socialist, as well as social democratic, support. As one can imagine, they are negatively related to bourgeois and progressive support (although, in the latter case, the coefficients are not significant except at the .5 level). In other words, pro-investment-control opinions are good predictors of left-socialist party choice (and social democratic party choice), and anti-investment-control attitudes are good predictors of support for the traditional bourgeois parties; but investment-control attitudes are unimportant for progress party support.[24] (Investment-control attitudes explain 8 percent of the left-socialist party variance.)

As in previous analyses, the comparison by investment-control opinions suggests that it is primarily attitudinal factors which propel voters left or right. In all the Danish analyses, class positional variables (union membership, class membership, and class identification) play a dominant role in explaining social democratic party support and a weaker, or nonexistent, role for either left-socialist or progress party support—even if unionized workers are important for left-socialist support. Social democratic party decomposition in Denmark, then, appears to be highly correlated with policy questions.

A comparison of the three countries on the issue of a controlled economy seems especially hard to make without placing attitudes and party choice in the context of social democratic performance. The substantive meaning of the question must certainly differ in Norway, where the entire postwar era is marked by major extensions in state controls in finance and industry; Sweden, where extensive labor market regulations and, more recently, state direction of investments have been attempted; and Denmark, where the social democrats have been repeatedly discouraged from, and frustrated in, pursuing more active and direct management of economic development. Thus, in Norway, it is likely that voters' responses to the survey questions are evaluative of the actual record and achievements, while in Denmark such responses seem to reflect desires about what should be done, or not done, in the field of economic policy. The difficulty of interpreting cross-national differences is that we have no way of ascertaining whether this is in fact the case. The comparative assessments that follow must therefore include an element of speculation.

For Denmark, it is possible to interpret the data to mean that elec-

[24] The age variable is insignificant (bivariate correlation between age and investment control = .071), indicating that generational differences play no important role in any of the attitudinal relations examined so far. Only in the social democratic party model does age have a significant independent effect, explaining roughly 5 percent of the social democratic "thermometer" variance.

toral concerns with a more thoroughly controlled economy has benefited the left socialists at the expense of the social democrats—although we should note that social democratic supporters also express quite strong desires to have the government direct investment. The issue of state control of investment can be viewed as a constituent element in the decomposition of Danish social democracy. Since the correlation between being working-class and unionized, on the one hand, and in favor of controls, on the other hand, is strong (.315 and .291, respectively), one may conclude that the desire for state controls is not limited to intellectuals, but is a rather keenly held demand within the historical core of the social democratic class base. In addition, since popular demand for a more controlled investment climate is so strong among the Danes, it appears more than likely that social democratic failures on this front have damaged the party's legitimacy and capacity to mobilize.

A Summary Evaluation

On virtually all attitudinal dimensions, the Danes present extreme scores. This suggests that Danish politics are considerably more politicized and polarized. Welfare state protest propelled voters to the right; demands for a more controlled economy moved them left. While in both instances, voters have moved away from the social democratic party, their directional choice seems to depend on a combination of two factors. One is their attachment to the working class. Those with strong ties to the unions and the working class tend to move left; those with weak ties, to the right. The other is the balance of opinion on antiwelfare versus procontrol issues.

Thus, among *workers* who support the Danish Progress party, there is substantial agreement that the state should control investment, but this is overshadowed by their disgust with excessive welfarism.[25] Among those workers who support left socialism, one finds that pro-welfare-spending and pro-investment-control attitudes are equally strong. In short, there is considerable evidence to suggest that the trend toward social democratic party decomposition requires political explanation; that the political fragmentation among wage-earner groups is a consequence of social democracy's record in social, housing, and economic policies. An "embourgeoisement thesis" certainly finds little empirical

[25] Pro-investment-control attitudes explain about 2 percent of the variance for Danish Progress party support *among workers alone*; antiwelfare attitudes explain nearly 18 percent.

support. Workers and white-collar employees may oppose the welfare state, but they also desire a radical economic program. The political drift of Danish workers does not indicate ideological or programmatic moderation but, rather, politicized protest.

Social democratic party decomposition in Denmark is also peculiar in class structural terms. Those who remain loyal to the party come primarily from its traditional core constituency—older, unionized manual workers whose party choice is guided by tradition, class identification, and party loyalty rather than by policy assessment. In contrast, those who exit for the redder pastures on the left, or the bluer pastures on the right, are generally younger and more motivated by policy concerns. Finally, the left-socialist parties seem to have attracted supporters, among manual workers and white-collar employees, around a set of political programs in opposition to social democracy. This suggests that the conditions for a social democratic realignment, both electorally and politically, are gloomy indeed, since a counteralignment, including younger and perhaps politically more aware wage earners, has already been forged on the left.

The connection between policies and social democratic party decline in Norway is less clear. At first glance, it would appear that the Norwegian electorate is the polar opposite of the Danish: it sanctions welfare enthusiastically, but rejects further radical advances in economic policy. As I have suggested, however, the greater disapproval on the latter issue may very well reflect voter assessments of actual DNA performance, rather than opposition to a controlled economy per se. We have seen that radicalism on economic policy issues has grown among left-socialist supporters, but waned among DNA as well as bourgeois-party voters. Yet, since left-socialist party strength has been so erratic, it is difficult to conclude that dissatisfaction with the DNA's economic policies has moved a substantial portion of voters to the left. On balance, to the extent that there is a connection, dissatisfaction probably pushes more voters to the right.

To be sure, the DNA displays signs of stagnation and decline. It has lost its formerly firm grip on the working-class vote but, unlike the Danish party, the DNA is not decomposing. My analyses suggest that welfare state issues have no bearing on the DNA's declining fortunes. (Perhaps economic policy questions do, but they will hardly have been the major catalyst of left-wing opposition.) As we shall see, this phenomenon was—in contrast to the Danish experience—largely the product of short-term issues, Common Market entry in particular. But the DNA has also failed to mobilize new white-collar strata within a broad wage-earner alliance, and there is some evidence that its politics have contributed to this failure. First, it seems that taxes and equalization policies alienate white-collar groups. In Norway, there is stronger resentment of steep tax progressivity than there is elsewhere—and this is an issue that clearly polarizes voters. If welfare program expansion unifies wage earners, taxes divide them. Secondly, support for a planned and controlled economy continues to exist, but the DNA's policy approach of late seems to inspire dissatisfaction.

Without a clear and novel economic program for the 1970s and 1980s, the DNA lost the initiative—especially since it had no equivalent to the Swedish, or even the Danish, plan for economic democracy. We must remind ourselves, however, that a majority of workers still support the DNA's policies strongly. Valen and Martinussen (1977, 54-71) have estimated the relative impact of salient policy issues on the DNA's dramatic election losses in 1973. In that election, remember, the party dropped from 46.5 percent to 35.3 percent of the vote, and the biggest victors were the left socialists, who suddenly scored 11.2 percent. By 1977, the DNA had recuperated most of its losses, and the left socialists returned to their accustomed 4-5 percent. This suggests that some of the DNA's electoral problems have to do with issues of a more temporary quality. Valen's data for 1969-1973 confirm this. In 1973, three issues exploded simultaneously: taxation, abortion, and Common Market entry.[26]

On all three issues the electorate was polarized, and the DNA lost substantially. Among those who believed that taxes were too high, the DNA lost 15 percent, most of which went to either the left socialists or the new Norwegian Progress party. Among antiabortionists, the DNA lost 10 percent, of which almost all went to the Christian people's party, while some proabortionists went from the DNA to the left. Of all the issues, the EEC controversy harmed the DNA most. A full 25 percent of EEC opponents who supported the DNA in 1969 defected to the left socialists, and between 1969 and 1973 the DNA lost 41 percent among EEC opponents. Clearly, then, the EEC issue was the single most disastrous one for the DNA, continuing to assert itself even after the referendum had been settled. Among the minority who favored EEC entry, there was less electoral volatility between 1969 and 1977 (20 percent changed party); among the majority who opposed EEC entry, 32 percent changed party. The proportion of changers was especially high among those who voted DNA in 1969.[27]

[26] The data reported here are derived from Valen and Martinussen (1977, tables 2.8-2.12) and Valen (1981, table 16.9).

[27] In comparison, the DNA lost only moderately on the abortion issue, and only among "pro-lifers" who shifted to the right.

Considering these findings together with the other analyses seen thus far, one would have to conclude that the roots of social democratic party "decomposition" in Norway are very different from those in Denmark, even if they do share the characteristic of springing from party policies, rather than from social structural forces. In Denmark, social, housing, and economic policies constitute the long-run basis of decomposition. In Norway, tax and (possibly) economic policies produce similar trends, although the party's sharp drop in 1973 was caused primarily by the short-run, ad hoc issues of EEC entry and abortion. The salience of flash issues, however, was so great that they may well have broken the legitimacy and loyalty traditionally accorded the social democrats.

As we contrast Denmark and Norway, it is also significant to note how the policies polarized the traditional social democratic core. In Denmark, welfare protesters went right and economic policy protesters left. In Norway, the EEC protesters moved left while "pro-lifers" moved right; as Valen and Martinussen (1977, table 2.12) show, these two issues completely overshadowed the tax issue in 1973. As abortion and the EEC have faded as issues, however, the tax issue has gained in prominence.

Within Scandinavia the Swedish social democrats are the most successful example of electoral aggregation and mobilization through policy. Or, to put it more cautiously, the SAP has managed to avert fragmentation and polarization within its electoral base. On social welfare issues, dissatisfaction does run quite high on average; the average, however, conceals a duality in which the welfare state is generally sanctioned by the social democrats' natural electorate but is increasingly rejected by their bourgeois opponents. The social welfare issue cannot be a significant source of electoral disaggregation for the SAP. The same can be said with respect to taxation. Housing policies were, until the 1970s, similarly supportive of social democratic electoral stability, and perhaps even a source of mobilization. But housing policies might well unleash decomposition trends in the foreseeable future. In regard to economic policies, wage-earner support for an extension of business-cycle controls is strong—whether motivated by the instrumental desire for full employment or the larger wish to curb the powers of bankers and industrialists. The stagnation and decline that marked SAP fortunes during the 1970s does, however, seem related to an eroding confidence in the party's conventional economic policy program. In this respect, my analyses support Korpi (1977) in his exchange with Lindhagen (1976, 1977).[28]

[28] The two Swedish sociologists engaged in a protracted debate in the pages of *Tiden*

If the SAP's loss of initiative helps explain its slack electoral performance in the 1970s,[29] it is very possible that the party would have fared much worse had it not been forced into opposition when economic conditions began to deteriorate seriously, and had it not faced political opponents persistently incapable of cohesion and, hence, of effective government. I believe there is considerable evidence to support the argument that the variable electoral performance of the three social democracies is chiefly the result of voter responses to their policy records, rather than to any intrinsic properties in the evolution of social structure. But this does not imply that social structural change is causally irrelevant. The electoral difficulties that all three social democratic parties face in the present era are caused by the interplay of how past reforms have shaped voters' political interests together with how the rise of the white-collar strata impose new conditions for political class alliances and policy programs.

What, to varying degrees, we witness in all three Nordic nations is the political death of social democracy's old, peasant-based reformist model. First of all, as presently conceived, the welfare state program can go no further. Secondly, the income-redistributive, egalitarian slant of this populist coalition threatens to halt any move toward a unified wage-earner alliance. Thirdly, the one overriding issue that can unite blue-collar and white-collar workers is that of effectively guaranteed full employment and, coupled with this, improvements in work life. Since social democracy's traditional package of policies has demonstrated its failure to make such guarantees effective, the chances for realignment hinge on whether the proposals for collective employee capital funds, or economic democracy, can bring social democracy back to positive-sum electoral politics.

---

on the sources of the SAP's decline during the 1970s. Lindhagen argues that the decline was the long-run effect of postindustrial changes in class structure. Korpi contends that these served only to boost the potential for social democratic power; the origins of stagnation, he says, must be sought in the SAP's loss of initiative in formulating effective policy responses for the new economic problems.

[29] Another factor was the nuclear power controversy (Holmberg 1981).

PART III

Social Democracy at the Crossroads

NINE

Toward a New Political
Realignment

SCANDINAVIAN SOCIAL DEMOCRACY, like social democracy elsewhere, is currently poised at a historical crossroads. To proceed with the postwar political formula, and the class alliances that underpin it, would almost certainly accelerate party decomposition. The postwar model is exhausted for international reasons as well. Since the Nordic economies are small and export-dependent, international economic expansion is an obvious necessity if zero-sum economic conflicts are to be avoided at home.

The new international division of labor poses additional problems for full-employment growth. High domestic labor costs will spark unemployment in the growing number of industries that can no longer compete with Korean steel or Singapore textiles—unless governments revert to subsidization of firms and jobs, or unless economic resources can be directed into new, dynamic outlets. The social democrats confront a real incompatibility between their broad welfare goals and continued economic vitality if those goals are not rearranged.

The new international economic order has altered domestic distributive conflicts. Higher import costs and restored export competitiveness must be financed by someone. Low profit margins, where government permits freedom of capital movement, would only provoke disinvestment and are thus a serious threat to the full-employment commitment. Across-the-board wage cuts are very difficult to undertake where the trade unions are powerful; workers will be disinclined to tolerate lowered wages over long periods while profits increase. Selective wage cuts (say, in export industries) would undercut the goal of wage solidarity, widen differentials, and seriously jeopardize trade union unity. Substantial cutbacks in public social expenditure would be tantamount to social democratic suicide. Finally, an attack on white-collar incomes—especially in the public sector—might please manual workers, but it would also destroy social democracy's capacity to unite blue-collar and white-collar wage earners.

A new international upswing might conceivably permit Scandinavian social democracy to escape its current political imprisonment, and proceed once again along the traditional policy road, were it not for additional forces. The "Keynes plus Beveridge" formula behind the postwar social democratic success story was, in many respects, politically exhausted even before the advent of international economic stagnation. First of all, the welfare state proved unable to deliver on the promise of greater equality as it established a proliferation of universal entitlements and necessarily luxurious benefits. Indeed, one of the earliest signs of exhaustion was the new-left critique of persistent inequality in the 1960s, a critique that social democracy was compelled to answer.

Secondly, the welfare state assumes that solidarity and entitlements are capable of raising economic productivity. Certainly welfare and labor market programs help socialize the risks of rapid industrial renovation. But they also permit—indeed, actively encourage—workers to leave the labor market, whether temporarily or permanently. The full-employment effect may be positive, but it comes at a high tax cost and perhaps even at a production cost. To put it differently, the overhead costs of maintaining full employment tend to spiral.

Finally, the assumed harmony between the welfare state and the private economy is increasingly being questioned. Democratic rights in work life are being demanded as a complement to social citizenship. Inequalities of wealth and economic power concentration are held to be unacceptable for general egalitarian reasons, but they are also a problematic consequence of solidaristic wage policies and structural reform of the economy. More collectivization of investment is held as indispensable for guaranteed full employment, equalization, and democracy.

No one policy can possibly address all these problems simultaneously, but the proposal for collective wage-earner funds and economic democracy does constitute the centerpiece of social democracy's realignment program. It aims to resolve the zero-sum distributive conflict between profits and wages (including the social wage). It promises lower production costs, higher investment levels, greater equality, and a first leap toward the promised democratic economy. Since, at present, social democracy has no other plan for the resolution of economic stagnation and the welfare state impasse, much rests on the movement's capacity to mobilize on the plan it does have. In the following pages, we shall first outline the two major plans, the Danish and Swedish, and then evaluate their political and electoral properties.

The 1975 program of the Swedish Social Democratic party proclaimed that, the struggle for political and social democracy having been completed, the time had come to bring full democratic citizenship rights into economic life. The Swedish party, along with other European socialist movements, is currently on the threshold of a fundamental programmatic shift in which the organization of capitalist production will once again be challenged.

There are two central elements in the new plan for a democratic economy: one emphasizes employee participation; the other, collectivization of ownership and control. The first of these is generally referred to as "industrial democracy" and involves the extension of worker participation and influence over microeconomic behavior (e.g. the division of labor, supervision, technology, health and safety issues, and company-level investment decisions). The second centers around macroeconomic issues (e.g. the accumulation of savings, investment allocation, and long-range capital formation strategies). In current usage, the latter element may be termed "economic democracy." Contemporary economic democracy plans, in Denmark as well as Sweden, all have one thing in common: they break with the orthodox prescription for nationalization and state ownership of the means of production.

All the prevailing plans for economic democracy are premised on two fundamental principles. First is a belief in the accumulation of collectively owned wage-earner capital funds (in contrast to individual profit-sharing systems). The second is that the wage-earner funds should be linked to some sort of industrial democracy.

Some European labor movements emphasize industrial democracy over economic democracy. This is the case in Norway, where the social democrats have already legislated work-life reforms granting wage earners influence over company-level managerial and executive decisions. The Norwegian labor movement, however, has no plan for economic democracy. In Germany, the idea of collective wage-earner funds had been raised by the German Trade Union Confederation (DGB) in the 1950s, but the SPD has refused to adopt it. Instead, the German labor movement has focused its attention on improving the existing co-determination system. After a protracted legal and parliamentary battle, the DGB and the SPD finally succeeded in extending co-determination to additional industrial branches and in strengthening worker representation (Sontheimer 1977). Industrial democracy was also given prominence in the Italian PCI- and CGIL-sponsored *Consiglia dei Fabricca* and in the French CFDT's *Autogestion* program. The British labor movement also emphasized participatory reforms with the ill-fated 1977 Bullock report (Nossiter 1978).

Economic democracy legislation is pursued by only a handful of labor movements. The German trade unions promoted the Gleitze plan of collective wage-earner funds, but without success (Zinn 1978; Nolan and Sabel 1982; SOU 1981). In Holland, the social democratic government proposed in 1976 a profits-based collective funds plan, but it was aborted with the 1977 change of government. The new bourgeois coalition has proposed, but not legislated, a revised plan (SOU 1981, 50). It is now only in Denmark and Sweden that social democratic plans for economic democracy are under serious consideration. In both cases, though most explicitly in Sweden, these proposals are linked to schemes for worker enterprise participation.

Economic democracy is both a radical break with the prevailing Keynesian model and a resurrection of a distant political past. The ideas that guide the contemporary plans have their roots in social democracy's original search for a workable alternative to either Bolshevism or syndicalism.

THE POLITICAL ORIGINS AND RESURRECTION OF ECONOMIC DEMOCRACY

Economic democracy plans derive from a multiplicity of historical origins. As Meidner himself suggests (1978), they can be traced back to profit-sharing ideas, to the influence of guild socialism, and to the immensely popular idea of workers' councils among left-wing socialists immediately after World War I (Cole 1969). There were more negative influences, too. Social democrats found themselves battling communists and syndicalists alike, and were compelled to draft a blueprint for socialism that would have left-wing ideological appeal as well as parliamentary reformist potential. When, during the interwar years, social democrats did go to elections with the traditional call for nationalization, they suffered painful electoral defeats, a lack of working-class enthusiasm, and devastating attacks from bourgeois quarters.

The first blueprint for economic democracy, as we now understand it, was drafted by Fritz Naphtali (1928), a close associate of Rudolf Hilferding. Naphtali's plan is an odd one since the social democrats in general, and Hilferding in particular, continued to insist that the route to socialism lay in the nationalization of heavy industry and finance capital (Gates 1974). Nevertheless, Naphtali's scheme of *Wirtschaftsdemokratie* suggested the establishment of social capital funds, to be financed through a levy on corporations. Most likely, his motive was to bolster the embattled system of workers' councils and codetermination. Prominent Swedish social democrats, like Wigforss and

Karleby in the 1920s, were inspired by similar ideas.[1] Wigforss rejected state socialization, since it would merely substitute one type of bureaucracy for another; but he did not provide a detailed plan for economic democracy.

In both Germany and Scandinavia, economic democracy was shipwrecked on the Great Depression and the rising tide of fascism. In Germany, the SPD leadership, guided by Hilferding, continued to adhere to its old nationalization measures for combatting the economic crisis. When in 1931 the ADGB trade unions presented a Swedish-style, deficit-financed job creation program (the Woytinsky plan), it was rejected by Hilferding as well as Naphtali (Gates 1974). In Scandinavia, the social democrats responded to the crisis by shelving radical socialization—to the extent that they had not already done so long ago—in response to the trade unions' demand for employment creation and the working-class electorate's cry for immediate relief. The Nordic socialists reversed the order of reformist priorities, placing social democracy before economic democracy. Hence, in Scandinavia, the trade unions' concern with mass unemployment prevailed over socialist dogma; in Germany, the ADGB and the SPD were at cross-purposes.

Economic democracy was originally a child of party intellectuals; postwar initiatives come from the trade unions. If indeed the promise of a socialist economy has been reawakened, this would appear to belie Lenin's dictum that trade unionism is incapable of advancing revolutionary goals. Yet, the reasons have less to do with ideology than with practical necessity. Union interest in economic democracy must first of all be understood in light of the altered roles of party and union in the postwar era. The social democratic parties are now forced to mobilize a broad wage-earner coalition, while trade unions retain their narrower class specificity. To promote economic democracy will accentuate the classic social democratic dilemma of how to reconcile left-wing ideological promises with the practical need for broad parliamentary majorities.

The unions' programmatic radicalism grows out of economic necessity. The reconciliation of wage militancy in a full-employment economy has imprisoned the unions in an increasingly narrow dilemma

---

[1] When in 1920 Branting formed the first social democratic government in Sweden, he immediately constituted a commission to recommend strategies for economic democracy. The commission report, published in 1923, held that it is impossible to introduce political democracy and then insist that inherited-property privileges remain unaltered. In this document, Wigforss coined the slogan that, five decades later, would become a rallying point in the LO's fight for economic democracy: "Democracy Cannot Stop at the Factory Gates" (Korpi 1981b; Wigforss [1923] 1981).

(especially where they are powerful, as in Sweden). Their wage-bargaining power is circumscribed by its inflationary effects and, in an open economy, also by its effects on export performance. Union power easily translates into declining investments and/or capital flight. Where unions accept voluntary or compulsory incomes policies, they frequently face rank-and-file disaffection and wildcat strikes (Panitch 1976; Crouch and Pizzorno 1978). Trade unions see a double-barreled industrial and economic democracy plan as the remedy to their dilemma. Greater employee participation and job control might help bridge the gap between central leadership and shop-floor demands. The accumulation of collective capital resources in wage-earner funds will allow trade unions improved control over investment decisions as well as capital formation for full employment. Whereas the fight between profits and wages is a zero-sum game, wage-earner funds offer the labor movement a trade-off—wage restraint in return for a share in future profits and control over the economy (Esping-Andersen and Friedland 1982). Furthermore, economic democracy addresses the growing problem of wealth and capital concentration. The goal of wealth redistribution is explicit in the formulation of all economic democracy plans.

Given the SPD's postwar decision to make peace with the capitalist economy, it is quite remarkable that a DGB-economist, Bruno Gleitze, was to formulate the first postwar scheme for collective wage-earner funds. The Gleitze plan spoke to the German unions' dual concern with the inherent limits of the co-determination system and their inability to exert much control over the increasingly concentrated and cartelized German capital structure (Lieberman 1977; Hallet 1973). Gleitze's is truly the parent of the subsequent Danish and Swedish plans, since it called for collective wage-earner funds ("social funds"), linked to co-determination and based upon the annual transfer of a certain percentage of business profits. The Gleitze plan, however, did not please all sections of the German labor movement,[2] and another version was promoted in 1972, when the SPD was electorally much stronger. But it, too, was rejected.

Economic democracy only became a political possibility in the early 1970s when first the Danish, and then the Swedish, labor movement proposed its legislation into existence. Given the power of the Scandinavian labor movements, compared with those in Germany or Hol-

---

[2] The similar Leber plan was actually implemented in the German construction industries.

land, their commitment to economic democracy could ensure its transition from utopia to reality.

The Politics of Economic Democracy in Scandinavia

Although it was Denmark that spearheaded a plan for economic democracy, the greatest chance for implementation lies in Sweden. The Norwegian labor movement has not yet contemplated economic democracy. Before we turn to the circumstances unique to each country's economic democracy battle, it is worthwhile first to examine what in their common legacy may help explain social democracy's commitment to the concept. Certainly the peculiar ideological heritage of the Scandinavian social democrats plays a role. They were among the first to shelve the demand for an immediate seizure of the means of production. In fact, Danish and Swedish state ownership is very modest by international standards (whereas in Norway it is quite considerable). Actually, socialization measures never entirely disappeared from party programs, though they were never entertained seriously after the 1920s.

In Sweden, we have seen, the postwar debate on economic policy turned to the more immediate question of labor market regulation. It was in the late 1960s that a theoretical discussion of economic policy re-emerged—and this time not in terms of central planning but, rather, in terms of how to steer the mobility of capital both geographically and sectorally (Martin 1975, 1979; Lindbeck 1975). Programmatically, the debate reinvented the theory of "functional socialism," according to which the relevant targets were the functions of private ownership rather than its legal property rights (Adler-Karlsson 1967). Simultaneously, the unions began to question the continued relevance of indisputable managerial rights to control the labor process (Korpi 1981b). Finally, the issue of income and wealth inequality enjoyed a powerful resurgence during the late 1960s.

The Danish social democrats were always more reluctant to engage in ideological debates on economic socialization. The brief Red Cabinet interlude in 1967 did stimulate greater attention to an active state-directed investment policy, but the defeat of the ITP plan and of the socialist coalition itself turned the labor movement back to conventional Keynesianism. Yet, the issue of wealth concentration was also forced upon Danish social democracy (Hansen 1973; Lykketoft 1973).

The debate about inequality and wealth concentration is important for subsequent economic democracy politics. In both Sweden and Denmark, the social democrats were at the point were they could declare that the struggle for the welfare state had reached fruition.

Concomitantly, the trade unions had pursued wage equalization with considerable dedication, in Sweden especially. Yet—from within social democracy as well as from the left socialists—there emerged growing criticism that income inequalities had remained intact and, indeed, that postwar policies had exacerbated the concentration of wealth and capital. From Stockholm, a government commission report on economic concentration demonstrated that Sweden might very well be one of the world's most concentrated economies in respect of ownership structure (SOU 1968; Åkerman 1973). The promise of more equality was given prominent attention in both Danish and Swedish party programs during the early 1970s.

These shifts in ideology also reflect the recognition that a programmatic renewal was necessary for the future. Scandinavian social democracy was becoming the victim both of its accomplishments and its shortcomings. The welfare state was financially endangered, for it presumed vigorous economic growth. By the late 1960s and early 1970s, there were indications that profitability was falling (Edgren et al. 1970; Bergström 1971) and that continued full employment, price stability, and export competitiveness would be difficult to sustain with the traditional package of liberal economic policy (Martin 1979, 1981; Esping-Andersen and Friedland 1982). Major cutbacks in either social benefits or market wages to restore profits would be politically difficult, given the power of the trade unions and the social democratic parties.

The search for an alternative economic policy flows ultimately from changes in the social structure and in the conditions for political alliances. Essentially, the problem for social democracy as it entered the 1970s was how to mold a policy that reconciled the interests of its conventional working-class base with those of the new white-collar strata. The future of social democracy is contingent on such a historical realignment, and it is the fate of economic democracy that will largely decide the prospects for that realignment.

The Swedish Plan

A Danish plan already existed when Rudolf Meidner, on behalf of the Swedish LO, began to draft his scheme for collective wage-earner funds. Yet, the Meidner plan, despite its similarity to the Danish scheme, was designed to accommodate peculiarly Swedish issues (Meidner 1978).

Meidner's task was dominated by three problems. First, coordinated solidaristic wage policies allowed the most dynamic companies "superprofits," because wages were restrained. It was difficult to compel workers in such companies to forgo potentially higher wage contracts without giving them something in return. It was therefore logical that workers as a group should be reimbursed out of the surplus profits. Secondly, capital concentration was in large measure fueled by the active labor market policies. The LO stipulated that Meidner's scheme should address wealth and capital concentration (LO 1976). Thirdly, the LO wanted more control over capital formation and stronger workplace democracy policies. In the late 1960s the LO had already begun to recognize that the active labor market policy alone was an insufficient instrument for balanced structural change. Though it had pressured the government to allow the fourth ATP pension fund to be used for capital investment, the LO sought a considerably stronger instrument for directing economic growth. Concomitantly, the efficacy of its labor-mobility policy was eroding as workers increasingly failed to move where the jobs would open and as the numbers engaged in various Labor Market Board activities rapidly grew. In the LO view, the chief culprit behind the imbalances was capital, not labor.

The deteriorating condition of the Swedish economy during the 1970s forced a reprioritization of the motives for economic democracy. Concern with wealth concentration and with greater worker partici- pation in management decisions subsided as anxiety grew over the sluggish rates of capital formation (Åsard 1978; Öhman 1979b). The problem crystallized after the 1974-1975 wage explosion, the erosion of export performance, and the continued sluggishness of international demand. With the mounting pressure for wage restraint, the LO chose to present economic democracy as the only acceptable quid pro quo: the labor movement would tolerate wage moderation on the condition that wage earners get a share of the resulting profits and some control over future capital formation. In this light, collective wage-earner funds became labor's formula for a new social contract that could move class conflict from a zero-sum to a positive-sum game.

Meidner's proposal for economic democracy was presented to the LO in 1975. Endorsed unanimously by the 1976 congress, it was then submitted to the social democrats for legislative consideration. But the party was ill-prepared for such a radical and complicated proposal, especially in light of the upcoming national elections. To buy time, a special investigatory commission was delegated to prepare a report by 1980-1981. (The first LO-SAP report had appeared in 1978, but was not well received.) The current proposal for wage-earner funds, drafted jointly by the LO and the Swedish Social Democratic party and pre- sented in spring 1981, deviates considerably from the initial plan, although the essential principles remain.

The original Meidner plan was both complex and clever. It called for a dual system of wage-earner funds: on one level, a system of enterprise-based funds and, on another level, a system of national development funds. The former system would be financed through a transfer of 20 percent of company profits per annum. The capital, in the form of stock options, would be administered and controlled by directly elected worker representatives within each enterprise. Meidner envisaged that part of the wage-earner fund's dividends would be targeted for investment in worker welfare and job enhancement. As the amount of collectively held stock could be expected to grow in relation to the amount of stock owned by private hands, the scheme anticipated a worker-majority representation in the long run.

The second tier of funds was designed with an eye to macroeconomic direction of capital. These funds were to be accumulated from a levy on total wages, not on profits. Their function was to ensure a regional redistribution and coordination of resources for more even economic development; their control was to be through leaders appointed by the unions and government. The Meidner plan, as well as its successor, is predicated on the prior passage of laws granting worker representatives access to company accounts. It also assumes that these representatives will have the skills and expertise necessary for complex financial accounting. Thus, one of the social democrats' last legislative accomplishments before leaving office in 1976 was an act (implemented in 1977) that grants unions almost complete access to company accounts. The Meidner plan contains the additional suggestion that revenues from the wage-earner funds be earmarked for worker education in managerial skills.

Given an annual transfer of 20 percent of profits in the form of stock ownership, it would be only a matter of time before wage earners hold a controlling share of the individual corporations. How rapidly this mechanism of "creeping socialism" works depends on the rate of profitability. Meidner suggests that effective union control of most major companies would be achieved within twenty-five to fifty years (Meidner 1978, 59). This process would certainly accelerate if it were to be decided that the employee funds should invest their capital primarily to boost company profits. Herein lies the brilliance of the Meidner plan. It seems to satisfy two apparently contradictory goals: on one hand, the pursuit of long-range profitability and high investment rates; on the other, a more equitable distribution of wealth, a gradual socialization of ownership, and an extension of worker representation in corporate management. In the short run, the plan would improve the companies' liquidity position and would make more capital available for expansion and technological change. In the long run, employees would exercise majority control and enjoy the rights of ownership.

In contrast to conventional socialization schemes, the Meidner plan contained another element of brilliance. In theory, if not in practice, there is no a priori reason for private stockholders to begin disinvesting should the plan be introduced. The wage-earner funds are designed to expand the companies' equity and to enhance profitability. This would benefit private stockholders; traditional private ownership suffers a setback *only relatively*.

Naturally, the Meidner plan provoked hostility from employers and the three bourgeois parties. Their attack, quite to the point, held that it was a proposal for "creeping socialism"; also, in their view, it violated the liberal tradition of individualism and freedom. Occasionally, there were complaints that economic democracy would destroy political democracy by concentrating too much economic power in the trade unions. On a more practical note, members of the Swedish Employers' Federation and the Association of Industrialists warned that incentives for technological innovation would decline, that the efficiency of the market mechanism would give way to bureaucratic rigidity and bottle-necks, and that, in the long run, Sweden would lose its international competitive edge (Meyerson 1979).

Although the bourgeois countercampaign was more feverish and ideologically sharp than probably at any time since the 1920s, employer organizations and the nonsocialist parties nevertheless sought to meet the challenge with alternative, less dangerous plans. The SAF suggested a variant on the voluntary profit-sharing theme: the employees would hold individual shares in a collectively administered fund and would have the right to cash in their shares after a given number of years. This plan, which may be interpreted as a policy of wage restraint in disguise, does speak to one element in Meidner's formula: namely, the accumulation of savings for investment. But it overlooks the other, more crucial element: the goal of transferring ownership and control to wage earners as a collectivity.

The LO rejects such proposals because they will cement existing inequalities and because they do not further a democratization of economic power. Low-income workers would probably be more tempted to sell their shares than would higher-paid employees; such schemes would increase income differentials among workers or, at any rate, weaken labor's collective solidarity with their stress on voluntarism and individual ownership rights. Yet, opinion polls suggest that individual profit-sharing schemes enjoy quite a favorable response among wage earners, especially among white-collar groups.

The Meidner plan was met with considerable skepticism within the labor movement, too. A major concern was its potential oligarchic consequences, as was the general question of how to ensure a representational system that speaks to growing demands for decentralized participatory democracy. The revised LO-SAP joint proposal for collective wage-earner funds delicately tries to avoid this question by leaving the exact structure of representation open to future debate.[3]

The plan confirms economic democracy's new role for the labor movement. Not only is it presented as the steppingstone for a recapitalization of Sweden's economy, it is also explicitly linked with the social democrats' economic crisis program *Framtid for Sverige* [A Future for Sweden]. The message to the Swedish electorate and to the business community is that labor is fully prepared to acquiesce in substantial reductions of consumption if, in return, it will get legislation on economic democracy. The joint program was first presented to the LO congress and then to the Swedish Social Democratic party congress in September 1981. In both cases it was carried nearly unanimously. On both occasions, the new version was proposed as a crisis measure that simultaneously promised to advance democratic socialism.

The revision deviates from the Meidner plan in several respects. First, the goal of extensive wealth redistribution and workplace democratization is played down in favor of savings and capital investment. Secondly, it is designed explicitly as a quid pro quo. The new proposal does not call for an automatic levy of 20 percent of all profits, but only that portion of profits which are "above average." If enacted, the rate of capital transfer will accordingly be much slower than originally envisaged. However, the crucial element is that the levy on profits will be complemented with a 1 percent deduction from total wages. The latter is admittedly a mechanism for wage restraint. Instead of the earlier firm-based worker funds, the new scheme calls for a more indirect financial arrangement. The transfer from profits and wages will first go to an extraordinary ATP pension fund, which in turn will lend capital to a series of wage-earner investment funds.[4]

This novel and seemingly cumbersome arrangement serves two vital functions. First, it serves to calm the fears of those who believe economic democracy will destroy the equilibrium of the capital market. The wage-earner funds, upon borrowing capital from the ATP fund,

[3] The process of revision included two new reports: *Wage-Earner Funds and Capital Formation* (LO and SAP 1978) and the final proposal, published in spring 1981 (LO and SAP 1981).

[4] These are organized into two national funds and twenty-four regional funds.

are compelled to provide a return on the borrowed capital. Hence, wage-earner fund investments will by necessity have to be profitable. The temptation to sink money into lame ducks in order to save jobs should be substantially reduced. It is also stipulated that the wage-earner funds will purchase stocks in the open stock market.[5] Secondly, the arrangement is designed to bring out a closer connection between collective necessity and individual interest. The idea of linking both the transfer of capital and the return on wage-earner fund investments to the ATP funds is intended to bolster the long-range financial viability of the pension system. Workers' future pensions thus become intimately contingent upon economic democracy.

The new plan was presented as a positive-sum consensual policy: one that would benefit wage earners as well as pensioners, labor as well as capital, democracy as well as the market. Yet, no political allies were readily forthcoming. The three nonsocialist parties all refused to lend their name to it,[6] and its opponents maintained their intense campaign against the proposal through the 1982 elections.

With its election victory in 1982, and VPK parliamentary support, the SAP managed in December 1983 to legislate the funds into existence. But this hardly settles the issue. For one thing, the critical TCO unions remain divided and, to a degree, negative concerning the funds. Moreover, neither the bourgeois parties nor the employers' organizations have resigned themselves to a *fait accompli*. In 1983, a public demonstration of Swedish employers in pin-stripe suits underscored their fervent opposition to any legislation; and the conservatives have promised that, as soon as they return to office, the legislated funds will be swiftly dismantled. The seriousness of the demonstration was left somewhat in doubt as the Stockholm stock exchange continued to boom, but the conservative warning signals a radical break with Swedish democratic tradition; it is the first time since the introduction of full parliamentary democracy that a Swedish party has refused to

[5] But since many Swedish companies are not even listed on the stock market, the plan calls for separate legislation that would compel nonquoted companies to open up for stock purchase.

[6] The social democrats had, for a period, pinned their hopes on a possible agreement with the liberal party, which for years has sponsored profit-sharing plans and has shown some sympathy toward the principle of building up capital funds. The liberals have occupied an electorally central place because of their urban, white-collar base. Tactically, the social democrats could anticipate that the liberals would fear losing white-collar support to a social democratic wage-earner fund proposal, especially if backed by the TCO unions. Yet, the liberals have in past years clearly moved toward an even closer alliance with the other two nonsocialist parties and, with them, have attacked the LO-SAP plan vociferously.

abide by decisions made through parliamentary majorities. The future of the wage-earner funds will therefore have to be tested once again at the 1986 elections.

The Danish Plan

The Danish social democrats were programmatically ahead of their Swedish brethren in respect of economic democracy. This vanguard position, unusual for Danish labor, may ironically be due to its relative lack of power. In the absence of any equivalent to the active labor market policy, the investment reserve bank, or savings accumulation in collective ATP funds, the Danish social democrats were confined to very conventional fiscal and monetary tools for macroeconomic management.

The original Danish proposal for economic democracy was drafted by Viggo Kampmann in close collaboration with the Metalworkers' Federation.[7] Presented to the union congress in 1969, it was approved unanimously. The plan was partly motivated by concerns similar to Meidner's; namely, the desire for a more democratic and socially responsible economy as well as for a more equal distribution of wealth. But Kampmann's main concern was with generating sufficient savings for sustained economic growth and full employment. He explicitly pointed to the chronic savings deficit in the Danish economy, and to the recurrent need for compelling unions to moderate their wage demands, as the plan's overriding priority (Kampmann 1970, 9-17).

Since the Kampmann plan is virtually identical to the Meidner proposal, there is no need to examine it in detail. It rejects voluntary profit-sharing schemes and insists that the wage-earner funds be collective (i.e. with no individual worker rights to the capital or dividends). Also, it suggests that the funds be financed by means of a transfer from company profits and total wages. But even if the Danish and Swedish plans began as very similar entities, their evolutionary paths were quite divergent.

After the Metalworkers' Federation endorsed Kampmann's proposal, it was forwarded to the LO congress for consideration, and then sent to the social democratic party (at the time, out of office). As in Sweden, the employers' organizations countered with proposals

[7] Kampmann was a prominent figure in the Danish Social Democratic party. He served as prime minister during the late 1950s and early 1960s until poor health forced him to resign.

for individual profit sharing. But all three of the Danish left-socialist, or communist, parties attacked it vehemently. The SF dismissed it as a ploy that "gives wage earners a chance to benefit employers with some good advice and economic concessions" (Sørensen 1972, 38). The leftist parties all maintained the traditional call for complete socialization of banks and high finance. The gist of the leftist attack was that economic democracy was little more than a disguised method of compulsory saving; it was, they argued, a regressive incomes policy in which workers were made to forgo wages in return for more investment.

An LO–social democratic commission was formed to prepare a commonly acceptable revision of Kampmann's plan. This revision, presented in 1971, deviates considerably from the principles embodied in the original, and it grants two important concessions to its non-socialist critics. First, it abandons the principle of profit-based transfers in favor of a levy on total wages amounting to 1 percent during the first year and .5 percent during the following eight years. Fund accumulation is to stop after nine years (Sørensen 1972, 54-60). The revision also includes a concession to those who favor a stronger individual attachment to wage-earner fund capital. Although the principle of collective ownership is maintained, individual employees will, at retirement, be paid a dividend.[8]

In light of these revisions, it is clear that the new Danish plan stops short of gradual socialization of capital ownership. Given the imposed ceiling on transfers, the leftist critique that the proposal amounts to little more than a compulsory savings scheme appears to be correct. Yet, if we also consider the social democrats' historical failure to extend public control over the capital market, even this relatively modest funding scheme would imply a decisive break with former economic policy. With some modifications of the details, the revised plan was accepted by the social democratic party in 1972 for future legislative action.

The subsequent politics of Danish economic democracy have been erratic and confusing. In 1973, the social democrats proposed to leg-

[8] The proposed system reflects a strong egalitarian commitment. Irrespective of their previous earnings history, all workers will be granted an identical flat-rate dividend. This principle follows the tradition of the Danish pension system—universal flat-rate pensions that have no relation to previous income. Since the Danish labor movement has been considerably less successful in equalizing market wages through a solidaristic wages policy, the equal flat-rate reimbursement system can be viewed as a special concession to the problems of low-wage workers.

islate the plan in connection with upcoming union-wage settlements. The idea was to ask for LO wage restraint in return for wage-earner funds. But the social democrats faced hostility from virtually all sections of the political spectrum. The left-socialist parties rejected the plan as a "sellout" of the working class; employers' organizations found it unacceptable, as did the nonsocialist parties; large sections of the working class were skeptical of its hidden incomes-policy implications, not to mention the powers it would concentrate at the top of the LO hierarchy. In general, the feeling was that the entire affair was too haphazard. When elections were called in late 1973, the plan was dropped as suddenly as it had emerged. The social democrats revitalized the plan in 1975 as a means of helping the Danish economy out of the deep recession. They were even prepared to compromise further on the principle of collective ownership. This time the unions refused. In 1978 the plan was once again resuscitated when the LO demanded that it be legislated in conjunction with a comprehensive incomes policy package. Although the LO was prepared to tolerate a freeze on wages in return for economic democracy, the initiative failed. The social democrats were at this point in a coalition government with the liberal party, and the government was doomed to fall if economic democracy were seriously proposed for legislation.

The absence of any potential political allies for the LO–social democratic plan, either on the right or the left, compelled the Danish labor movement to reassess its ideas for collective wage-earner funds. Since 1978, it has promoted an entirely redesigned plan. The current proposal—known as the *Overskudsdeling* plan—fuses elements of traditional profit-sharing plans with earlier economic democracy schemes. The motives are familiar: the buildup of collective savings for capital formation, a reduction of economic inequality, and a more democratic form of economic decisionmaking. The new plan suggests a transfer of 10 percent of profits from private-sector firms into collectively administered wage-earner funds. It has abandoned the old idea that the funds be under central LO control. The profit transfer, which would be compulsory, will first go to a central clearing fund, which in turn will make local investments. Employees will locally administer the equity of their collective capital. The fund capital takes the form of shareholdings, mainly in the firms to which individual funds are linked, and each employee—whether in the private sector or the public sector—will have a claim on a share of the equity. Like the previous scheme, the system of shareholding rights is redistributive, since all employees receive identical shares irrespective of their previous earnings or employment record.

The *Overskudsdeling* plan is markedly less centralistic than the previous one in its emphasis on local employee influence. This is unquestionably a concession to repeated critiques from the workers themselves concerning a centralized, LO-controlled fund system. But when the plan was presented to parliament in the spring of 1981—once again in connection with an incomes policy package for wage restraint—it immediately fell.

ECONOMIC DEMOCRACY AND SOCIAL DEMOCRATIC REVITALIZATION

The process of social democratic party decomposition has, we have seen, advanced quite far in Denmark. The Swedish party has experienced a decade of stagnation. With the political need to forge a new, lasting, and broad wage-earner alliance, and with little else to offer as an economic strategy under current economic conditions, the future of social democracy is heavily dependent on the fate of economic democracy.

The question facing social democracy is therefore twofold. First, will it be capable of winning over popular opinion to economic democracy, as opposed to the bourgeois parties' remarketization strategy? Second, can it forge a workable political coalition of white-collar and blue-collar groups behind an economic revitalization based on wage-earner funds?

Analyses of electoral support for collective wage-earner funds must take into consideration the alterations that have been made in the plans over time. One must also keep in mind the different design and content of the Danish and Swedish proposals. We may begin with the mid-1970s. For Denmark, this means support for the LO–social democratic party plan for a centralized system of collective funds financed primarily through the wage bill, giving employees the right to cash in their individual shares after a certain number of years. For Sweden, it means support for Meidner's original plan as it was adopted by the LO congress in 1976. The Swedish electorate will therefore be expressing opinions on a plan that is more "radical" than the Danish scheme.

It is clear from the data that economic democracy through collective wage-earner funds commands only lukewarm support. In Denmark, the situation was particularly bleak for the social democrats, for in

TABLE 9.1. Support for Economic Democracy Legislation in Denmark
by Party Preference and Social Class, 1977
(% favoring)

	No Economic Democracy	Employers' Plan	LO–Social Democratic Plan	N =
PARTY PREFERENCE				
Left Socialists	31	38	31	(81)
Social Democrats	38	39	23	(371)
Bourgeois-Party				
Supporters	65	34	1	(336)
Progressives	65	31	4	(94)
Entire Sample	51	34	15	(1,127)
CLASS POSITION				
Unskilled Workers	44	36	20	(149)
Skilled Workers	43	29	28	(124)
Lower White Collar	56	34	10	(139)
Middle and Higher				
White Collar	35	58	7	(138)

SOURCE: Danish electoral survey, 1977.
NOTE: LO = Landsorganisationen.

no single group is there majority support. In Sweden, there is relatively
strong support among left socialists, SAP voters, and workers; and
some support is even to be found among the critically important white-
collar voters. (See Tables 9.1 and 9.2.) The tabular data are not immediately comparable because the Danish survey invited respondents
to choose from among three alternatives: the LO–social democratic
plan, the employers' proposal for individual profit-sharing schemes,
and no economic democracy at all. Clearly, the largest portion favors
no reform whatsoever, and the employers' plan enjoys more than twice
as much support as the labor movement's plan.

Table 9.1 presents the irony that left socialists are the most favorably
disposed to wage-earner funds, even if these parties do express strong
and persistent critiques of the social democratic proposals. The employers' profit-sharing plan is equally popular across the party spectrum, and is especially favored by the unskilled worker and the middle-
level white-collar employee. This is again puzzling, since one would
expect profit-sharing plans to be least attractive among the lowest-
paid sectors of the working class. The skilled workers, who are a

TABLE 9.2. Support for Economic Democracy Legislation in Sweden
by Party Preference and Social Class, 1976
(%)

	Support	Neutral/No Opinion	Oppose	N =
PARTY PREFERENCE				
Left Socialists	62	19	19	(94)
Social Democrats	57	27	16	(1,063)
Bourgeois-Party Supporters	12	19	69	(1,124)
CLASS POSITION				
Workers	45	28	28	(1,284)
Lower White Collar	31	27	42	(210)
Middle White Collar	29	20	51	(443)
Entire Sample	33	24	43	(2,536)

SOURCE: Swedish electoral Survey, 1976.
NOTE: Due to rounding errors, percentages do not always total 100.

bastion within the LO, are somewhat more keen on wage-earner funds
than the others. But the overall conclusion must be that this economic
democracy plan is vastly unpopular across all classes and parties. Even
if manual workers could be persuaded, it is clear that a white-collar
coalition would not materialize easily.[9]

The findings for Sweden suggest that the SAP also faces considerable
popular opposition to economic democracy—at least as expressed in
the Meidner plan. But in Sweden the distribution of opinion is vastly
different. Among social democrats and left socialists a relatively convincing majority is present; an equally convincing opposition is expressed by bourgeois-party voters. Within the working class, one finds

[9] The debate on economic democracy has stretched over a long period and has been
marked by confusion and pervasive apathy. A poll taken in the Århus municipality
found that only 21 percent of respondents "understood the proposal well" (Buksti et
al. 1978, 9). Gallup polls in 1973 found only 11 percent who would support economic
democracy, and this figure fell to 8 percent in 1975. Unfortunately, the Gallup data
are misleading: respondents were forced to choose between economic democracy and
workplace democracy when, in fact, the plan calls for a combination of both. Another
series of polls, taken by Observa, show substantially higher levels of support which,
furthermore, rose over the years (from 13 percent in 1973 to 29 percent in 1976 and
1977); opposition to the plan declined from 57 percent to 40 percent. The validity of
these data should be superior, since respondents were simply asked to vote for, or
against, the LO–social democratic plan. Clearly, the distribution of popular support
will vary considerably, depending on how the questions are worded and how alternatives
are presented.

less than majority support and many undecideds, and the level of support drops even further among the white-collar strata. Assuming the possibility of winning over many of the undecided voters, however, a wage-earner majority is not an unrealistic goal. Still, that mobilization would have to be substantial.

In both countries, the wage-earner plans originated within the LO, and one would naturally expect that the trade unions would be a crucial center of mobilization. Do the data suggest that these powerful union organizations might be capable of solidifying member support? Among manual worker trade unionists, the level of support for wage-earner funds is virtually identical to that among manual workers generally. Since almost all workers are unionized, this is to be expected. White-collar unionism seems more decisive. In Denmark this does seem to make a difference, since unionized white-collar employees are twice as likely (21 percent) as white-collar employees in general to favor economic democracy. In Sweden, it makes no difference (again, virtually all white-collar employees are organized under the TCO).

Generational differences may prove to be the most decisive factor in the long run. First of all, if we consider economic democracy to be the cornerstone of the future social democratic realignment, then the movement will have to count on the enthusiasm of the young. Secondly, since recent social democratic losses have been acute among the younger cohorts—especially among the newly entering voters— economic democracy must be considered the centerpiece of social democratic remobilization of the young.

In Denmark, there is no generational effect on support for economic democracy. Younger voters are no more likely to support (or oppose) it than older voters.[10] In Sweden, the situation is different. Among the youngest voters, 40.4 percent favor economic democracy, and the level of support decreases linearly as age increases. Among the oldest group (sixty-five and older), support drops to 29.6 percent. Interestingly, such age differences disappear among manual workers (44.4 and 42.1 percent, respectively), but are present among lower-level white-collar employees (40.4 percent among those eighteen to twenty-four years

---

[10] In an earlier study (Esping-Andersen 1981a), regressing support for economic democracy on social class (manual/nonmanual), age, union membership, and size of workplace, I found that only class was significantly related. Voters' positions on welfare spending and investment controls ($R = -.153$ and $.171$, with $F = 8.10$ and 9.03, respectively) were considerably more important when controlling for class ($R = -.146$, $F = 6.63$).

old, 31.7 percent among those twenty-five to thirty-four, and 34.3 percent among those thirty-five to sixty-four).[11]

So far, one would have to conclude that the economic democracy plan in Denmark would fail to perform its desired function of re-mobilizing the electorate around a realigned social democratic program. After 1978, however, the Danish LO and Social Democratic party launched the entirely new plan for collective wage-earner-based profit sharing, a plan that is markedly less centralistic but retains the elements of capital formation, redistribution, and individual entitlements.

Having abandoned the oligarchic features of the old scheme, the recent one ought to attract broader citizen support. One would also anticipate that the deep economic recession will induce greater concern for capital formation. According to recent survey data, it appears that economic democracy has indeed become more popular. In one study (Buksti et al. 1981), 40 percent of the population support its ideas while 25 percent oppose; the "don't knows" remain numerous. This same survey suggests that the new plan is popular among leftists (71 percent in favor), social democrats (51 percent in favor), and supporters of centrist parties (close to 50 percent in favor). However, the study is marred because it does not directly pose the question of whether one favors or opposes the plan.[12]

The 1981 Danish electoral survey is a more appropriate starting point for an assessment of electoral shifts, even if the question formulation is again unfortunate.[13] At any rate, aggregate support for economic democracy has risen dramatically between 1977 and 1981. If we exclude the "don't knows" (32 percent of the sample), 39.4 percent say that they favor economic democracy, with or without the controversial central fund, and 60.6 percent oppose it. Among workers, 43 percent agree; among the white-collar strata, 44 percent. The new proposal, therefore, does seem to contain the seeds of a wage-

[11] The percentage is zero among those sixty-five and older, but the sample is too small (N = 8).

[12] Instead, the study asks a battery of questions that address the essential principles behind the new plan, and then adds up the pros and cons. This may have been done in order to avoid provoking negative responses simply by virtue of the bad name that "economic democracy" has acquired. In any event, the absence of a direct question means that these data cannot be compared with those of other studies.

[13] Respondents could chose between "don't know," "reject the plan," or "support the plan, with or without central funds." Because the central fund principle was included in the wording of the question, there can be little doubt that it generated confusion, since the new plan explicitly rejects a central fund.

earner coalition. When one examines level of support by party preference, the terrain has again shifted. There is a 58 percent majority in favor among left socialists; among social democrats, a 57 percent majority. In contrast, bourgeois-party supporters score 73 percent *against* the plan. In brief, whether because of the new plan or altered economic circumstances, the attitudinal profile has undergone a dramatic shift. Pervasive indifference or hostility in all sections of Danish society has given way to a more polarized climate in which the socialist bloc stands in confrontation against the bourgeois parties. At the same time, however, this is a climate in which all wage-earner categories present similar preferences. It is therefore not wrong to speculate that economic democracy may help bridge the divisions that wreaked havoc on Danish politics in general, and social democracy in particular, during the 1970s.

The Danish data for 1981 are surprisingly similar to those for Sweden in 1976. Unfortunately, there are no data for Sweden recent enough to gauge public opinion after the introduction of the new proposal in 1981 and, what is more important, after the SAP's victory in the recent election. According to Holmberg's data (1981, table 12.7) for 1979, there was a slight drop in support between 1976 and 1979. Though the opinion balance declined from −9 to −13, this shift conceals a polarizing trend. Support actually grew among social democrats (from +38 in 1976 to +43 in 1979), while declining more sharply among bourgeois voters. Since the wage-earner funds issue once again dominated the 1982 election (which nevertheless produced considerable social democratic gains) there is reason to expect that the concept has increased in popularity.

CONCLUSIONS

The social democratic parties have been forced to pin their hopes on economic democracy for a set of interlocked reasons. First of all, it is the only existing plan that permits labor to escape from the economic dilemma in which it finds itself. Given the international economy, a resumption of domestic economic growth with full employment would have to demand considerable wage sacrifices from the trade unions. Not only is it extraordinarily difficult for social democratic governments repeatedly to demand union wage restraint, but the problem becomes almost unbearable if wage concessions are not shouldered equally among the population, especially if the resulting higher profits are not invested in new production and jobs. Since economic democracy grants employees a share of the profits they produce, gives them leverage over investments, and also imposes the burden of wage restraint in a solidaristic way, it offers an acceptable alternative to the status quo as well as to the conservatives' neoliberal version of economic policy.

The second reason is of a more ideological and programmatic nature. Everyone, the social democratic leadership included, would agree that social democracy can no longer draw support on the basis of its postwar "Keynes plus Beveridge" program. Not only have such policies become practically incompatible with the new realities of the 1970s, but they also fail to address the kinds of issues that resonate with the new electorate: equality, restored full employment, improvements in work life, employee participation in the economy, less bureaucracy, and more balanced development. Even if it evidently cannot speak to all such desires, economic democracy is at present the only realistic centerpiece around which a programmatic renewal can be built.

The third reason has to do with the class basis upon which a social democratic realignment must be formed. The old rural alliance has de facto been dead for many years, and social democracy would have everything to lose and nothing to gain by reverting to a strictly working-class-based politics. Class politics in the orthodox sense would seal the fate of socialism forever: manual workers are diminishing in number, and the white-collar strata persistently refuse to slide into the ranks of proletarian unity. Thus, social democracy must forge a program that can unite these classes. Because economic democracy speaks to their shared desire for full employment, improvements in work life, and employee participation, and because it does not directly demand a narrowing of earnings and income differentials between salaried employees and workers, economic democracy may well hold such promise.

Survey data obviously cannot tell us whether economic democracy will become the catalyst for political realignment. Yet, if we examine the trends in electoral preference, there are some indications that it may. Granted that enthusiastic majorities are far from being present, we nevertheless have to note that support, in Denmark at least, is growing and that a manual-nonmanual labor alliance does seem within reach. What seems certain is that the issue is pushing politics back to the traditional left-right axis. If, as it seems, broad sections among the white-collar strata can be swayed toward the left on this issue, the process of social democratic party decomposition may be arrested. There is, in any case, no indication that economic democracy fuels decomposition.

311

Social democracy offers to the world one of the most durable and successful labor movements ever, and Scandinavian social democracy stands as the international model. Close scrutiny of why Scandinavian social democracy originally succeeded to such a degree, why it managed to consolidate political hegemony, and also why its fate has come to diverge fundamentally in the three Nordic nations should tell us why social democracy—or its equivalent—has failed to implant itself similarly in other nations. Moreover, when we acknowledge that Scandinavia presents social democracy in its "purest" form, we are perhaps better equipped also to distill its essence and emerge with a theory that is applicable to the multitude of "less pure" cases.

My intention has been to offer a theoretical reinterpretation of the conditions that make for a successful social democratic road to power. As discussed in Chapter 1, our understanding of the phenomenon has been guided primarily by the traditional debates that took place within Marxist socialism during the early decades of this century. According to one orthodox interpretation, exemplified most clearly in Kautskyanism and Leninist Marxism, the process of proletarianization and class structural change endemic to capitalist societies constitutes the prime mover of socialist ascendance. Revisionist Marxism, followed by postwar pluralist social science, rejected class polarization as a causal force. Instead, the process of social differentiation would eventually push socialist movements in the direction of "end of ideology."

Neither position appears to be fully satisfactory as an interpretation. Orthodox Marxism clearly overstates class development as a historically autonomous force. Yet, to abandon an emphasis on class mobilization and class formation is to throw out the baby with the bath water. The second great failure among extant studies, is their disregard for the dialectics that are set in motion once socialist parties gain access to state power and implant, however successfully, their reforms and policies. If democratic socialist parties choose a strategy for mobilization that relies on policies, then we must study their capacity in that context. The reinterpretation of social democracy offered in this book, therefore, has argued that the conditions for class alliances, combined with the effects of state policies on class formation, are the most important factors for social democratic success and failure. In order to explain how these two forces have interacted to produce social democratic ascendance and, especially in the case of Denmark, decomposition, we have been forced to direct our attention back to historical circumstances that surrounded early industrialization and the struggles over democratization of the state.

The first conclusion of this study is, accordingly, that the historical position of farmers and the peasantry has been of incomparable importance for labor movement development. To put it as strongly as possible, social democratic ascendance would have been difficult—if not impossible—had it not been for the democratic impulse that originated from a politically articulate, organized peasantry during the nineteenth-century battle for political democracy and parliamentarism. This helped set the stage for the really crucial precondition of social democracy—namely, the capacity for realignment during the interwar era. That realignment required a coalition between peasants and the working class, and it made possible the package of reform policies upon which social democratic power in the postwar era has been based. The nature and institutional content of these reform policies, moreover, have been decisive. For with these policies it was possible to construct a new world of social solidarity and political efficacy among the electorate that would help sustain the social democratic "project."

Just as the peasantry helped decide the initial fortunes of social democracy, the rising new middle strata of white-collar and technical employees now occupy center stage and will determine whether social democracy can renew itself for a new era of mobilization and power. The realignment for a broad wage-earner alliance, however, is decisively conditioned by social democracy's previous political accomplishments, by its ability to sever its ties with the traditional farmer coalition, and by its competence at constructing a new policy package on which a wage-earner coalition can be built. In summary, the fate of social democracy hinges on the interaction between class alliances and political reforms. Let us now briefly survey how these basic forces have operated in the evolution of the social democratic parties.

TEN

Preconditions and Conditions
for Social Democracy

THE PROCESS of industrialization and democratization was less turbulent in Scandinavia than it was in many other places. But this alone cannot account for the relative ease with which social democracy came to prominence in the Nordic countries, for the same could be said for the Netherlands, Great Britain, and the United States, not to mention Switzerland. A historical comparison of the Scandinavian nations, moreover, brings to light sharp differences with respect to the period of early capitalism, the attainment of parliamentary democracy, and the early stature of the labor movements. In all three countries, there is little doubt that peasants and farmers played a central role in securing an easy transition to democracy and in guaranteeing its permanence. Their political independence and self-articulated demands on the state helped ensure perennial conflicts and antagonisms within the bourgeois bloc that, in turn, made reactionary political coalitions unlikely at the same time that they made progressive, populist coalitions between labor and peasants possible. Furthermore, being both independently organized and politically astute, the Scandinavian peasantry was a far cry from the "sack of potatoes" to which Marx had likened the French peasantry.

Scandinanvian farmers and peasants could join forces with embryonic working-class movements in the early struggles against the conservatives, the aristocracy, and the bourgeoisie. This contrasts sharply with the situation elsewhere in Europe, where labor movements remained isolated political ghettoes of the working class, as well as with developments in Russia. Granted, Russian peasants and workers did join hands in the 1917 revolution, but the peasants were indeed a "sack of potatoes."

Clearly, though, the position of the Scandinavian peasantry during the nineteenth-century struggles for democracy could not, by itself, guarantee social democratic ascendance. The two class movements may have found common ground in the quest for universal and equal suffrage but, as subsequent events showed, there was little else that fundamentally united them. Farmers saw organized labor as a threat, especially where farming depended on rural wage labor; the working class naturally opposed high food prices.

The Nordic countries continued to exhibit a unique political constellation after the attainment of democracy. The farmers developed independent parties—in Denmark, two—whose political agendas were as frequently in opposition to the conservatives as they were to the socialists. Castles (1978) is therefore correct when he emphasizes the lack of bourgeois unity to explain why social democracy has been so unusually successful in Scandinavia. This meant that the socialist parties could not be isolated and crushed. Even the revolutionary DNA of Norway was permitted to operate without repressive incursions; indeed, the DNA was asked to form a government in 1927.

The turning point came with the Great Depression. Despite the optimistic predictions of Kautskyanism, there developed no proletarian force that socialist parties could rely upon to furnish the desired absolute parliamentary majority for state power. Left to run its course, moreover, the economic crisis was clearly weakening working-class unity and the socialist cause, Leninist theory notwithstanding. The precondition for a social democratic realignment was therefore the presence of a political ally; electorally as well as in terms of influence, the peasantry held the key.

The roots of the social democratic realignment of the 1930s cannot be found in the independent actions of the labor movements—whether they "opportunistically" betrayed the proletarian cause, embraced "social fascism," or they clung faithfully to the correct revolutionary line. If this were so, how would we explain the dramatic convergence among the Nordic social democrats in the 1930s? The three Scandinavian labor parties could hardly have been more divergent than they were during the 1920s. Their realignment around the "people's home" model in the 1930s could occur because the political state of the peasantry permitted it; this was not the case in most European nations at the time. In Germany, where the outcome was exceptionally dramatic, the SPD was just as committed to parliamentarism and reformism as its Scandinavian sister parties; and the party itself was probably even stronger. The conditions for a laborer-farmer coalition, however, were completely absent.[1]

[1] Paradoxically, the United States exhibited one of the closest parallels to the Scandinavian laborer-farmer alliance when, in the formation of Roosevelt's New Deal realignment, the Democratic party succeeded in building the North-South, working-class–farmer alliance. Yet, in the United States, unlike Scandinavia, neither labor nor the farmers championed autonomous and independent political organizations with sufficient force to manufacture the alliance independently. Instead, it was, so to speak, manu-

If, then, the peasantry held the key to the social democratic realignment of the 1930s, the next question is how social democracy could construct a viable political program based on the new political coalition. In strategic terms, socialist mobilization could no longer proceed (if ever it could) on orthodox Kautskyan foundations, which included prohibitions against participation in nonsocialist coalitions or minority governments. Ideologically the social democrats were compelled to define their historical task and responsibilities as an affair of "the people," not of the proletariat alone.

The long-term issue, however, was the packaging of a durable and viable policy formula that could genuinely synthesize the conflicting interests of farmers and workers. What, in terms of reformist policy, has now become virtually synonymous with social democracy constitutes precisely this kind of robust synthesis. Full-employment Keynesianism and welfare-statism could be made acceptable to farmers once it was recognized that working-class purchasing power is good for farm incomes. A commitment to income redistribution—especially to farmers—became the cornerstone of the realignment. The Keynesian welfare state model of social democracy could transform politics into a positive-sum affair because, from the perspective of the socialists, it promised to strengthen the cause of working-class political mobilization and shift the balance of power in their favor. And, for the peasantry, it prolonged the economic viability of farming and promised higher incomes. Hence, to the extent that the realignment genuinely secured positive-sum class politics, the electoral dilemma of socialism, as described by Przworski, would not necessarily assert itself. In Scandinavia, it certainly did not. Through realignment, the social democratic parties succeeded in weakening their left-socialist and communist opposition.

⌐The Heightened Importance of Politics

It is likely that Scandinavian social democracy, like that of Germany, would have decomposed in the 1930s had it not been for the farmer-based alliance and the full-employment, welfare state policy realignment. But, once in place, the new "people's home" formula became the basis of continued social democratic power. A commitment to Keynesian-style welfare state politics is surely not a sufficient precon-

factured on their behalf by the key political brokers of the New Deal. A scholarly comparison of the American New Deal with the Scandinavian realignment has yet to be undertaken.

dition for sustained political mobilization, as the cases of Britain and post-1969 Germany, for example, illustrate. A large variety of policies can be, and have been, launched in the name of Keynes or under the rhetoric of welfare and social progress. It is in this context that the institutional content and social structural repercussions of social democratic reforms come to be decisive. Social democratic class formation becomes increasingly mediated by state policies.

In ideology as well as strategic practice, the full-employment welfare state must be premised on a reversal of the steps undertaken to achieve the Good Society. Social citizenship, it must be convincingly argued, should precede economic citizenship; socialist reforms must be assumed to have the capacity to alter the existing capitalist social structure in a way that is advantageous, both for the immediate living conditions of the individual and for the long-term social democratic capacity to sustain and broaden its following.

Throughout this book, analyses of social and economic policymaking have served to identify the conditions under which particular reforms help generate decomposing tendencies in social democracy as well as the conditions under which they may enhance social democratic power. The basic criterion, I have argued, is whether reforms consistently have the capacity to breed a broader, stronger, and even politically hegemonic unity and solidarity. That is why social democratic welfare state reforms must embark upon a gradual marginalization of pure market relations in the satisfaction of citizens' living standards; decommodification is a prerequisite to reducing the natural compulsion of wage earners to compete.

It is also why social programs have to strive for universality in terms of financial responsibilities as well as benefits. Where social democracy expands the role of the state in civil society in order to obtain its objectives, policies that divide or compartmentalize the population will help generate politicization and conflict against the state and, consequently, against social democracy. Furthermore, as the importance of the state grows, its intervention in society will increasingly affect social stratification. Selective policies will easily result in the superimposition of new social cleavages, while universalist policies should help to narrow traditional cleavages. Economic and labor market policies follow the same political logic. Sustained full employment is the single most important means of preventing dualism and fundamental cleavages among wage earners; it is the ultimate precondition for trade union strength and labor movement unity.

The direct influence of social democratic reforms on party decomposition is most evident by far in Denmark, where several key reforms have succeeded in establishing powerful new divisions among the electorate, primarily with respect to old-age pensions, housing, and left-right polarization of wage earners. Consequently, the reforms have promoted the erosion of Danish social democracy itself. In this respect, the Norwegian and the Swedish social democratic parties have both managed to construct a substantially stronger and universally shared consensus. As shown in Chapter 8, the correlations between voter behavior and voter perceptions of social democratic policies confirm this line of argument. Even though it would have been desirable to have had empirical data that addressed my hypotheses more directly, it does seem clear that the differential impact of welfare reforms in the Nordic countries has been powerful in sustaining or eroding political loyalties. In terms of economic policy, it also seems quite evident that the modest capacity of Danish social democracy to live up to the promise of full employment, coupled with its chronic inability to gain control over economic development, has contributed to an accelerating decomposition.

Yet, even if we conclude that Swedish social democratic reforms have been more successful in securing continued party power and mobilization, we find that as Scandinavian social democracy entered the 1970s, stagnation and decompositional symptoms appeared in all three countries. Social democracy seems, at best, exhausted; at worst, dying. If we are to explain this new order, if we are to isolate the conditions required for the revitalization of social democracy, then we must turn our attention once again to the social structural change and the importance of class coalitions for the social democratic road to power.

FROM PEOPLE'S PARTY TO
WAGE-EARNER PARTY

Since reforms have played such a decisive role in determining the fortunes of the Nordic social democratic parties in the postwar era, we must confront an obvious question. Why has social democratic reformism had such disparate results? In particular, how do we explain the Danish social democrats' especially dismal performance?

We can immediately discard the argument that the Danish social democrats, unlike their Norwegian or Swedish brethren, exemplify a more cautious and less ambitious party, a party whose dedication to fundamental transformation is somewhat lacking. The Danish social democrats have repeatedly attempted to follow virtually the same reformist agenda that the Swedes have promoted. The Danish Social

Democratic party, however, has been electorally weaker than the other two throughout the entire postwar era. Moreover, class relations in Denmark developed in such a way that the influence of farmers as well as the traditional urban petite bourgeoisie subsided much later than it did in Sweden. In short, Danish social democratic reformism has been perennially constrained by a need to compromise with the bourgeois parties.

In this, the Danish case dramatically illustrates what can be identified as the essential underlying condition for social democratic renewal in general—namely, a capacity to realign by breaking with the historical farmer coalition and forging a new wage-earner coalition between the rising middle strata (bureaucrats, technicians, and intellectuals), on one hand, and the traditional working class, on the other. This re-alignment is not conditioned merely by the emergence of white-collar employees as the dominant group. Equally important—if not more so—is the social democrats' capacity to recast their political agenda and formulate a new policy package that has the quality of trans-forming zero-sum conflicts into a positive-sum synthesis of wage-earner demands.

It is in the process of class realignment that the variable fate of Scandinavian social democracy must ultimately be explained. We can see that the conditions for this essential realignment were considerably more present in Sweden than elsewhere. For one thing, class structural development in Sweden procceded very rapidly during the 1940s and 1950s, peaking in the 1960s. The role of the small peasants and larger farmers declined decisively during the 1950s, while that of the white-collar strata grew rapidly. At a very early date, therefore, the SAP was forced to—and could also afford to—provoke a political break with its former allies. This break, furthermore, occurred in a context of conflict over ATP pension reform—a proposal that held unique prom-ise for mobilizing manual workers as well as white-collar employees. The SAP victory on this policy question helped reverse the party's declining position, and it permitted the party to enter a new era of political and ideological radicalism as well as electoral success. The electoral survey data indicate that the SAP succeeded in mobilizing white-collar voters in a positive fashion; that is, without simultane-ously losing support among its traditional working-class base.

While the Swedish social democrats blossomed during the 1960s, the Norwegians and especially the Danes entered an era of stagnation and decay. The conditions for realignment were not similarly present in either of these countries, though for different reasons. Alliance with the peasantry had permitted the DNA much greater scope for far-reaching social and economic reform than the Danish party had been afforded. The Norwegian peasantry never commanded the degree of economic and social power that has characterized their Danish brethren; considerably more "proletarianized," the Norwegian peasantry could to a greater degree be counted upon to support the same sort of policies that the urban working classes favored. At the same time, the persistent cultural and political influence of localism and regionalism meant that the DNA was prohibited from shifting its allegiance away from traditional allies. Furthermore, it is significant that the Norwegian equivalent of the ATP reform was introduced by a bourgeois government in the late 1960s, and that overall the policies of the bourgeois parties hardly diverged from those of the DNA. In Norway, unlike Sweden, the social democrats were locked into a continuation of the traditional class alliance and were unable to create a new policy profile that would move it decisively toward a wage-earner alliance. Thus, stranded between its declining class allies on the periphery and the rising white-collar strata in the cities, the party appears increasingly unable to act decisively in any direction.

While the Norwegian party commanded broad consensus on its social policies as well as, until the 1970s, its economic policies, decomposition began over the issue of Common Market entry. Subsequently, owing to drastic incomes settlements and a resolve to maintain full employment by means of objectionable policies, party decomposition continued. The incomes settlements of 1973 and 1976, one may hypothesize, had particularly powerful decompositional effects—further trapping the party in the old coalition with the peasantry while alienating white-collar voters on the longstanding issue of income redistribution. When, in addition, the bourgeois parties successfully attacked the DNA's unproductive and expensive subsidization policies, the conditions for a realignment with white-collar employees were destroyed.

In Denmark, the conditions that could have allowed a realignment were notably lacking. First of all, both the rural and the urban petite bourgeoisie were much slower to decline than in Sweden. Furthermore, their political and economic influence continued to be far greater than elsewhere. Until the 1960s, Danish agriculture remained the dominant element in the economy and could, even in the 1970s, compel entry into the EEC. Also, the craft-dominated nature of urban enterprise meant that large sections of the working class were wedded to the economic interests of the petite bourgeoisie. These circumstances help explain why the Danish social democratic performance throughout the 1950s was so mediocre, why no significant social reforms could be undertaken until the 1960s, why the party was chronically frustrated in its attempts to enhance public control over economic performance, and why Danish social democratic reformism ultimately had the decompositional effects it did.

The political necessity of adhering to the bourgeois parties was perhaps most evident in the catastrophic housing reform of the 1960s, but it could also be seen in the aborted attempt to parallel the Swedish realignment with an ATP-style reform. Overall, the Danish social democrats were forced to acquiesce in compromises that had the effect of dividing the same electorate that it relies upon for political power. Structural divisions were established between renters and homeowners, between productive workers and welfare state clients, and between different kinds of pensioners. The political fragmentation of the electorate translated into intractable equity conflicts and eroding support for the welfare state in general and the social democratic party in particular. The result was evident not only in the internationally unparalleled tax revolt that exploded in 1973, but also in social democracy's inability to stem the rise of a large left-socialist opposition (supported primarily by the very same white-collar elements upon which a social democratic renewal would have to be based).

Even if an initial attempt at class realignment was undertaken by the Swedish social democrats in the 1960s, it was clearly not founded on a sufficiently strong and persuasive policy base. The SAP, in the late 1960s and early 1970s, began to build a new policy profile for the future, but clearly fell short. The workplace democratization reforms can be viewed as one element, but the advent of economic stagnation helped expose two decisive shortcomings. One was the conflict between salaried employees and manual workers over income distribution and tax equity in the financing of the full-employment welfare state. The other was the inappropriateness of the SAP's existing battery of economic policies for dealing with the new economic realities. It was, undoubtedly, very fortunate for the SAP that it was forced into opposition exactly when its political capacity to manage the economy had been exhausted. While the party clearly slipped into negative-sum electoral dilemmas—the SAP began to lose support among its core working-class constituency—it nonetheless managed to stem the tide as the bourgeois parties assumed office.

Toward a Social Democratic Renewal?

We may conclude that Scandinavian social democracy has entered a new stage. Today, the movement's traditional policies and coalitions are not only exhausted, but they actually thwart the parties' likelihood of regaining power. The present era can be viewed as a historical crossroads similar to that of the 1930s. If the peasantry then held the key to the social democratic future, today the white-collar strata occupy that position. Consequently, the question is how a new wage-earner alliance can be forged?

A first attempt to answer this question must be directed at the class character of the new middle strata. Classical Marxist theory generally assumed that, except for a limited stratum of top-level salaried positions, the historical trend would proletarianize and hence universalize conditions among wage earners. By and large, events have proved this theory false. In some cases, it is true, large numbers of white-collar employees increasingly exhibit collectivist tendencies parallel to those of traditional workers, and the boundaries between routine clerical workers and manual workers are indeed blurred. Nevertheless, there is no doubt that a) the white-collar strata are extraordinarily differentiated, and b) such issues as income distribution and earnings differentials constitute fundamental lines of conflict between salaried employees and manual labor. In short, it seems quite inconceivable that all wage-earner strata are moving in the direction of a massive convergence of interests.

If I am correct in assuming that fundamental class-interest differences will continue to mark relations between manual workers and white-collar employees, then the Kautskyan formula for social democratic class formation remains as obsolete today as it was fifty years ago. White-collar employees will not automatically embrace working-class platforms. On the other hand, Przworski's pessimistic scenario may be equally wrong. True, the social democrats' future must depend on some kind of alliance with the salaried strata, but this does not necessarily mean that the social democratic project will die. The fundamental question that social democracy faces today has to do with what political package will permit a new positive-sum coalition.

This book has brought to light a number of tentative answers to this question. The first refers back to the legacy of previous social democratic reforms. The chances of building a durable wage-earner alliance are substantively curtailed wherever previous reforms have fragmented and divided the electorate in bitter equity struggles over state policies. One reason why a social democratic renewal seems so much more likely in Sweden is that each of the SAP's vast array of reforms has been uniquely tailored to attract broad, if not universal, approval.

The second answer will undoubtedly prompt considerable dismay among those who believe that egalitarianism is the very essence of socialism. From all available evidence, it seems exceedingly clear that a continued socialist commitment to effective income redistribution will alienate white-collar strata and thus block any chance of a broad wage-earner alliance. That this is a crucial issue seems evident for all three countries. In Norway, the DNA's commitment to massive redistribution—either through sharply progressive taxes, as in the 1950s and 1960s, or through incomes policy settlements, as in the 1970s—has repelled white-collar groups from the social democratic camp and, in recent years, pushed them toward the conservative party. In Denmark, social democratic policy has not been so aggressively committed to income redistribution and narrowed earnings differentials, but the party's successful attempts in the 1970s to reduce the earnings and privileges of public-sector employees may help explain why that stratum has turned away from social democracy in recent years—despite the fact that social democratic government is the single best guarantee of public-sector job security. In Sweden, the story appears much the same. In the late 1970s and early 1980s, the SAP was compelled to participate in reforms that essentially rendered taxes less progressive. The emergence of "leapfrogging" and the erosion of coordinated, solidaristic wage bargaining in recent years is symptomatic of the limits of an aggressive redistributive agenda.

The problem of income equality and redistribution poses a severe dilemma for social democracy—not merely because these constitute a core element of socialist ideology, but primarily because powerful labor organizations (unskilled unions especially) insist on equalization. It is tempting to conclude that unless social democracy abandons this classical goal, its chances of political resurgence will be slim. However, the third answer may provide a way out of this political dilemma.

A recast social democratic economic policy must necessarily form the centerpiece of the new realignment. Almost all categories of wage earners have in common a fundamental interest in sustained full employment, wage growth, and improved working conditions (including a general democratization of economic relations). One area in which the objective positions of manual workers and salaried employees have clearly converged is the issue of job security and the desire for an improved work life. As shown in Chapter 9, the balance of class power is such that some form of economic democracy through collective wage-earner funds appears to be the only plausible policy alternative to traditional welfare-statism. Whether or not the socialization of capital and investments has ideological appeal among the electorate is of secondary importance. The crucial point, as electoral survey data show, is that wage earners exert a very powerful demand for greater public control of economic development, both to ensure sustained full employment and to enhance the position of wage earners vis-à-vis employers.

Economic democracy, then, in whatever form it might eventually take, will have to be the cornerstone for a broad wage-earner alliance. And, to return to the dilemma of equality, social democracy's traditional working-class clientele—the unions especially—will have to accept the sort of equality that economic democracy entails instead of the more conventional desire for income equalization among wage earners. Whether or not the economic democracy plan can perform the task of uniting wage earners, and thus return social democracy to a new era of positive-sum politics, remains to be seen. It seems clear, though, that without this type of reform program, the trend toward social democratic party decomposition will continue.

Election Results in
the Nordic Countries

TABLE A.1. Party Vote in Danish National Elections, 1920-1981
(% of electorate)

	Left Socialists[a]	Social Democrats	Center Parties[b]	Bourgeois Parties[c]	Turnout[d]
1920	.4	32.2	12.1	53.9	(77.0)
1924	.5	36.6	14.0	47.2	(78.6)
1926	.4	37.2	12.6	48.4	(77.0)
1929	.3	41.1	12.5	44.8	(79.7)
1932	1.1	42.7	12.1	43.4	(81.5)
1935	1.6	46.1	11.7	35.6	(80.7)
1939	2.4	42.9	11.5	36.0	(79.2)
1943	—	44.5	10.3	39.7	(89.5)
1945	12.5	32.8	10.1	41.6	(86.3)
1947	6.8	40.0	11.4	40.0	(85.8)
1950	4.6	39.6	16.4	39.1	(81.9)
1953	4.3	41.3	11.3	39.9	(80.6)
1957	3.1	39.4	13.1	41.7	(83.7)
1960	7.2	42.1	8.0	39.0	(85.8)
1964	7.0	41.9	6.6	40.9	(85.5)
1966	11.7	38.2	10.5	39.0	(88.6)
1968	9.1	34.2	17.0	39.0	(89.3)
1971	12.1	37.3	16.1	32.3	(87.2)
1973	11.1	25.6	16.1	54.0	(89.0)
1975	11.3	29.9	25.9	42.4	(88.2)
1977	10.3	37.0	16.4	35.1	(88.6)
1979	11.5	38.3	13.8	36.0	(85.6)
1981	15.1	32.9	18.2	34.7	(83.2)

SOURCES: Mackie and Rose (1974a, 1974b, 1976, 1978, 1980, 1982).

NOTE: Percentages do not add up to 100 because insignificantly small parties have been excluded.

[a] Left-socialist parties include only the Danish Communist party (DKP) until 1960; thereafter, also the Danish Socialist People's party (SF) and, after 1968, the Danish Left-Socialist party (VS).

[b] Center parties include only the Danish Radical Liberals (RV) and the Danish Justice party (Retsforbundet) until 1971; thereafter, also the Danish Christian People's party (KF) and, after 1973, the Danish Center Democratic party (CD), which was a splinter from the Danish Social Democratic party.

[c] The bourgeois parties include the Danish Conservative party and the Danish Liberal party (Venstre). Note that, after 1973, the Danish Progress party (Fremskridts partiet) is included with the bourgeois-party votes.

[d] As a percentage of total eligible voters.

TABLE A.2. Party Vote in Norwegian National Elections, 1921-1981
(% of electorate)

	Left Socialists[a]	Social Democrats[b]	Center Parties[c]	Conservative Parties[d]	Turnout[e]
1921	—	30.5	35.7	33.3	(67.9)
1924	6.1	27.2	33.9	32.5	(69.9)
1927	4.0	36.8	33.4	25.4	(68.1)
1930	1.7	31.4	36.9	30.0	(77.6)
1933	1.8	40.1	32.3	21.8	(76.4)
1936	.3	42.5	29.2	22.6	(84.0)
1945	11.9	41.0	29.7	17.0	(76.4)
1949	5.8	45.7	31.8	15.9	(82.0)
1953	5.1	46.7	29.8	18.4	(79.3)
1957	3.4	48.3	31.3	16.8	(78.3)
1961	5.3	46.8	28.5	19.3	(79.1)
1965	7.4	43.1	29.2	20.3	(85.4)
1969	4.4	46.5	30.0	18.8	(83.8)
1973	11.2	35.3	30.4	22.2	(80.2)
1977	4.6	42.3	26.0	26.4	(82.9)
1981	5.2	37.2	19.9	36.2	(82.0)

SOURCES: Mackie and Rose (1974a, 1974b, 1978, 1982).

NOTE: Percentages do not add up to 100 because insignificantly small parties have been excluded.

[a] Left-socialist parties include the Norwegian Communist party and, after 1961, also the Norwegian Socialist People's party. In 1973, these were merged into the Socialist Election Alliance (SV). In 1975 a new party, the Norwegian Left-Socialist party (SV) took the place of the previous alliance, but excluded the communists.

[b] The Norwegian Labor party (DNA); in 1921 and 1924 also includes the Social Democratic Workers' party. The two were united in 1927.

[c] Includes the liberals, the Norwegian Farmers' party (renamed the Norwegian Center party in 1959), the Norwegian Radical People's party (1921-1936), the Norwegian Christian People's party (after 1933), and the Joint Nonsocialist Election Alliance (after 1949). After 1973, also includes the New Liberal People's party.

[d] Includes the Norwegian Conservative party (Højre) and, until 1936, the Norwegian National Liberal Party. After 1973, also includes the Anders Langes party (renamed the Norwegian Progress party in 1977).

[e] As a percentage of total eligible voters.

APPENDIX

TABLE A.3. Party Vote in Swedish National Elections, 1920-1982
(% of electorate)

	Left Socialists[a]	Social Democrats	Center Parties[b]	Conservative Party	Turnout[c]
1920	6.4	36.1	36.0	27.9	(55.3)
1921	7.8	39.4	30.2	25.8	(54.2)
1924	5.1	41.1	27.7	26.1	(53.0)
1928	6.4	37.0	27.1	29.4	(67.4)
1932	8.3	41.7	25.8	23.5	(68.6)
1936	7.7	45.9	27.2	17.6	(74.5)
1940	4.2	53.8	24.0	18.0	(70.3)
1944	10.5	46.7	26.5	15.9	(71.9)
1948	6.3	46.1	35.2	12.3	(82.7)
1952	4.3	46.1	35.1	14.4	(79.1)
1956	5.0	44.6	33.2	17.1	(79.8)
1958	3.2	46.2	30.9	19.5	(77.4)
1960	4.5	47.8	31.1	16.5	(85.9)
1964	5.2	47.3	30.2	13.7	(83.9)
1968	3.0	50.1	30.0	12.9	(89.3)
1970	4.8	45.3	36.1	11.5	(88.3)
1973	5.3	43.5	34.5	14.3	(90.8)
1976	4.8	42.8	35.2	15.6	(91.8)
1979	5.6	43.2	28.9	20.3	(90.7)
1982	5.6	45.9	21.4	23.4	(91.4)

SOURCES: Mackie and Rose (1974a, 1974b, 1977, 1980, 1983).

NOTE: Percentages do not add up to 100 because insignificantly small parties have been excluded.

[a] Left-socialist parties include only the Swedish Left-Socialist party until 1921; thereafter, the Swedish Communist party (VPK). (The Swedish Left-Socialist party disappeared after 1921.) Between 1930 and 1944, also includes the Swedish Socialist party (Kilbomskommunisterna).

[b] Center parties include the Swedish Center party (until 1957 called Bondeförbundet) and the Swedish Liberal party (Folkepartiet).

[c] As a percentage of total eligible voters.

BIBLIOGRAPHY

BOOKS, ARTICLES, AND MISCELLANEOUS MATERIALS

Åkerman, N.
1973   *Klassamhället i Siffror.* Stockholm: Prisma.
Aasard, E.
1978   *LO och Löntagarfonderna.* Uppsala: Raben & Sjögren.
Aasheim, N. (ed.).
1970   *Frigjøring, Gjenreisning og Velstand: Etterkrigs Historie I.* Oslo: Universitetsforlaget.
1971   *Frigjøring, Gjenreisning og Velstand: Etterkrigs Historie II.* Oslo: Universitetsforlaget.
Abraham, D.
1981   *The Collapse of the Weimar Republic.* Princeton: Princeton University Press.
Abramson, P.
1971   "Social Class and Political Change in Western Europe." *Comparative Political Studies* 4.
Adams, C. T.
1975   "Interests, Parties, and the Public Role in Housing." In A. J. Heidenheimer et al. (eds.), *Comparative Public Policy.* New York: St. Martin's Press.
Adler, M.
1926   *Politische oder Soziale Demokratie.* Berlin: Laubsche Verlag.
1978   "Wandlung der Arbeiterklasse" [1933]. In T. Bottomore and M. Rubel (eds.), *Austro-Marxism.* Oxford: Oxford University Press.
Adler-Karlsson, G.
1967   *Funktionssocialism.* Lund: Prisma.
Alford, R.
1963   *Party and Society.* Chicago: Rand McNally.
Andersen, B.
1973   *Grundprincipper i Socialpolitiken.* Copenhagen: Det Danske Forlag.
1974   *Samfundsanalyse og Erhvervsstruktur.* Copenhagen: Paludan.

Andersson, R., and R. Meidner.
1973   *Arbetsmarknadspolitik och Stabilisering*. Stockholm: Prisma.

Anners, E.
1976   *Den Socialdemokratiska Magtapparaten*. Boraas: Askild & Kärnekull.

Anton, T.
1975   *Governing Greater Stockholm*. Berkeley: University of California Press.

Aukrust, O.
1965   *Norges Økonomi etter Krigen*. Oslo: Statistisk Sentralbyrå.

Bäck, M.
1974   *Partier och Organisationer*. Uppsala: Uppsala University Press.

Barrington Moore, J.
1967   *The Social Origins of Dictatorship and Democracy*. Boston: Beacon Press.

Baude, A.
1978   *Från Fattigdom till Velfärd*. Stockholm: Liber.

Bauer, O.
1978   "Political and Social Revolution" [1919]. In T. Bottomore and M. Rubel (eds.), *Austro-Marxism*. Oxford: Oxford University Press.

Bell, D.
1973   *The Coming of Post-Industrial Society*. New York: Basic Books.
1977   "Memoir: Anthony Crosland and Socialism." *Encounter* 49.
1978   *The Cultural Contradictions of Capitalism*. New York: Basic Books.

Bendix, R.
1964   *Nation-Building and Citizenship*. New York: John Wiley & Sons.

Bentzel, R.
1952   *Indkomstfordelingen i Sverige*. Stockholm: Prisma.

Bergh, T.
1977   "Norsk Økonomisk Politikk, 1945-65." In T. Bergh (ed.), *Vekst og Velstand*. Oslo: Universitetsforlaget.

Berglind, H.
1974   "Unemployment and Redundancy in a Post-Industrial La-

bor Market." Paper presented at the Eighth World Congress of Sociology, Toronto.

Berglind, H., and A. Lindquist.
1972   *Utslagningen på Arbetsmarknaden.* Lund: Studentlitteratur.

Berglind, H., and B. Rundblad.
1978   *Arbetsmarknaden i Sverige.* Stockholm: Esselte Studium.

Berglund, S., and V. Lundström.
1979   "The Scandinavian Party System(s) in Transition? A Macro-Level Analysis." *European Journal of Political Research* 7.

Bergström, V.
1971   "Industriel Utveckling, Industrins Kapitalbildning och Finanspolitiken." In E. Lundberg (ed.), *Svensk Finanspolitik i Teori och Praktik.* Stockholm: Aldus.

Berkling, A. L.
1982   *Fraan Fram till Folkhemmet: Per Albin Hansson som Tidningsman och Talare.* Falköping: Metodica.

Bernstein, E.
1971   *Evolutionary Socialism* [1899]. New York: Schocken Books.

Bertold, O.
1938   *Pionerer.* Copenhagen: Fremad.

Bertold, O., E. Christiansen, and P. Hansen.
1954-   *En Bygning Vi Rejser,* vols. 1 and 2. Copenhagen: Fremad.
1955

Bille, L.
1972   *Danske Partiprogrammer, 1945-1970.* Copenhagen: Gyldendal.

1974   *S-SF.* Copenhagen: Gyldendal.

Bille, L., et al.
1975   *Danmark, 1966-1970: En Historisk-Økonomisk Oversigt.* Copenhagen: Berg.

Bjerke, J.
1966   *Langtidslinier i Norsk Økonomi, 1865-1960.* Oslo: Statistisk Sentralbyrå.

Bjerke, K.
1961   "Indkomstfordelingen i Danmark Før og Efter Krigen." *Socialt Tidsskrift* 37.

Björn, L.
1976   *Labor Parties and the Distribution of Incomes in Capi-*

talist Democracies. Ph.D. dissertation, University of North Carolina, Chapel Hill.

Blauner, R.
1964 *Alienation and Freedom*. Chicago: University of Chicago Press.

Boberg, K., et al.
1974 *Bostad och Kapital*. Lund: Prisma.

Bonke, S.
1976 "Traek af Bygge—og Anlaegssektorens Udvikling." *Kontekst 32*.

Borre, O.
1977 "Recent Trends in Danish Voting Behavior." In K. Cerny (ed.), *Scandinavia at the Polls*. Washington D.C.: American Enterprise Institute.
1979 "The Impacts of Strains on Public Attitudes and Political Party Systems." Paper presented at Council for European Studies Conference, Washington D.C.

Borre, O., and J. Stehouwer.
1970 *Fire Folketingsvalg, 1960-1968*. Århus: Akademisk Boghandel.

Borre, O., et al.
1976 *Vaelgerne i 70'erne*. Copenhagen: Akademisk Forlag.

Branting, H.
1913 "Ekonomisk och Social Arbetarpolitik." In *Tal och Skrifter*, vol. 7. Stockholm: Tiden.

Briggs, A.
1961 "The Welfare State in Historical Perspective." *European Journal of Sociology* 1.

Bryld, C.
1976 *Det Danske Socialdemokrati og Revisionismen*, vol. 2. Copenhagen: GMT.

Buksti, J., et al.
1978 *ØD Undersøgelsen i Aarhus Kommune*. Århus: Arbeiderbevaegelsens Oplysningsforbund.
1981 *Befolkningens Holdninger til Overskudsdeling*. Århus: Institut for Statskundskab.

Bull, E.
1922 *Den Skandinaviske Arbeiterbevaegelse*. Kristiania: Det Norske Arbeiderparti.
1947 *Arbeiterklassen i Norsk Historie*. Oslo: Tidens Norsk Forlag.

1976   "Arbeiderbevaegelsens Stilling i de tre Nordiske Land, 1914-1920" [1922]. *Tidsskrift for Arbeiderbevaegelsens Historie* 1.

Burnham, W. D.
1970   *Critical Elections and the Mainsprings of American Elections.* New York: Norton.

Butler, D., and R. Rose.
1960   *The British General Election of 1959.* London: Macmillan.

Butler, D., and D. Stokes.
1971   *Political Change in Britain.* New York: St. Martin's Press.

Cameron, D.
1976   "Inequality and the State: A Political-Economic Comparison." Paper presented at APSA meeting, Chicago.
1978   "The Expansion of the Public Sector: A Comparative Analysis." *American Political Science Review* 72.

Cappelen, Å.
1981a   "Intektspolitikken i Norge i Etterkrigstiden." *Vardøger* 11.
1981b   "Noen Hovedtraek ved Norsk Økonomi etter 2 Verdenskrig." In B. A. Lundvall (ed.), *Inntektspolitikk i Norden, 1945-80.* Copenhagen: Nordisk Forum.

Carlsson, G., and K. Karlsson.
1970   "Age Cohorts and the Generation of Generations." *American Sociological Review* 35.

Carlsson, S.
1966   "Den Sociala Omgrupperingen i Sverige efter 1866." In A. Thompson (ed.), *Samhälle och Riksdag.* Stockholm: Almqvist & Wicksell.

Castells, M.
1972   "Urban Renewal and Social Conflict in Paris." *Social Science Information* 2.

Castles, F.
1978   *The Social Democratic Image of Society.* London: Routledge & Kegan Paul.

Christiansen, T.
1975   *1970'ernes Social Reform.* Copenhagen: Gyldendal.

Cole, G. D. H.
1969   *A History of Socialist Thought,* vol. 4. London: Macmillan.

Crosland, C. A. R.
1967   *The Future of Socialism*. New York: Schocken Books.
Crouch, C., and A. Pizzorno (eds.).
1978   *The Resurgence of Class Conflict in Western Europe since 1968*. New York: Holmes & Meier.
Dahl, H. F.
1969   *Fra Klasskamp til Nasjonal Samling*. Oslo: Pax.
1971   *Norge Mellom Krigene*. Oslo: Pax.
Dahlkvist, M.
1975   *Staten, Socialdemokratin och Socialismen*. Lund: Prisma.
Dahlström, E.
1965   *Svensk Samhällsstruktur i Sociologisk Belysning*. Stockholm: Svenska Bokforlag.
Damgaard, E.
1973   "Party Coalitions in Danish Law Making, 1953-1970." *European Journal of Political Research* 1.
1974   "Stability and Change in the Danish Party System over Half a Century." *Scandinavian Political Studies* 9.
Damgaard, E., and J. Rusk.
1976   "Cleavage Structures and Representational Linkages: A Longitudinal Analysis of Danish Legislative Behavior." *American Journal of Political Science* 20.
Dich, J.
1973   *Den Herskende Klasse*. Copenhagen: Borgen.
Donnison, D.
1967   *The Government of Housing*. London: Penguin.
Downs, A.
1957   *An Economic Theory of Democracy*. New York: Harper & Row.
Duverger, M.
1964   *Political Parties*. London: Methuen.
Dybdahl, V.
1975   *Industrialisering og Folkestyre*. Copenhagen: Gyldendal.
Edgren, G., et al.
1970   *Lönebildning och Samhällsekonomi*. Stockholm: Raben & Sjögren.
Eidem, R., and B. Öhman.
1979   *Economic Democracy*. Stockholm: Arbetslivcentrum.
Elmer, Å.
1960   *Folkpensioneringen i Sverige*. Lund: Gleerups.
1978   *Svensk Socialpolitik*. Lund: Gleerups.

Elmgren, B.
1969   *Politik och Jämtlikhet*. Stockholm: Prisma.
Elvander, N.
1966   *Interesseorganisationerne i Sverige*. Lund: Gleerups.
1972   *Svensk Skattepolitik, 1945-1970*. Uppsala: Raben & Sjö-
          gren.
1974a   "Staten och Organisationerne på Arbetsmarknaden i de
          Nordiska Länderna." In L. Brantgärde (ed.), *Konfliktlös-
          ning på Arbetsmarknaden*. Lund: Gleerups.
1974b   "In Search of New Relationships: Parties, Unions, and
          Salaried Employees' Associations in Sweden." *Industrial
          and Labour Relations Review* 28.
1980   *Skandinavisk Arbetarrörelse*. Helsingborg: Liber.
Engels, F.
1951   "The Housing Question" [1872]. In K. Marx and F. En-
          gels, *Selected Works*. Moscow: Foreign Language Pub-
          lishing House.
Epstein, L.
1967   *Political Parties in Western Democracies*. New York:
          Praeger.
Eriksen, K., and G. Lundestad.
1972   *Norsk Innenrikspolitik*. Oslo: Universitetsforlaget.
Erixon, L.
1982   *Tillväkst och Strukturförandringar i Svensk Industri un-
          der 70-talet*. Stockholm: Institute for Social Research.
Esping-Andersen, G.
1978   "Social Class, Social Democracy, and the State." *Com-
          parative Politics* 11.
1980   *Social Class, Social Democracy, and State Policies*. Co-
          penhagen: Nyt Fra Samfundsvidenskaberne.
1981a   "From Welfare State to Economic Democracy." *Political
          Power and Social Theory* 2.
1981b   "Politics against Markets: De-commodification in Social
          Policy." Paper presented at the Arne Ryde Symposium on
          the Economics of Social Security, Lund.
1982   "The State as a System of Stratification." Paper presented
          at Council for European Studies conference, Washington
          D.C.
Esping-Andersen, G., and R. Friedland.
1982   "Class Coalitions in the Making of West European Econ-
          omies." *Political Power and Social Theory* 3

Esping-Andersen, G., and W. Korpi.
1984   "From Poor Relief to Institutional Welfare States." In
        R. Eriksson et al. (eds.), *Welfare Research and Welfare
        Society*. New York: M. E. Sharpe.
Esping-Andersen, G., R. Friedland, and E. Wright.
1976   "Class Conflict and the Capitalist State." *Kapitalistate*
        4-5.
Flora, P.
1981   "Solution or Source of Crisis? The Welfare State in His-
        torical Perspective." In W. J. Mommsen (ed.), *The Emer-
        gence of the Welfare State in Britain and Germany*. Lon-
        don: Croom Helm.
Franzen, T., et al.
1975   *Skatters och Offentliga Utgifters Effekter paa Innkomst-
        fördelingen*. Stockholm: Stockholm University, Depart-
        ment of Economics.
Friis, H.
1971   "Socialvidenskab og Socialpolitik: Nogle Danske Erfar-
        inger." In *Økonomien Bag Socialpolitiken*. Copenhagen:
        Thanning & Appel.
Frykman, T.
1983   "Vem bor i Ägd Bostad?" *At Bo* 1.
Fulcher, J.
1976   "Joint Regulation and Its Decline." In R. Scase (ed.),
        Readings in the Swedish Class Structure. London: Per-
        gamon Press.
Furåker, B.
1976   *Stat och Arbetsmarknad*. Kristianstad: Arkiv.
Furre, B.
1971   *Norsk Historie, 1905-1940*. Oslo: Det Norske Samlaget.
Galbraith, J. K.
1969   *The New Industrial State*. London: Penguin.
Galenson, W.
1949   *Labor in Norway*. Cambridge: Harvard University Press.
1952   *The Danish System of Labor Relations*. Cambridge: Har-
        vard University Press.
1968   *Comparative Labor Movements*. New York: Russell &
        Russell.
Gates, R.
1974   "Von der Sozialpolitik zur Wirtschaftspolitik." In
        H. Mommsen et al. (eds.), *Industrielles System und Poli-*

tisches Entwicklung in der Weimarer Republik. Düsseldorf: Droste Verlag.

Gay, P.
1970   *The Dilemma of Democratic Socialism.* New York: Collier.

Geiger, T.
1978   *Welfare and Efficiency.* Washington D.C.: National Planning Commission.

Gerschenkron, A.
1943   *Bread and Democracy in Germany.* Berkeley: University
of California Press.

Glans, I.
1975   "Årets första Folketingsval." *Statsvetenskapligt Tidskrift*
3.

Glenn, N.
1977   *Cohort Analysis.* Beverly Hills, Calif.: Sage.

Gorz, A.
1967   *A Strategy for Labor.* Boston: Beacon Press.

Goul Andersen, J.
1977   *Mellemlagene i Danmark.* Aarhus: Politica.

Goul Andersen, J., and I. Glans.
1981   "Socialklasser og Partivalg i 1970'erne." *Politica* 13.

Gramsci, A.
1978   *Selections from Political Writings, 1921-1926.* New York:
International Publishers.

Grønlie, T.
1977   "Norsk Industripolitikk." In T. Bergh and H. Pharo (eds.),
Vekst og Velstand. Oslo: Universitetsforlaget.

Guldbrandsen, L., and U. Torgerson.
1978   "Concern with Redistribution as an Aspect of Postwar
Norwegian Housing Policy." *Acta Sociologica* 21.
1981   "Høyre—Den Offentlige Sektorens Parti?" In T. Bjørk-
lund and B. Hagtved (eds.), *Høyrebølgen.* Oslo: Asche-
houg.

Gustavsson, B.
1982   "Löntagarfonder: Demokrati och Effektivitet." *Tiden* 6.

Haarr, A.
1982   *I Oljens Tegn.* Olso: Tanum Norli.

Hallet, G.
1973   *The Social Economy of West Germany.* London: Macmillan.

Hamilton, R.
1967   *Affluence and the French Worker in the Fourth Republic.*
        Princeton: Princeton University Press.
1972   *Class and Politics in the United States.* New York: John
        Wiley & Sons.

Hancock, D.
1972   *Sweden: The Politics of Postindustrial Change.* Hinsdale,
        Ill.: Dryden Press.

Hansen, B.
1973   *Velstand uden Velfaerd.* Copenhagen: Fremad.

Hansen, E. J.
1980   *Levevilkår i Velfaerdsstaten.* Copenhagen: Social Forsk-
        nings Instituttet.

Hansen, S. Å.
1974   *Økonomisk Vaekst i Danmark.* Copenhagen: Akademisk
        Forlag.

Hansson, P. A.
1982   *Från Fram till Folkhemmet: A Collection of Writings and
        Speeches by P. A. Hansson,* edited by A. L. Berkling.
        Falköping: Metodica.

Heberle, R.
1951   *Social Movements.* New York: Appleton-Century-Crofts.

Heclo, H.
1974   *Modern Social Politics in Britain and Sweden.* New Ha-
        ven: Yale University Press.

Heidenheimer, A., et al.
1975   *Comparative Public Policy.* New York: St. Martin's Press.

Heiman, E.
1929   *Soziale Theorie des Kapitalismus: Theorie der Sozial Po-
        litik.* Tübingen: Mohr.

Hentilää, S.
1974   "Orsaken till Reformismens Gennombrott i Svensk So-
        cialdemokrati." *Arkiv 5.*

Hewitt, C.
1977   "The Effects of Political Democracy and Social Democ-
        racy on Equality in Industial Societies." *American Soci-
        ological Review 42.*

Hibbs, D.
1977   "Political Parties and Macroeconomic Policy." *American
        Political Science Review 71.*
1978   "On the Political Economy of Long-Run Trends in Strike
        Activity." *British Journal of Political Science 8.*

Higgins, W., and N. Apple.
1982   "Vad gör Reformistarna när de Reformerar?" *Häften för Kritiska Studier* 15.

Himmelstrand, U., et al.
1981   *Beyond Welfare Capitalism: Issues, Actors, and Forces in Societal Change*. London: Heineman.

Hirschman, A. O.
1970   *Exit, Voice, and Loyalty*. Cambridge: Harvard University Press.

Høgh, E.
1956   "Vaelgeradfaerd." *Sociologiske Meddelelser* 3.

Højland, M., and C. Vesterø Jensen.
1979   *Skattepolitik*. Copenhagen: Suenson Forlag.

Holmberg, S.
1981   *Svenska Väljare*. Stockholm: Publica.

Hull Kristensen, P., and J. Annersted.
1980   *Innovative Kapabiliteter i de Skandinaviske Lande*. Roskilde: Roskilde Universitets Center.

Huntford, R.
1971   *The New Totalitarians*. London: Penguin.

Huntington, S.
1975   "The United States." In M. Crozier, S. Huntington, and J. Watanuki (eds.), *The Crisis of Democracy*. New York: New York University Press.

Hyman, H. H.,
1959   *Political Socialization*. New York: Free Press.

Ibsen, F., and K. Vangskjaer.
1976   "Indkomstpolitiske Eerfaringer i Danmark: Helhedsløsningen i 1963." *Nordisk Tidskrift for Politisk Økonomi* 4.

Jackman, R.
1974   "Political Democracy and Social Equality." *American Sociological Review* 39.

Johannesson, J.
1982   *On the Outcome of Swedish Labor Market Policy from the 1960's up to 1981*. Berlin: Wissenschaftszentrum.

Johansson, S.
1974   *När er Tiden Mogen? En Fråga inför Program Kommisionen*. Karlskrona: Tidens Forlag.
1982   "When Is the Time Ripe?" *Political Power and Social Theory* 3.

Johnston, T. L.
1962   *Collective Bargaining in Sweden*. London: Allen & Unwin.

Jörberg, L.
1976   "Industrialization in Scandinavia." In F. Cippola (ed.), *The Economic History of Europe*. London: Fontana.

Jungen, E.
1931   "Socialpolitik och Socialism." *Tiden* 23.

Kampmann, V.
1970   *Økonomisk Demokrati*. Copenhagen: Fremad.

Karleby, N.
1926   *Socialism inför Verkligheten*. Stockholm: Tiden.

Kassalow, E.
1969   *Trade Unions and Industrial Relations: An International Comparison*. New York: Random House.

Kautsky, K.
1943   *The Road to Power* [1909]. Chicago: S. A. Bloch.
1971   *The Class Struggle* [1892]. New York: Norton.

Kerr, C., et al.
1964   *Industrialism and Industrial Man*. London: Penguin.

King, A.
1975   "Overload: Problems of Governance in the 1970's" *Political Studies* 23.

Kirschheimer, O.
1968   "The Transformation of Western European Party Systems." In J. Palombara and M. Weiner (eds.), *Political Parties and Political Development*. Princeton: Princeton University Press.

Kjeldstadli, K., and V. Keul (eds.).
1973   *DNA—Fra Folkebevegelse till Statsstøtte*. Oslo: Pax.

Klingman, D.
1976   *Social Change, Political Change, and Public Policy: Norway and Sweden, 1875-1965*. Beverly Hills, Calif.: Sage.

Kolberg, J. E. and P. A. Pettersen.
1981   "Om Velfaerdsstatens Politiske Basis." *Tidsskrift for Samfunnsforskning* 22.

Kolberg, J. E., and A. Viken.
1978   "Trygdhetsens Struktur." *Tidsskrift for Samfunnsforskning* 19.

Korpi, W.
1972   "Some Problems in the Measurement of Class Voting." *American Journal of Sociology* 78.

1977   "Vad Hotar Arbetarrörelsen?" *Tiden* 3.
1978   *The Working Class in Welfare Capitalism.* London: Routledge & Kegan Paul.
1980a   *Fonder för Ekonomisk Demokrati.* Stockholm: Sveriges Kommunaltjänestemanna Förbund.
1980b   "Social Policy and Distributional Conflict in the Capitalist Democracies." *West European Politics* 3.
1981a   *Den Demokratiska Klasskampen.* Stockholm: Tiden.
1981b   "Från Undersåte till Medborgare: Socialistiska Tankegångar hos Ernst Wigforss." *Tiden* 6.

Korpi, W., and M. Shalev.
1980   "Strikes, Power, and Politics in the Western Nations, 1900-1976." *Political Power and Social Theory* 1.

Krag, J. O. and K. B. Andersen.
1971   *Kamp og Fornyelse.* Copenhagen: Fremad.

Kristensen, O. P.
1981   "Voter Attitudes and Public Spending: Is There a Relationship?" Paper presented at the Sixth Nordic Political Science Congress, Åbo.

Kuhnle, S.
1975   *Patterns of Political and Social Mobilization.* Beverly Hills, Calif.: Sage.
1978   "The Beginnings of the Nordic Welfare States." *Acta Sociologica* 21 (supp.).

Kuhnle, S., and L. Solheim.
1981   "Party Programs and the Welfare State: Consensus and Conflict in Norway, 1945-1977." Paper presented at the European Consortium for Political Research joint sessions, Lancaster, England.

Kuusi, P.
1964   *Social Policy for the Sixties.* Helsinki: Finnish Social Policy Association.

Kvavik, R.
1976   *Interest Groups in Norwegian Politics.* Oslo: Universitetsforlaget.

Lafferty, W.
1971   *Economic Development and the Response of Labor in Scandinavia.* Oslo: Universitetsforlaget.

Landauer, K.
1959   *European Socialism: A History of Ideas and Movements,* vols. 1 and 2. Berkeley: University of California Press.

Lange, P., and M. Vanicelli.
1979   "From Marginality to Centrality: Italian Unionism in the
         1970's." Paper presented at the Annual APSA Meeting,
         Washington D.C.
Lederer, E., and J. Marschak.
1926   "Der Neue Mittelstand." In *Grundriss der Sozialöko-
         nomik*, vol. 9, no. 1. Tübingen: Verlag von Mohr.
Leion, A.
1970   *Indkomstfördelingen i Sverige*. Falköping: Landsorgani-
         sationen & Prisma.
Leiserson, M.
1959   *Wages and Economic Control in Norway*. Cambridge:
         Harvard University Press.
Lenin, V. I.
1929   *What Is to Be Done?* [1909]. New York: International
         Publishers.
1939   *Imperialism: The Highest Stage of Capitalism* [1924]. New
         York: International Publishers.
1943   *The State and Revolution* [1919]. New York: Interna-
         tional Publishers.
Lewin, L.
1967   *Planhushålningsdebatten*. Stockholm: Almqvist & Wick-
         sell.
Lieberman, S.
1977   *The Growth of European Mixed Economies, 1945-1970*.
         New York: John Wiley & Sons.
Lindbeck, A.
1972   *Swedish Economic Policy*. Berkeley: University of Cali-
         fornia Press.
1975   *Svensk Ekonomisk Politik*. Stockholm: Bonniers.
1976   "Stabilization Policy in Open Economies with Endoge-
         nous Politicians." *American Economic Review* 66.
Lindhagen, J.
1972   *Socialdemokratin's Program*. Stockholm: Tiden.
1976   "Åren Vi Forlorade." *Tiden* 10.
1977   "Men å andra sidan." *Tiden* 8.
Lindström, S.
1979   *Sweden's Economic Situation during the 1979 Election
         Campaign*. New York: Swedish Institute Pamphlets.
Lipset, S. M.
1960   *Political Man*. New York: Doubleday, Anchor.

1964   "The Changing Class Structure and Contemporary European Politics." In S. Graubard (ed.), *A New Europe?* Boston: Beacon Press.

LO (Landsorganisationen).

1951   *Fackföreningsrörelsen och den Fulla Sysselsättningen.* Stockholm: LO.

1961   *Samordnad Näringsliv.* Stockholm: LO.

1970   *Indkomstfördelingen i Sverige* [by A. Leion]. Stockholm: LO & Prisma.

1976   *Kollektiv Kapitalbildning genom Löntagarfonder.* Stockholm: LO.

1980   *Lönepolitik och Solidaritet.* Stockholm: LO.

LO and SAP (Sveriges Socialdemokratiska Arbetarparti).

1978   *Löntagarfonder och Kapitalbildning.* Stockholm: Tiden.

1981   *Arbetarrörelsen och Löntagarfonderna.* Stockholm: Tiden.

Logue, J.

1975   "Beyond Welfare Socialism: The Case of the Danish Socialist People's Party." Paper presented at the Society for the Advancement of Scandinavian Studies workshop, Madison, Wisc.

Lorenz, E.

1974   *Arbeiderbevegelsens Historie II, 1930-1973.* Oslo: Pax.

Lund, O. and M. Langholm.

1967   *Folketrygden.* Oslo: Johan Grundt Tanum Forlag.

Lundberg, E.

1968   *Instability and Economic Growth.* New Haven: Yale University Press.

Lykketoft, M.

1973   *Kravet om Lighed.* Copenhagen: Fremad.

Mackie, T., and R. Rose.

1974a   *The International Almanac of Electoral History.* New York: Free Press.

1974b   "General Elections in Western Nations during 1973." *European Journal of Political Research* 2.

1976   "General Elections in Western Nations during 1975." *European Journal of Political Research* 4.

1977   "General Elections in Western Nations during 1976." *European Journal of Political Research* 5.

1978   "General Elections in Western Nations, 1977." *European Journal of Political Research* 6.

1980   "General Elections in Western Nations during 1979." *European Journal of Political Research* 8.

1982   "General Elections in Western Nations during 1981." *European Journal of Political Research* 10.

1983   "General Elections in Western Nations during 1982." *European Journal of Political Research* 11.

Madsen, H. J.

1980   "Class Power and Participatory Equality: Attitudes towards Economic Democracy in Denmark and Sweden." *Scandinavian Political Studies* 3.

Mallet, S.

1975   *Essays on the New Working Class*. St. Louis, Mo.: Telos Press.

Mannheim, K.

1959   *Essays in the Sociology of Knowledge*. London: Routledge & Kegan Paul.

Marshall, T. H.

1950   *Citizenship and Social Class*. Cambridge: Cambridge University Press.

1964   *Class, Citizenship, and Social Development*. Chicago: University of Chicago Press.

Martin, A.

1973   *The Politics of Economic Policy in the United States*. Beverly Hills, Calif.: Sage.

1975   "Is Democratic Control of Capitalism Possible? Some Notes towards an Answer." In L. Lindberg et al. (eds.), *Stress and Contradiction in Modern Capitalism*. Lexington, Mass.: D. C. Heath.

1979   "The Dynamics of Change in a Keynesean Political Economy: The Swedish Case and Its Implications." In C. Crouch (ed.), *State and Economy in Contemporary Capitalism*. London: Croom Helm.

1981   "Economic Stagnation and Social Stalemate in Sweden." In U.S. Congress, Joint Economic Committee, *Monetary Policy, Selective Credit Policy, and Industrial Policy in France, Britain, West Germany, and Sweden*. Washington D.C.: United States Congress.

Marx, K.

1964   *Class Struggles in France* [1895]. New York: International Publishers.

1967   *Capital*, vol. 1 [1872]. New York: International Publishers.

1978   "Critique of the Gotha Program" [1875]. In R. Tucker
            (ed.), *The Marx-Engels Reader*. New York: Norton.
Marx, K., and F. Engels.
1967   *The Communist Manifesto* [1848] London: Penguin.
Mason, T.
1977   *Sozialpolitik im Dritten Reich*. Opladen: Westdeutscher
            Verlag.
Mayer, K.
1955   *Class and Society*. New York: Random House.
Meidner, R.
1974   *Samordning och Solidarisk Lönepolitik*. Stockholm: Prisma.
1978   *Employee Investment Funds*. London: Allen & Unwin.
1979   *Employee Investment Funds and Capital Formation*. New
            York: Swedish Institute Pamphlets.
Meier, C.
1975   *Recasting Bourgeois Europe*. Princeton: Princeton Uni-
            versity Press.
Meyerson, P. M.
1979   *Capital Accumulation and Ownership Structure in Swed-
            ish Industry: The Employee Fund Debate in Perspective*.
            New York: Swedish Institute Pamphlets.
Michels, R.
1962   *Political Parties* [1915]. New York: Collier.
Miliband, R.
1972   *Parliamentary Socialism*. London: Merlin.
1977   *Marxism and Politics*. Oxford: Oxford University Press.
Mills, C. W.
1951   *White Collar*. New York: Oxford University Press.
1967   *The Sociological Imagination*. London: Oxford Univer-
            sity Press.
Mjøset, L.
1981   "Socialdemokratisk Økonomisk Politikk i Norge etter
            Krigen." *Vardøger* 11.
Mogensen, G. V.
1967   *Økonomiske Udviklingslinier, 1945-65*. Copenhagen: Gad.
1975   *Socialhistorie*. Copenhagen: Akademisk Forlag.
Molin, B.
1967   *Tjänstepensionsfrågan: En Studie i Svensk Partipolitik*.
            Lund: Akademisk Forlag.
Möller, G.
1938   "The Unemployment Policy." *Annals of the American
            Academy* 197.

Mommsen, H., et al.
1974a   *Sozialdemokratie Zwischen Klassenbewegung und Volks-partei.* Frankfurt: Atheneum Verlag.
1974b   *Industrielles System und Politische Entwicklung in der Weimarer Republik.* Düsseldorf: Droste Verlag.
Moore, J. Barrington.
1967   *The Social Origins of Dictatorship and Democracy.* Boston: Beacon Press.
Mortensen, H.
1969   *Arbejderflertallet.* Copenhagen: Røde Hane.
Munck, I., et al.
1980   "Økonomisk udvikling og Industripolitik i Danmark efter 1958." *Nordisk Forum* 28.
Myrdal, A. and G. Myrdal.
1934   *Kris i Befolkningsfrågan.* Stockholm: Tiden.
Naphtali, F.
1928   *Wirtschaftsdemokratie, Ihr Wesen, Weg und Ziel.* Berlin: Allgemeine Deutsche Gewerkschaftsbund.
Nasenius, J.
1974   *Delad Velfärd.* Lund: Scandinavian University Books.
Neumann, F.
1944   *Behemoth: The Structure and Practice of National Socialism.* New York: Oxford University Press.
Neumann, S.
1965   *Permanent Revolution.* New York: Praeger.
Nielsen, H. J.
1975   "To-i-et Partiet." In *Småborgerskab og Politisk Krise i Danmark.* Roskilde: Roskilde Universitets Center.
1976   "The Uncivic Culture: Attitudes towards the Political System in Denmark, and Vote for the Progress Party, 1973-1975." *Scandinavian Political Studies* 11.
1979   *Politiske Holdninger og Fremskridtsstemme.* Copenhagen: Politiske Studier.
Nielsen, K., and T. Grønnebaek-Hansen.
1979   "Placering af Fondsmidlerne." Paper presented at seminar, "Medbestemmelse og Økonomisk Demokrati."
Nielsen, M.
1973   *Enhed i Arbejderbevaegelsen.* Copenhagen: Fremad.
Nolan, M., and C. Sabel.
1982   "Cycles of Reform and Revolution in German Social Democracy." *Political Power and Social Theory* 3.

Nordvik, H.
1977   "Krisepolitikken og den Teoretiske Nyorientering af den
         Økonomiske Politikken i Norge i 1930-årene." *Historisk
         Tidskrift 56.*

Nossiter, B.
1978   "Britain's Cautious Step towards Industrial Democracy."
         Working Papers for a New Society July/August.

O'Connor, J.
1973   *The Fiscal Crisis of the State.* New York: St. Martin's
         Press.

Offe, C.
1972   "Advanced Capitalism and the Welfare State." *Politics
         and Society 4.*

Öhman, B.
1979a   *Employee Funds.* New York: Swedish Information Serv-
         ice.
1979b   *Wage Earner Funds.* Stockholm: Sveriges Offentliga
         Utredningar.
1981a   "Solidarisk Lönepolitik och Löntagarfonder." Mimeo.,
         Stockholm University.
1981b   *Principfrågar for Fondmodeller.* Stockholm: Liber Forlag.

Øjen, Ø
1968   "Norges Befolkning." In N. Rogoff Ramsøy (ed.), *Det
         Norske Samfunn.* Oslo: Gyldendal.

Økonomisk Råd.
1967   *Den Personlige Indkomstfordeling og Indkomst-
         udjævningen i Danmark.* Copenhagen: Det Økonomiske
         Råd.

Olsen, E.
1962   *Danmarks Økonomiske Historie siden 1720.* Copen-
         hagen: Gads Forlag.

Olsen, H., and G. Hansen.
1981   *De Aeldres Levevilkår 1977.* Copenhagen: Socialforsk-
         nings Instituttet.

Olsen, O. Jess.
1980   *Industripolitik i Danmark, Norge og Sverige.* Copen-
         hagen: Paludan.

Olsen, P., and V. Kampmann.
1948   "Indkomstudjaevningen i Danmark." *Socialt Tidsskrift*
         24.

Olsson, G.
1966   *Nordisk Arbetsmarknad.* Stockholm: Raben & Sjögren.
Olsson, I.
1980   *Den Solidariska Lönepolitikens Resultat.* Stockholm: Landsorganisationen.
Panitch, L.
1976   *Social Democracy and Industrial Militancy: The Labour Party, the Trade Unions, and Income Policy, 1945-74.* London: Cambridge University Press.
1981   "Trade Unions and the Capitalist State." *New Left Review* 125.
Pannekoek, A.
1914   *Olika Riktninger inom Arbetarrörelsen.* Lund: Arkiv.
Parkin, F.
1972   *Class Inequality and Political Order.* New York: Praeger.
1979   *Marxism and Class Theory: A Bourgeois Critique.* London: Cambridge University Press.
Paterson, W., and I. Campbell.
1974   *Social Democracy in Postwar Europe.* London: Croom Helm.
Paterson, W., and A. Thomas (eds.).
1977   *Social Democratic Parties in Western Europe.* London: Croom Helm.
Pedersen, P.
1977   "Aspekter af Fagbevaegelsens Vaekst i Danmark, 1911-1976." Mimeo., Århus University, Department of Economics.
Pelling, H.
1961   *The Origins of the Labour Party.* Oxford: Clarendon Press.
Perlman, S.
1926   *A Theory of the Labor Movement.* New York: Macmillan.
Perrin, G.
1969   "Reflections on Fifty Years of Social Security." *International Labor Review* 99.
Petersson, O.
1977   *Väljarna och Valet 1976.* Stockholm: Liber Forlag.
Philip, K.
1939   *Den Dansk Kriselovgivning, 1931-38.* Århus: Studier fra Århus Universitet, Økonomisk Institut.

Pinker, R.
1971   *Social Theory and Social Policy.* London: Heineman.
Polanyi, K.
1957   *The Great Transformation.* Boston: Beacon Press.
Poulantzas, N.
1975   *Classes in Contemporary Capitalism.* London: New Left
         Books.
Preller, L.
1949   *Sozialpolitik in der Weimar Republik.* Stuttgart: Mittel-
         bach Verlag.
Przworski, A.
1975   "Party Strategy, Political Ideology, and Class Voting."
         Grant proposal to the National Science Foundation, Uni-
         versity of Chicago, Department of Political Science.
1980   "Social Democracy as an Historical Phenomenon." *New
         Left Review* 122.
Przworski, A., and J. Sprague.
1977   "A History of European Socialism." Paper presented at
         APSA meeting, Washington D.C.
Przworski, A., and E. Underhill.
1977   "The Process of Class Formation from Karl Kautsky to
         Recent Controversies." *Politics and Society* 7.
Przworski, A., E. Underhill, and M. Wallerstein.
1978   "The Evolution of Class Structure in Denmark 1901-1960,
         France 1901-1968, Germany 1882-1933 and 1950-1961,
         and Sweden 1900-1960." Basic data tables, research re-
         port, University oif Chicago, Department of Political Sci-
         ence.
Rasmussen, E.
1933   "Socialdemokraternes Stilling til det Sociale Spørgsmål,
         1890-1901." In P. Engelstoft and H. Jensen (eds.), *Maend
         og Meninger i Dansk Socialpolitik, 1866-1901.* Copen-
         hagen: Nordisk Forlag.
Regini, M.
1980   "Changing Relations between Labour Unions and the State
         in Italy." In G. Lembruch and P. Schmitter (eds.), *Varia-
         tions in Patterns of Corporatist Policy Formation.* Lon-
         don: Sage.
Rehn, G.
1948   "Ekonomisk Politik vid Full Sysselsättning." *Tiden* 40.

351

Renner, K.
  1953   *Wandlungen der Modernen Gesellschaft*, vol. 3 of *Nach-gelassene Werke*. Wien: Wiener Volksbuchhandlung.
Rimlinger, G.
  1971   *Welfare Policy and Industrialization in Europe, America, and Russia*. New York: John Wiley & Sons.
Ringen, S.
  1979   "Inntektsfordelingen i Norge." Mimeo., Harvard University, Department of Sociology.
Rødseth, T.
  1977   *Inntektsfordelingen i Norge*. Oslo: Norges Offentlige Utredninger.
Rogoff-Ramsøy, N.
  1974   *Norwegian Society*. Oslo: Universitetsforlaget.
Rokkan, S.
  1966   "Numerical Democracy and Corporate Pluralism." In R. Dahl (ed.), *Political Oppositions in Western Democracies*. New Haven: Yale University Press.
  1970   *Citizens, Elections, Parties*. Oslo: Universitetsforlaget.
Rokkan, S., and J. Meyriat.
  1969   *International Guide to Electoral Statistics*. The Hague: Mouton.
Rose, R., and G. Peters.
  1978   *Can Government Go Bankrupt?* New York: Basic Books.
Rose, R., and D. Urwin.
  1971   "Social Cohesion, Parties, and Strains in Regimes." In M. Dogan and R. Rose (eds.), *European Politics*. Boston: Little, Brown.
Rusk, G., and O. Borre.
  1974   "The Changing Party Space in Danish Voter Perceptions." *European Journal of Political Research* 2.
Ryder, N.
  1965   "The Cohort as a Concept in the Study of Social Change." *American Sociological Review* 30.
SAF (Sveriges Arbetsgiverförbund).
  1978   *Direct and Total Wage Costs for Workers, 1958-1966*. Stockholm: SAF.
  1980   *Wages and Total Labour Costs for Workers, 1968-1978*. Stockholm: SAF.
Samuelsson, K.
  1968   *From Great Power to Welfare State*. London: Allen & Unwin.

1974   *Om Bostad och Bostadspolitik.* Stockholm: Raben & Sjögren.

SAP (Socialdemokratiska Arbetar Partiet).

1944   *Arbetarrörelsens Efterkrigsprogram* Stockholm: Tiden.

1969   *Jämtlikhet.* Stockholm: Prisma.

1981a   *Framtid för Sverige.* Stockholm: Tiden.

1981b   *Ekonomisk Demokrati och Löntagarfonder: Kreditpolitik.* Stockholm: SAP Parti Kongress.

Särlvik, B.

1966   "Political Stability and Change in the Swedish Electorate." *Scandinavian Political Studies* 1.

1970   "Voting Behavior in Shifting Election Winds," *Scandinavian Political Studies* 5.

1974   "Social Bases of the Parties in Developmental Perspective." In R. Rose (ed.), *Electoral Behavior.* New York: Free Press.

1977   "Recent Electoral Trends in Sweden." In K. Cerny (ed.), *Scandinavia at the Polls.* Washington D.C.: American Enterprise Institute.

Sartre, J. P.

1968   *The Communists and Peace.* New York: Braziller.

Sawyer, M.

1976   *Income Distribution in OECD Countries.* Paris: OECD Occasional Studies.

Scase, R.

1976   *Readings in the Swedish Class Structure.* London: Pergamon Press.

1977   *Social Democracy in Capitalist Society.* London: Croom Helm.

Schmidt, E. I.

1971   *Dansk Økonomisk Politik.* Copenhagen: Fremad.

Schmitter, P., and W. Streeck.

1981   *The Organization of Business Interests.* Berlin: Wissenschaftzentrum Discussion Papers.

Schumpeter, J.

1970   *Capitalism, Socialism, and Democracy.* London: Allen & Unwin.

Schwerin, D.

1980   "The Limits to Organization as a Response to Wage-Price Problems." In R. Rose (ed.), *Challenge to Governance.* Beverly Hills, Calif.: Sage.

1981a   *Corporatism and Protest.* Kent, Oh.: Kent Popular Press.
1981b   "Norway's Corporate Incomes Policy: Second-Best Institutions." *Polity* 13.

Seierstad, S.
1974   "The Norwegian Economy." In N. Rogoff-Ramsøy (ed.), *Norwegian Society.* Oslo: Universitetsforlaget.

Sejersted, F.
1978   "Norsk Økonomi etter Krigen med saerlig vekt paa Strukturendringene i Industrin." Paper presented at Historisk Institut, Oslo University.

Severin, F.
1969   *Från Socialism till Velfärd.* Udevalla: Natur & Kultur Forlag.

Shalev, M.
1980   "Socialism and the Welfare State in Democratic Politics." Mimeo., Tel Aviv University, Department of Labor Studies.

Socialdemokratiet.
1945   *Fremtidens Danmark.* Copenhagen: Socialdemokratiet.
1961   *Vejen Frem.* Copenhagen: Socialdemokratiet.
1964   *1964—Et Afgørende År.* Copenhagen: Socialdemokratiet.
1969   *Det Nye Samfund.* Copenhagen: Socialdemokratiet.
1975   *Solidaritet, Lighed og Trivsel: En Samfundsdebat.* Copenhagen: Fremad
1977   *Solidaritet, Lighed og Trivsel.* Copenhagen: Socialdemokratiet.

Söderpalm, S. A.
1976   *Direktörsklubben: Storindustrin i Svensk Politik under 1930- och 1940-tallet.* Stockholm: Raben & Sjögren.

Södersten, B.
1974   *Svensk Ekonomi.* Stockholm: Raben & Sjögren.

Sontheimer, K.
1977   *Handbuch des Politischen Systems der Bundesrepublik.* Munich: Piper Verlag.

Sørensen, H.
1972   *Økonomisk Demokrati.* Copenhagen: Gyldendal.

Sørensen, K.
1967   "Denmarks Political Development." *Scandinavian Political Studies* 2.

Spånt, R.
1975   *Förmögenhetsfordelingen i Sverige.* Stockholm: Prisma.

1976   *Den Svenska Inkomst Fördelingens Utveckling*. Uppsala: Studia Oeconomica Uppsaliensia.

Ståhlberg, A. C.
1981   *ATP Gynnar Höginnkomsttagarna*. Stockholm: Institute for Social Research Reprint.

Stark, T.
1977   *The Distribution of Income in Eight Countries*. Background Paper no. 4 of the Royal Commission on the Distribution of Income and Wealth. London: Her Majesty's Stationery Office.

Steincke, K. K.
1920   *Fremtidens Forsørgelsesvaesen*. Copenhagen: Schultz.

Stephens, J.
1976   *The Consequences of Social Structure Change for the Development of Socialism in Sweden*. Ph.D. dissertation, Yale University, Department of Sociology.
1979   *The Transition from Capitalism to Socialism*. London: Macmillan.

Stephens, J., and E. Huber Stephens.
1982   "The Labor Movement, Political Power, and Workers' Participation in Europe." In *Political Power and Social Theory* 3.

Stevenson, P.
1974   "Monopoly Capital and Inequalities in Swedish Society." *Insurgent Sociologist* 1.

Stjernquist, N.
1966   "Sweden: Stability or Deadlock?" In R. Dahl (ed.), *Political Oppositions in Western Democracies*. New Haven: Yale University Press.

Strachey, J.
1933   *The Coming Struggle for Power*. New York: Covici Friede.
1956   *Contemporary Capitalism*. London: Oxford University Press.

Sturmthal, A.
1943   *The Tragedy of European Labor, 1918-1939*. New York: Columbia University Press.

Svensson, P.
1974   "Support for the Danish Social Democratic Party, 1924-1939." *Scandinavian Political Studies* 9.

Swedish Institute.
1977   *Housing and Housing Policy in Sweden*. Stockholm: Swedish Institute.

TCO (Tjänstemännens Centralorganisation).
1981   *Västeuropäiska Skattesystem och Fackföreningsrörelsens Syn paa Skatterna.* Stockholm: TCO.
Tennstedt, F.
1976   "Sozialgeschichte der Sozialversicherung." In M. Blohmke et al. (eds.), *Handbuch der Sozialmedizin,* vol. 3. Stuttgart: F. Enke Verlag.
Therborn, G.
1976   "The Evolution of the Swedish Class Structure." In R. Scase (ed.), *Readings in the Swedish Class Structure.* London: Pergamon Press.
Therborn, G., et al.
1978   "Sweden before and after Social Democracy." *Acta Sociologica* 21 (supp.).
Tholin, L.
1982   *Sweden's Economic Situation—Prospects for 1982.* New York: Swedish Information Service.
Thomas, A.
1977   "Social Democracy in Denmark." In W. Paterson and A. Thomas (eds.), *Social Democratic Parties in Western Europe.* London: Croom Helm.
Thon, S.
1968   *Økonomisk Politik i Norge, 1945-65.* Oslo: Elingård.
Tilton, T.
1974   "The Social Origins of Liberal Democracy: The Swedish Case." *American Political Science Review* 68.
1979   "A Swedish Road to Socialism: Ernst Wigforss and the Ideological Foundations of Swedish Social Democracy." *American Political Science Review* 73.
Timm, H.
1952   *Die Deutsche Sozialpolitik und der Bruch der Grossen Koalition im März 1930.* Düsseldorf: Droste Verlag.
Tingsten, H.
1941   *Den Svenska Socialdemokratins Idehistoria.* Stockholm: Tiden.
1954   "Stability and Vitality in Swedish Democracy." *The Political Quarterly* 2.
Titmuss, R. M.
1962   *Income Distribution and Social Change.* London: Allen & Unwin.
1974   *Social Policy.* New York: Pantheon.

Togeby, L.
1968   *Var de så Røde?* Copenhagen: Fremad.
Tsuru, S.
1961   *Has Capitalism Changed?* Tokyo: Iwanami Shoten.
Tufte, E.
1978   *Political Control of the Economy.* Princeton: Princeton University Press.
Tyrell, R. Emmett.
1977   *The Future That Does Not Work: Social Democracy's Failures in Britain.* New York: Doubleday.
Uhr, C. G.
1977   "Economic Development in Denmark, Norway, and Sweden." In K. Cerny (ed.), *Scandinavia at the Polls.* Washington D.C.: American Enterprise Institute.
Ussing, N.
1953   "En Fordeling af Skatter og Sociale Ydelser i 1949 på Sociale Grupper." *Socialt Tidsskrift* 29.
Uusitalo, H.
1975   *Income and Welfare.* Helsinki: University Research Reports.
Valen, H.
1978   "The Storting Election of 1977: Realignment or Return to Normalcy?" *Scandinavian Political Studies* 1.
1981   *Valg og Politikk.* Oslo: Gyldendal.
Valen, H., and D. Katz.
1964   Political Parties in Norway. Oslo: Universitetsforlaget.
Valen, H., and W. Martinussen.
1972   *Velgere og Politiske Frontlinier.* Oslo: Gyldendal.
1977   "Electoral Trends and Foreign Politics in Norway." In K. Cerny (ed.), *Scandinavia at the Polls.* Washington D.C.: American Enterprise Institute.
Valen, H., and S. Rokkan.
1974   "Conflict Structure and Mass Politics in a European Periphery." In R. Rose (ed.), *Electoral Behaviour: A Comparative Handbook.* New York: Free Press.
Vesterø Jensen, C.
1982   "Det Tvedelte Pensionssystem i Danmark." Mimeo., European University Institute, Florence.
Vogel, J.
1974   "Taxation and Public Opinion in Sweden: An Interpretation of Recent Survey Data." *National Tax Journal* 27.

357

Warren, B.
1972   "Capitalist Planning and the State." *New Left Review* 72.
Wedderburn, D.
1974   *Poverty, Inequality, and Class Structure*. London: Cambridge University Press.
Wendt, P.
1962   *Housing Policy: The Search for Solutions*. Berkeley: University of California Press.
1976   *Byggeri og Boligforhold*. Copenhagen: Akademisk Forlag.
Westergaard, J. H., and M. Reisler.
1975   *Class in Capitalist Society*. London: Heineman.
Westergård Andersen, H.
1974   *Dansk Politik igår og Idag*. Copenhagen: Fremad.
1976   *De Nordiske Velfærdsstater efter 1939*. Copenhagen: Gyldendal.
Wigforss, E.
1938   "The Financial Policy during Depression and Boom." *Annals of the American Academy* 197.
1941   *Från Klasskamp till Samverkan*. Stockholm: Tiden.
1971   *Vision och Verklighet*. Stockholm: Tiden.
1980   *Skrifter i Urval*. Stockholm: Tiden.
1981   "Arvskatten 1928." In Wigforss, *Minnen*, vol. 2. Stockholm: Tiden.
Wilensky, H.
1975   *The Welfare State and Equality*. Berkeley: University of California Press.
1976   *The New Corporatism, Centralization, and the Welfare State*. Beverly Hills, Calif.: Sage.
Wilhjelm, P.
1971   *Dansk Boligpolitik: Forbrydelse eller Dumhed?* Copenhagen: Røde Hane.
Wolfe, A.
1978   "Has Social Democracy a Future?" *Comparative Politics* 11.
Worre, T.
1980   "Class Parties and Class Voting in the Scandinavian Countries." *Scandinavian Political Studies* 3.
Wright, E. O.
1979   *Class Structure and Income Determination*. New York: Academic Press.

Zeitlin, M.
1966   "Political Generations in the Cuban Working Class."
          American Journal of Sociology 71.
1974   "Corporate Ownership and Control." *American Journal
          of Sociology* 79.
Zeitlin, M., and S. Norich.
1979   "Management Control, Exploitation, and Profit Max-
          imization." *Research in Political Economy* 2.
Zeuthen, F.
1944   "Socialpolitiske Problemer i Danmark efter Krigen." *Na-
          tionaløkonomisk Tidsskrift* 4.
Zinn, K. G.
1978   "The Social Market in Crisis." In S. Holland (ed.), *Beyond
          Capitalist Planning*. Oxford: Basic & Blackwell.
Zweig, F.
1971   *The Worker in Affluent Society*. New York: Free Press.

GOVERNMENT DOCUMENTS AND PUBLICATIONS

Denmark

Boligministeriet (Ministry of Housing).
1968   *Housing in the Nordic Countries*. Copenhagen: Statens
          Trykningskontor.
Danmarks Statistik.
1974   *Statistisk Årbog 1974*. Copenhagen: Statistisk Kontor.
1976   *Levevilkår i Danmark, 1976*. Copenhagen: Statistisk
          Kontor.
1978   *Statistisk Årbog 1978*. Copenhagen: Statistisk Kontor.
1981a   *Statistisk Årbog 1981*. Copenhagen: Statistisk Kontor.
1981b   *Statistisk Ti-Års Oversigt, 1981*. Copenhagen: Statistisk
          Kontor.
Handelsministeriet (Ministry of Commerce).
1973-   *Perspektiv Plan II, 1972-1987*. Copenhagen: Statens Tryk-
1974   ningskontor.

Norway

NOS (Norges Offentlige Statistikk).
1978   *Historisk Statistikk*. Oslo: NOS.

Statistisk Sentralbyrå (SSB).
1911   *Statistisk Årsbok*. Oslo: SSB.
1927   *Statistisk Årsbok*. Oslo: SSB.
1933   *Statistisk Årsbok*. Oslo: SSB.
1934   *Statistisk Årsbok*. Oslo: SSB.
1945   *Statistisk Årsbok*. Oslo: SSB.
1953   *Statistisk Årsbok*. Oslo: SSB.
1963   *Statistisk Årsbok*. Oslo: SSB.
1965   *Norges Økonomi etter Krigen*. Samfunnsøkonomiske Studier no. 12. Oslo: SSB.
1966   *Historisk Statistik for Norge*. Oslo: SSB.
1971   *Statistisk Årsbok*. Oslo: SSB.
1973   *Økonomisk Utsyn 1973*. Oslo: SSB.
1974   *Statistisk Årsbok*. Oslo: SSB.
1978   *Kreditmarkedsstatistikk 1974-76*. Oslo: SSB.
1980   *Statistisk Årsbok*. Oslo: SSB.
1981   *Statistisk Årsbok*. Oslo: SSB.

Sweden

SEP (Sekretariatet för Ekonomisk Planering).
1970   *Långtidsutredningen 1970*. Stockholm: SEP.
SOU (Sveriges Offentliga Utredningar).
1966-   *Koncentrationsutredningarna I-V*. Stockholm: SOU.
1968
1981   *Löntagarna och Kapitalväksten*. Report no. 5. Stockholm: SOU.
Statistiska Centralbyron (SCB).
1931   *Statistisk Årsbok*. Stockholm: SCB.
1933   *Statistisk Årsbok*. Stockholm: SCB.
1942   *Statistisk Årsbok*. Stockholm: SCB.
1952   *Statistisk Årsbok*. Stockholm: SCB.
1960   *Statistisk Årsbok*. Stockholm: SCB.
1961   *Statistisk Årsbok*. Stockholm: SCB.
1964   *Almänna Valen*. Stockholm: SCB.
1965   *Statistisk Årsbok*. Stockholm: SCB.
1971   *Statistisk Årsbok*. Stockholm: SCB.
1973   *Inkomst och Förmögenhet*. Stockholm: SCB.
1975a   *Levnadsförhållanden*. Stockholm: SCB.
1975b   *Almänna Valen 1973*. Del Rapport 3. Stockholm: SCB.
1976   *Statistisk Årsbok*. Stockholm: SCB.

1978   *Social Rapport om Ojämlikheten i Sverige, 1977-1978.* Report no. 22. Stockholm: SCB.
1980   *Statistisk Årsbok.* Stockholm: SCB.
1981a   *Statistisk Årsbok.* Stockholm: SCB.
1981b   *Almänna Valen 1979.* Del Rapport 3. Stockholm: SCB.
Swedish Ministry of Economic Affairs.
1976/77- *The Swedish Budget,* current annual issues. Stockholm:
1982/83 Ekonomi Departementet.
Swedish National Audit Board.
1982   "The Structure of Pensions in Sweden." Memorandum dated 27 April, Stockholm.

NORDIC COUNCIL OFFICIAL PUBLICATIONS

NBO (Nordisk Bostadskooperativorganisation).
1977   *Bostadspolitisk Utveckling i Norden.* Oslo: NBO.
Nordic Housing Administration.
1981   *Boligudgifter og Boligudgiftsandele i de Nordiske Lande.* Copenhagen: Ministry of Housing.
Nordisk Råd.
1980   *Nordisk Statistisk Årbog.* Copenhagen: Nordisk Råd.
1981   *Nordisk Statistisk Årbog.* Copenhagen: Nordisk Råd.
NU (Nordisk Udredningsserie).
1966-   *Social Tryghed i de Nordiske Lande.* Copenhagen: So-
1980   cialministeriet.
1978   *Arbejdsmarknadspolitiken: Mål & Midler.* Oslo: Nordisk Ministerråd.
1980a   *Individinriktatede Sysselsätningsåtgärder i de Nordiska Ländarna.* Oslo: Nordisk Ministerråd.
1980b   *Företagsinriktade Sysselsätningsskapande Åtgarder i de Nordiska Länderna.* Oslo: Nordisk Ministerråd.

INTERNATIONAL DOCUMENTS AND STATISTICS

ILO (International Labor Organization).
1960   *Yearbook of Labor Statistics.* Geneva: ILO.
1970   *Yearbook of Labor Statistics.* Geneva: ILO.
1979   *Yearbook of Labor Statistics.* Geneva: ILO.
IMF (International Monetary Fund).
1973   *International Financial Statistics,* supplement. Washington D.C.: IMF.

1976   *International Financial Statistics*, supplement. Washington D.C.: IMF.

OECD (Organization for Economic Cooperation and Development).

1970   *National Accounts, 1950-1968.* Paris: OECD.

1978   *Economic Survey: Norway.* Paris: OECD.

1980a   *National Accounts, 1961-1978.* Paris: OECD.

1980b   *The Tax-Benefit Position of a Typical Worker.* Paris: OECD.

1981   *Economic Survey: Norway.* Paris: OECD.

United Nations.

1966   *Major Problems in European Postwar Housing.* Geneva: United Nations.

1967   *Economic Survey of Europe.* Geneva: United Nations.

1979   *Annual Bulletin of Housing and Building Statistics for Europe.* Geneva: United Nations.

INDEX

Adler, Max, 20-21, 30, 152
agrarian parties, in Scandinavia. *See* Liberal party (Denmark), Center party (Norway, Sweden)
agriculture and agrarian structure: Denmark, 42-45, 206-208, 210, 212, 320; Norway, 45-48, 78, 198, 217, 223-224, 236; Scandinavia compared, 314, 318-319; Sweden, 48-51, 82, 200-202, 314, 318-319
Alford, Robert, 27n, 114
Anders Langes Parti. *See* Progress party (Norway)
Austro-Marxism, 20-26

Bang, Gustav, 76, 146
Bauer, Otto, 21, 152
Bebel, August, 10, 146
Bernstein, Eduard, 7, 15, 17, 19-21, 25, 29
Bismarck, Otto von, 10, 19, 145-146, 153
Bjerregård, Ritt, 178
Bondeförbundet. *See* Center party (Sweden)
Borten, Per, 103
Branting, Hjalmar, 21, 83-84, 86n, 151, 200-201, 293n
Bull, Edvard, 15
Burnham, Walter Dean, 114

Castles, Frances, 37, 73n, 112, 156, 315
Center Democratic party (Denmark), 96-99 passim
Center party: Norway, 80, 100-103 passim, 106, 116, 199, 222, 314-315; Sweden, 83, 85-86, 106-108, 110-111, 161, 202-203, 314-315
Christian People's party (Norway), 104, 106, 222, 283
class, social: *definition*, 26-27; *class alliances*, 18-19, 21, 27, 36-38, 71-73, 76, 89-90, 103, 108, 112, 204, 310-313, 316-324 passim; *class formation*,

10-11, 19, 24-26, 30-36, 140-141, 319; *class identification*, 257-258; *class structure*, compared, 51-57, 89, 130, 139-141, 319, 322, Denmark, 42-45, Norway, 45-48, Sweden, 48-51, 108; *class voting*, 33, 120-139 passim, 250-285 passim, 305-310; *petite bourgeoisie*, 29, 36-37; *white collar*, and class alliances, 29-30, 37, 89-90, 99, 108, 112-113, 176, 221, 226-227, 236, 243, 285, 289, 318-324 passim, and party support, 15-16, 29-30, 123-132 passim, 162-163, 252-255, 306-310 passim, political attitudes, 252-282 passim, in class structure, 29-30, 37, 44-45, 48, 51, 56-57, 108, 139-141, and trade unions, 62-64; *working class*, 27-28, political attitudes, 254-285 passim
collective bargaining. *See* trade unions
Comintern. *See* International (Third)
Communist party: Denmark, 65-66, 75-78 passim, 91-92, 98, 116, 206; Norway, 66-68, 78-81 passim, 101, 116, 198; Sweden, 68-70, 84-85, 107, 109, 111, 116, 138, 273, 301, 307
Conservative party: Denmark, 74, 97-99, 116, 273; Norway, 78, 101-102, 105, 116, 273; Sweden, 82-83, 85-87, 111-112, 116, 202-203, 273
cooperative movements, 85-86, 120
Crosland, C. A. R., 23-24, 28, 148n, 192

Danmarks Kommunistiske Parti. *See* Communist party (Denmark)
decommodification, 31-36, 148, 317. *See also* social democracy (welfare state)
defense policy: Denmark, 92-94, 212; Norway, 101-102; Sweden, 107
Det Norske Arbeiderparti (DNA). *See* Social Democratic party (Norway)
Duverger, Maurice, 4-5

363

laissez-faire economics, attitudes toward, 271-274
Larsen, Axel, 92
left-socialist parties: Denmark, 94, 116, 124, 137, 259-260, 280, 282, 306-307; Norway, 137, 282. *See also* Communist party, Socialist People's party
Lenin, Vladimir Illich, 10-14 passim, 18-19, 24-25, 293
Leninism and social democracy, 11-14, 24-26, 244-245, 315
Liberal party: generally, 150-151, 159; Denmark, 74, 76-77, 97-98, 116, 208, 314-315; Norway, 78, 101-103, 116, 199; Sweden, 82-83, 85-87, 109, 116, 202-203
liberalism, 7, 13, 29, 84, 148, 158, 200
LO (Landsorganisationen). *See* trade unions
Luxemburg, Rosa, 10, 146

Marshall, T. H., 16, 34, 157
Marx, Karl, 11-12, 29, 146, 195, 314
Meidner, Rudolf, 111, 175, 201n, 227n, 229n, 231-232, 234, 296-300 passim, 302, 305, 307
Michels, Roberto, 5, 16, 92
middle classes. *See* class
Mills, C. Wright, 16, 132
Möller, Gustav, 84, 87, 151, 203
Moore, Barrington, 28, 36n
Myrdal, Alva, 158
Myrdal, Gunnar, 88, 107, 158

Naphtali, Fritz, 292-293
Norges Kommunistiske Parti (NKP). *See* Communist party (Norway)
North Atlantic Treaty Organization (NATO). *See* defense policy
nuclear power issue, 111

oil economy of Norway, 224-225, 242-243
organized capitalism, theory of, 9-10

parliamentarism, in Scandinavia, 73-74, 78, 82-83
Perlman, Selig, 14-15
Pio, Louis, 74

Polanyi, Karl, 146
political distinctiveness of class, defined, 114-115, 122-123. *See also* class (voting)
political generations: defined, 132-133; and party support, 115, 132-139, 254-255, 308-309
Poulantzas, Nicos, 16, 27, 30
Progress party: Denmark, 97, 116, 124, 137, 249, 257-259, 260, 280-281; Norway, 103-104, 116, 249, 283
Przworski, Adam, 6-10 passim, 13-14, 27, 36, 51n, 52, 77, 94, 127, 191, 273, 316, 322

Radical-Liberal party (Denmark), 74, 76-77, 91-94, 97-98, 164, 207, 212
Rehn, Gösta, 107, 229, 230
Renner, Karl, 20
revisionist theory, 7, 19, 147
Rokkan, Stein, 16, 46, 47, 52, 66n, 71n, 72n, 123n, 163, 197, 199, 221-222

Sandler, Rikard, 201
Schumpeter, Joseph, 8, 15, 23-24, 28
social citizenship, 16, 34-35, 145-178. *See also* social democracy (welfare state)
social class. *See* class
social democracy: *defined*, 4-9; *economic policy*, comparisons and general, 35-36, 86-88, 100-101, 105, 107-108, 191-243 passim, 270-274, 317-318, Denmark, 194-196, 205-215, Norway, 196-199, 215-227, Sweden, 199-204, 227-236; *housing policy*, comparisons and general, 179-180, 246, Denmark, 93, 96, 180-186, 190, 321, Norway, 180-183, 186-187, 190, Sweden, 180-183, 187-190, 230-231; *welfare state*, comparisons and general, 22, 35-36, 100-101, 145-178 passim, 245-246, 315-316, Denmark, 152, 155, 157-178 passim, 321, Norway, 153, 155-178 passim, 321, Sweden, 152-153, 155-178 passim
Social Democratic party: *class alliances*, comparisons and general, 18-19, 21, 27, 36-38, 71-73, 89-90, 176, 204, 243, 285, 289, 310-313, 316-324,

LIBRARY OF CONGRESS CATALOGING
IN PUBLICATION DATA

Esping-Andersen, Gøsta, 1947-
  Politics against markets.

  Bibliography: p.
  Includes index.
  1. Socialism—Scandinavia—History—20th century.
  2. Socialist parties—Scandinavia—History—20th century.
  3. Scandinavia—Politics and government.
  I. Title.
HX319.E87 1985   320.5'315'0948   84-42882
ISBN 0-691-09408-X (alk. paper)
ISBN 0-691-02842-7 (pbk.)